PSYCHO-SOCIAL ASPECTS OF HEALTH AND ILLNESS

About the Editors

Dr. Shikha Dixit is a Professor of Psychology in the Department of Humanities and Social Sciences at Indian Institute of Technology Kanpur, Kanpur. She is engaged in teaching and research at IIT Kanpur since last twenty years. Her interests includes health psychology, social representations and social cognition. She has studied the psychological outcomes of chronic and life threatening such as cancer, HIV, myocardial infarction and mental illness.

Dr. Arun Kumar Sharma is P.K. Kelkar Chair, and Professor of Sociology, Indian Institute of Technology Kanpur, Kanpur. He teaches courses in research methods, statistical inference, health, and social demography. He has been working in the areas of development and health for more than 35 years. His research interests include evaluation of rural development programmes, situation analysis of HIV/AIDS, mapping of high risk groups, and maternal and child health.

PSYCHO-SOCIAL ASPECTS OF HEALTH AND ILLNESS

Edited by

Shikha Dixit
Professor of Psychology
Department of Humanities and Social Sciences
IIT Kanpur

Arun Kumar Sharma
Professor of Sociology
Department of Humanities and Social Sciences
IIT Kanpur

CONCEPT PUBLISHING COMPANY PVT. LTD.
NEW DELHI - 110 059

ISBN-13: 978-93-5125-276-4

First Published 2017

Published and Printed by

Concept Since 1974

Concept Publishing Company Pvt. Ltd.
A/15-16, Commercial Block, Mohan Garden
New Delhi-110059 (India)
T: 25351460, 25351794, *F*: 091-11-25357109
E: publishing@conceptpub.com, W: www.conceptpub.com

Cataloging in Publication Data--Courtesy: D.K. Agencies (P) Ltd. <docinfo@dkagencies.com>

Symposium on Health (2013 : Department of Humanities and Social Sciences, Indian Institute of Technology Kanpur)

Psycho-social aspects of health and illness / edited by Shikha Dixit, Arun Kumar Sharma.
pages cm

"This book is the outcome of a Symposium on Health held in November 2013 in Humanities and Social Sciences Department of Indian Institute of Technology, Kanpur"--Preface.

Includes bibliographical references and index.
ISBN 9789351252764

1. Public health--India--Congresses. 2. Medical care--India--Congresses. 3. Mental illness--India--Congresses. 4. Clinical health psychology--India--Congresses. I. Dixit, Shikha, editor. II. Sharma, A. K., 1953- editor. III. Indian Institute of Technology Kanpur. Department of Humanities and Social Sciences, organizer. IV. Title.

RA529.S96 2013 DDC 362.10954 23

PREFACE

This book is the outcome of a symposium on health held in November 2013 in Humanities and Social Sciences Department of Indian Institute of Technology, Kanpur. The purpose of conducting this symposium was to discuss psychological and sociological issues in health, which has been one of the priority research areas of the department. Since, we have been working in this area for a long time, we were given the responsibility of organizing this symposium. We invited a small number of experts working in diverse sectors of health in different types of organizations — Universities, Government, NGOs, and research centres — who had established themselves as expert in some sub-field of health. We decided to include a number of themes in the symposium, such as health cognition, adaptation and conceptualization; health care and health initiatives; mental health and mental illness; and health challenges. We stressed on exploring how laypersons represent health and illness and what are the psychosocial issues involved in common sense models of health representations. We also wanted to explore emerging issues in health policy and planning such as the role of AYUSH and the relationship between social structure and health. Needless to say, there is a dearth of studies on mental health issues in India. Therefore, an attempt was also made to review the concept of mental health, to identify issues in mental health research and to explore social representations of mental health in the Indian context. Further, we thought that there is a need to focus on psychological aspects of health among women and children and initiate debate on health in defense services. While a good amount of work has been done in the field of reproductive health there is a dearth of studies on health among the defence personnel. In the recent past media has often reported cases of extreme mental distress in defence personnel and its implications for formal and informal organizations of defence services. Keeping this in mind, a special session was planned for discussion on mental health issues in the defence forces with special attention to suicide.

Looking at the success of the seminar the department encouraged us to produce a book containing significant contributions on health from diverse perspectives. At this stage all the chapters presented in the symposium were peer reviewed. A few more chapters were invited from eminent scholars working in this field. On the basis of the reviews some chapters were identified for publication in this volume. These chapters were sent to reviewers once again. The comments received from reviewers were sent to the authors for their consideration and modification in the chapter. It took almost more than a year to get the final versions of the chapters keeping in mind that each one of them must make an original and significant contribution to knowledge on the subject.

Apart from us, a number of people have contributed to this book. First of all, we would like to thank Humanities and Social Sciences Department of the Indian Institute of Technology Kanpur, for providing us a generous grant for organizing the symposium. We take this opportunity to specially thank the contributors of this volume for participating in the symposium and expressing their views on the topics discussed. Their active participation in the symposium and their enthusiasm was a major motivator behind conceptualization of this volume. We also thank the anonymous academic reviewers who spent their valuable time in reviewing the papers. Thanks are due to different contributors for bearing with us in revising their chapters a couple of times in the light of the reviewers' comments, and also meeting deadlines. We also express our gratitude to our colleagues from the department and our Ph.D. students who have helped us at various stages in organizing the symposium and producing this book. Special thanks are due to our Ph.D. Scholars Bidisha Banerjee, Aarti Singh, Anu Malik, Nidhi Yadav, Amithy Jasrotia, Vikas Dubey and T. Shukkoor. All of them worked to make the symposium a success. We would like to end this preface by specially acknowledging Ms. Nidhi Yadav for helping us with various tasks during the process of editing and finalizing this manuscript.

Shikha Dixit
A.K. Sharma

CONTENTS

LIST OF TABLES

LIST OF FIGURES

LIST OF CONTRIBUTORS

Alankrita Maurya, Independent Researcher, Mumbai.

Aneesh Kumar, Assistant Professor, Christ University, Bengaluru.

Anjali Gireesan, Assistant Professor, Mithibai College of Arts and Science, Mumbai.

Aparna Mehrotra, Visiting Faculty (Psychology), College of Nursing, Bharati Vidyapeeth, Belapur, Navi Mumbai.

Arun Kumar Sharma, Professor of Sociology, Department of Humanities and Social Sciences, IIT Kanpur.

Bidisha Banerjee, Assistant Professor, Christ University, Bengaluru.

Dharitri Panda, Joint Secretary, Ministry of Health and Family Welfare.

Dinika Anand, Research Fellow, Defence Institute of Psychological Research (DIPR), Delhi.

Gurpreet Kaur, Scientist, Defence Institute of Psychological Research (DIPR), Delhi.

Lilly Ganju, Scientist and Head, Immunomodulation Division, Defence Institute of Physiological Research (DIPAS), Delhi.

M. Akram, Associate Professor, Department of Sociology, Aligarh Muslim University, Aligarh.

Nutan Prabha Jain, Professor, IIHMR University, Jaipur.

P.M. Kulkarni, Professor, Centre for the Study of Regional Development, School of Social Sciences, Jawaharlal Nehru University, New Delhi.

Purnima Awasthi, Assistant Professor, Department of Psychology, Banaras Hindu University, Varanasi.

R.C. Mishra, Professor, Department of Psychology, Faculty of Social Sciences, Banaras Hindu University, Varanasi.

Rajbala Singh, Associate Professor, Department of Humanities and Social Sciences, The LNM Institute of Information Technology, Jaipur.

S.D. Gupta, President, IIHMR University, Jaipur.

Shikha Dixit, Professor of Psychology, Department of Humanities and Social Sciences, IIT Kanpur.

Sibnath Deb, Professor, Department of Applied Psychology, School of Physical, Chemical and Applied Sciences, Pondicherry University.

Snigdha Pareek, Officer, Programmes, Population Services International, Jaipur.

Soumi Awasthy, Scientist and Head, Intelligence and Aptitude Division, Defence Institute of Psychological Research (DIPR), Delhi.

U.P. Shahi, Professor, Department of Radiotherapy and Radiation Medicine, Institute of Medical Sciences, Banaras Hindu University, Varanasi.

Updesh Kumar, Scientist 'F' and Head, Mental Health Division at Defence Institute of Psychological Research (DIPR), R&D Organization (DRDO), Ministry of Defence, Delhi.

Introduction

The study of health and illness is a vibrant and active research area in the social sciences and there is a need to explore the various aspects related to this area using an interdisciplinary perspective. For such an exploration, mainly from psychological and sociological perspectives, a symposium was organized in the Department of Humanities and Social Sciences at IIT Kanpur. The symposium was geared towards understanding and discussion of following aspects: Health cognitions; health care and health initiatives; mental health and mental illness; and health challenges.

The chapters presented in the symposium and the discussion that ensued motivated us to prepare the present manuscript. Some chapters were selected from the chapters presented in the symposium and a few other chapters were added to create a text that would provide the readers with a glimpse of health related conceptualizations and issues, viewed both from psychological and sociological lenses.

The nature and level of the articles included in the edited volume is suited for researchers interested in the area of health and illness. Since, both psychological and sociological perspectives are reflected in the articles included in the text, this volume might be a good research resource for researchers and other health professionals who are interested in an interdisciplinary social scientific perspective. The level of the text is such that it is relevant for students, researchers and professionals. The future potential of this volume lies in the fact that this would enable scholars interested in the study of health and illness to explore the issues in this area from a lens that makes it possible to look at certain issues both from different perspectives. In addition to this, a discussion on health finance also brings into focus the financial aspects of health care. The articles selected for the volume present topics and ideas pertaining to various aspects related to health and illness mainly but not necessarily in the Indian context. The articles specifically explore psychological and sociological dimensions related to health beliefs, adaptation and conceptualization; health care in different contexts; aspects of mental illness; health concerns of children in India; reproductive health and other concerns.

The text is broadly divided into four sections. Each section intends to provide an insight into some aspect of health and illness. The **first section** on **'Health Cognitions'** presents chapter that explore issues related to cognizing illness, understanding illness beliefs, perception about severity of life threatening illness and the relationship between illness beliefs and well-being. The chapters in this section are in line with the psychological perspective. The First chapter on 'Conceptualization of Perceived Illness Severity in Cancer Patients' presents a study that attempts to understand cancer patients' perceived illness severity. The results are relevant as far as understanding patients' cognition about their illness condition and coping with illness is concerned. On the basis of preliminary interviews with patients and doctors, questionnaires were constructed to assess the difference between patients' perceived severity and their biomedical severity. The items were related to severity of symptoms, severity at the time of diagnosis, severity at present, severity as compared to earlier condition and doctor's control over the disease. Further, a semi-structured interview schedule was developed to explore the conceptualization of disease severity in patients. The findings revealed a significant difference between patients' perceived and biomedical severity. As compared to the doctors' judgement, patients reported their disease severity as less. Analysis of the qualitative responses of patients resulted in ten themes pertaining to perceived illness severity: symptoms, physical effects, social effects, effects of treatment, body-image, duration of illness, controllability, social comparison, psychological impact and global severity.

The Second chapter on 'Health Beliefs and Behaviour during Acculturation: The Case of the Kharwar Tribal Group' deals with health beliefs and health behaviours. Health occupies an important place in the life of human beings because of its direct relationship with survival. Concern for health seems to be universal, but the way in which people in different cultures understand health and manage their health problems shows considerable variation. All cultures nurture certain ideas about health, and people in all cultures share certain beliefs about causation, prevention, treatment, and control of illness, which have profound effect on their health behaviour. With acculturation health-related understanding and practices of individuals seem to present interesting variations. This chapter focusses on physical and mental health of women of the *Kharwar tribal* group undergoing acculturation for the last couple of decades. In a series of three studies health beliefs and behaviours of the *Kharwar* women, including the problems of their mental health, were examined using observation, interview, group discussion, and testing procedures. The analyses revealed diarrhoea, fever, child mortality, conjunctivitis, unwanted pregnancies, and arthritis as the major health problems reported by women. In a later study, cough/cold, headaches and skin diseases were also added to the previous list of health problems. Younger women reported conjunctivitis, headaches and unwanted pregnancies more frequently, whereas elderly women reported arthritis and skin diseases more frequently as health problems. Younger women generally considered themselves responsible for health problems, whereas elderly women largely attributed health problems to supernatural causes. The stressors of women's life were found rooted mainly in financial and familial constraints. Also there was evidence for the expression of psychological difficulties in somatic forms.

The Third chapter is about 'Illness Beliefs, Optimism, Subjective Well-Being and Post-Traumatic Growth of Cervix Cancer Patients' . This chapter examines the relationship of illness beliefs and optimism with subjective well-being and post-traumatic growth in a sample of 100 uneducated cervix cancer patients. The participants belonged to middle class families and their age ranged from 30 to 60 years. Measures of illness causation and control beliefs, optimism, subjective well-being, and post-traumatic growth were administered. The analysis of data revealed that patients believed more strongly in 'external' than 'internal' causes of illness. They also held a stronger belief in 'doctor' and 'supernatural' controls of illness as compared to 'self' control. With respect to growth outcomes, scores were higher on 'relating to others' and 'new possibilities than 'spiritual change', 'personal strength', and 'appreciation of life'. Regression analysis brought out optimism, supernatural control, self-control, and supernatural causation as significant predictors of 'subjective well-being' and 'post-traumatic growth' of cancer patients.

The Fourth chapter entitled 'Common Sense Model of Illness Representations: Issues and Implications' does not report any study but provides conceptual discussion pertaining illness cognition. The prevalence of chronic illness is legion. However, with the advancement in medical science, mortality risk from chronic illness can be now managed more effectively. As a result of this, the life expectancy has increased significantly in last few decades. However, increased life expectancy has given rise to various psychological challenges that patients have to face while going through different phases of their illness. Thus, one of the important challenges in the area of health psychology is to understand those factors that influence an individuals' understanding regarding illness condition as well as adherence to treatment. Scholars have shown keen interest in studying how patients create their own models or representations of illness. Studies have also focussed upon how such representations influence patients' illness related behaviour such as, coping with illness, adaptation process and adherence to treatment regimen. Much of the researches in this area have focussed upon cognitive factors underlying patients' motivation to manage illness condition effectively. In this context, Leventhal's Common Sense Model (CSM) of illness representations has received significant attention from researchers. The CSM follows a self-regulatory approach that highlights importance of various cognitive and affective processes underlying it. This chapter analyses the common sense model of illness representations and highlights some important issues in this area. The chapter suggests in what manner certain features of CSM can be useful for adopting positive health behaviours as well as for developing patient centred health management.

The **second section** deals with **'Health Care and Health Initiatives'**. This section presents a multidimensional and a diverse discussion of health care, ranging from alternative systems to health financing in India. This section includes discussions on conceptualization of health care as an Indian experience as well as an evaluation of implications of psychoneuroimmunology. Both sociological and psychological perspectives find an expression in this section. There are four chapters in this section.

The first chapter focusses on 'Alternative Systems of Health Care and National Health Missions'. Following the framework of National Health Policy (NHP) 1983 in India, National Rural Health Mission (NRHM) 2005-07 recognized the importance of alternative systems of health care. As early as 1995, the Central Government had created the Department of Indian System of Medicine and Homoeopathy (ISM&H). NHP 2002 and Five Year Plans also committed to it. The new approach is expected to lay emphasis on upgradation of standards, quality control, research, and awareness generation. With a small budget devoted to Ayurveda, Yoga and Naturopathy, Unani, Siddha and Homoeopathy (AYUSH) in the Twelfth Five Year Plan, the National Health Mission (NHM) has accorded increased importance to alternative systems. Yet, there is a dearth of scientific, i.e. evidence based research on therapeutic aspects of AYUSH and on issues involved in integration of scientific and alternative systems. Arguments are examined in favour of and against AYUSH and suggest that there is a need for exercising caution in promoting AYUSH as part of the public health programme.

The second chapter in this section deals with health finance. The chapter on 'Financing Health Care in India: Reforms and Challenges' is based on research from secondary data and literature. It outlines the concept of health financing and its sources, the status of health in India and its linkage with spending, the health reforms that have taken place in the country and its impact on the health indicators. In the course of the analysis, the focus has been on public health spending specially by the Federal government, the financing mechanism of Natural Rural Health Mission (NHRM), National Urban Health Mission (NUHM) and the Rashtriya Swasthya Bima Yojana (RSBY). It has also dwelt on Health Research financing. The chapter has concluded with the challenges that lie in the road ahead in achieving the Millennium Development Goals (MDGs). It has been analyzed that through its latest health reforms public health spending has increased over last decade it is not enough to reach the MDG targets and along with increasing the quantity of spending the quality of spending has to be focussed upon to achieve desired outcomes and improve customer satisfaction and provide financial protection.

The third chapter on 'Disease, Illness and Health Care: A Sociological Conceptualization of the Indian Experience' discusses some major issues of health care. Health is a universal need of mankind. However, the health outcomes are not uniform across regions. In India, the life expectancy at birth is much lower than in many neighbouring countries; the infant and maternal mortality rates are very high, even from the standards of the South and East Asian countries. Most of the States of India are yet to witness the epidemiological transition and much of the deaths are associated with communicable diseases. Huge differences and inequities in health outcomes are visible among the various States imbibing several social, spatial and occupational categories. The unmet health needs of the vulnerable populations pose serious question marks on the comprehensiveness of the prevailing medical care system with heavy dependence on the bio-medical approach. This necessitates looking beyond the grand narratives related to disease, illness, treatment and health care. The existing grand narratives fail to address the varying impacts of the plurality of 'discourses' and 'simulations'; the growth of 'habitus' and 'world views'; and the divides between the 'public' and 'private' spheres. This chapter aims to understand the social situations which perpetuate the disease and illness conditions and discard the health coverage goals in India. The conditions of 'diseases' of vulnerable groups in India, very often, are not getting the recognitions of 'illness' or 'sickness' and miss the required intervention of treatment through 'medical and health care intervention'. Lack of optimum public facilities and absence of quality of life factors often mitigate the differences between the 'symptoms and pains' of pathological conditions of 'disease' and social conditions of 'resource deprivation' creating 'illness doubts' and 'health illusions' within the overall understanding of illness and health care discourses. The chapter suggests that several conditions like lack of public health facilities, absence of basic health goods (BHGs), social discrimination and marginalization, medical indifference, corporatization, overmedicalization, profit orientation and privatization create the disease-friendly 'habitus' and 'social worlds' for the vulnerable and distance them from the interventions of health care. Under these conditions, the poorly designed health programmes and policies and their deficient implementations make the contributions of limited health care facilities insignificant.

The fourth chapter in this section on 'Psychoneuroimmunology: Implications for Health and Immune System' provides a rather different picture of health care as compared to other articles in this section. This review chapter intends to present a holistic picture of the way our health, well-being and daily functioning are intertwined. Psychoneuroimmunology is the scientific field of study investigating the link between tri-directional communication between nervous system, endocrine system, and immune system; and the implications of these linkages for physical health. This multi-disciplinary research area explains the dynamics between behavioural factors (like mood, emotions and thought processes), the neurological system (like reflex systems and neuro-endocrine system) and the immune system (cellular structure and immune system constitution). Psychoneuroimmunology is based on aspects like emotions which play an important role in the development of physical diseases, different stressors that produce different responses in the body, and methods which help to mitigate the effects of stress and boost immunity. This Chapter attempts to draw together current and past literature in the domain ranging from factors like stress and unconscious reservoir which impact the immune system at one end to the interventions like relaxation training, hypnosis and meditation at the other end. Through the chapter an effort is made to determine the underlying link between mind, behaviour and immunity and the related implications that such cross-disciplinary studies would facilitate in promoting good health.

The **third section** of the volume articulates some aspects of **'Mental Health and Mental Illness'**. Mental health and illness is an area that requires attention and focus. This section presents an analysis of pertinent research questions and a discussion on involvement of families in caring for mentally ill persons and healing traditions. This section also includes a chapter that explores the social representations of mental health, mental illness and health seeking in urban middle class Indians. There are three chapters in this section. Mental illness issues are explored both from sociological and psychological perspectives. The first chapter on 'Mental Illness and Mental Health: Questions for Research' posits that in years to come mental illness and unhappiness will pose enormous challenges to health care delivery as well as to social system. Sociology of health in India is dominated by studies of reproductive and public health issues. The reason is that for a long time health discourse concentrated on the reduction of population growth which was caused by a rapid mortality transition. Little attention has been paid to mental health issues. As a consequence of it, mental health facilities in India are far from being adequate and mental illness is highly stigmatized. This chapter attempts to seek attention of social scientists to the vector of mental health issues. It includes discussion of mental illness and mental health, relationship between social structure and mental health, and policy perspectives on mental health in India. It is argued that the relationship between mental illness and mental health is not dualistic: absence of mental illness does not mean happiness and mental disorder does not necessarily lead to unhappiness. The chapter shows that due to paucity of resources and other priorities, it may not be possible for the state to fight against all the sources of alienation and disintegration, and treatment and rehabilitation. In the complex world of today both state and civil society have to work together for a better system in which all social needs of all citizens are satisfied, and in which no class of people remain under stress or develop distress.

The second chapter in this section presents a review of studies related to the 'Concept of Mental Illness, healing traditions, and involvement of families in caring in the Indian context'. Mental illness researches in India are mostly focussed on understanding the patients' perspective despite families' involvement in treatment and care. Thus, the care giving experiences of families require attention. This review chapter aims to understand the role and involvement of families in mental illness care in the Indian context by exploring the Indian concepts of mental illness and different healing traditions. Studies conducted using explanatory models perspectives have also been reviewed. At the end, the review identifies some research issues.

The third research chapter in this section explores the lay collective meanings of mental health and mental illness. This chapter presents a qualitative study that explores the 'Social Representations of Mental Health, Mental Illness and Health seeking Behaviour in the Urban Middle Class Indians'. The findings of the study suggest that the commonsense understanding of mental health and mental illness in the Indian urban middle class comprises polymorphic representations. These polymorphic representations of mental health and mental illness were found to be deeply rooted in the social and cultural contexts of Indian urban middle class society. The lay understanding of health seeking behaviour also reflected polymorphic representations in terms of awareness about health services with a reluctance to use them.

An important aspect that needs to be explored in any discussion of health and illness are the challenges that health professionals and researchers face. Some such challenges in the Indian context pertain to reproductive health, health challenges and concerns in the domain of child health care and also the health issues in other domains such as armed forces. The fourth section on 'Health Challenges' presents chapters related to some of these issues. The first article in this section explores the issues and challenges related to 'Health and Illness Concerns of Children in India'. This is a review based research chapter which aims at understanding the present scenario of health, health care services, and related issues with regard to children in India. In a developing country like India there are many issues pertaining to child health care and illness. Children are deprived and neglected of basic needs and health care facilities. Children are also at risk of abuse, disability and maltreatment. It has been observed that there is an increase in the prevalence of health compromising behaviours among children like change in eating habits, alcohol abuse and other changes in lifestyle which has a synergistic effect on both physical and mental health. Stress and environmental factors also affect children's health in all realms. The chapter calls for the need of awareness and interdisciplinary approach towards building a healthier society, based on the principles of rationality and inclusion, catering to the majority needs of its population.

The second chapter of this section discusses 'Early Childhood Mortality in India'. Recent trends and prospects for the near future are articulated in this chapter. In spite of an impressive decline in childhood mortality in India in the recent years, there are questions about the pace of decline and whether the level will fall to reasonably low level in the future, in particular, whether the Millennium Development Goal of lowering the under-five mortality rate will be attained. Based on an assessment of recent trends in the under-five mortality rate in India and in large States, the chapter shows that India is likely to reach close to the Millennium Development Goal for under-five mortality rate at the national level. However, some of the States have a long way to go. The chapter also discusses the prospects of rapid decline in childhood mortality in the foreseeable future.

One of the major health challenges is reproductive health. The third chapter in this section discusses 'Psychological Aspects of Reproductive and Sexual Health'. Reproductive health is a major concern for both women and men. Reproductive health conditions make a major contribution to the global burden of disability, accounting for 21.9 per cent of DALYs lost for women and 3.1 per cent for men annually. The chapter discusses reproductive health with life-cycle approach and psychological aspects based on review of literature. The chapter argues that there are multiple points of intersection between psychological aspects of reproductive health.

The last chapter in this section presents a discussion on the issue of suicide. Suicide is one of the most extreme and therefore visible manifestations of stress and mental ill health.

This chapter explores the 'Causes and Prevention of Suicides in the Military'. A single incidence of suicide within the organization results in long-term repercussions in terms of morale and motivation level of the troops, and is indicative of inadequacies at the systemic level to provide coping resources to the soldiers. In the military context, it is not only committed suicide, but also suicide ideation, suicidal behaviours, and attempts at self-harm that are a cause of concern. Such negative behavioural manifestations are reflective of the intensity of stress and emotional disturbance felt by the military personnel due to various reasons. Suicide is a complex phenomenon behind which lie a host of causes as well as multidimensional and overlapping risk factors. It has been a challenge to find out the causes leading to suicidal behaviours and structuring preventive measures. Based on a series of research studies, the present chapter elaborates upon the risk factors for suicide in military environments. A model is proposed that provides a comprehensive explanation of the interplay among various domains of a soldier's life, *viz.* personal, familial, interpersonal, occupational and environmental, and the dynamics of risk *versus* protective benefits caused by this interplay. It is argued that a comprehensive programme for suicide prevention should focus not only on minimizing the risk factors, but must equally emphasize upon building soldier strengths and inculcating resilience at the individual, interpersonal and organizational fronts.

As is evident from the above discussion about the contents, this book covers a wide spectrum of health issues from theoretical standpoints to practical concerns. Instead of merely documenting the status of health in India, chapters of this book will serve the diverse, critical and interdisciplinary needs of the research professionals and students. Since, the book includes chapters from different perspectives and the contributors are from diverse disciplines, such as psychology, population studies, sociology, and administration, it provides a holistic understanding of health issues in India. Thus, academicians, planners and NGOs working in the field of health will benefit from the book. In addition, this book would be useful to doctoral and post-doctoral students working on health in different universities in India and abroad. Although, not written with any specific group of students as the target, this book will also serve the needs of students doing courses in health psychology and sociology of health.

SECTION I

Health Cognitions, Adaptation and Conceptualization

1

Conceptualization of Perceived Illness Severity in Cancer Patients

Aparna Mehrotra and *Shikha Dixit*

The present study aims at understanding the difference between cancer patients' perceived illness severity and their biomedical disease severity. Since, one of the aims of this work was also to understand the conceptualization of disease severity in cancer patients, dimensions of patients' perceived severity were explored through qualitative interviews with cancer patients.

Disease severity is an important variable in connection to understanding the relation between disease state and its consequences. Review of literature suggested that studies have linked patients' disease severity and health outcomes such as, coping and adjustment (Kershaw, Northouse, Kritpracha, Schafenacker & Mood. 2004; List, Rutherford, Stracks, Haraf, Kies & Vokes, 2002; Manne, Sabbioni, Bovbjerg, Jacobsen, Taylor & Redd, 1994; Northouse, Dorris & Charron-Moore, 1995; Shapiro, Lopez, Schwartz, Bootzin, Figueredo, Braden, *et al.*, 2001). These studies demonstrated that health outcomes of patients were influenced mainly by their biomedical disease stage.

However, the relationship between the biomedical aspects of disease and psychological outcomes has not been consistent in the studies. Some researchers found that health outcomes were independent of the biomedical status of disease. Kazak, Barakat, Meeske, Christakis, Meadows, Casey, *et al.* (1997), found no difference in post-traumatic stress levels between the childhood leukemia patients and their peers. Glanz and Lerman (1992) found that women suffering from breast cancer reported different levels of psychological distress associated with diagnosis and treatment. The abovementioned studies suggest that the medical condition of a person can have limited influence on his/her psychosocial outcomes.

Research pertaining to disease stage and its impact on the psychological health of individuals has also reported contradictory findings. Some studies have reported high correlation between the early stage of disease and negative psychological outcomes; whereas in some studies, later stages or recurrence was reported to have more negative impact on patients' psychological health. Cassileth, Lusk, Strouse, Miller, Brown, Cross, *et al.* (1984), found poorer mental health scores among recently diagnosed patients as compared to patients who were diagnosed four months earlier. They included arthritis, diabetes, cancer, renal disease and dermatologic disease patients in their study. One of the conclusions of this study was that adjustment to chronic illnesses was not dependent on the illness diagnosis. Derogatis, Morrow, Fetting, Penman, Piasetsky, Schmale, *et al.* (1983), conducted a study to assess the prevalence of psychiatric disorders among newly admitted cancer patients. They found that a large number of patients were diagnosed with a psychiatric condition. In contrast to the abovementioned results, some studies suggested that high stress was reported by cancer patients who were facing recurrence (Northouse, Dorris & Charron-Moore, 1995). Patients also reported that adjustment with recurrence was more difficult as compared to adjustment with the initial diagnosis (Cella, Mahon & Donovan, 1990).

These contradictory findings question the role of biomedical disease stage in predicting psychological outcomes in patients. Holland and Holahan (2003) found that perceived social support was important in predicting psychological well-being and positive health behaviours in cancer patients. Further, this relationship was mediated by approach coping strategies. There was no effect of disease stage and treatment related variables on the well-being of patients. Bombardier, D'Amico and Jordan (1990) have discussed the role of appraisal in chronic illness and have demonstrated that appraisal of a chronic illness condition predicted coping and psychosocial adjustment in patients. On a similar note, Dunkel-Schetter, Feinstein, Taylor and Falke (1992) reported no effect of factors related to cancer (as reflected in type of cancer, time since diagnosis and treatment) on patients' coping strategies. A study on acute myocardial infarction patients (Greco, A., Stecca, P., Pozzi, R., *et al.*, 2014) demonstrated that although disease severity had an impact on the depression levels of patients, this relationship was fully mediated by personal control variables such as illness representations, perceived social support and self-efficacy. Laubmeier and Zakowski (2004) studied patients' perception of illness in the form of Perceived Life Threat (PLT) and found that PLT and not the disease stage significantly predicted distress and quality of life among patients. Heijmans, Foets, Rijken, Schreurs, de Ridder and Bensing (2001) have demonstrated that chronically ill patients' perception of their illness was different from their doctors' view. Juth, Silver and Sender (2015) have explored the relationship between objective and subjective disease severity among cancer patients and their caregivers. They found that subjective disease severity in adolescent and young cancer patients as well as their caregivers was independent from the medical indicators of severity. The indicators that were used to assess medical severity were: healthcare utilization, medical costs and risk prognosis. Items from illness perception questionnaire were used as an indicator of subjective disease severity.

As it is clear in the studies discussed above, the biomedical stage or the medical indicators of severity of disease are not the sole predictors of health outcomes in patients. Studies have demonstrated a difference between patients' perceptions and the biomedical evaluation of the disease. Thus, it becomes important to understand patients' perspective regarding their disease severity. The present chapter attempts to understand cancer patients' perception regarding their disease severity as well as to demonstrate the differences between severity assessment by cancer patients and their doctors in the Indian scenario.

Aim

The present work was concerned with understanding cancer patients' perceptions regarding their disease severity. In this connection, it was imperative to study the difference between patients' perceived and biomedical severity in order to establish the rationale for studying patients' perceived illness severity. Therefore, the first aim of this study was to empirically explore whether a significant difference exists between cancer patients' perceived severity and biomedical judgment of severity. The second step of this study was to understand the way cancer patients conceptualize their disease severity. Therefore, the second aim focused on the exploration of perceived illness severity in patients.

In the present study, disease severity judged by patients has been termed as Perceived Illness Severity (PIS) and severity judged by doctors has been termed as Objective Illness Severity (OIS).

Method

Data was collected on 30 cancer patients. In order to fulfil the first aim mentioned above, a Likert type rating scale was used to gather information regarding cancer patients' disease severity. The concerned doctors of the participants also participated in the study to provide the biomedical assessment of patients' disease severity.

Since, the second aim of this study was to understand cancer patients' conceptualization of their disease severity qualitative in-depth interviews were conducted in order to fulfil this aim.

Participants

The purpose of this study was to assess the disease severity of cancer patients from the patients' perspective and from the biomedical perspective. Therefore, patients having a clear diagnosis of cancer were contacted in the hospital setting for participation. Patients who showed their willingness to participate in the study were included. The sample consisted of 21 female and 9 male cancer patients admitted in two cancer hospitals of Northern India. Of these 30 cases, 13 per cent patients were diagnosed with breast cancer, 43 per cent with cervical and ovarian cancer, 23 per cent with oral and larynx cancer, 10 per cent with gallbladder and liver cancer and 3 per cent each with rectum, testes and lung cancer. It has been reported that these cancers have most frequent occurrence in the Indian context (Rao & Ganesh, 1998). Patients' average age was 48 years (SD-11.27) and average years of education were 8.87 (SD-6.45). Information regarding perceived illness severity was obtained from patients. The oncologists treating the patients were contacted for information regarding patients' biomedical disease stage.

Measures

Two scales were constructed for the present study. The scales were developed in Hindi language keeping in view the target sample that was predominantly Hindi speaking. A brief description of the scales is as follows:

The quantitative scales intended to measure the severity of cancer patients from the perspective of patients (*Perceived illness severity scale*) and medical professionals (*Objective illness severity scale*). In order to construct these scales, initial interviews were conducted with 5 patients and 5 oncologists. Their responses suggested that dimensions such as, symptom severity, controllability, severity at the time of diagnosis and overall severity were important to assess severity of patients. The items were constructed on the basis of the interview responses obtained from patients and oncologists.

Perceived Illness Severity Scale: A 5-item scale was developed to assess patients' perception of their disease severity. First item (How severe are the symptoms of your disease according to you?) measured patients' perception of their symptom severity. Second item was used to measure patients' perceived severity at the time of diagnosis (How severe was your disease according to you at the time of diagnosis?). Third item (According to you, how severe is your disease at present?) measured the overall perceived severity according to patients. Fourth item assessed the way patients felt about their condition at present in comparison to their earlier condition (As compared to earlier condition, how is your condition now according to you?). Fifth item assessed patients' perception of doctors' control over their illness (According to you, how much control the doctor has on your disease?).

Existing literature in health psychology and psycho-oncology suggests that the dimensions explored in the interviews were present in the literature, but not in similar form. According to the common sense model of illness representation proposed by Leventhal, Meyer and Nerenz (1980), patients label their disease on the basis of symptoms. However, in the present study the perceived severity of those symptoms was taken into account and not only the mere presence or absence of those symptoms. Second item was constructed to measure patients' perceived severity at the time of diagnosis. Literature suggests that cancer induces distress in patients since the time it is diagnosed (Holland, 1998). Research has demonstrated that distress at the time of diagnosis is high (Trask & Griffith, 2004; Trask, Paterson, Hayasaka, Dunn, Riba & Johnson, 2001). Therefore, patients' perceived severity at the time of diagnosis was taken into account. The third item measured overall perceived severity of patients. It was similar to the measure used by Marks, Richardson, Graham and Levine (1986), in which they had used only one item to measure perceived disease severity (How ill do you think you are now?). The fourth item measured patients' perception of disease severity at present as compared to their earlier condition. The rationale behind the inclusion of the fourth item was to understand whether distress level in patients varies with time. Fifth item measured the level of control that patients perceived their doctors had on their disease. In the present study, control referred to patients' perception of doctors' control on their disease. High controllability referred to lower level of perception of illness severity. Patients were asked to rate each item on a 5-point scale from *very less severe to very much severe*. The minimum score on this scale was 5 and maximum was 25. High scores indicated higher perceived severity. The internal consistency of the scale was good, with an overall Cronbach's alpha of 0.75.

Objective Illness Severity Scale: In order to measure patients' severity according to the biomedical perspective, a similar measure (as used with the patients) was used. However, the items were modified to represent the judgement of the oncologists. The oncologists were asked to rate patient's severity on the basis of their medical condition on a 5-point scale. High score denoted high disease severity. The reliability score of this scale was found to be good (Cronbach alpha = 0.81).

Qualitative Interviews: Semi-structured qualitative interviews were conducted with patients to understand their conceptualization and sense making of disease severity. The interview schedule generally focused on the following questions: (a) Since when are you in hospital? (b) When and why did you first go for a medical check-up? What changes did you perceive in yourself that prompted you to go for a check-up? (c) What were those symptoms that made you feel that you were sick? (d) Did you feel that your symptoms were severe? If yes, then what were the reasons for that feeling? (e) According to you what is the meaning of severity of disease? and (f) What aspects of your life have been affected by your disease and how? The initial questions were asked to establish a rapport with patients. Questions (d), (e) and (f) focused more on the conceptualization of disease severity in patients.

Procedure

Permission was taken from the hospital administration to meet the patients and their concerned oncologists. Patients and their family members were then asked for their consent and were briefed about the purpose of the study. Only about 10 per cent of contacted patients declined to participate in the study. Scales and semi-structured interviews were used to elicit information from patients. Patients were requested to rate their illness severity on the items of perceived illness severity scale. Patients were then interviewed using the semi-structured interviews. The interview responses were noted verbatim. On an average, 1.5-2 hours were spent with each patient. The concerned oncologists of patients were contacted and patients' medical information and their disease severity (according to the medical judgement) were obtained. In case of patients as well as the doctors, the questions were interviewer-administered.

Results and Interpretation

Perceived versus Objective Illness Severity

The main aim of this study was to examine the difference between patients' perceived illness severity and their biomedical severity. SPSS for Windows version 13.0 was used to analyze the data. Original scores and the mean scores of patients and oncologists along with the *t*-tests are presented in Table 1.1. The results demonstrate that cancer patients, as compared to their oncologists, perceived their disease as less severe. Independent *t*-tests were conducted to investigate the significance of mean differences.

Table 1.1: Aggregate Scores, Means and *t*-values of the Five Items of Perceived Illness Severity and Objective Illness Severity Scales

Perceived and Objective Severity Scores, Means and t-values ↓ → *Items of the Scale*	*PIS Scores*	*PIS Means (n = 30)*	*OIS Scores*	*OIS Means (n = 30)*	*t-value*
Severity of symptoms	84	2.80	113	3.77	2.82**
Severity of disease at the time of diagnosis	95	3.17	113	3.77	1.68
Severity of disease at present	72	2.40	119	3.97	4.76**
Condition as compared to earlier	62	2.07	109	3.63	4.24**
Doctors' control on the disease	66	2.20	102	3.40	4.50**
Aggregate scores	379	12.63	556	18.53	5.02**

Note: PIS = Perceived Illness Severity, OIS = Objective Illness Severity.
Significance Level = ** $p < 0.01$.

All the *t*-values were significant except for the severity at the time of diagnosis. As far as severity of symptoms was concerned, results suggested that patients perceived their symptoms as less severe than the oncologists and the difference was found to be significant [t (58) = 2.82, $P < 0.01$]. For the 2nd item that measured the severity at the time of diagnosis, the mean difference was not significant. The 3rd item that assessed the severity of the patient at present, demonstrated a significant difference [t (58) = 4.76, $P < 0.01$]. Fourth item measured patients' severity at the given time as compared to their earlier condition. The *t*-test for this item was significant which suggested that there was a difference between the perspective of patients and oncologists [t (58) = 4.24, $P < 0.01$].

As far as the control dimension was concerned, there was a significant difference between the patients' and the doctors' view [t (58) = 4.50,

$P < 0.01$]. Patients perceived that doctors had more control over their disease. The overall severity of patients reflected by the aggregate scores indicated a significant difference between perceived and biomedical severity [t (58) = 5.02, $P < 0.01$]. The results suggested that there was a significant difference between the perceived and objective illness severity of cancer patients.

Graphical Representation

The difference between the two severities has been presented graphically in order to give a clear picture. Figure 1.1 is a line diagram representing the level of perceived and biomedical disease severity assessed for each patient. X-axis represents patients and Y-axis represents the perceived and objective severity. As the legend describes, the higher line represents the objective severity and the lower one represents the perceived severity of patients. It is clear from the graph that the perceived severity of patients is lower in most of the cases.

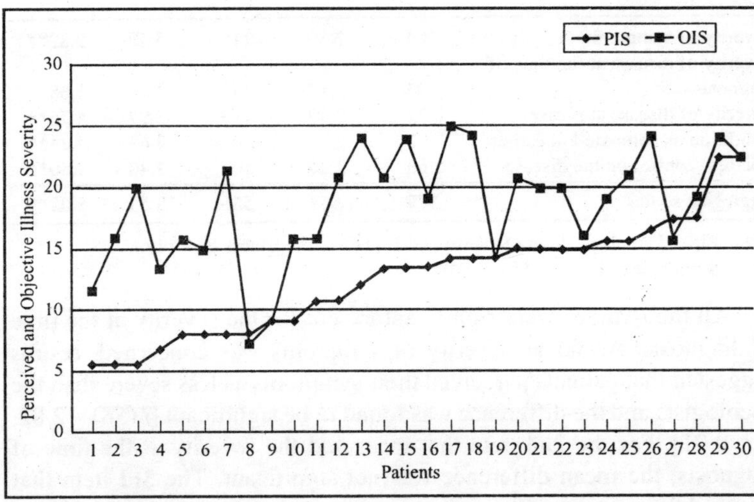

Figure 1.1: Graphical Representation of the Perceived and Objective Illness Severity of Patients

Qualitative Interviews

The aim of the qualitative interviews was to understand patients' perceptions regarding their disease severity. Therefore, questions were framed to understand the way patients make sense of their condition and the way they construe disease severity. The responses of patients were noted verbatim. During the interviews, the first observation by the researcher was patients' willingness to talk about their condition. It was patients' willingness to share their perceptions which encouraged the researcher to continue the interviews with them.

The qualitative responses of patients were transcribed and were read and reread several times. The contents of the responses were analyzed. The method used to analyze the data was theoretical thematic analysis as the purpose was theory driven (Braun & Clarke, 2006) and the aim was to focus on those aspects of data which reflected the dimensions of perceived illness severity. Initial codes were extracted from the transcribed data. In the present work, semantic and latent coding was done to identify dimensions related to patients' perceived severity.

In patients' responses, features pertaining to perceived illness severity were identified in the form of codes. Among the list of codes, those codes were identified that were reported by at least 50 per cent patients. Codes belonging to one broad theme were identified and categorized. Ten such broad themes or dimensions of severity emerged from the data analysis. It was observed that patients judged their severity on many more dimensions than just physical discomfort or the biomedical stage of the disease. Table 1.2 presents the dimensions of perceived illness severity of cancer patients along with the codes.

Table 1.2: Dimensions of Perceived Illness Severity Identified in the Interview Responses of Patients

Sl. No.	*Broad Dimensions of Severity*	*Codes Pertaining to the Severity Dimensions*
(1)	*(2)*	*(3)*
1.	Symptoms	(a) Pain in the body
		(b) Weight loss
		(c) Weakness as an indication of disease
		(d) Tiredness as an indication of disease
		(e) Nausea
		(f) Dryness of body
		(g) Tumour
		(h) Loss of appetite
		(i) Headache
2.	Physical effects of disease	(a) Overall side effects
		(b) Spells of unconsciousness
		(c) Difficulty in walking
		(d) Lack of efficiency

(Con

Table 1.2 (*Contd.*)

(1)	*(2)*	*(3)*
		(e) Decreased daily activities
		(f) Lack of strength
		(g) Memory loss
		(h) Difficulty in talking
		(i) Lack of sleep
		(j) Fatigue after the onset of disease
		(k) Weakness as an after-effect of disease
3.	Social effects of the disease	(a) Dependence on others
		(b) Unfulfilled responsibilities
4.	Effects of treatment	(a) Fear of treatment
		(b) Effects of chemotherapy and radiation
		(c) Severity due to hospitalization
		(d) Severity due to being bedridden
		(e) Hair fall
		(f) Spots on the body
		(g) Feeling of nausea
		(h) Heaviness in head
		(i) Dizziness
		(j) Bothersome bodily sensations
		(k) Gastric problem
		(l) Severity due to medicines
		(m) Constipation
5.	Body image	(a) Changed physical appearance
		(b) Hair fall
		(c) Changed skin texture and colour
		(d) Darkening of body
6.	Duration of illness	(a) Severity because of long duration of illness
		(b) Severity because of long treatment
7.	Controllability	(a) Severity because of lack of controllability
8.	Social comparison	(a) Severity felt when compared to other patients
9.	Psychological Impact	(a) Psychological impact of cancer in the form of stress, anxiety, depression, changed life view, etc.
10.	Global severity	(a) Cancer labelled as a severe disease

Discussion

Difference between Patients' Perceived and Objective Illness Severity: A Discussion of Results in the Light of Existing Research

On the basis of literature reviewed, it was hypothesized that patients' own perception of their disease severity would differ from the severity judged by the doctors. The results demonstrated that there was a significant difference between patients' perceived severity and their biomedical severity on various dimensions such as, severity of symptoms, severity at a given time, patients' severity as compared to their earlier condition, controllability and overall severity. Patients perceived their disease as less severe as compared to the oncologists' judgement. The results have been discussed in the following section using varied theoretical approaches and empirical evidence:

The difference in perceived and biomedical severity can result from the unawareness of patients. In the Indian context, some patients are not aware of the exact condition or stage of their disease. Thus, they rely on their experiences to judge severity. In many cultures cancer is understood as a very severe and fatal disease (Wang, Chen, Chen & Huang, 2004). In order to protect patients, doctors hide the diagnosis of cancer (Oken, 1961). In a study by Baird, RN and Eliasziw (2011), significant difference was found between perceived disease severity of coronary artery bypass graft patients and their spouses. The spouses perceived their partners' disease to be more severe than patients. Baird, *et al.*, have explained these inconsistencies on the basis of the different information that patients and their spouses receive about the disease. Wang, *et al.* (2004), stated that it is important to study the disclosure dimension culturally because in Asian, Arab and African countries, major emphasis is laid on family which influences disease disclosure.

Similar results as found in the present work were reported by Abudi, Bar-Tal, Ziv and Fish (1997). They studied the severity of symptoms reported by Parkinson's patients. Abudi, *et al.*, found that the severity reported by patients was less for some Parkinson's symptoms. The results were explained on the basis of patients' ability to cope with the limitations of disease. It is important to understand patients' severity (even if it is less than the biomedical severity) because the caregivers often fail to understand the perceptions of patients and expect the patients to feel bad even if the patients do not feel the impact of severity (Muhlenkamp & Joyner, 1986). The expectations of caregivers lead to discrepancy.

In another study on diabetes and osteoarthritis patients, general practitioners (GPs) evaluated patients' condition as more serious than the judgement of osteoarthritis patients (Heijmans, Foets, Rijken, Schreurs, de Ridder & Bensing, 2001). However, for diabetes patients, the researchers found mixed results. On some dimensions (life-threatening disease, progressiveness of disease and physical and social impairments) the GPs judged patients' condition as more serious, whereas on some dimensions (changing course, possibility of medical control, pain and visible bodily changes) the patients judged their condition as more serious. In case of diabetes, patients reported less medical control over their disease. Researchers have suggested that discrepancy in disease related stress is higher for a disease that lacks a clear treatment policy. In the present work, patients reported high perceptions of control by the doctors over their disease. This could be due to differences in awareness and knowledge about the disease. Heijmans, *et al.* (2001), have described taking two disease categories as a limitation of their study. They have suggested that, since every chronic disease has different problems, the results of their study cannot be generalized to other disease groups. Cancer is considered as a terminal disease. Therefore, it is important to understand cancer patients' perceptions regarding their disease separately. Cassileth, *et al.* (1984), have reported that even in chronic illnesses, patients learn to adapt to the disease that can result in lowered perception of severity.

Scholars have suggested that people interpret situations in unique ways and these interpretations of the situations affect their emotions and behaviour (Pawlik & Rosenzweig, 2000). Dember (1960) has defined perception as a process in which the behaviour of a person is triggered by a stimulation that impinges on the senses. The incoming stimulus and behaviour both have a wide range of possibilities and behaviour is a result of the perception of the external environment.

Miller, Brody and Summerton (1988) have reported that patients differ in their understanding of medical problems. Construal of stressful events also depends on the dispositional styles of people. People can be high on monitoring or blunting and their dispositional styles affect their reaction to the situation.

The first item of perceived and objective illness severity scale assessed patients' symptom severity from the perspective of patients and doctors. A significant difference was found between the two perspectives. Radley (1994) has stated that the meaning of illness depends on the person who is making the judgement. Doctors diagnose a disease on the basis of the symptoms or signs that patients show, whereas, patients come to know of their illness when they perceive any change in their body functions. Severity judged by the doctors is a clinical process. On the other hand, patients judge their condition on the basis of many factors such as, disease symptoms (pain, discomfort, etc.), affected relationships, economic burden due to disease, and stress caused by the disease, etc. Wiginton (1999) has noted that patients' own perception is the main cause of varying representations of lupus. Wiginton has further mentioned the importance of studying patients' perceptions regarding their illness, as this understanding can assist the medical professionals to provide better healthcare.

As noted by the cognitive theorists, it is the perception of situations and not the situations themselves that affect the responses of people (Bandura, 1986). These cognitive representations are formed by past experiences and the decisions about the present situations are made on the basis of these experiences. People suffering from same disease can have entirely different cognitive representations of their illness depending on their specific past experiences.

In the present study, overall the patients' perception of severity was significantly lower than the doctor's judgement. However, it is possible that sometimes patients perceive their severity as more than actual. Facing a chronic disease (e.g. cancer) is a traumatic event for the patients. Foa, Steketee and Rothbaum (1989) have discussed the cognitive basis of post-traumatic stress disorders. People have mental structures of traumatic events in their memories. When a person faces a traumatic event that matches with the existing features, it activates the fear memory and stimulates the fear structure. People have representations of cancer in their minds as a life-threatening disease. Diagnosis of cancer can trigger the fear structure in people. Because of this fear network, it is very likely that the patient perceives the severity of the disease as more than the actual.

It is important to study the patients' perspective of illness from a holistic perspective because illness experience is not only affected by the biological condition of the person but is given a meaning by the shared categories of the culture, gender, ethnicity, social position and age (Kleinman & Seeman, 2000). Cultural differences in illness perceptions have been studied widely. According to Baumann (2003): "Health beliefs and practices arise from normative or collective cultural values that interact with an individual's unique experiences, beliefs, and values that have been learned in and adapted to a particular context" (p. 242). Baumann has noted that in the Western cultures, biomedical approach is predominantly used in order to understand illness; whereas in socio-centric cultures, disease has also been understood on the basis of emotional, social and religious perspectives. On the basis of Baumann's observation, it can thus be surmised that it is important to study Indian cancer patients' perceptions of their disease.

According to the transactional model of stress (Lazarus & Folkman, 1984), the individual's perception of threat is strongly related to distress and quality of life than the objective or real event. Laubmeier and Zakowski (2004) found that compared to disease stage, perceived life threat was more strongly related to psychological distress and quality of life among cancer patients. Cameron, Leventhal and Leventhal (1993) found that the presence of symptoms was not the only predictor of care seeking in patients. Care seeking was also influenced by representations of factors related to health threat. Studies pertaining to the communication styles of physicians have demonstrated that physicians vary in their levels of sensitivity towards patients' perceptions of their own illness. It has been observed that physicians generally emphasize more on the medical aspects of patients' disease and overlook the psychosocial aspects (Verhaak, 1988).

Chronic illness changes the way of life and the self becomes vulnerable. Patients tend to think about the moral meanings of illness (Charmaz, 2000). The findings of the present study are supported by the constructivist approach which is participant centred, experience-based and relativistic (Wiginton, 1999). Overall, the results of the quantitative study suggested that disease severity in cancer patients was different from the biomedical perspective that relies on the clinical judgement of the disease. The biomedical perspective can be appropriate for the treatment of the patients. However, in order to understand the psychosocial status of cancer patients, it is important to understand disease severity from their perspective.

Qualitative Exploration of Dimensions of Perceived Illness Severity in Cancer Patients

The quantitative section demonstrated a difference between cancer patients' perceived disease severity and their biomedical severity. Further, qualitative interviews were conducted in order to explore the dimensions on which patients judged their disease severity. The results demonstrated that patients judged their disease severity on various dimensions related to their physical, psychological and social aspects of life. Ten dimensions were identified from the data. The first dimension pertained to the general physical symptoms of cancer. Leventhal, *et al.* (1980), have also mentioned that patients have schema pertaining to the symptoms of disease. The second dimension was related to the physical effects of cancer. Third dimension was perception of severity due to affected social relationships. Responses of patients suggested that patients also judged their condition on the basis of treatment side-effects. Judging one's condition on the basis of treatment effects can lead to negative psychological state. An important dimension of patients' perceived severity was distorted body-image. Patients judged their condition as more severe in case of altered physical appearance. Sixth and seventh dimensions were severity due to the duration and controllability of cancer. Time-line and controllability dimensions were also part of Leventhal's common sense model of illness. Results demonstrated that patients also perceived their condition as severe on the basis of comparing their condition with other patients. Patients reported the negative psychological impact of cancer as a basis to judge the severity of their disease. The last dimension reflected the overall perceived severity of patients due to the label of cancer as a severe disease. There was an overlap between perceived illness severity and the common sense model of illness. However, this overlap was observed only for three dimensions. Difference between perceived illness severity dimensions and the common sense model could be noted on the basis of the goals of the two models. The common sense model purported to understand patients' representations of their disease on specific dimensions; whereas, perceived illness severity intends to measure cancer patients' perceptions of severity.

Conclusion

The present study examined the difference between cancer patients' perceived illness severity and the biomedical judgement of their disease severity. The results suggested a significant difference between two types of severities. The findings of the present study can have major implications for patients suffering from cancer. Disparity in patients' and medical experts' views can lead to miscommunication and can affect the well-being and healthcare behaviour of patients. Understanding of cancer patients' perceptions can assist the healthcare providers to develop psycho-educational intervention programmes. This study was part of a larger study that was conducted to demonstrate the impact of perceived severity of cancer patients on their coping strategies. A perceived illness severity scale was constructed on the basis of the dimensions that were explored in the present study. Understanding patients' severity judgement on various dimensions suggests a holistic and patient-centred approach to cater to the psychosocial needs of patients. Adopting this approach can lead to an enhancement of positive coping strategies in patients, thereby increasing their quality of life.

REFERENCES

Abudi, S., Bar-Tal, Y., Ziv, L. and Fish, M. (1997). "Parkinson's Disease Symptoms — Patients' Perceptions", *Journal of Advanced Nursing*, 25, 54-59.

Baird, D.L., RN, M.N., Eliasziw, M. (2011). "Disparity in Perceived Illness Intrusiveness and Illness Severity between Cardiac Patients and their Spouses", *Journal of Cardiovascular Nursing*, 26, 6, 481-86.

Bandura, A. (1986). *Social Foundations of Thought and Action: A Social Cognitive Theory*, Englewood Cliffs, NJ: Prentice Hall.

Baumann, L.C. (2003). "Culture and Illness Representation", in L.D. Cameron and H. Leventhal (eds.), *The Self-regulation of Health and Illness Behaviour* (pp. 242-53). London: Routledge.

Bombardier, C. H., D'Amico, C. and Jordan, J.S. (1990). "The Relationship of Appraisal and Coping to Chronic Disease Adjustment", *Behavioural Research and Therapy*, 28(4), 297-304.

Braun, V. and Clarke, V. (2006). "Using Thematic Analysis in Psychology", *Qualitative Research in Psychology*, 3, 77-101.

Cameron, L., Leventhal, E. A. and Leventhal, H. (1993). "Symptom Representations and Affect as Determinants of Care Seeking in a Community-dwelling, Adult Sample Population", *Health Psychology*, 12(3), 171-79.

Cassileth, B.R., Lusk, E.J., Strouse, T.B., Miller, D.S., Brown, L.L., Cross, P.A. and Tenaglia, A.N. (1984). "Psychosocial Status in Chronic Illness: A Comparative Analysis of Six Diagnostic Groups", *The New England Journal of Medicine*, 311(8), 506-11.

Cella, D.F., Mahon, S.M. and Donovan, M.I. (1990). "Cancer Recurrence as a Traumatic Event", *Behavioural Medicine*, 16(1), 15-22.

Charmaz, K. (2000). "Experiencing Chronic Illness", in G.L. Albrecht, R. Fitzpatrick and S.C. Scrimshaw (eds.), *Handbook of Social Studies in Health and Medicine* (pp. 277-92), London: Sage Publications.

Dember, W.N. (1960). *The Psychology of Perception*, New York: Holt, Rinehart and Winston.

Derogatis, L.R., Morrow, G.R., Fetting, J., Penman, D., Piasetsky, S., Schmale, A.M., *et al.* (1983). "The prevalence of Psychiatric Disorders among Cancer Patients", *The Journal of the American Medical Association*, 249, 751-57.

Dunkel-Schetter, C., Feinstein, L.G., Taylor, S.E. and Falke, R.L. (1992). "Patterns of Coping with Cancer", *Health Psychology*, 11(2), 79-87.

Foa, E., Steketee, G. and Rothbaum, B.O. (1989). "Behavioural/Cognitive Conceptualizations of Post-traumatic Stress Disorder", *Behaviour Therapy*, 20, 155-76.

Glanz, K. and Lerman, C. (1992). "Psychosocial Impact of Breast Cancer: A Critical Review", *Annals of Behavioural Medicine*, 14(3), 204-12.

Greco, A., Steca, P., Pozzi, R., Monzani, D., D'Addario, M., Villani, A., Rella, V., Giglio, A., Malfatto, G. and Parati, G. (2014). "Predicting Depression from Illness Severity in Cardiovascular Disease Patients: Self-efficacy Beliefs, Illness Perception and Perceived Social Support as Mediators", *International Journal of Behavioural Medicine*, 21, 221-29.

Heijmans, M., Foets, M., Rijken, M., Schreurs, K., de Ridder, D. and Bensing, J. (2001). "Stress in Chronic Disease: Do the Perceptions of Patients and their General Practitioners Match?", *British Journal of Health Psychology*, 6, 229-42.

Holland, J.C. (1998). *Psycho-oncology*, New York: Oxford University Press.

Holland, K.D. and Holahan, C.K. (2003). "The Relation of Social Support and Coping to Positive Adaptation to Breast Cancer", *Psychology and Health*, 18(1), 15-29.

Juth, V., Silver, R.C. and Sender, L. (2015). "The Shared Experience of Adolescent and Young Adult Cancer Patients and their Caregivers", *Psychooncology*, Published online in Wiley Online Library (wileyonlinelibrary.com), DOI: 10.1002/pon.3785.

Kazak, A.E., Barakat, L.P., Meeske, K., Christakis, D., Meadows, A.T., Casey, R., Penati, B. and Stuber, M.L. (1997). "Post-traumatic Stress, Family Functioning and Social Support in Survivors of Childhood Leukemia and their Mothers and Fathers", *Journal of Consulting and Clinical Psychology*, 65(1), 120-29.

Kershaw, T., Northouse, L., Kritpracha, C., Schafenacker, A. and Mood, D. (2004). "Coping Strategies and Quality of Life in Women with Advanced Breast Cancer and their Family Caregivers", *Psychology and Health*, 19(2), 139-55.

Kleinman, A. and Seeman, D. (2000). "Personal Experience of Illness", in G.L. Albrecht, R. Fitzpatrick and S.C. Scrimshaw (eds.), *Handbook of Social Studies in Health and Medicine* (pp. 230-242), London: Sage Publications.

Laubmeier, K.K. and Zakowski, S.G. (2004). "The Role of Objective *versus* Perceived Life Threat in the Psychological Adjustment to Cancer", *Psychology and Health*, 19(4), 425-37.

Lazarus, R. and Folkman, S. (1984). *Stress, Appraisal and Coping*, New York: Springer.

Leventhal, H., Meyer, D. and Nerenz, D. (1980). "The Common-sense Representation of Illness Danger", in S. Rachman (ed.), *Contributions to Medical Psychology* (Vol. 2, pp. 7-30), New York: Pergamon Press.

List, M.A., Rutherford, J.L., Stracks, J., Haraf, D., Kies, M.S. and Vokes, E.E. (2002). "An Exploration of the Pretreatment Coping Strategies of Patients with Carcinoma of the Head and Neck", *Cancer*, 95(1), 98-104.

Manne, S.L., Sabbioni, M., Bovbjerg, D.H., Jacobsen, P.B., Taylor, K.L. and Redd, W.H. (1994). "Coping with Chemotherapy with Breast Cancer", *Journal of Behavioural Medicine*, 17(1), 41-55.

Marks, G., Richardson, J.L., Graham, J.W. and Levine, A. (1986). "Role of Health Locus of Control Beliefs and Expectations of Treatment Efficacy in Adjustment to Cancer", *Journal of Personality and Social Psychology*, 51(2), 443-50.

Miller, S.M., Brody, D.S. and Summerton, J. (1988). "Styles of Coping with Threat: Implications for Health", *Journal of Personality and Social Psychology*, 54(1), 142-48.

Muhlenkamp, F.A. and Joyner, A.J. (1986). "Arthritis Patients' Self-reported Affective States and their Caregivers' Perception", *Nursing Research*, 35(2), 24-27.

Northouse, L.L., Dorris, G. and Charron-Moore, C. (1995). "Factors Affecting Couples' Adjustment to Recurrent Breast Cancer", *Social Science and Medicine*, 41(1), 69-76.

Oken, D. (1961). "What to Tell Cancer Patients", *Journal of the American Medical Association*, 175, 1120-28.

Pawlik, K. and Rosenzweig, M.R. (2000). *International Handbook of Psychology*, London: Sage Publications.

Radley, A. (1994). *Making Sense of Illness: The Social Psychology of Health and Disease*, London: Sage Publications Limited.

Rao, D.N. and Ganesh, B. (1998). "Estimate of Cancer Incidence in India in 1991", *Indian Journal of Cancer*, 35(1), 10-18.

Shapiro, S.L., Lopez, A.M., Schwartz, G.E., Bootzin, R., Figueredo, A.J., Braden, C.J., and Kurker, S.F. (2001). "Quality of Life and Breast Cancer: Relationship to Psychosocial Variables", *Journal of Clinical Psychology*, 57(4), 501-19.

Trask, P.C. and Griffith, K.A. (2004). "The Identification of Empirically Derived Cancer Patient Subgroups Using Psychological Variables", *Journal of Psychosomatic Research*, 57, 287-95.

Trask, P.C., Paterson, A.G., Hayasaka, S., Dunn, R.L., Riba, M. and Johnson, T. (2001). "Psychosocial Characteristics of Individuals with Non-stage IV Melanoma", *Journal of Clinical Oncology*, 19(11), 2844-50.

Verhaak, P.F. (1988). "Detection of Psychological Complaints by General Practitioners", *Medical Care*, 26(10), 1009-20.

Wang, S., Chen, C., Chen, Y. and Huang, H. (2004). "The Attitude Toward Truth Telling of Cancer in Taiwan", *Journal of Psychosomatic Research*, 57, 53-58.

Wiginton, K.L. (1999). "Illness Representations: Mapping the Experience of Lupus", *Health Education and Behaviour*, 26(4), 443-53.

2

Health Beliefs and Behaviour During Acculturation
The Case of the *Kharwar* Tribal Group

R.C. Mishra

In this chapter the focus is on health beliefs and behaviour of women of the *Kharwar* tribal group. This is a population that has not been much studied by psychologists. The chapter presents a brief description of the tribal context of India. Then the cultural and psychological characteristics of tribal people are outlined in order to argue how these can be used in meeting the challenges of their health. Major issues related to the health of *Kharwar* women are discussed in some detail with the help of studies dealing with physical and mental health problems of the *Kharwar* women. These studies show how the health problems of the *Kharwar* women are different from those of other (cultural) groups of the Indian society. Towards the end, it is argued that a culturally sensitive, ecologically valid, and economically viable programme of health management is needed in order to ensure effective participation of tribal people in general, and of the *Kharwar* women in particular, in various health related programmes.

The Tribal Context of India

The culturally plural nature of Indian society is a significant feature that distinguishes it in several respects from many other societies of the world. Several ethnic, religious, and linguistic groups constitute the cultural mosaic of the country, but these groups also show enormous differences with respect to their socio-cultural features. Such a cultural diversity provides Indian researchers with the opportunity for carrying out cross-cultural research next door, a privilege, which is not available to researchers at other places. Among the various cultural groups, some constitute mainstream of the Indian society, whereas others exist as peripheral groups trying to seek entry (or being pushed for entry) into the larger mainstream society.

Characterized by the existence of a number of caste groups the mainstream Indian society represents a vertical structure, which is generally not found anywhere else in the world. The tribal people represent an outcaste group; they do not form part of the mainstream of the Indian society. They are popularly known as *Adivasi*, which means the original inhabitants of the country. They are regarded as people indigenous to the soil. A majority of them lives in naturally isolated forests and hilly regions. Hence, they are also known as *Vanavasi* (forest dwellers). Constitutionally, these groups are named as Scheduled Tribes (ST) or *Anusuchit Janajati*. They are listed in the Constitution of India for special privileges in matters like education and employment. In other parts of the world, such populations are named as "aboriginal" or "indigenous" or "native" peoples.

A point to be noted here is that the term "tribal" is defined nowhere in the Constitution of India. As a result, a lot of debate revolves around the use of this term. In his book, "The Time of Tribes", Maffesoli (1996) argues that in certain respects all of us seem to belong to a tribal group. However, according to Article 342 of the Constitution of India, the ST represents the tribes or tribal communities, which may be notified by the President of India from time to time. This means that the existing list of tribal groups cannot be taken as final. The Census of India enumerates only such tribal communities as are scheduled under the relevant constitutional order that is in force at the time of the census.

In anthropological and sociological writings, the term "tribal" is used to refer to a group of people who: (1) claim themselves as indigenous to the soil; (2) generally inhabit forest and hilly regions; (3) largely pursue a subsistence level economy; (4) have great regard for traditional religious and cultural practices; (5) believe in a common ancestry; and (6) have strong in-group ties. Mishra (2007a) argues that none of these characteristics strictly applies to all tribal people. For practical purposes, tribal groups today represent a "federally determined and locally recognized category". In some psychological research, they are also identified on the basis of "strong identity" of a tribal, just like any other ethnic group in a multicultural society.

Tribal people do not represent a homogeneous group today. However, a majority of them still retains its traditional cultural features despite being exposed to many historical and cultural influences in earlier decades. Reports indicate that the tribal represents the most neglected group of the Indian society even today (Sivanand, 2001). The Central and State governments have introduced a variety of developmental programmes to bring about changes in different spheres of their life with a view to raise their socio-economic level. These changes are currently witnessed in the life of tribal populations, both at the group and individual levels. On the other hand, the participation of tribal people in change programmes has been quite diverse depending mainly on the region of the country where they live.

Classification of Tribal Groups

Tribal populations have been classified in many different ways. These classifications are based on several indicators of socio-economic development and cultural transformations in their life. A dominant classification, based on economic activities, classifies them into four distinct groups, namely hunting-gathering group, rudimentary agricultural group, irrigation agricultural group, and urban, industrial wage-earning group (Mishra, Sinha & Berry, 1996). In recent years, some individuals of agricultural groups are also engaged in business or wage employment. The lifestyle of such individuals differs from that of other members who still live a traditional life. The wage-earning people have adopted some of the cultural and psychological qualities of the members of other groups. On the other hand, the hunting-gathering and, to some extent, rudimentary agricultural groups (e.g. the *Birhor* and *Asur* in Jharkhand) display little impact of other cultural groups or of the development programmes. In official records, these groups are labelled as "primitive" or "backward" tribes. It is the members of these groups who are in the main focus of most of the developmental activities of the Government. While there are enormous differences in the life of "primitive" and "other" tribal groups, in many parts of the country, differences are also obvious between the life of "tribal" groups and "Christian tribal" groups.

People generally hold a negative view of tribal peoples. In scholarly writings and official documents, terms like "primitive culture", "educational backwardness", "cultural backwardness" and "intellectual deficits" have often been used. These expressions suggest that tribal people in general are culturally inferior, behaviourally unsophisticated, and intellectually underdeveloped compared to members of other groups. Such conceptions held about tribal people do not have any reasonable basis or empirical support. The strengths of tribal culture and life generally go unnoticed by people who do not know them closely. Hence, most of the evaluative judgements about tribal groups largely reflect the stereotypical perceptions of the larger population rather than the reality.

Acculturation in the Tribal Context

Tribal populations in India have been subjected to variety of acculturative influences during the last century. Several changes have been imposed (perhaps deliberately) on the life of tribal people in recent years. Initially, these changes came through Christian missionaries; they provided tribal people with a model of change in the form of church organization, western education and inculcation of western values (Roy, 1931). Special programmes have been developed for integration of the tribal communities in the mainstream society (Saxena, 1983). While this influence has not altogether vanished from the life of tribal people, in recent years a major acculturative influence has come through industrialization and urbanization going on in tribal regions. So much so, that Vidyarthi (1970) calls it "industry-based urban explosion". The impact of such developments has resulted in uprooting of tribal populations from their original habitat and in disintegration of their cultural context.

The implementation of tribal development and welfare schemes has introduced several changes in the lives of tribal people. The Government of India evolved a policy of "integration" of tribal people with the mainstream society. Guided by the spirit of this policy attempts have been made towards bringing about changes in the economic, social, cultural and political life of the tribal people, although the overall result of such efforts has not been very encouraging (Saxena, 1983).

In spite of apparent difficulties with regard to these programmes, some influences of the outside world have reached some sections of the tribal population. Among others (e.g. agriculture, education) health programmes along with introduction of modern medicines have gained popularity, particularly in the less isolated villages. However, change in the tribal way of life has not been felt so distinctly; particularly, the relatively isolated and traditional groups have been less affected by these programmes than the more acculturated groups.

Health in the Tribal Population

During the last decades much has been said and written about tribal people of India, including the problems of their health. Distributed in some 427 communities tribal people constitute about 8.6 per cent of the total Indian population, representing the weakest section of the Indian society. In spite of all efforts towards change, the life of tribal people is still organized according to certain beliefs, rituals, customs, and taboos, which are different from those of the general population. In addition, their economic, political, social, and cultural traditions are so different from other groups of the Indian society that they can be regarded as distinct cultural groups (Mishra, *et al.*, 1996).

Psychologists, who have worked with tribal groups, maintain that the barriers of their development in the health domain are mainly cultural in nature. The kind of changes in behaviour the development programmes require are often inconsistent with behaviours that have been practiced and encouraged in tribal communities for generations. The traditional knowledge and skills, with which they could survive in their respective environments for centuries, carry a lot of value even today. During the last decades, however, the tribal populations have experienced acculturation through their exposure to the outside world, contact with other cultural groups, and government initiated activities going on in their regions.

Health is one of the areas of human life in which social psychological principles seem to have direct applications. The World Health Organization (1988) defines health as a state of physical, mental, social, and spiritual well-being of individuals, not merely the absence of disease and infirmity. While there is a notion of health held by medical practitioners, research suggests that the meaning of health and disease is constructed differently across cultures (Helman, 1990; Radley, 1994). People hold different viewpoints about health and illness. They also nurture different types of beliefs and engage in different types of practices with regard to the maintenance of health and treatment of diseases. Even the practitioners of different medicinal systems (e.g. Allopathic, Homoeopathic, *Ayurvedic*, and *Unani*) do not agree on issues such as the meaning of health, causes of ill-health, prevention or treatment of health problems, and so on (Singh, Tripathi, Verma, & Mishra, 1999). Behaviours associated with maintenance and promotion of health or prevention and treatment of illness have been the main subjects of study in health psychology (Matarazzo, 1980) in general and in cross-cultural health psychology in particular (Berry, Poortinga, Breugelmans, Chasiotis, & Sam, 2011).

The role of psychosocial factors in behaviours, which keep people healthy and those that produce long-term and debilitating diseases, has been well documented (Berry, Poortinga, Segall & Dasen, 2002). On the other hand, there is much less understanding of how people in different societies and cultures explain the causes of ill-health, which types of treatment they believe in, who they generally turn to when caught ill, and what system(s) of medicine they often use to cure the ailment. The significance of these issues for health and illness has been highlighted in some previous work (Furnham, 1988). For organizing any disease prevention and health promotion programme, full understanding of peoples' cultural values, traditions, beliefs and patterns of family interaction is considered necessary.

There is no doubt that people everywhere accept the importance of health in life, but almost all of us in our life time fall ill and consult someone for cure. Research suggests that the current professional practice of health is based on the assumption that diseases (e.g. fever) are universal, and that their treatment recipes (e.g. Paracetamol) have universal appeal. In such a conception of human health, cultural factors are altogether ignored (McName & Gergen, 1992; Capewell, 1994; Lewis, Fernandez & Kleinman, 1994; Beardsley & Pederson, 1997; Tanaka-Matsumi & Draguns, 1997; Misra & Verma, 1999). Based on the analysis of health and disease concepts Antonovsky (1979) had suggested that health was influenced by specific social and cultural contexts. Helman's (1985, 1990) analysis shows that culture influences health behaviour through the generation of specific knowledge, beliefs, customs and habits. These factors need to be accommodated for meaningful understanding and management of health problems in any society.

Viewed from this cultural perspective, the portrayal of a universal picture of health or well-being of individuals appears a highly challenging task. In order to ensure the relevance of health research, we need to focus on local cultural contexts and community conceptions of health including the health beliefs, attitudes and behaviour of individuals. Women are regarded as more vulnerable group than men for many health problems, and there are also certain health problems that are specifically related to women (e.g. pregnancy related problems, cancer of cervix or breast). Studies of health, being widely carried out with male samples, seem to reflect a gender bias. In fact, women's point of view with respect to many health problems is present in such a faint degree that it hardly gets resonated in health psychology literature. Indian researchers have conducted some good studies on health beliefs and behaviour of women suffering from diseases like cancer and diabetes

(Mishra, Awasthi & Singh, 2004; Awasthi, Mishra & Shahi, 2006; Awasthi & Mishra, 2007, 2008, 2013), but the studies are confined to patients seeking treatment in hospitals. The women of normal population have been studied only as control groups. Contrasts in samples have been created by the inclusion of educated and uneducated women from rural and urban settings, but the cultural perspective is missing in these studies.

In the following sections, we will look at some studies carried out with women of the *Kharwar* tribal cultural group living in Naugarh region of eastern U.P. The studies were carried out with the objective of grasping women's viewpoint on several issues pertaining to their health.

The *Kharwar* Group and the Field Setting

The *Kharwar* tribal group, with which the studies were carried out, lives in the hilly regions of Naugarh Block of Chandauli district (earlier part of Varanasi) in eastern U.P. They represent a tribal community now settled in villages as agriculturalists. They consider themselves as *Rajput* (descendants of ruling Hindu warrior classes of North India), and engage in many of their cultural practices (e.g. worshipping weapons). Their houses are built of mud walls and tiled roofs with enough space to store agricultural produce. They have a community *Panchayat*, a village *Pradhan* (the headman) and a *Baiga* (the priest). The *Baiga* occupies a prominent place in their life. Prior to cultivation of land and harvest, he engages with the family in propitiating the local deities. He also decides the auspicious days for initiating a number of activities by the people of the community.

The Naugarh region is characterized by acute shortage of water providing people with very limited irrigation facilities. Hence, the *Kharwar* living in this region grow mainly the crops of the rainy season. These are often eaten up by the wild animals roaming around. Guarding crops against animals is a round-the-clock activity for the *Kharwar*. The agricultural produce can barely feed them for 3-4 months. For the rest of the year, they have to depend mainly on forest being engaged in activities like hunting and gathering.

There is great scarcity of drinking water in the whole region. During the summer the water level goes down, and the hand pumps installed in villages stop lifting water. In this state of affairs, people in many villages depend on *Chuan* (the seepage water), which appears to be a major cause of diarrhoea for people. Medical facilities are generally not available in villages. So much so, that even today one has to walk or ride a bicycle for about 10-20 km. to avail very basic medical facilities. Some *Kharwar* have good knowledge of herbs, roots and seeds that carry medicinal value, but people generally do not use them much nowadays. They prefer tablets and capsules that are handy and involve no efforts. The overall health status of the community is poor. There are very few schools to cater to children's need of primary education.

A few NGOs have started programmes of primary education and healthcare in some villages, but the facilities to serve to the health needs of people are very meagre. On the whole, the *Kharwar* life is characterized by many difficulties and constraints. Due to pressure of economy, the new generation is moving away from villages in search of wages. Consequently, a number of changes can be noticed in some families, while the majority continues to live a traditional life.

Health in the *Kharwar* Community

During the initial visits to the field in the early 1990s, we observed that people suffered from a number of health problems. With respect to health behaviour, we found that for the first few days they watched the progress of the disease. A common belief was that poison accumulated in one's body due to several reasons came out in the form of a disease. If the illness did not go away, people consulted the local *Baiga* (the priest), who would tell what kind of *Puja* (worship) was to be performed, and which god had to be propitiated. Then the traditional healers were consulted. Doctors were consulted at the last stage when the patient had been completely taken over by the disease. A number of changes in these practices are taking place nowadays, especially in the new generation, which prefers to consult a practitioner of modern (Allopathic) system of medicine instead of going to a *Baiga* or a healer.

Physical Health Problems of the *Kharwar* Women

In the previous decades Naugarh happened to be in the red column of the newspapers, especially during the summer when acute shortage of drinking water and infant deaths due to diarrhoea were often reported. To understand and intervene into the problems faced by the people of this region, an informal study (Mishra, 1997) was organized. It started with a series of visits made to a number of villages, but mainly to those villages from where the sad episodes of life were reported in the newspapers. A team, consisting of an educationist, a psychologist, a horticulturist, and a medical scientist, travelled together, walked through the villages, camped there, chatted with men and women about life in villages, and asked about problems they faced in day-to-day lives. The team also explored their knowledge of agriculture, flora and fauna, discussed the problems of their health, and probed into the support systems available to the community for healthcare. These discussions were recorded (soon after discussions) and later subjected to content analysis.

In this informal study, discussions were held with 100 women, aged 27-60 years, on various issues related to health. The analysis revealed the following major health problems with the percentage of women reporting each one of them: diarrhoea (96%), fever (90%), child mortality (70%), conjunctivitis (68%), unwanted pregnancy (65%), delivery deaths (56%), arthritis (34%), and eye defects (30%). It may be noted that women were allowed to mention as many problems as they could.

We also asked women to tell the main causes of the abovementioned health problems. Here again, women could mention multiple causes of health problems. In general, women attributed five different causes to their health problems. These included food, water, bad habits, evil eye, and evil spirits. The percentage of women attributing these different causes to health problems varies considerably, but an obvious point to be noted is the presence of physical, behavioural and supernatural causes of health problems in their attributions. The analysis indicated that food and personal habits were largely held responsible for fever, food and evil spirits for diarrhoea, personal habits and evil eye for conjunctivitis, water and personal habits for arthritis, evil spirits and personal habits for eye defects as well as unwanted pregnancy, evil spirits and evil eye for delivery deaths and child mortality. A noteworthy point in this respect is the perceived importance of personal habits and evil spirit for almost all kind of health problems in the community.

The study also explored the major support systems of the *Kharwar* women that could be mobilized during the crisis situations. Here again, the participants could mention multiple supports. The analysis revealed that family occupied the first place (100%) in the hierarchy of supports. The other supports were relatives (86%), friends (76%), neighbours (68%) and local healers (36%). The supports included physical (e.g. time, money, food, and medicines), social (e.g. company, advice, and suggestion) and emotional (e.g. sharing, affection, and trust) supports. The percentage of women reporting these supports from the family was 100, 96 and 88 respectively. Noteworthy is the high percentage of all the three kind of supports. Relatives, neighbours and friends were also mentioned as the people providing these supports. It might be noted that none of the participants mentioned a doctor or hospital as support in healthcare.

Health Cognition and Practices of Young and Elderly *Kharwar* Women

In health psychology literature there is enough evidence to suggest that young and old people not only experience different health problems, but they also perceive them differently. Mishra (2009) analyzed the health cognition and practices of the *Kharwar* women by using a standard questionnaire, which probed into the meaning of health, major health problems, control agency for illnesses, responsibility for illnesses, prevention from illnesses and ways of maintaining good health. A local research assistant interviewed women individually. The responses were content-analyzed by two independent judges.

The findings revealed that the participants generally described health as a disease-free state, characterized by body strength. In addition to the health problems noted in Mishra (1997) study, the participants also mentioned cough/cold, headaches, and skin diseases as their major health problems. The distribution of reported health problems according to the age of women (i.e. below 30 years and above 50 years) revealed that all the problems were well represented in the cognition of both young and elderly women. Among others, diarrhoea and fever appeared to be the most important problems of health. Significant differences in the cognition of health problems according to age were found observed on conjunctivitis, headaches, unwanted pregnancy, child mortality (young/elderly), arthritis and skin diseases (elderly/young).

Women generally mentioned multiple causes of health problems, which could be grouped into three broad categories, namely environmental (weather, food, and water), personal (own behaviour, carelessness, and habits) and supernatural (evil eye, evil spirits, and local deities). With respect to the attribution of environmental causes, a significant difference between the young and elderly women was noted on child mortality alone (young/elderly). Younger women mentioned personal causes more frequently than the elderly women. Differences between the two groups were significant on fever, conjunctivitis, arthritis, cold/cough, headaches, skin diseases and unwanted pregnancy. Except for unwanted pregnancy and child mortality, the elderly women attributed supernatural causes to health problems more frequently than the younger women did. Significant differences between the groups were noted on conjunctivitis, arthritis, headaches, skin diseases, unwanted pregnancy, and child mortality.

The participants did not regard doctor as an important agent of control for illnesses. The local *Vaidya* (herbal medicinal practitioner) and healer were considered as main control agents. The younger women preferred to consult a doctor, while the elderly women preferred to consult a healer. However, both the groups attributed the lowest level of control to self.

With respect to health maintenance, a majority of women indicated food/water, cleanliness and personal habits as major factors. Compared to elderly women, the younger women more often considered doctor as an important factor in health maintenance. With respect to illness prevention, the findings revealed that both the groups considered food, water and cleanliness as the most important factors. The participants also mentioned medical check-up and satisfaction of spirits as other factors, but a significant difference between young and elderly women was observed with respect to the satisfaction of spirits.

Stressors and Mental Health Problems of the *Kharwar* Women

The analysis of physical health problems of women in the *Kharwar* community threw up many health-related questions. Looking at the hardships of life in the villages and the pressures of social and cultural change being imposed from outside, we wondered if these conditions would not lead to the experience of mental health problems on the part of women. Some previous research with culturally changing tribes in Bihar (now Jharkhand) had indicated that changes introduced in the traditional life of people were often conflict-ridden and tensional (Sinha, Mishra, & Berry, 1992; Mishra & Kothiyal, 1995; Mishra, *et al.*, 1996; Mishra, 2007b). However, when these are "forced" on people without seeking their options, they tend to be disruptive for groups and stressful for individuals. High stress and greater incidence of health problems among acculturating societies and individuals are now well documented in research (Sam & Berry, 2006; Sam, 2006). Although many stressors associated with such changes have been pointed out in studies (Berry, 2006), analyses have less frequently been made of the stressors, which individuals perceive as operating in their specific contexts. The extent to which such stressors were present in the changing cultural context of the *Kharwar*, and the extent to which they were stress producing for the *Kharwar* women, were not known.

Mishra and Vajpayee (1996) made an attempt to analyze the stressors in the life of *Kharwar* women and compare them with those found in the life of another community (i.e. *Yadav*) living the same villages, but not undergoing any major cultural change. The assumption was that (a) women of the *Kharwar* community would experience different variety of stressors than those of the *Yadav* community; and (b) that women of the *Kharwar* community would experience greater mental health problems than those of the other community. In the study we observed and interviewed a group of 60 women, aged 24-58 years. In the observation we focused on the activities in which women of these groups actively participated. While some of the activities could be put into the category of "light work" (e.g. preparing meals, sweeping, washing dishes, and making rope, etc.), many of the activities also appeared to be strenuous (e.g. fetching water, mending house, making flour, sowing potatoes, and rice plantation, etc.). Nevertheless, the participants generally reported none of these activities as "stress-producing". They formed part of the day-to-day life of the *Kharwar* women to which they seemed to have adapted.

The analysis of stressors revealed that these were largely related to financial and familial constraints. The ten major problems and the percentage of the *Kharwar* women expressing worry about them were: money (93%), child education (87%), treatment and care of the sick (80%), child mortality (80%), guarding the crops from wild animals (67%), drinking water (65%), diminishing forest resources (57%), money-lenders (47%), unwanted pregnancy (43%), and disabled/old parents or grandparents (37%). Although the women of the *Yadav* community also mentioned many of these problems almost to the same level, the percentage of women reporting problems like guarding crops from animals (37%), drinking water (13%), diminishing forest resources (23%), and unwanted pregnancies (10%) was fairly low in comparison to that of the *Kharwar* women.

Analysis of the mental health scores indicated that *Kharwar* women reported significantly greater number of psychological and psycho-physiological problems of health than did the *Yadav* women. The difference between the two groups was not significant on the problems of physical health.

Major Issues of Health in Tribal Populations

Studies carried out with the *Kharwar* women bring certain issues relating to health that need some reflection and discussion. In the following pages, we will examine five main concerns that often arise in studies of tribal populations.

(a) *Continuity and Change in the Notion of Health*

The findings of our studies indicate that the problems of health, including the strategies of their prevention and treatment, are represented in the cognition of the *Kharwar* women almost in the same way that they are found in other groups. Surveys (e.g. Dubey, 1993) carried out with the *Kharwar* of the Naugarh region indicate that they have been in contact with people of other groups for almost a century from now. Some two decades ago, they were introduced to the modern medical facilities as a part of the development programme going on in their region. Since then, the health of women and children has been particularly in the focus of all health related activities organized either by the government machinery or by the NGOs. These interventions seem to have considerable influence on health related ideas of the *Kharwar* community. The notion of health held by *Kharwar* women at the present time is much similar to the one held by people of the mainstream society. The ideas were not the same in the previous decades (see Mishra, 1997 study).

(b) *Cultural Specificity of Health Problems*

In studying health problems of the *Kharwar* women the expectation was that they would mention some culture-specific problems. This expectation was not borne out of the findings. There was nothing culture-specific about the health problems reported by the *Kharwar* women. The only difference noted was with regard to the language used to describe some of the health problems. For example, conjunctivitis was called *Laali* (red eye disease), headache as *Adhakapari* (half skull pain), and diarrhoea as *Petjhari* (upset stomach). These terms come from the language widely spoken in the Naugarh region, and are possibly shared by the members of other (non-tribal) groups. On the other hand, differences noted with respect to the frequency with which diseases are reported indicate that the cognition of health problems, including their causation and control, does vary across individuals in the population. For example, headaches, problems of eye, unwanted pregnancies, and child mortality were of greater concern for younger women, whereas arthritis and skin diseases were of greater concern for relatively elderly women.

(c) *Salience of Factors in Health Problems*

Analysis of the factors related to disease causation revealed that personal factors were considered important more by young than elderly women. On the other hand, supernatural factors showed considerable variation between the young and elderly women according to health problems. This suggests that although women believe in co-existence of multiple agencies of control (e.g. personal, environmental and supernatural) for health problems, they assign different weights to each control agency for different health problems. This feature generally characterizes the cognition and behaviour of culturally changing individuals and communities (Mishra, *et al.*, 1996). Health problems attributed to multiple causes (e.g. food, habits, and evil spirits) in the studies (Mishra, 1997, 2009) indicate that culturally rooted belief systems are not easily displaced in the course of acculturation.

Some studies (e.g. Dalal, 1999) indicate that people of traditional societies often hold external factors (e.g. fate, God) responsible for health problems more than internal (personal) or environmental factors. The findings with *Kharwar* women do not offer strong support to this notion. *Kharwar* women did believe in supernatural causes of illness, but they also admitted the importance of personal and environmental factors in disease causation. The belief that health problems do have an outside locus is clearly reflected, but the role of an individual's own behaviour in its causation is also acknowledged.

(d) *Agency of Disease Control*

The findings indicated that women in general did not consider 'doctor' as an important agent of disease control. In previous decades, a doctor was generally not known to people of the *Kharwar* community. Even in recent years, the traditional system of health care (e.g. consulting a *Vaidya* or a healer) is more often used than consulting a doctor. This happens for two reasons: (a) the doctor is not easily available in villages; and (2) people do not have money to afford the cost of doctor's consultation.

A weak tendency towards the use of modern medicinal system for healthcare was also evident on the part of women. Studies indicate that in the process of social and cultural change, traditional institutions of the society often undergo change, and that individuals participate in this process differently. In case of the *Kharwar*, the traditional healthcare system is not eroded; it still functions as a vital health care system for the community. This system needs to be strengthened in order to fulfil people's day-to-day health requirements locally without dependence on others. Its utility is recognized and pleaded for in studies (e.g. Joshi, 2000).

(e) *Acculturation and Mental Health*

Reduction in mental health status of individuals undergoing acculturation is a commonly reported finding (Berry, 1990; Mishra, *et al.*, 1996). A number of stressors are postulated for explaining the lowered level of mental health (Berry, 2006; Mishra, 2007b). In the *Kharwar* community, the stressors seem to be more of economic and social than of personal nature. Women mentioned money, child's education, care of the sick, drinking water, and dwindling forests as major stressors of their life. Apparently all these conditions are related to people's survival, and in this sense, they may be regarded as "culture-specific stressors". Thus, while we do not find much evidence for cultural specificity in respect of physical health problems, the evidence is fairly strong in the case of mental health problems. The *Kharwar* women reported more psycho-physiological than merely physiological (physical) problems of health. This finding is consonant with previous findings obtained with other tribal groups (see Mishra, *et al.*, 1996); it reconfirms the claim that, in the course of acculturation, psychological difficulties of traditional groups and individuals are often expressed in somatic forms.

Concluding Comments

The studies described in this chapter present a picture of physical and mental health problems of women belonging to the *Kharwar* tribal group of Uttar Pradesh. The findings indicate that the *Kharwar* women have a clear understanding of the major health problems they face in day-to-day life, although some of the problems are also labelled differently in the local language. Women believe in multiple causation of illness and multiple illness control agencies. Despite having a strong belief in supernatural causes of illness, women also hold personal behaviours to be partly responsible for health problems. Although their mental health problems are not serious at the moment, with increasing demands of change, the risk of running into them is likely to be enhanced. People concerned with health and well-being of tribal populations may find these findings useful for organizing health services locally in effective ways. The situation calls for the programmes of social and cultural change to be carried out in sensitive ways, so that, the tribal people can find enough space for integrating the strengths of their traditional culture and life with those that are highly valued in modern times.

REFERENCES

Antonovsky, A. (1979). *Health, Stress and Coping*, San Francisco: Jossey Bass.

Awasthi, P., Mishra, R.C. and Shahi, U.P. (2006). "Health Beliefs and Behaviour of Cervix Cancer Patients", *Psychology and Developing Societies*, 18(1), 37-58.

Awasthi, P. and Mishra, R.C. (2007). "Role of Coping Strategies and Social Support in Perceived Illness Consequences and Controllability among Diabetic Women", *Psychology and Developing Societies*, 19(2), 179-97.

Awasthi, P. and Mishra, R.C. (2008). "A Comparative Study of Chronic Illness Beliefs of Cancer and Diabetic Women", *Journal of Indian Health Psychology*, 3(1), 27-49.

Awasthi, P. and Mishra, R.C. (2013). "Can Social Support and Control Agency Change Illness Consequences? Evidence from Cervix Cancer Patients", *Open Journal of Medical Psychology*, 2(3), 115-23.

Beardsley, L. and Pederson, P. (1997). "Health and Culture Centred Intervention", in J.W. Berry, M.H. Segall and C. Kagitcibasi (eds.), *Handbook of Cross-cultural Psychology*, Vol. 3, *Social Behaviour and Applications*. Boston: Allyn and Bacon.

Berry, J.W. (1990). "Psychology of Acculturation: Understanding Individuals Moving between Cultures", in R. Brislin (ed.), *Applied Cross-cultural Psychology* (pp. 232-53). Newbury Park: Sage.

Berry, J.W. (2006). "Stress Perspectives on Acculturation", in D. Sam, and J.W. Berry (eds.), *The Cambridge Handbook of Acculturation Psychology* (pp. 43-57), Cambridge: Cambridge University Press.

Berry, J.W., Poortinga, Y.H., Segall, M. and Dasen, P.R. (2002). *Cross-cultural Psychology: Research and Applications* (2nd ed.), Cambridge: Cambridge University Press.

Berry, J.W., Poortinga, Y.H., Breugelmans, S.M., Chasiotis, A., and Sam, D. (2011). *Cross-cultural Psychology: Research and Applications* (3rd ed.), Cambridge: Cambridge University Press.

Capewell, S. (1994). *Are Health and Illness Defined by Society or by Doctor?*, Proceedings of Royal College of Physicians, 24, 181-86.

Dalal, A.K. (1999). "Health Beliefs and Coping with Chronic Illness", in G. Misra (ed.), *Psychological Perspectives on Stress and Health* (pp. 100-125). New Delhi: Concept.

Dubey, V.K. (1993). *The Agony of Life*, Varanasi: National Council of Development Communication.

Furnham, A. (1988). *Lay Theories: Everyday Understanding of Problems in the Social Sciences*, Oxford: Pergamon.

Helman, C. (1985). *Psyche, Soma, and Society: The Social Construction of Psychosomatic Disorders, Culture, Medicine, and Psychiatry*, 9(1), 1-26.

Helman, C. (1990). *Culture, Health and Illness*, London: Wright.

Joshi, P.C. (2000). "Relevance and Utility of Traditional Medical Systems (TMS) in the Context of a Himalayan Tribe", *Psychology and Developing Societies*, 12(1), 5-29.

Lewis-Fernandez, R. and Kleinman, A. (1994). "Culture, Personality and Psychopathology", *Journal of Abnormal Psychology*, 103(1), 67-71.

Maffasoli, M. (1996). *The Time of Tribes*, Thousand Oaks: Sage.

Matarazzo, J.D. (1980). "Behavioural Health and Behavioural Medicine: Frontiers for a New Health Psychology", *American Psychologist*, 35(9), 807-17.

McName, S. and Gergen, K.J. (1992). *Therapy as Social Construction*, London: Sage.

Mishra, R.C. and Kothiyal, D. (1995). "Stress in Relation to Varying Experiences of Culture Change", in O.P. Misra and S.K. Srivastava (eds.), *Ecological Perspectives and Behaviour* (pp. 89-102), Hardwar: Gurukul Kangri University.

Mishra, R.C., Sinha, D., and Berry, J.W. (1996). *Ecology, Acculturation and Psychological Adaptation: A Study of Adivasis in Bihar*, New Delhi: Sage.

Mishra, R.C. and Vajpayee, A. (1996). "Mental Health Problems of Women in a Culturally Changing Community", *Indian Journal of Mental Health and Disabilities*, 1, 8-15.

Mishra, R.C. (1997). "Family Support and Health Care in a Cultural Changing Village Community in Northern India", *Social Science International*, 13(1 & 2), 10-18.

Mishra, R.C., Awasthi, P. and Singh, S.K. (2004). "Illness Causation Beliefs and Perceived Illness Consequences in Diabetic Women", *Psychological Studies*, 49, 238-44.

Mishra, R.C. (2007a). "Psychological Perspective on Educational Development of Tribals", in M.B. Sharan and D. Suar (eds.), *Psychology Matters: Development, Health and Organization* (pp. 01-17), New Delhi: Allied Publishers.

Mishra, R.C. (2007b). "Studies of Acculturation Attitudes and Acculturative Stress: Generalizability of Findings on Tribal Peoples", in M.B. Sharan and D. Suar (eds.), *Psychology Matters: Development, Health and Organization* (pp. 45-57), New Delhi: Allied Publishers.

Mishra, R.C. (2009). "Health Cognition and Practices", in A. Shukla (ed.), *Culture: Cognition and Behaviour* (pp. 264-76), New Delhi: Concept.

Misra, G. and Verma, S. (1999). "Introduction: Concerns in the Study of Stress and Health", in G. Misra (ed.), *Psychological Perspectives on Stress and Health* (pp. 25-38), New Delhi: Concept.

Radley, A. (1994). *Making Sense of Illness: The Social Psychology of Health and Disease*, London: Sage.

Roy, S.C. (1931). "The Effect on the Aborigines of Chotanagpur of their Contact with Western Civilization", *Journal of Bihar and Odisha Research Society*, 17(4), 358-94.

Sam, D. (2006). "Acculturation and Health", in D. Sam and J.W. Berry (eds.), *The Cambridge Handbook of Acculturation Psychology* (pp. 452-68), Cambridge: Cambridge University Press.

Sam, D. and Berry, J.W. (2006). *The Cambridge Handbook of Acculturation Psychology*, Cambridge: Cambridge University Press.

Saxena, K.B. (1983). "Tribal Development in Bihar: An Appraisal", *Bulletin of the Bihar Tribal Research Institute*, 25, 1-108.

Sinha, D., Mishra, R.C., and Berry, J.W. (1992). "Acculturative Stress in Nomadic and Sedentary Tribes of Bihar (India)", in S. Iwawaki, Y. Kashima, K. Leung (eds.), *Innovations in Cross-cultural Psychology* (pp. 396-407), Lisse: Swets & Zeitlinger.

Singh, T., Tripathi, K.N., Verma, S., and Mishra, R.C. (1999). "The Notion of Health in Theory and Practice", in G. Misra (ed.), *Psychological Perspectives on Stress and Health* (pp. 66-84), New Delhi: Concept.

Sivanand, M. (2001). "The Good Doctors of Settling", *Reader's Digest*, 159, 110-17.

Tanaka-Matsumi, J., and Draguns, J. (1997). "Culture and Psychopathology", in J.W. Berry, M.H. Segall, and C. Kagitcibasi (eds.), *Handbook of Cross-cultural Psychology*, Vol. 3, *Social Behaviour and Applications* (pp. 449-91), Boston: Allyn & Bacon.

Vidyarthi, L.P. (1970). *Socio-cultural Implication of Industrialization in a Case Study of Tribal Research*, Ranchi: Council of Cultural and Social Research.

World Health Organization (1988). *Charter for Action to Achieve Health for All (Ottawa Charter)*, Geneva: WHO.

3

Illness Beliefs, Optimism, Subjective Well-being and Post-Traumatic Growth of Cervix Cancer Patients

P. Awasthi, R.C. Mishra and *U.P. Shahi*

The role of positive psychological factors in coping with challenging life circumstances is increasingly recognized (Love & Sabiston, 2011). Post-Traumatic Growth (PTG) is an important psychological positive change an individual experiences after a life threatening event. Research (Calhoun & Tedeschi, 2001) suggests that PTG outcomes are manifested in three broad kinds of change in an individual: changes in the perception of self, changes in interpersonal relationships, and changes in the philosophy of life. Studies of PTG have been carried out with variety of populations, such as bereaved individuals, people suffering from chronic illnesses like cancer, CAD, HIV/AIDS and disabilities, parents coping with medical problems of their children, survivors of road accidents or house fires, rape victims, and sexual abuse survivors (Bozo, Gundogdu & Buyukasik-Colak, 2009). Among others, PTG is found most commonly displayed by cancer patients. Reports indicate that about 60-90 per cent of all cancer survivors report positive changes (Fromm, Andrykowski & Hunt, 1996; Petrie, Buick, Weinman & Booth, 1999), which are viewed as beneficial in terms of improved personal resources, enhanced sense of purpose, greater spirituality, closer ties with others, and changes in life priorities (see Bozo, 2009). It is also indicated that patients hold certain health beliefs, which significantly influence their adaptive resources, such as hope of recovery and decision about the future course of action (Dalal, 2000).

Illness Beliefs and Health Behaviour

Recent studies (Hagger & Orbell, 2003) in the field of health psychology have revealed illness belief structure to be a supportive tool for understanding the psychosocial aspects of medical conditions including cancer. Being embedded in a socio-cultural context, people acquire a variety of beliefs about causes, consequences, controllability and outcomes of various diseases that prevail in a given society. As an integral part of the cognitive system (Gilbert, 1991), and also possibly of the neural system (Tondon, 2012), beliefs determine people's health cognition, treatment strategies, treatment compliance, perceived treatment outcomes, social support seeking, self-care, personal growth, and coping with illness (Kiecolt-Glasser, *et al.*, 1985; Peterson, Seligman & Vaillant, 1988).

When individuals are confronted with an unexpected life-threatening illness, they try to place the illness into a meaningful cognitive framework (Taylor, 1983). Part of this process entails understanding of the causes of illness. Beliefs about the causes of illness have been identified as essential dimensions of common sense understanding and representation of illness (Lau, Bernard & Hartman, 1989). A common sense understanding of the causes of illness is often a social construction derived from the cultural models of illness (Mishra, 2009). Kelley (1973) considers causal beliefs as critical because they are linked directly to how people make sense of an unexpected event. Causal understanding is also essential to sustain positive expectations and selection of ways of illness management (Kleinman, 1980).

It has been observed (e.g. Dijker and Koomen, 2003) that when people suffer from a chronic illness, their self-perception gets blurred. To regain self-sensibility, they try to make sense of the illness by extending their formulations about illness beyond medical explanations. Research in India reveals that in explaining health problems, people attribute causality either to themselves (e.g. careless attitude, bad habits) or to external factors (e.g. environmental hazards, god's wish) (Dalal & Pandey, 1988; Dalal & Singh, 1992; Shweder, 2008). In Indian studies, a coexistence of both sets of factors has been reported (Mishra, 2009). In view of these evidences, it may be argued that in the Indian cultural context, in which concepts of gods, goddesses, spirits, and fate are transmitted to children as indispensable lessons, individuals are likely to consider external factors to be responsible for health problems more than individual factors. The beliefs in external factors inculcate among individuals an attitude of acceptance of their own and other's sufferings. They provide people not only with mental and physical strength and relief from psychological strain, but also a coherent meaning to life. The attribution of causality to external factors is likely to lead to a strong belief in external control of illness. The acquisition of external control belief and PTG may mutually influence each other.

Growth, however, does not occur as a direct result of life crisis. Individual's struggle with the new reality in the aftermath of life crisis is crucial in determining the extent to which PTG occurs. Cognitive rebuilding, which takes into account the changed reality of one's life after trauma, produces schemas, which are more resistant to being shattered. These results are experienced as growth (Tedeschi & Calhoun, 2004).

Optimism, Subjective Well-Being (SWiB), and Post-Traumatic Growth (PTG)

Researchers have shown the importance of optimism in several health related contexts (Scheier, Carver & Bridges, 2001). As a broad sense of confidence, optimism keeps people engaged in efforts toward desired goals and results in positive behavioural outcomes (Carver, Lehman & Antoni, 2003) and adaptive coping (Stanton & Snider, 1993). Studies indicate that in cancer patients, optimism tends to reduce the level of stress at the time of diagnosis of cancer and sustains this process for some time (Carver, *et al.*, 1993; Epping-Jordan, *et al.*, 1999). PTG has also been reported to have positive association with optimism, hope and strong social resources (Park, Cohen & Murch, 1996; Park, 1998; Sears, Stanton & Danoff-Burg, 2003; Urcuyo, Boyers, Carver & Antoni, 2005). It seems that optimism may predict better SWB and PTG in cancer patients in the long-term.

In recent years, life span perspectives (which focus on well-being) have highlighted the role of SWB in positive growth. With respect to effects on SWB, subjective perceptions of health have been found to carry greater weight than objective perceptions of health (Watten, Vassend, Myhrer & Syversen, 1997). Life satisfaction (a cognitive component of SWB) has become a broader measure of quality of life, because it reflects values, which transcend physical pleasures and ephemeral emotions (Park, 2004). Studies have revealed that intrapersonal (e.g. belief system, schemas, prejudices, etc.) interpersonal, and socio-cultural variables account for a greater amount of variance in the SWB of individuals than demographic variables (Gilman & Huebner, 2003). Studies also (e.g. Furr & Funder, 1998) reveal that individuals with lower SWB are at risk of a variety of psychological and social problems, such as depression and maladaptive relationships. Although many studies on SWB of adults have been conducted, in patient populations, SWB has become the focus of empirical research only in recent years. Patients' beliefs regarding chronic illnesses may provide researchers with an understanding of the causes of SWB. Thus, the importance of illness beliefs may widen their effects on SWB.

Correlates of Subjective Well-Being

Staudinger, Baltes and Fleeson (1999) indicate that regulation of SWB occurs through psychosocial resources of individuals. Studies demonstrate a strong positive association of SWB with adaptive coping skills, perceived internal control, social support, and materially advantaged environment in life situations of the people; these factors empower individuals to deal effectively with adverse circumstances (Moos & Mitchell, 1982; Bourland, Stanley & Snyder, 2000). Studies reveal a positive association of SWB with self-esteem, internal locus of control and future orientation among cancer patients. Preventing relapse and hospitalization, promoting social support, and enhancing sense of freedom have also emerged as good predictors of SWB for cancer patients (Spiegel, 1999; Rowland & Baker, 2005). A longer period of time since the diagnosis of cancer has been found to be associated with greater perceived positive changes, suggesting that, during the first few weeks or months after being diagnosed with chronic illness, patients have to adjust to their diagnosis and to side-effects of medication (Cordova, Cunningham, Carlson & Andrykowski, 2001; Tomich & Helgeson, 2002). Although SWB is seen to improve over the course of therapy in cancer patients (Pinquart & Forhlich, 2009), the observed improvement in SWB in patients would probably not be found where the cancer progresses extensively.

Health Beliefs and Health Outcomes in Chronic Illness

Studies in India have generally attempted to examine the health beliefs of individuals by analyzing their attributions to health problems. In some studies with cervix cancer patients, (e.g. Kohli & Dalal, 1998; Dalal, 2000) the relationship between causal explanations of the disease and psychological recovery from it have been examined. These studies indicate that patients attribute their illness to metaphysical factors (e.g. fate, God's will, *karma*) more often than to other factors. Dalal and Pandey (1988) interviewed accident victims during their hospitalization, and found that people attributed the causes of their accident to metaphysical factors and self more often than to external situations. Attribution of accident to "*karma*" was positively correlated with the psychological recovery of patients. Such type of attribution was more characteristic of permanently than of temporarily disabled patients. Agrawal and Dalal (1993) studied patients who had been diagnosed a week earlier as suffering from myocardial infarction (MI). They observed that the patients of different ages, education and income levels believed in *karma*, God, and a "just world". Those who believed in *karma* as a cause of MI also showed high expectation for recovery.

Broota (1997) examined the effect of surgical stress on "belief in God" and superstition by comparing major surgery patients, minor surgery patients and a matched group of patients from the normal population. Results indicated that major surgery patients not only had greater "belief in God", but they were also more superstitious than the other two groups. An interesting finding of this study was a reduction in the level of "belief in God" and superstition among major surgery patients after operation, which did not happen in the case of minor surgery patients. These findings bring out the functional importance of beliefs in the sense that they provide great relief to individuals suffering from anxiety, which is quite a common experience of major surgery patients prior to operation.

Awasthi, Mishra and Shahi (2006) examined the health beliefs of cervix cancer patients and compared them with those of the normal women. The samples were selected taking into consideration whether women were educated or uneducated, and whether they came from rural or urban settings. Findings revealed that individual and psychosocial causes were more strongly represented in the belief system of patients than environmental and supernatural causes. The patients scored lower and differed significantly from the non-patient group with respect to their belief in psychosocial and environmental causes. Uneducated women held a stronger belief in psychosocial, supernatural and environmental causes than the educated. Urban women believed more strongly in individual, psychosocial and environmental causes of illness than rural women. On the other hand, rural women believed more strongly in supernatural causes than urban women. The study suggested the coexistence of internal (individual psychosocial) and external (supernatural, environmental) causes of illness in the belief system of patients.

With respect to illness controllability, the findings revealed that cancer patients believed more strongly in doctors' control than normal women. Educated group believed more strongly in self-control than uneducated group. Rural group believed more strongly in supernatural control than urban group. With regard to belief about illness outcomes, cancer patients tended to show greater hope for improvement as compared to normals. The beliefs of uneducated subjects in various causes, consequences, controllability, and outcomes of illness were stronger than those of educated subjects.

Some findings from breast cancer survivors bring out evidence for positive changes. For example, Taylor (1983) observed that 53 per cent of the breast cancer patients reported deriving benefits from their cancer experience. Similarly, 83 per cent of the patients construed at least one benefit from their experience with cancer (Sears, Stanton & Danoff-Burg, 2003). Cordova, Cunningham, Carlson and Andrykowski (2001) observed that, compared to the control group, breast cancer patients showed a pattern of greater PTG. With respect to growth outcomes Tomich, Helgeson, and Vache (2005) found that, patients reported not only greater appreciation of life, self-improvement, and re-prioritizing, but also felt enabled to help others with an enhanced belief in faith as compared to controls.

Bozo, Gundogdu, and Buyukasik-Colak (2009) investigated the relationship between dispositional optimism and Post-Traumatic growth (PTG) in post-operative breast cancer patients and examined the moderating role of social support between dispositional optimism and PGT. Results revealed that cancer survivors, high on dispositional optimism and perceived social support, were more likely to develop PTG than those who were low on dispositional optimism and perceived social support. Among different sources of social support, only the support perceived from a private person moderated the relationship between dispositional optimism and PTG.

Positive outcomes and personal growth may be associated with several factors, which include personal characteristics (e.g. gender, illness perception, temperament, and personality traits), characteristics of the environment (e.g. social support, and living conditions), characteristics of the negative event (e.g. stressfulness, duration, and controllability) and coping responses (e.g. problem-focussed coping, and emotion-focussed coping) (Schaefer & Moos, 1992).

A glance at the studies discussed above indicates that very little work has been done linking health beliefs and optimism to SWB and PTG. The association among different kind of illness beliefs, SWB, and PTG has not been examined in the context of cancer. In the present study an attempt was made to analyze the relationship of illness beliefs (illness causation and illness controllability) and optimism with SWB and PTG in a sample of women patients of cervix cancer.

Focus on cervix cancer in the study is because of its most common occurrence and high incidence among Indian women. It is estimated that every year about 1,42,000 new cases of cervix cancer are registered and about 77,000 women die of the disease. At the present time India accounts for almost the one-third of the global burden of cervical cancer, and by 2025 the number of new cervical cancer cases in India is projected to increase to 2,26,084 (WHO, 2009). Uneducated women patients are included because the number of cervical cases is very high in such populations. It also suggests that the lack of education is possibly a major reason for the existence of cervix cancer among women (Manjunatha, 2013). Psychological growth of women cannot be ensured unless they experience some positive growth-related changes in difficult circumstances created by the cancer.

Guided by the abovementioned picture, the present study attempts to analyze some psychological aspects of cervix cancer patients. In the light of general findings reported in this field of research, it was hypothesized that:

1. Patients holding strong belief in external causes of illness would show greater SWB and PTG as compared to those holding strong belief in internal causes of illness.
2. Patients scoring high on "self" and "doctor" control agency of illness would show greater SWB and PTG than those who score high on belief in "supernatural" control agency.
3. Patients with high dispositional optimism would show greater SWB and PTG than those with low dispositional optimism.

Method

Participants

The study was carried out at Varanasi with 100 uneducated women suffering from the cancer of cervix. Women were drawn in equal number from rural and urban areas. The age of participants ranged from 30 to 60 years, and they generally belonged to middle class families. Participants were selected from some medical centers and hospitals, which they visited for treatment (e.g. radiotherapy, chemotherapy or both) and for routine check-up after recovery. The participants had the history of cervix cancer at least for two months.

Measures

Illness Causation Belief Measure

It comprised 20 items related to four factors, i.e. individual, psychosocial, supernatural, and environmental causes derived from a factor analysis of the items (see Awasthi, *et al.*, 2006). These factors explained approximately 80 per cent of variance in the scores, with alpha values of 0.93 and above. The individual and psychosocial causes represented the internal causes of illness; supernatural and environmental causes represented the external causes of illness. The participants rated each item on a 5-point scale in terms of the perceived degree of its importance in the causation of cancer ("very much" =5, "very little" =1). The scores on these measures ranged from 5 to 25. Test-retest reliability of the measure ranged between 0.73 and 0.92 for different causes.

Illness Controllability Belief Measure

It consisted of 3 items, which assessed the degree to which the participant believed that the disease was controllable by "self", "external agents" or a "doctor" (see Awasthi, *et al.*, 2006). Each item was rated on a 5-point scale, ranging from "not at all" (1) to "very much" (5). Test-retest reliabilities of the scales were 0.90, 0.93, and 0.91 respectively.

The Life Orientation Test-Revised

Developed by Scheier and Carver (1985) and revised by Scheier, *et al.* (1994), this test consists of 6 items, each rated on a 5-point scale, ranging from "strongly agree" to "strongly disagree". The scores on these measures ranged from 6 to 30. Items 1, 3, and 6 are positively keyed (strongly agree = 5, strongly disagree = 1), whereas items 2, 4, and 5 are negatively keyed and scored in reversed direction (strongly agree = 1, strongly disagree = 5).

Satisfaction with Life Measure

This measure was developed by Pavot and Diener (1993). It consists of 5 items, each rated on a seven point scale. The scores range is 5 to 35. The participants are asked to mark one of the seven points that they consider most appropriate (in terms of degree of importance) for a given item. The alpha coefficient for the scale is 0.87 and test-retest reliability is 0.82. This scale has been widely used to assess SWB in cross-cultural studies.

Post-Traumatic Growth Inventory (PTGI)

The PTGI was developed by Tedeschi and Calhoun (1996). It consists of 21 items divided into five sub-scales: new possibilities (5 items), relating to others (7 items), personal strength (4 items), spiritual change (2 items) and appreciation of life (3 items). Each item is answered on a scale ranging from 0 (I did not experience this change as a result of my crisis) to 5 (I experienced this change to a very great degree). The internal consistency coefficient of the scale is 0.90, the test-retest reliability over a two-month interval is 0.71 and its construct validity is acceptable. In the present study, the internal consistency reliability of the PTGI calculated by Cronbach's alpha was 0.79.

Results

Mean, SD, and Correlation of Illness Beliefs and Optimism with SWB and PTG Measures

Means and standard deviations on different measures employed in the study are given in Table 3.1. The values of correlation of illness causation, controllability and optimism with SWB and PTG measures are presented in Table 3.2. The analysis revealed that "Individual causation" was negatively correlated with SWB, spiritual change, and appreciation of life measures, suggesting that attribution of disease to individual causation reduces SWB, spiritual change, and appreciation of life. "Supernatural" and "environmental" causes were positively related to SWB, representing greater experience of SWB and PTG with attribution to supernatural and environmental causes of illness. "Self-control" was positively correlated with personal strength, indicating that belief in "self-control" enhances patients' perception of personal strength. "Doctor-control" was negatively correlated with spiritual change and appreciation of life, indicating that belief in doctor-control reduces the perception of spiritual change and appreciation of life. "Supernatural-control" and "optimism" were positively correlated with SWB and all the measures of PTG, indicating that supernatural-control and optimism are linked to greater experience of SWB and PTG.

Table 3.1: Mean Scores of Women Patients on Various Measures of Illness Belief, Subjective Well-Being, Optimism and Post-Traumatic Growth

Illness Causation Belief	*Mean*	*Standard Deviation*
Individual	15.06	5.33
Psychosocial	15.96	4.87
Supernatural	17.19	5.94
Environmental	16.18	5.42
Illness Controllability Belief		
Self	1.24	0.53
Doctor	3.48	1.28
Supernatural	2.41	1.61
Optimism	19.35	5.13
Subjective Well-being	25.44	5.90
Post-Traumatic Growth		
Relating to Others	26.46	5.43
New Prospects	14.00	5.93
Personal Strength	9.50	4.53
Spiritual Change	5.96	3.06
Appreciation of Life	9.62	3.90
Overall Post-Traumatic Growth	65.54	19.39

Table 3.2: Inter-correlations of Scores on Illness Beliefs, Optimism, Life Satisfaction and Post-Traumatic Growth Measures

Illness Causation/ Controllability/ Optimism	*Subjective Well-being*	*Post-Traumatic Growth*					
		Relating to Others	*New Prospects*	*Personal Strength*	*Spiritual Change*	*Apprecia-tion of Life*	*Overall*
Individual	−0.256*	−0.158	−0.096	−0.031	−0.355**	−0.341**	−0.206
Psychosocial	−0.086	−0.106	−0.030	−0.038	−0.167	−0.163	−0.107
Supernatural	0.348**	0.259**	0.150	0.259**	0.666**	0.617**	0.408**
Environmental	0.380**	0.295**	0.163	0.311**	0.406**	0.411**	0.352**
Self	0.159	0.171	0.185	0.313**	−0.124	−0.062	0.145
Doctor	−0.035	−0.002	0.154	0.099	−0.344**	−0.324**	−0.050
Supernatural	0.685**	0.603**	0.431**	0.464**	0.804 **	0.694**	0.676**
Optimism	0.830**	0.832**	0.696**	0.556**	0.497**	0.442**	0.743**

$^{*}P \leq 0.05$, $^{**}P \leq 0.01$.

Multiple Regression Analysis

A step-wise Multiple Regression Analysis was carried out using illness beliefs and optimism as predictor variables, and SWB (Table 3.3) and PTG (Table 3.4) as the criterion variables.

Findings revealed that "optimism" ($b = 0.65$), "supernatural-control" ($b = 0.29$), and "environmental causation" ($b = 0.12$) accounted for approximately 78 per cent of variance in the scores on SWB ($F_{3,}$ 96,

115.69, $p < 0.01$) and made positive predictions (higher SWB). The highest contribution was made by "optimism", which accounted for approximately 68 per cent of variance (F_1, 98, 216.56, $p < 0.01$) in the scores. "Supernatural-control" and "environmental causation" accounted for approximately 8 per cent and 1 per cent of variance in the scores respectively.

Table 3.3: Summary of Step-wise MRA on Subjective Well-being Measure

Sl. No.	*Predictor Variables*	*Multiple R*	R^2	R^2 *Change*	*Df*	*F*	*Beta Weights*
1.	Optimism	0.830	0.688		1,98	216.56**	0.65
2.	Supernatural Control	0.879	0.772	0.084	2,97	164.30**	0.29
3.	Environmental Causation	0.885	0.783	0.011	3,96	115.69**	0.12

$^*P \le 0.05$, $^{**}P \le 0.01$.

Table 3.4: Summary of Step-wise MRA on Various Domains of Post-Traumatic Growth Measure

Sl. No.	*Predictor Variables*	*Multiple R*	R^2	R^2 *Change*	*Df*	*F*	*Beta Weights*
(a)	*Relating to Others*						
1.	Optimism	0.832	0.692		1,98	220.10**	0.71
2.	Supernatural Control	0.854	0.729	0.037	2,97	130.26**	0.23
(b)	*New Possibilities*						
1.	Optimism	0.696	0.484	0.484	1,98	91.93**	0.70
(c)	*Personal Strength*						
1.	Optimism	0.556	0.309		1,98	43.77**	0.31
2.	Self-Control	0.592	0.351	0.042	2,97	26.23**	0.30
3.	Supernatural Control	0.656	0.430	0.079	3,96	24.17**	0.35
(d)	*Spiritual Change*						
1.	Supernatural Control	0.804	0.647		1,98	179.76**	0.56
2.	Supernatural Causation	0.821	0.674	0.027	2,97	100.42**	0.25
3.	Optimism	0.829	0.688	0.014	3,96	70.54**	0.14
(e)	*Appreciation of Life*						
1.	Supernatural Control	0.694	0.481		1,98	90.82**	0.51
2.	Supernatural Causation	0.722	0.521	0.040	2,97	52.78**	0.27
	Overall Post-Traumatic Growth						
1.	Optimism	0.743	0.552		1,98	120.68**	0.54
2.	Supernatural Control	0.814	0.663	0.111	2,97	95.25**	0.39

$^*P \le 0.05$, $^{**}P \le 0.01$.

"Optimism" (b = 0.71) and "supernatural-control" (b = 0.23) accounted for approximately 73 per cent of variance in the scores on relating to others measure (F_2, 97, 130.26, $p < 0.01$) and made positive predictions. The highest contribution was made by "optimism", which accounted for approximately 69 per cent of variance (F_1, 98, 220.10, $p < 0.01$) in the scores. "Supernatural-control" accounted for approximately 4 per cent of variance in the scores. "Optimism" (b = 0.70) accounted for approximately 48 per cent of variance in the scores on new possibilities measure (F_1, 98, 91.93, $p < 0.01$) and made positive predictions.

With respect to the prediction of personal strength, results indicated that "optimism" ($b = 0.31$), "self-control" ($b = 0.30$), and "supernatural-control" ($b = 0.35$) explained approximately 43 per cent of variance the in the scores (F_3, 96, 24.17, $p < 0.01$). Highest contribution was made by "optimism", which accounted for approximately 31 per cent of variance in the scores (F_1, 98, 43.77, $p < 0.01$). "Self-control" accounted for approximately 4 per cent of variance in the scores. "Supernatural-control" accounted for approximately 8 per cent of variance in the scores.

On spiritual change measure, "supernatural-control" (b = 0.56), "supernatural causation" ($b = 0.25$), and "optimism" ($b = 0.14$) accounted for approximately 69 per cent of variance in the scores (F_3, 96, 70.54, $p < 0.01$) and made positive predictions. "Supernatural-control" contributed approximately 65 per cent (F_1, 98, 179.76, $p < 0.01$), "supernatural causation" contributed approximately 3 per cent, and "optimism" contributed approximately 1 per cent of variances in the scores.

Regarding the prediction of appreciation of life, results indicated that "supernatural-control" (0.51) and "supernatural causation" (0.27) emerged as positive predictors and accounted for approximately 52 per cent of variance in the scores (F_2, 97, 52.78, $p < 0.01$). Supernatural-control contributed approximately 48 per cent (F_1, 98, 90.82, $p < 0.01$) and supernatural causation contributed 4 per cent of variances in the scores.

With respect to the prediction of overall PTG, results indicated that "optimism" ($b = 0.54$) and "supernatural-control" ($b = 0.39$) accounted for approximately 66 per cent of variance in the scores (F_2, 97, 95.25, $p < 0.01$) and made positive predictions (greater post-traumatic growth). Optimism contributed approximately 55 per cent (F_1, 98, 120.68, $p < 0.01$) and supernatural control contributed approximately 11 per cent of variance in the scores.

Discussion

The findings revealed that supernatural and environmental causes were more strongly represented in the belief system of women patients than individual and psychosocial causes. Women believed in self, doctor, and supernatural control of illness, but held a stronger belief in doctor and supernatural control as compared to self-control. In terms of growth outcomes, patients could relate themselves to others, experienced new possibilities, personal strength, and spiritual changes, and they also appreciated their life. They scored higher on relating to others and new possibilities than on spiritual change and appreciation of life. The findings strongly support the hypothesis that patients holding strong belief in external causes of illness would show greater SWB and PTG as compared to those holding strong belief in internal causes of illness. These results are consonant with other Indian studies carried out with orthopedic (Dalal & Pandey, 1988), tubercular (Dalal & Singh, 1992) and heart (Agarwal & Dalal, 1993) patients, which report attributions of illness to "God's will" and "Karma" as major influences on patients' health behaviour. These processes help patients in dealing with their health problems and making peaceful adjustment with life threatening conditions. Western researchers (e.g. Axelrad, 1982; Witenburg, 1983; Taylor, Lichtman & Wood, 1984; Affleck, McGrade & McQueeny, 1985; Timko & Janoff-Bulman, 1985) have reported external attributions to be related to mal-adaptation, and internal attribution to positive adaptation. This proposition certainly goes against our results.

Since, cervix cancer is a chronic illness, causal beliefs might be particularly relevant in this case. Studies (e.g. Irvine, Cox & Gonder-Frederick, 1992) indicate that internal attribution is conducive to positive disease-related outcomes, whereas external attribution is related to lower levels of psychological distress (Sinzato, *et al.*, 1985). The latter result may, however, be specific to cancer. External attribution may be most useful when cancer patients appraise their disease experience as one for which nothing can be done to modify the event. For some patients, external attribution provides a way of coping with the emotional distress. Other evidences also suggest that external beliefs may lead to avoidance of a range of physical and psychosocial distress (Asmundson, Larsen & Stein, 1998; Brooks, Daglish & Alison, 2013), and reinforce patients' adjustment to different domains of life.

The finding concerning patients' beliefs in supernatural causes are corroborated by several other studies indicating that higher attribution to supernatural factors provides a defense against stress reactions. Furnham, Akande, and Baguma (1999) observed that people from developing countries believed in more social, fatalistic and supernatural explanations for health and illness than people from developed countries. It seems that people's belief in God raises the level of personal energy to bear with chronic health condition and cope with it effectively.

Studies have often indicated that illness is not necessarily associated with low life satisfaction (Diener, Suh, Lucas & Smith, 1999). A high percentage of satisfied individuals has been reported even among those who clearly have severe health problems (Manocchia, Keller & Ware, 2001; Murdaugh, *et al.*, 2006). Moreover, even within later parts of the life span, which is characterized by an accumulation of losses within different domains (e.g. health, functional ability, social network) and a relative decline of gains, life satisfaction remains relatively stable (Fujita & Diener, 2005).

In the present study, positive association of external causes with SWB may be interpreted in terms of rural background of women. Researchers have indicated that people from different geographic locations appear to respond differently on measures of well-being. It has been found that rural dwellers are more satisfied with their personal lives than their urban counterparts, particularly regarding personal life, relationships and community connection (Cummins, *et al.*, 2001). In India, attribution to external forces has been found to be the best resource that makes the sufferers perceive life worth even in the phase of life-threatening situations (Mishra, 1997).

The findings do not fully substantiate the hypothesis that patients, who score high on "self" and "doctor" control agency of illness, would show greater SWB and PTG than those who score high on belief in supernatural control agency. The pattern of results was, in fact, opposite to the prediction of supernatural-control that enhanced the perception of SWB and experience of PTG in all domains. The positive role of belief in supernatural control of illness can be interpreted in terms of the Hindu worldview and religious philosophy. Theoretical writings (e.g. Radhakrishnan, 1926) and empirical studies lay great emphasis on the theory of *karma* (Agarwal & Dalal, 1993; Dalal, 2000; Dalal & Pandey, 1988; Dalal & Singh, 1992; Gokhale, 1981). This theory holds that all good or bad deeds accumulate over our previous births, and that the present sufferings are the outcome of the misdeeds of the previous births, not only of the present life. Paranjpe (1987) has indicated that search for explanation of sufferings is the cornerstone of Indian philosophical traditions. By endorsing causes of an event to supernatural factors, patients get relieved from holding themselves responsible for health problems, although they may still continue treatment as their duty (*karma*). The supernatural control belief may be considered as a positive belief, and the wider body of illness perception research (Hagger, *et al.*, 2003) suggests that positive illness beliefs are associated with better health outcomes.

In the present chapter, "self-control" enhanced the perception of personal strength among women patients. Researchers (Dempster, *et al.*, 2011; Hagger & Orbell, 2003) have indentified the role of self-control beliefs in encouraging constructive reactions to serious illnesses. Findings indicate that individuals, who believe that their health and illness are under their own control, are more likely to engage in health promoting activities than those who believe that it is under the control of other factors (Rochelle & Fidler, 2013). Thus, patients, who believe that they have control over their illness, are better adjusted to illness than those who do not believe in self-control (Lazarus, 1983; Taylor, Lichtman & Wood, 1984). Although self-control beliefs have sometimes been accused of generating "illusions of control", they still have positive consequences for patients in terms of facilitating psychological adaptation, and hence, termed as "healthy illusions" (Taylor, 2005).

The findings fully support the hypothesis that patients with high dispositional optimism would show greater SWB and PTG than those with low dispositional optimism. This finding can be explained in terms of women's optimistic beliefs that negative events are less likely to occur in the near future because of the medical treatments they were undergoing. Optimists generally tend to engage in activities, which enhance chances of experiencing positive outcomes. Studies report that optimists are more likely than pessimists to adapt to the stressful circumstances and tend to employ emotion-focussed coping strategies (e.g. acceptance, humour, positive reframing of the situation) and experience better emotional outcomes (Scheier & Carver, 1987; Scheier, Carver & Bridges, 1994). Optimists then differ from pessimists in their stable coping tendencies and in the kind of coping responses that they spontaneously generate when given hypothetical coping situations (Scheier, Weintraub & Carver, 1986). Optimistic women are less likely to have negative emotional outcomes from diagnosis and treatment of breast cancer compared to pessimistic women (Carver, *et al.*, 1993, missing in ref. list; Epping-Jordanmet, *et al.*, 1999; Stanton & Snider,

1993). This suggests that optimism has a generalized beneficial effect on the experience of SWB and PTG.

In this study "optimism" has made the highest contribution to SWB and PTG. This finding is similar to those described in many studies (Bozo-Ozlem, *et al.*, 2009; Carver & Scheier, 2005; Deimling, Bowman, Sterns, Wagner & Kahana, 2006; Schou, Ekeberg, Sandvik, Hjermstad & Ruland, 2005). It appears that optimism becomes a powerful predictor of SWB and PTG once the immediacy and intensity of the physical and psychosocial stressors of the initial diagnostic and treatment period are over. Peterson and Seligman (1984) have defined optimism and pessimism as the ways in which people explain experiences in their lives, i.e. as explanatory styles. People, who have an optimistic explanatory style, attribute problems to instable, external, and specific causes, whereas people, who have a pessimistic style, attribute problems to stable or permanent, internal, and global causes (Gillham, Shatte, Reivich & Seligman, 2001). Peterson and Steen (2002) have noted that people's explanatory style influences how they respond to difficulties in their lives. Pessimists see the difficulty as permanent and unchangeable, whereas optimists see the difficulty as temporary and changeable. Dykema, Bergbower and Peterson (1995) indicated that the optimists' perception of the world as filled with fewer hassles affects their overall well-being. However, as Peterson & Steen (2002) note, more attention needs to be focussed on the mechanisms that lead from explanatory style to adaptational outcomes.

Another predictor that also made great contribution to SWB and PTG is the belief in supernatural-control. This belief is beneficial particularly where opportunities for internal control are low and severe consequences of cancer are generally high. Recent research suggests that different beliefs may be prominent at different disease stages (DeJong, *et al.*, 2012; Hurt, *et al.*, 2012). It seems that supernatural-control belief is beneficial particularly for the survivors of cancer. Attribution theory suggests that causal beliefs of people for negative events concerning external factors influence their affective response and behavioural reaction to physical and mental health conditions (e.g. Weiner, 1985). Such beliefs can be useful in understanding why and how people respond to illnesses (e.g. Dijker & Koomen, 2003; Weiner, 1993; Weiner, 1988). Researchers (Irvine, *et al*, 1992) have revealed that internai belief is conducive to positive disease-related outcomes, whereas external belief is related to lower levels of psychological distress (Sinzato, *et al.*, 1985). The latter finding supports our study.

The present study brings out the importance of illness beliefs and optimism in SWB and PTG. Findings indicate that illness beliefs and optimism may enhance the perception of SWB and PTG in cancer patients. Hence, assessment of patients' illness beliefs and optimism should be made an integral part of all psychological intervention programmes. The finding pertaining to belief in "self-control" of illness can be used to enhance the feeling of "personal strength" among cancer patients. Since factors such as belief in external causation of illness, belief in supernatural control, and optimism carry the potential to enhance feelings of SWB and PTG, healthcare professionals may use these beliefs in helping patients to view cancer as manageable. Specific intervention programmes can be developed to help patients learn the value of illness beliefs and optimism for enhancing SWB and PTG in times of traumatic experiences.

Though the study has explored some important psychological predictors of SWB and PTG of cervix cancer patients, there are also some limitations. Further, study may explain the associations among illness beliefs, optimism, SWB, and PTG at other time points along the cancer trajectory, such as at the diagnosis of cancer and at the time of cancer recurrence. The associations among these variables may be explored in patients with other cancer diagnoses. If this relationship is confirmed, then intervention studies using cognitive therapy to strengthen illness control beliefs and optimism may be designed and tested. A comparative study of females and males may also provide some further insights in this respect.

In the present study, the age range of patients was fairly wide (i.e. 30 to 60 years), but we have not used age as a factor in the present analyses. Future studies may develop age-specific psychological profiles of the patients and compare them. The impact of rural-urban residence and educated and uneducated background on illness beliefs, optimism, SWB and PTG of women patients also need to be examined seriously.

REFERENCES

Affleck, G., McGrade, B.J., Allen and D.A. McQueeny, M. (1985). "Mothers' Beliefs about Behavioural Causes for their Developmentally Disabled Infants' Condition: What do they Signify?" *Journal of Pediatric Psychology*, 10(3), 293-303.

Agarwal, M. and Dalal. A.K. (1993). "Causal Beliefs and Psychological Recovery of Myocardial Infarction Patients", *Journal of Social Psychology*, 133(3), 385-94.

Asmundson, G.J.G., Larsen, D.K. and Stein, M.B. (1998). "Panic Disorder and Vestibular Disturbance: An Overview of Empirical Findings and Clinical Implications", *Journal of Psychosomatic Research*, 44(1), 107-20.

Awasthi P., Mishra, R.C. and Shahi, U.P. (2006). "Health Beliefs and Behaviour of Cervix Cancer Patients", *Psychology and Developing Societies*, 18(1), 37-58.

Axelrad, K.J. (1982). "Locus of Control and Causal Attributions as they Relate to Expectations for Coping with a Heart Attack", *Dissertation Abstract International*, 42(12), 4924-13.

Bourland, S., Stanley, M. and Snyder, A. (2000). "Quality of Life in Older Adults with Generalized Anxiety Disorder", *Ageing and Mental Health*, 4(4), 315-23.

Bozo O., Gundogdu E. and Buyuksik-Colak, C. (2009). "The Moderating Role of Different Sources of Perceived Social Support on the Dispositional Optimism — Post-traumatic Growth Relationship in Post-operative Breast Cancer Patients", *Journal of Health Psychology*, 14(7), 1009-20.

Brooks, J.M., Daglish, J. and Wearden, A.J. (2013). "Attributions, distress and Behavioural Responses in the Significant Others of People with Chronic Fatigue Syndrome", *Journal of Health Psychology*, 18(10), 1288-95.

Broota, K.D. (1997). "Belief and their Functional Significance", *Trends in Social Science Research*, 4, 133-39.

Calhoun, L.G. and Tedeschi, R.G. (2001). "Post-traumatic Growth: The Positive Lessons of Loss", in R.A. Neimeyer (ed.), *Meaning Reconstruction and the Experience of Loss* (pp. 157-72), Washington, DC: American Psychological Association.

Carver, C.S., Lehman, J.M. and Antoni, M.H. (2003). "Dispositional Pessimism Predicts Illness-related Disruption of Social and Recreational Activities among Breast Cancer Patients", *Journal of Personality and Social Psychology*, 84(4), 813-21.

Carver, C.S., Pozo, C., Harris, S.D., Noriega, V., Scheier, M.F., Robinson, D.S., Ketcham, A.S., Moffat, F.L. Jr. and Clark, K.C. (1993). "How Coping Mediates the Effect of Optimism on Distress: A Study of Women with Early Stage Breast Cancer", *Journal of Personality and Social Psychology*, 65(2), 375-90.

Carver, C.S. and Scheier, M.F. (2005). "Optimism", in C.R. Snyder and S.J. Lopez (eds.), *Handbook of Positive Psychology* (pp. 231-43), New York: Oxford University Press.

Cordova, M., Cunningham, L., Carlson, C. and Andrykowski, M. (2001). "Post-traumatic Growth Following Breast Cancer: A Controlled Comparison Study", *Health Psychology*, 20(3), 176-85.

Cummins, R.A., Eckersley, R., Pallant, J., Van Vugt, J., Shelly, J., Pusey, S.M. and Misajon, R. (2001). *Australian Unity Well-Being Index: Survey 2, Report 1.0*, Australian Centre on Quality of Life, School of Psychology, Deakin University, Melbourne.

Dalal, A.K. (2000). "Living with a Chronic Disease: Healing and Psychological Adjustment in Indian Society", *Psychology and Developing Societies*, 12, 67-81.

Dalal, A.K. and Pandey, N. (1988). "Psychological Recovery of the Accident Victims with Temporary and Permanent Disability", *International Journal of Psychology*, 23(1), 25-40.

Dalal, A.K. and Singh, A.K. (1992). "Causal Beliefs and Recovery from Surgery", *Psychology and Health*, 6(3), 193-203.

Deimling, G.T., Bowman, K.F., Sterns, S., Wagner, L.J. and Kahana, B. (2006). "Cancer-related Health Worries and Psychological Distress among Older Adult: Long-term Cancer Survivors", *Psycho-Oncology*, 15(4), 306-20.

DeJong, H., Hillcoat, J., Perkins, S., *et al.* (2012). "Illness Perceptions in Bulimia Nervosa", *Journal of Health Psychology*, 17(3), 399-408.

Dempster, M., McCorry, N.K., Brennan, E., Donnelly, M., Murray, L.J. and Johnston, B.T. (2011). "Do Changes in Illness Perceptions Predict Changes in Psychological

Distress among Oesophageal Cancer Survivors?" *Journal of Health Psychology*, 16(3), 500-09.

Diener, E., Suh, E.M., Lucas, R.E. and Smith, H.E. (1999). "Subjective Well-being: Three Decades of Progress", *Psychological Bulletin*, 125(2), 276-302.

Dijker, A.J.M. and Koomen, W. (2003). "Extending Weiner's Attribution — Emotion Model of Stigmatization of Ill Persons", *Basic and Applied Social Psychology*, 25(1), 51-68.

Dykema, J., Bergbower, K. and Peterson, C. (1995). "Pessimistic Explanatory Style, Stress, and Illness", *Journal of Social and Clinical Psychology*, 14(4), 357-71.

Epping-Jordan, J.E., Compas, B.E., Osowiecki, D.M., Oppedisano, G., Gerhardt, C., Primo, K. and Krag, D.N. (1999). "Psychological Adjustment in Breast Cancer: Processes of Emotional Distress", *Health Psychology*, 18(4), 315-26.

Fromm, K., Andrykowski, M.A. and Hunt, J. (1996). "Positive and Negative Psychosocial Sequelae of Bone Marrow Transplantation: Implications for Quality of Life Assessment", *Journal of Behavioural Medicine*, 19(3), 221-40.

Fujita, F. and Diener, E. (2005). "Life Satisfaction Set Point: Stability and Change", *Journal of Personality and Social Psychology*, 88(1), 158-64.

Furnham, A., Akande, D. and Baguma, P. (1999). "Beliefs about Health and Illness in Three Countries: Britain, South Africa and Uganda", *Psychology, Health and Medicine*, 4(2), 189-201.

Furr, R.M. and Funder, D.C. (1998). "A Multimodal Analysis of Personal Negativity", *Journal of Personality and Social Psychology*, 74(6), 1580-91.

Gilbert, D.T. (1991). "How Mental System Believe", *American Psychologist*, 46(2), 107-09.

Gillham, J.E., Shatté, A.J., Reivich, K.J. and Seligman, M.E.P. (2001). "Optimism, Pessimism, and Explanatory Style", in E.C. Chang (ed.), *Optimism & Pessimism* (pp. 53-75), Washington, DC: American Psychological Association.

Gilman, R. and Huebner, E.S. (2006). "Characteristics of Adolescents Who Report Very High Life Satisfaction", *Journal of Youth and Adolescence*, 35(3), 311-19.

Gokhale, B.G. (1961). *Indian Thought Throughout the Ages: A Study of Some Dominant Concepts*, Mumbai: Asia Publishing House.

Hagger, M.S. and Orbell, S. (2003). "A Meta-analytic Review of the Common sense Model of Illness Representations", *Psychology & Health*, 18(2), 141-84.

Hurt, C.S., Weinman, J., Lee, R., *et al.* (2012). "The Relationship of Depression and Disease Stage to Patient Perceptions of Parkinson's Disease", *Journal of Health Psychology*, 17(7), 1076-88.

Irvine, A.A., Cox, D. and Gonder-Frederick L. (1992). "Fear of Hypoglycemia: Relationship to Physical and Psychological Symptoms in Patients with Insulin-dependent Diabetes Mellitus", *Health Psychology*, 11(2), 135-38.

Kelley, H.H. (1973). "The Processes of Causal Attribution", *American Psychologist*, 28(2), 107-28.

Kiecolt-Glaser, J.K., Glaser, R., Williger, D., Stout, J., Messick, G., Sheppard, S., Ricker, D., Romisher, S.C., Briner, W., Bonnell, G. and Donnerberg, R. (1985). "Psychosocial Enhancement of Immunocompetence in a Geriatric Population", *Health Psychology*, 4(1), 25-41.

Kleinman, A. (1980). *Patients and Healers in the Context of Culture*, Berkley: University of California Press.

Kohli, N. and Dalal, A.K. (1998). "Culture as a Factor in Causal Understanding of Illness: A Study of Cancer Patients", *Psychology and Developing Societies*, 10(2), 115-29.

Lau, R.R., Bernard, T.M. and Hartman, K.A. (1989). "Further Explorations of Common-sense Representations of Common Illnesses", *Health Psychology*, 8(2), 195-219.

Lazarus, R.S. (1983). "The Costs and Benefits of Denial", in S. Bresnitz (ed.), *Denial of Stress*, New York: International Universities Press.

Love, C. and Sabiston, C.M. (2011). "Examining Physical Activity as a Moderator of the Relationship between Social Support and Psychological Growth among Young Adult Cancer Survivors", *Psycho-Oncology*, 20(3), 278-86.

Manjunatha S. (2013). "A Sociological Study on the Women Cancer Patients in Bengaluru City, India", *International Research Journal of Social Sciences*, 2(7), 8-13.

Manocchia, M., Keller, S. and Ware, J.E. (2001). "Sleep Problems, Health-related Quality of Life, Work Functioning and Healthcare Utilization among the Chronically Ill", *Quality of Life Research*, 10(4), 331-45.

Mishra, R.C. (1997). "Family Support and Health Care in a Culturally Changing Village Community in Northern India", *Social Science International*, 13, 10-13.

Mishra, R.C. (2009). "Health Cognition and Practices", in A. Shukla (ed.), *Culture: Cognition and Behaviour* (pp. 264-76), New Delhi: Concept.

Moos, R. and Mitchell, R. (1982). "Social Network Resources and Adaptation: A Conceptual Framework", in T.A. Wills (ed.), *Basic Processes in Helping Relationships*, New York: Academic Press.

Murdaugh, C., Moneyham, L., Jackson, K., Phillips, K. and Tavakoli, A. (2006). "Predictors of Quality of Life in HIV-infected Rural Women: Psychometric Test of Chronic Illness Quality of Life Ladder", *Quality of Life Research*, 15(5), 777-89.

Paranjpe, A.C. (1987). *The Nature of Suffering and Its Remedy: A Perspective from the Cultural Tradition of India*, Unpublished Manuscript, Simon Fraser University, Canada.

Park, C.L. (1998). "Stress-related Growth and Thriving through Coping: The Roles of Personality and Cognitive Processes", *Journal of Social Issues*, 54, 267-77.

Park, C.L., Cohen, L.H. and Murch, R.L. (1996). "Assessment and Prediction of Stress-related Growth", *Journal of Personality*, 64(1), 71-105.

Park, N. (2004). "The Role of Subjective Well-being in Positive Youth Development", *The Annals of the American Academy*, 591(1), 25-39.

Pavot, W. and Diener, E. (1993). "Review of the Satisfaction with Life Scale", *Psychological Assessment*, 5(2), 164-72.

Peterson, C., Seligman, Martin E. and Vaillant, George E. (1988). "Pessimistic Explanatory Style is a Risk Factor for Physical Illness: A Thirty-five-year Longitudinal Study", *Journal of Personality and Social Psychology*, 55 (1), 23-27.

Peterson, C. and Seligman, M.E.P. (1984). "Causal Explanations as a Risk Factor for Depression: Theory and Evidence", *Psychological Reoiebo*, 91, 347-74.

Peterson, C. and Steen, T.A. (2002). "Optimistic Explanatory Style", in C.R. Snyder and S.J. Lopez (eds.), *Handbook of Positive Psychology* (244-56), Oxford University Press.

Petrie, K.J., Buick, D.L., Weinman, J. and Booth, R.J. (1999). "Positive Effects of Illness Reported by Myocardial Infarction and Breast Cancer Patients", *Journal of Psychosomatic Research*, 47(6), 537-43.

Pinquart, M. and Frohlich, C. (2009). "Psychosocial Resources and Subjective Well-being of Cancer Patients", *Psychology and Health*, 24(4), 407-21.

Radhakrishnan, S. (1926). *The Hindu View of Life*, Mumbai: Blakie.

Rochelle, T.L. and Fidler, H. (2013). "The Importance of Illness Perceptions, Quality of Life and Psychological Status in Patients with Ulcerative Colitis and Crohn's Disease", *Journal of Health Psychology*, 18(7), 972-83.

Rowland, J. and Baker, F. (2005). "Introduction: Resilience of Cancer Survivors Across the Lifespan", *Cancer*, 104(11), 2543-48.

Schaefer, J.A. and Moos, R.H. (1992). "Life Crises and Personal Growth", in B.N. Carpenter (ed.), *Personal Coping: Theory, Research, and Application* (pp. 149-70), Westport, CT: Praeger.

Scheier, M.F. and Carver, C.S. (1985). "Optimism, Coping, and Health: Assessment and Implications of Generalized Outcome Expectancies", *Health Psychology*, 4(3), 219-47.

Scheier, M.F. and Carver, C.S. (1987). "Dispositional Optimism and Physical Well-being: The Influence of Generalized Expectancies on Health", *Journal of Personality*, 55(2), 169-210.

Scheier, M.F., Carver, C.S. and Bridges, M.W. (1994). "Distinguishing Optimism from Neuroticism (and Trait Anxiety, Self-mastery, and Self-esteem): A Reevaluation of the Life Orientation Test", *Journal of Personality and Social Psychology*, 67(6), 1063-78.

Scheier, M.F., Carver, C.S. and Bridges, M.W. (2001). "Optimism, Pessimism, and Psychological Well-being", in E.C. Chang (ed.), *Optimism and Pessimism: Implications for Theory, Research, and Practice* (pp. 189-216). Washington, DC: American Psychological Association.

Scheier, M.F., Weintraub, J.K. and Carver, C.S. (1986). "Coping with Stress: Divergent Strategies of Optimists and Pessimists", *Journal of Personality and Social Psychology*, 51(6), 1257-64.

Schou, I., Ekeberg, O., Sandvik, L., Hjermstad, M. J. and Ruland, C.M. (2005). "Multiple Predictors of Health-related Quality of Life in Early Stage Breast Cancer", Data from a year follow-up study compared with the general population, *Quality of Life Research*, 14(8), 1813-23.

Sears, S.R., Stanton, A.L. and Danoff-Burg, S. (2003). "The Yellow Brick Road and the Emerald City: Benefit Finding, Positive Reappraisal Coping, and Post-traumatic Growth in Women with Early-stage Breast Cancer", *Health Psychology*, 22(5), 487-97.

Shweder, R.A. (2008). "The Cultural Psychology of Suffering: The many Meanings of Health in Odisha, India (and Elsewhere)", *Ethos*, 36(1), 60-77.

Sinzato, R., Fukino, O., Tamai, H., Isuzu, H., Nakagawa, A. and Ikemi, Y. (1985). "Coping Behaviour of Severe Diabetics", *Psychotherapy and Psychosomatics*, 43(4), 219-26.

Spiegel, D. (1999). "A 43-year Old Women Coping with Cancer", *Journal of American Medical Association*, 282(4), 371-78.

Stanton, A.L. and Snider, P.R. (1993). "Coping with a Breast Cancer Diagnosis: A Prospective Study", *Health Psychology*, 12(1), 16-23.

Staudinger, U., Baltes, P. and Fleeson, W. (1999). "Predictors of Subjective Physical Health and Global Well-being: Similarities and Differences between the United States and Germany", *Journal of Personality and Social Psychology*, 76(2), 305-19.

Tandon, P.N. (2011). "Belief: A Scientific Perspective", in P.N. Tondon, R.C. Tripathi and N. Srinivasan (eds.), *Expanding Horizons of the Mind Science(s)*, (pp. 235-47), New York: Nova Science Publishers.

Taylor, S.E. (1983). "Adjustment to Threatening Life Events: A Theory of Cognitive Adaptation", *American Psychologist*, 38(11), 1161-73.

Taylor, S.E. (2005). "On Healthy Illusions", *Daedalus*, 134(1), 133-35.

Taylor, S.E., Lichtman, R.R. and Wood, J.V. (1984). "Attributions, Beliefs about Control, and Adjustment to Breast Cancer", *Journal of Personality and Social Psychology*, 46(3), 489-502.

Tedeschi, R.G. and Calhoun, L.G. (1996). "The Post-traumatic Growth Inventory: Measuring the Positive Legacy of Trauma", *Journal of Traumatic Stress*, 9(3), 455-71.

Tedeschi, R.G. and Calhoun, L.G. (2004). "Post-traumatic Growth: Conceptual Foundations and Empirical Evidence", *Psychological Inquiry*, 15(1), 1-18.

Timko, C. and Janoff-Bulman, R. (1985). "Attributions, Vulnerability, and Psychological Adjustment: The Case of Breast Cancer", *Health Psychology*, 4(6), 521-44.

Tomich, P. and Helgeson, V. (2002). "Five Years Later: A Cross-sectional Comparison of Breast Cancer Survivors with Healthy Women", *Psycho-Oncology*, 11, 154-69.

Tomich, P.L., Helgeson, V.S. and Vache, E.J.N. (2005). "Perceived Growth and Decline following Breast Cancer: A Comparison to Age-matched Controls 5-years Later", *Psycho-Oncology*, 14, 1018-29.

Urcuyo, K.R., Boyers, A.E., Carver, C.S. and Antoni, M.H. (2005). "Finding Benefit in Breast Cancer: Relations with Personality, Coping, and Concurrent Well-being", *Psychology and Health*, 20(2), 175-92.

Watten, R.G., Vassend, D., Myhrer, T. and Syversen, J.N. (1997). "Personality Factors and Somatic Symptoms", *European Journal of Personality*, 11(1), 57-68.

Weiner, B. (1985). "An Attribution Theory of Achievement Motivation and Emotion", *Psychological Review*, 92(4), 548-73.

Weiner, B. (1988). "Attribution Theory and Attribution Therapy: Some Theoretical Observations and Suggestions", *British Journal of Clinical Psychology*, 27(1), 99-104.

Weiner, B. (1993). "On Sin *versus* Sickness: A Theory of Perceived Responsibility and Social Motivation", *American Psychologist*, 48(9), 957-65.

Wittenberg, S.H., Blanchard, E.B., Suls, J., Tennen, H., McCoy, G. and McGoldrick, M.D. (1983). "Perceptions of Control and Causality as Predictors of Compliance and Coping in Hemodialysis", *Basis and Applied Social Psychology*, 4, 319-36.

World Health Organization (2009). *The Global Burden of Disease: 2004 Update*, Geneva: WHO.

4

Common Sense Model of Illness Representations: Issues and Implications

Rajbala Singh

Advancement in medical science has given biological cure to various chronic illnesses. The biological cure of chronic illnesses has also given rise to life expectancy with a set of psychological challenges. The basic nature of chronic illnesses can be characterized by its different level of uncertainty throughout illness episodes. As a result, patients need to bring lot of behavioural changes in terms of lifestyle, adaptation to illness and adherence to demanding nature of treatment process. Thus, adaptation to chronic illness condition is psychologically very demanding and challenging (White, 2001).

What is Chronic Illness?

According to Kaptein, *et al.* (2003), originally the word chronic has been derived from Greek word 'chronos' which means 'time'. Similarly, 'chronikos' in Greek refers to 'during a long period of time'. Thus, the element of time is a core concept in defining any chronic illness. Illnesses such as, asthma, arthritis, cancer, heart attack, etc. are good examples of chronic illnesses because they exist in a sufferes's life for a long time and even for the whole life. According to Leventhal, Halm, Horowitz, Leventhal and Ozakinci (2004), certain characteristics are common across majority of chronic illnesses: (a) they systematically affect physiological system and impose significant limitations on physical and social functioning; (b) they are latent in nature; (c) they cannot be cured fully, but can be controlled and managed; (d) many chronic illnesses, but not all have pernicious tendency. As noted by Kaptein, *et al.* (2003), three characteristics of illness have been outlined in epidemiological studies: duration, severity of functional limitation and use of healthcare services. Any illness condition can be labelled as chronic if it lasts for at least three months or recur for a number of times. The functioning of individuals should be severely affected in a manner that they are unable to perform work and other daily activities. In addition, help of medical care services are required for a long period of time.

At this juncture it is also important to know the difference between three terms that are often used interchangeably: disease, illness and sickness. These three concepts belong to three different domains, medicine, psychology and sociology respectively. In general, these three concepts are understood as same but theoretically they are different. In bio-medical science disease refers to a state of physiological dysfunction for which any physiological basis exists (Kaptein, *et al.*, 2003; Mishra & Verma, 1999). Unlike disease, illness is a subjective concept. An illness can be present without being diseased. People associate different subjective symptoms such as pain, weakness, headache, etc. while reporting any illness. The word 'sickness' has been coined by sociologists, which is related to someone's 'social identity' or role people assume to play once they have been labelled as sick by given society (Mishra & Verma, 1999). The social tagging of being 'sick' may occur without actual presence of disease or illness.

What is Self-Regulation?

Compared to other species, humans have the ability to exercise control over mind and behaviour. Humans can resist their own impulses, thought processes, emotions, motivation, etc. (Baumeister, 1999). According to Carver and Scheier (1982), the notion of control provides a framework for self-regulation. Scholars have given numerous definitions of self-regulation. The common theme of all definitions of self-regulation incorporates "ability to change, alter or modify one's own behaviour" (Hagger, 2010, p. 57). According to Hagger, this definition refers to certain characteristics of self-regulation such as; self-regulation is related to conscious, planned, intentional and goal directed action and behaviour reflected by an individual.

As noted by Cameron and Leventhal (2003), self-regulation can be construed as a "systematic process involving conscious efforts to modulate thoughts, emotions and behaviours" (p. 1). It is a 'dynamic motivational' construct that comprises setting goals, planning appropriate strategies to achieve these goals, appraisal of goals and strategies and revision of selected goals and strategies. It follows the principle of TOTE (Test, Operate, Test, Exit).

Self-Regulation *vs.* Regulation

The difference between regulation and self-regulation can be understood from the locus of control perspective. As noted by Zeidner, Boekaerts and Pintrich (2000), it is important to know whether goal for regulation emanated from internal world, i.e. self-system or from external world, i.e. social system. Thus, if an individual is setting a goal and its related procedures at own, it will be an example of self-regulation. On the other hand, if the desired goal setting and related procedures are determined by others, it will be known as regulation by external factors.

Self-Regulation *vs.* Self-Management

The distinction between self-regulation and self-management has not been clearly spelt out. According to Zeidner, *et al.* (2000), for the ease of understanding it can be assumed that in self-regulation people inclined to follow self-set goals whereas in self-management individuals follow goals set by an external agent such as, health professional in case of a chronic illness. However, distinction made by Zeidner, *et al.* (2000), is not universally accepted.

Common Sense Model of Illness Representations: Basic Assumptions

According to Leventhal, Leventhal and Cameron (2001), there are three basic assumptions of common sense-model of self-regulation:

- **(a)** ***Individual as an active problem solver:*** This model assumes that human beings are bestowed with active problem solving capacity. The term 'problem solving' suggests that most of the human actions are purposeful and goal directed. In the context of health and illness, individuals are thought of as active problem solvers, who try to make sense of their somatic state and of changes in that state. Individuals by their self-regulating systems try to avoid or control changes that are perceived as signs of illness. Here the process of adaptation with illness is similar to problem solving.
- **(b)** ***Process of adaptation:*** It is based on individual's 'common sense belief.' Thus, the individual's understanding of disease influences representation, coping and outcome.

(c) ***Representation of disease:*** In self-regulation model, representation of disease may be distinct from objective biomedical representation. Here the representation of disease threat is influenced by individuals' perceptions, attitudes and beliefs regarding his environment. Beliefs of environment include family, friends, doctors, mass media, and other cultural factors.

Overall, common sense model of illness representation suggests that individuals on the basis of their experiences develop their own illness models or mental representations that give them lay understanding of their disease and also give guidelines regarding coping and adaptation in the context of illness. According to Hagger, Chatzisarantis and Griffin (2004), three basic sources of information mould this mental representation: (i) lay information, assimilated and stored in individual's mind from various sources such as, social interaction, and cultural beliefs about illness, etc., (ii) Information from significant others such as, parent, spouse, doctor, etc., and (iii) Individual's experience with illness. This includes bodily cues regarding current illness, past experiences with illness and previous knowledge in coping with illness, etc.

Self-Regulation and Common Sense Model of Illness Representations

According to Cameron and Leventhal (2003), a health model cannot be called a self-regulation model unless it has three essential components: feedback, motivation and goals. Only having elements of cognitive, affective and behavioural components will not make any health model a self-regulation model.

Cameron and Leventhal (2003) have contrasted common sense models with other health models such as, health belief model, reasoned action model and transactional model. In health belief model and reasoned action model, individual is conceived as a 'rational decision-maker' who calculates the cost and benefit for adopting health behaviour in question. Up to this point, both the models fulfil the initial phase of self-regulation, i.e. setting goals. However, they fail to take into account other aspects such as, emotional processes. Emotional processes include behavioural decisions. Such decisions are dynamic processes, where feedback processes apparaise individuals' health behaviour and suggest them whether to engage in specific health behaviour or not. Transactional model of health behaviour proposes the phases of selection, adaptation and maintenance of a change in health behaviour. This model recognizes that behaviour is dynamic in nature. However, it is less successful in explaining the role of emotional processes, the nature of psychological processes at each stage and the influence of socio-environmental factors on health behaviour. Common sense model on the other hand emphasizes that health behaviour is dynamic in nature and successfully explains both cognitive and emotional representation when an individual faces an illness threat.

Dimensions of Illness Representations

As noted by Croyle and Barger (1993), Jenkins was one of the pioneering researchers who empirically examined the dimensions of illness representations. Jenkins (1966) found that differences in perception of tuberculosis were associated with education, socio-economic status and ethnicity (white & non-white). Further, in another study, Jenkins and Zyzanski (1968) studied the dimensions of belief and feeling pertaining to three diseases of poliomyelitis, cancer and mental illness. Jenkins and Zyzanski used semantic differential scale consisted of 16 questions related to disease and employed factor analysis method. Jenkins and Zyzanski found three dimensions of illness representation common across the three diseases: personal involvement, human mastery, and social acceptability. Though Jenkins and Zyzanski's work had been considered one of the earliest works, but their work was criticized by scholars for using single item scale to measure the structural basis of illness beliefs (Turk, Rudy & Salovy, 1986).

Contemporary to Jenkins, Leventhal with his coworkers investigated the effect of fear arousing messages on coping with health threats. In their studies they found that neither the level of fear message (high fear, low fear) nor the action plan alone was capable of influencing individuals to adopt any health action. It was effective only when both the levels of fear (high, low) were presented with an action plan (Leventhal, Jones & Trembly, 1966). Individual's tendency to engage in any health action such as stop smoking occurred only when individual also got an action plan preceded by a fear arousing message (Leventhal, Watts & Pagano, 1967). The findings of these studies gave a realization to the researchers that it is important to study how people process illness related information when exposed to a health threat.

Later, Leventhal, Meyer and Nerenz (1980) and Leventhal, Nerenz and Steele (1984) proposed a structural model of illness representation by assuming humans as an active problem solver. Turk, *et al.* (1986), studied common sense model of illness and explored the dimensional structure underlying an individual's illness representations with the help of factor analysis method. They found four dimensions of illness model: seriousness, personal responsibility, controllability, and changeability. They advocated that these four dimensional structure reflect an individual's 'implicit model of illness.'

As noted by Petrie and Pennebaker (2004), early researches to identify dimensions of illness representations employed open ended interviews/ semi-structure interviews with patients suffering from chronic illness. The patients were asked variety of questions that aimed to gauge their understanding and belief about illness. The interviews were designed to encourage patients to elicit their ideas about illness in an in-depth manner. Initial researches on common sense model of representation yielded four dimensions of illness representations (Leventhal, *et al.*, 1980; Leventhal, *et al.*, 1984; Leventhal & Nerenz, 1985): *identity* (abstract labels and concrete symptoms associated with an illness), *timeline* (patients' belief regarding duration of illness. It also included individual's perception regarding whether the illness is acute, chronic or cyclic), *consequences* (patient's belief regarding what would be the outcome of the illness), and *cause* (patient's beliefs regarding what would have caused his/her illness). Further, Lau and Hartman (1983) provided support for Leventhal's work. The findings of Lau and Hartman study provided strong support for identity and consequences dimensions of Leventhal's model but weak support for timeline component. In addition, findings of Lau and Hartman's study added another dimension to illness representations: cure control (patient's beliefs regarding whether illness is controllable or uncontrollable).

Measurement of Illness Representations

The results obtained from open ended/semi-structured interviews provided both generic and specific understanding regarding illness. However, due to reliability issues with these methods, researcher motivated to develop a systematic and robust psychometric tool to assess illness representations. In this connection, Weinman, Petrie, Moss-Morris and Horne (1996) developed illness perception questionnaire (IPQ) to assess five dimensions of illness representations. Later, Moss-Morris, *et al.* (2002), added few more dimensions to illness representations such as, timeline cyclical, illness coherence and emotional representation and developed revised illness perception questionnaire (IPQ-R). Broadbent, Petrie, Main and Weinman (2006) developed brief illness perception questionnaire. According to Croyle and Barger (1993), broadly scholars have adopted three methods, factor analysis, cluster analysis and multidimensional scaling to study illness representation statistically.

Common Sense Model of Illness Representations: Issues

According to Leventhal, Leventhal and Breland (2011), Common Sense Model (CSM) of illness representation involves higher order cognitive processes in molding illness representation. CSM is more focussed upon numbers of features with "common sense" characteristics. However, it would be more justified to say that CSM is a process orient model than just a mere theoretical model. The following section broadly discusses certain issues in the area of CSM followed by implications of CSM.

Common Sense Model of Illness Representations: Dynamic *vs.* Static

According to Leventhal, *et al.* (2011), the common sense model of illness representation is a 'dynamic system model'. Individuals actively update their common sense models regarding potential health threats, coping strategies treatment plans and appraisals regarding treatment received. Along with this, changes in disease process, feedback from significant others such as, medical professionals, friends, spouse, etc. also influence individuals' model of illness representations (Leventhal, Halm, Horowitz, Leventhal & Ozakinci, 2004). Information from various sources such as, perceived changes in one's biological function, observation of these changes in similar others or through mass media shapes the representation of illness. The success and failure of a coping strategy serves to revise an illness representation.

According to Leventhal, *et al.* (2001), individual uses his/her problem solving capacity while going through different episodes of illness. At this level, interaction occurs between concrete and abstract features of illness representation and concrete and abstract features of self. The concrete features of illness representation such as, labelling of disease, anticipated symptoms, experiential part of treatment, etc. interact with concrete level of self such as, individual's perceived ability to tolerate the pain and discomfort due to disease and treatment. On the other hand, abstract features of illness representation such as, belief about life and death, anticipated injury from serious treatment (chemotherapy, surgery, etc.) interact with abstract features of self such as, optimism-pessimism, self-efficacy, etc. The meanings generated from the interaction between higher order variables are assumed to be important for planning and execution of goal directed behaviour.

Although CSM claims to be a dynamic model, there is dearth of empirical researches focussed on whether and how illness representations change (Fischer, 2010).

Levels of Representations: Unilateral or Bilateral

According to Diefenbach and Leventhal (1996) and Leventhal, Diefenbach and Leventhal (1992), individuals deal with any health threat on the basis of two types of representations. These representations occur simultaneously and interactive in nature (Whitmarsh, Koutantji & Sidell, 2003):

(a) Perception of health threat or cognitive representation.
(b) Emotional reaction to health threat or emotional representation.

Cognitive Representation

According to CSM, both external and internal stimuli trigger illness representations when an individual encounters any health threat. At this point of time, pre-stored existing schematic structures of health/illness serve as a basis for the interpretation of new illness related cues or information. In other words, individuals on the basis of their prior experiences with illness give meaning and interpretation to incoming illness related experiences (Diefenbach & Leventhal, 1996). The illness related threat or illness related stimulus can come from either external and/or internal source.

According to Diefenbach and Leventhal (1996), when a stimulus comes from an internal source such as, any somatic cue then its representation depends on its similarity with already available illness schema in the mind. The existing illness schemata may be an individual's past experience with diseases or it may be rooted in an imagined one. In this case, the matching process between current somatic cue and existing schemata will generally revolve around five dimensions of illness cognition: Identity, timeline, cure control, consequence and causes of the illness. The detailed discussion regarding these illness representation dimensions can be found later in the present chapter.

According to Cameron, Leventhal and Leventhal (1993), the illness representation model guides selection of coping strategies as well perception of illness outcomes. It is important to mention here that the flow between illness cognition, coping and outcome is not unidirectional, but bi-directional. It may follow both top down and bottom up processes.

Emotional Representation

Any somatic cue may evoke emotional response when it is interpreted as threatening or signal of coming health threat (Leventhal, Brissette & Leventhal, 2003). For example, for a girl, a lump in the breast will not be threatening unless it is labelled as a possible cancerous lump. In this case, it may invoke anxiety and fear of body image. Similarly, a pain in the chest will not invoke an emotional response such as, depression, fear, etc., unless it is labelled as a sign of heart attack. Emotional representation is important for understanding reaction to health threat.

According to Hale, Treharne and Kitas (2007), it is important for a health professional to understand and acknowledge multiple levels of representations as these representations influence patients' orientation regarding treatment and health behaviours across time. Unawareness of these representations by a health professional will be detrimental for patients' adherence to treatment.

Does CSM Involve Cognitive Structures?

CSM describes a wide range of cognitive processes of attention, perception, motivation, interpretation, etc. in response to variety of illness related information. Basic researches conducted in the area of social cognition throws light on underlying structures of illness representation such as, role of prototype, etc. as well as rules or heuristics involved in the formation of illness representations. The following section discusses the role of prototype and heuristics in relation to CSM of illness representations.

Role of Prototypes in CSM

Bishop and Converse (1986) used prototype approach to study illness representations. Bishop and Converse found that symptom sets with high prototype were rated more as an indication of disease than the low or medium prototype symptom set. In addition, Bishop and Converse also reported that subjects recalled more symptoms for high prototypical symptom set than other symptom sets. Bishop and Converse concluded that organization and processing of physical symptoms happen as per individuals' pre-existing beliefs regarding relationship between specific symptoms and diseases. In another study, Bishop (1991) used 'prototype construct' as a model for cognitive structure and suggested that an individual's available cognitive structures serve as a source to provide meaning for illness. Prototypes are best examples or standards in the memory to which new things are compared. Similarly, people compare physical symptoms with the prototype of similar illness symptoms stored in the memory. It is important to note that selection of prototype does not require a perfect match between the symptom and prototype rather significant resemblance between two is important. Bishop asked the subjects to rate whether symptom sets with different prototypicality represented a specific disease. Results demonstrated that subject's decision was faster for high prototypical symptom set than others. Bishop concluded that disease prototypes play a significant role in recognition of a disease state, retrieval and processing of information related to illness episodes. As noted by Croyle and Barger (1993), findings of these studies suggested that a "closer fit between a symptom and prototype facilitate processing of symptom information" (p. 33). Thus, cognitive structures exert an impact on not only reporting of symptoms but also on whole illness experience.

Role of Heuristics in CSM

According to Leventhal, *et al.* (2003), evidences in research literature indicate involvement of variety of heuristics in the development of illness representations. The first heuristic is symmetry. The symmetry heuristic suggests that people combine their abstract experience with labels. For example, Bauman, Cameron, Zimmerman and Leventhal (1989) in a lab studies found that subjects reported symptoms when they were informed that their blood pressure is very high. According to Leventhal, *et al.* (2003), the connection between these two is bi-directional, i.e. "labels seek symptoms and symptoms seek labels" and it gives depth to the representation. Individuals use age illness heuristic and stress illness heuristic when they have to make a decision regarding whether perceived underlying physiological changes are due to disease process or due to non-disease process such as, ageing or due to over work, etc.

According to Leventhal, *et al.* (2004), locational heuristic refer to reporting of perceived symptoms such as breathlessness and pain to its location such as, respiratory system or muscles than its possible source such as myocardial infarction. While using the prevalence heuristics, individuals tend to underestimate the severity of symptoms if they perceive that in a given environment many individuals report similar symptoms. Affective heuristics indicate that the feeling of anxiety and depression positively affect individuals' perception that regarding being ill (Croyle & Jemmott, 1991).

Does Coping Mediates the Relationship between Illness Representations and Illness Outcomes?

CSM proposes that illness representations influence choice of coping strategy to cope with the disease that in turn influences outcome appraisals (Leventhal, *et al.*, 1980). In other words, this model proposes that a mediational relationship exists among illness cognition, coping processes and outcome; where coping is thought to mediate the relationship between illness representations and illness outcomes. However, it is debatable whether illness representations directly influence illness outcomes or through coping.

Studies of Heijmans (1998, 1999) and Moss-Morris, Petrie and Weinman (1996) on different chronic disease groups, reported that patient's illness representations are more important in predicting adjustment to illness and coping strategies are less important in predicting adjustment to illness. Similarly, Scharloo, *et al.* (1998), did not found coping as a mediating factor between illness representations and illness outcomes and thus reported that illness representations affect illness outcomes directly not through coping. In another study, Rutter and Rutter (2002) tested the mediational role of coping between illness representations and illness outcomes. They reported that coping sometimes mediated the link between illness representations and illness outcomes. The consequence dimension of illness representations was related with illness outcomes, both directly and indirectly through coping. Indirectly, consequence was related to psychological adjustment through venting emotions and through behavioural disengagement. Carlisle, John, Fife-Schaw and Lloyd (2005) examined the relationship between illness representation, coping strategies and illness outcome among women suffering from rheumatoid arthritis. They found that dimensions of illness representation were strongly related to dimensions of illness outcomes. In their study, only the coping strategies of avoidance and resignation were partially found to mediate between illness identity and illness outcomes of disability and psychiatric morbidity.

Heijmans (1998) examined the role of illness representations on coping and adaptive outcomes in chronic fatigue syndrome. The study demonstrated that both illness representations and coping strategy, especially passive coping were related to the different dimensions of illness outcome. However, the results of regression analysis revealed the low power of illness representation in predicting coping strategies. In a meta-analytic review of CSM, Hagger and Orbell (2003) reported that illness representation dimensions are related to coping processes and illness outcomes. However, Hagger and Orbell were unable to make any judgement regarding the mediational role of coping between illness representation and illness outcome because studies used in the meta-analysis were largely cross-sectional. In addition, there are few researches that have tested the mediational relationship among illness cognition, coping and illness outcome.

Implications of Common Sense Model of Illness Representations

Common Sense Model (CSM) has been found successful in examining how individuals make sense of their illness in day-to-day life and how such sense making influences coping with illness and appraisal of illness outcomes. CSM may have important implications for adopting positive health behaviour in general and making overall treatment process more effective by gauging the disparity between objective and subjective model of illness. In addition, scholars have also acknowledged the significance of CBT for patients suffering from chronic illness (Taylor, 2006; White, 2001). The present chapter proposes that CSM could serve as a basc for CBT to make treatment and health interventions more effective.

CSM has been studied with wide range of illness such as, myocardial infarction, chronic fatigue syndrome, irritable bowel syndrome, diabetes, HIV, etc. Although, CSM has been widely studied in disease populations, CSM may have significant implications for non-disease population in terms of adopting healthy health behaviours such as, how to utilize healthcare, how to drive oneself for self-care, etc. (Rau & Williams, 2013). However, such relationship need to be examined through empirical researches as there are dearth of studies in this area.

According to Leventhal, *et al.* (2011), CSM offers an avenue for a better personalized treatment. In general, patients and health professionals bring diverse set of knowledge domain. Health professionals adopt a rather crude 'bio-medical perspective' where the focus is upon observing symptoms, recording the history of illness episodes and related symptoms followed by diagnosis and treatment. This indicates that traditionally a physician deals with a disease in a way we deal with variety of objects and its functioning in day-to-day life. On the contrary, patients perceive themselves more than an object. Patients may bring novel clusters of complicated symptoms. There are number of factors such as, social and cultural context of patient, media resources, personal and emotional factors, etc. that may influence patients' complaint regarding illness as well as may influence or interfere patients' adherence to the treatment regime. Thus, awareness regarding the disparity between objective and subjective model of illness may bring better outcomes for health interventions. According to Leventhal, *et al.*, variety of psycho-social factors may influence following processes essential for designing an effective health intervention:

- *Information Sharing:* Patients speak about the nature and history of complaint, and collaborate with health professionals during physical examination.
- *Diagnosis:* It refers to defining the complaint in biomedical term and explaining its meaning to the patient.
- *Recommendation for Management:* It refers to making a patient specific 'treatment protocol'.

Leventhal, *et al.* (2011), proposed that first two steps which are, information sharing and diagnosis, aim to creation of common representation of illness condition (for both patient and health professional) whereas step three aims to set up a health management. Thus, treatment regime and health intervention guided by common representations may bring more favourable results as it aims to capture both subjective and objective indices of illness condition.

CSM has been found successful in studying patients' subjective understanding regarding physical illness. On the other hand, Cognitive Behaviour Therapy (CBT) has been widely used for treatment of mental illness. The comprehensive details regarding implications of CBT for psychiatric disorders can be witnessed in the work of Beck (1995).

Scholars have acknowledged significance of CBT for patients suffering from chronic illness (White, 2001, Sperry, 2008; Taylor, 2010). Halford and Brown (2009) proposed that CBT can be used as an adjunctive treatment for patients suffering from chronic physical illness. They suggested that chronic illness condition may serve as potential risk factor for psychological symptoms similar to different psychiatric disorders. Coates, *et al.* (1983), in a study on patients receiving chemotherapy found that patients rated non-physical side effects such as anger, anxiety, etc. more severe than physical side effects of vomiting, nausea or hair loss. According to Watanabe, Stewart, Jenkins, Bhugra and Furukawa (2008), the treatment of physically ill should also take into account associated psychiatric symptoms such as, depression, anxiety, post-traumatic stress disorder, etc. Results of these studies indicate that both patients suffering from chronic physical illness and mental illness experience similar kind of psychological symptoms. Thus, it would be appropriate to rationalize the importance of CBT as an adjunctive treatment for patients suffering from chronic illness.

The present chapter asserts that CBT as an adjunctive treatment could be more successful if it utilizes CSM to understand the subjective understanding of illness. CSM would be highly informative as it gauges both cognitive and emotional representation of illness. There is a lot of similarity in basic postulates of CSM and CBT.

The basic postulate of CSM emphasizes that cognitive and emotional representations take place simultaneously. Similarly, CBT affirms that cognition influence emotional reactions and behaviour in a significant manner (Westbrook, Kennerley & Kirk, 2011). CSM assumes that individual's lay model of illness rests upon their belief system and is also detrimental to coping and appraisal of illness outcomes. In CBT, belief is the center figure in deciding the perception of consequences (Westbrook, *et al.*, 2011). CSM suggests that illness schema guides action planning or coping responses as well as appraisal of illness outcomes. CBT supports that negative schemas about self, world or future will activate the feeling of depression and helplessness (Westbrook, *et al.*, 2011). Thus, present chapter proposes that CBT as an adjunctive treatment can be more effective if it utilizes information obtained from CSM. However, relevance of CSM for CBT needs to be investigated empirically.

Conclusion

The common sense model of illness representations has been found very useful in understanding patients' subjective experience regarding their illness. The CSM focuses upon beliefs and ideas patients hold about their illness condition that in turn may play a crucial role in selection of coping strategies with illness as well as in perception of illness related outcomes. The CSM may be instrumental for adopting positive health behaviour in day-to-day life. In addition, CSM may play a very important role in bridging the gap between objective and subjective model of illness. The understanding about patients' common sense model of illness would help both health professionals while planning health interventions and patients to understand a clear picture about their illness condition. CSM may have also major implication for CBT as an adjunctive treatment. However, such associations need to be examined empirically.

REFERENCES

Bauman, L.J., Cameron, L.D., Zimmerman, R.S. and Leventhal, H. (1989). "Illness Representations and Matching Labels with Symptoms", *Health Psychology*, 8(4), 449-69.

Baumeister, R.F. (1999). "The Nature and Structure of the Self: An Overview", in R.F. Baumeister (ed.), *The Self in Social Psychology* (pp. 1-24), Philadelphia: Psychology Press.

Beck (1995). *Cognitive Therapy: Basics and Beyond*, New York: Guilford Press.

Bishop, G.D. (1991). "Understanding the Understanding of Illness: Lay Disease Representations", in J.A. Skelton and R.T. Croyle (eds.), *Mental Representations in Health and Illness* (pp. 32-59), New York: Springer-Verlag.

Bishop, G.D. and Converse, S.A. (1986). "Illness Representations: A Prototype Approach", *Health Psychology*, 5(2), 95-114.

Broadbent, E., Petrie, K.J., Main, J. and Weinman, J. (2006). "The Brief Illness Perception Questionnaire (BIPQ)", *Journal of Psychosomatic Research*, 60, 631-37. doi:10.1016/j.jpsychores.2005.10.020

Cameron, L.D. and Leventhal, H. (2003). "Self-regulation, Health and Illness: An Overview", in L.D. Cameron and H. Leventhal (eds.), *The Self-Regulation of Health and Illness Behaviour* (pp. 1-14), London: Routledge.

Cameron, L.D., Leventhal, E.A. and Leventhal, H. (1993). "Symptom Representations and Affect as Determinants of Care Seeking in a Community Dwelling Adult Sample Population", *Health Psychology*, 12(3), 171-79.

Carlisle, A.C.S., John, A.M.H., Fife-Schaw, C. and Lloyd, M. (2005). "The Self-regulatory Model in Women with Rheumatoid Arthritis: Relationship between Illness Representations, Coping Strategies, and Illness Outcome", *British Journal of Health Psychology*, 10(4), 571-87.

Carver, C.S. and Scheier, M.F. (1982). "Control Theory: A Useful Conceptual Framework for Personality — Social, Clinical, and Health Psychology", *Psychological Bulletin*, 92(1), 111-35.

Coates, A., Abraham S., Kaye S.B., Sowerbutts, T., Frewin, C., Fox, R.M. and Tattersall, M.H. (1983). "On the Receiving End — Patient Perception of the Side-effects of Cancer Chemotherapy", *European Journal of Cancer & Clinical Oncology*, 19(2), 203-08.

Croyle, R.T. and Barger, S.D. (1993). "Illness Cognition", in S. Maes, H. Leventhal and M. Johnston (eds.), *International Review of Health Psychology* (Vol. 2, pp. 22-49), Chichester: John Wiley & Sons.

Croyle, R.T. and Jemmott, J.B.I. (1991). "Psychological Reactions to Risk Factor Testing", in J.A. Skeleton and R.T. Croyle (eds.), *Mental Representations in Health and Illness* (pp. 85-103), New York: Springer.

Diefenbach, M. and Leventhal, H. (1996). "The Common-sense Model of Illness Representation: Theoretical and Practical Considerations", *Journal of Social Distress and the Homeless*, 5(1), 11-38.

Fischer, M., Scharloo, M., Abbink, J., van't Hul, A., van Ranst, D., Rudolphus, A., Weinman, J., Rabe, K. and Kaptein, A.A. (2010), "The Dynamics of Illness

Perceptions: Testing Assumptions of Leventhal's Common-sense Model in a Pulmonary Rehabilitation Setting", *British Journal of Health Psychology*, 15, 887-903. doi: 10.1348/135910710X492693

Hagger (2010): "Self-regulation: An Important Construct in Health Psychology Research and Practice", *Health Psychology Review*, 4(2), 57-65.

Hagger, M.S. and Orbell, S. (2003). "A Meta-analytic Review of the Common-sense Model of Illness Representations", *Personality and Health*, 18(2), 141-84.

Hagger, M.S., Chatzisarantis, N.L.D. and Griffin, M. (2004). "Coping with Sports Injury: Testing a Model of Self-regulation in a Sports Setting", in D. Lavallee, M. Jones and J. Thatcher (eds.), *Coping and Emotions in Sport* (pp. 150-30), New York: Nova Science.

Hale, E.D., Treharne, G.J. and Kitas, G.D. (2007). "The Common-Sense Model of Self-regulation of Health and Illness: How Can We Use it to Understand and Respond to Our Patients' Needs", *Rheumatology*, 46(6), 904-06.

Halford, J. and Brown, T. (2009): "Cognitive-behavioural Therapy as an Adjunctive Treatment in Chronic Physical Illness", *Advances in Psychiatric Treatment*, 15, 306-17. doi: 10.1192/apt.bp.107.003731

Heijmans, M. (1998). "Coping and Adaptive Outcome in Chronic Fatigue Syndrome: Importance of Illness Cognitions", *Journal of Psychosomatic Research*, 45(1), 39-51.

Heijmans, M. (1999). "The Role of Patients' Illness Representations in Coping and Functioning with Addison's Disease", *British Journal of Health Psychology*, 4(2), 137-49.

Jenkins, C.D. (1966). "Group Differences in Perception: A Study of Community Beliefs and Feelings about Tuberculosis", *American Journal of Sociology*, 71(4), 417-29.

Jenkins, C.D. and Zyzanski, S.J. (1968). "Dimensions of Belief and Feelings Concerning Three Diseases — Poliomyelitis, Cancer, and Mental Illness: A Factor Analytic Study", *Behavioural Science*, 13(5), 372-81.

Kaptein, A.A., Scharloo, M., Helder, D.I., Kleijn, W.C., van Korlaar, I.M. and Woertman, M. (2003). "Representations of Chronic Illness", in L.D. Cameron and H. Leventhal (eds.), *The Self-Regulation of Health and Illness Behaviour* (pp. 97-118), London: Routledge.

Lau, R.R. and Hartman, K.A. (1983). "Common Sense Representations of Common Illnesses", *Health Psychology*, 2(2), 197-85.

Leventhal, H., Brissette, I. and Leventhal, E.A. (2003). "The Common Sense Models of Self-regulation of Health & Illness", in L.D. Cameron and H. Leventhal (eds.), *The Self-Regulation of Health and Illness Behaviour* (pp. 42-61), London: Routledge.

Leventhal, H., Diefenbach, M. and Leventhal, E.A. (1992). "Illness Cognition: Using Common Sense to Understand Treatment Adherence and Affect Cognition Interaction", *Cognitive Therapy and Research*, 16(2), 143-63.

Leventhal, H., Jones, S. and Trembly, G. (1966). "Sex Differences in Attitude and Behaviour Change under Conditions of Fear and Specific Instructions", *Journal of Experimental Social Psychology*, 2(4), 387-99.

Leventhal, H., Halm, E., Horowitz, C., Leventhal, E.A. and Ozakinci, G. (2004). "Living with Chronic Illness. A Contextualized, Self-regulation Approach", in R.S. Sutton, A. Baum and M. Johnston (eds.), *The Sage Handbook of Health Psychology* (pp. 197-240), India: Sage Publications.

Leventhal, H., Leventhal, E.A. and Breland, J.Y. (2011). "Cognitive Science Speaks to the 'Common-Sense' of Chronic Illness Management", *Annals of Behavioural Medicine*, 41(2), 152-63.

Leventhal, H., Leventhal, E.A. and Cameron, L. (2001). "Representations, Procedures and Affect in Illness Self-regulation: A Perceptual-cognitive Model", in Baum, A., Revenson, T.A. and Singer, J.E. (eds.), *Handbook of Psychology* (pp. 19-47), Mahwah: Lawrence Erlbaum Associates.

Leventhal, H., Meyer, D. and Nerenz, D. (1980). "The Common Sense Model of Illness Danger", in S. Rachman (ed.), *Medical Psychology*, (Vol. 2, pp. 7-30), New York: Pergamon.

Leventhal, H., Nerenz, D.R. and Steele, D.A. (1984). "Illness Representations and Coping with Health Threats", in A. Baum, S.E. Taylor and J.E. Singer (eds.), *A Handbook of Psychology and Health* (pp. 219-52), Hillsdale: Lawrence Erlbaum Associates.

Leventhal, H. and Nerenz, D. (1985). "The Assessment of Illness Cognition", in P. Karoly (ed.), *Measurement Strategies in Health* (pp. 517-54), New York: John Wiley & Sons.

Leventhal, H., Watts, J.C. and Pagano, F. (1967). "Effects of Fear and Instructions on How to Cope with Danger", *Journal of Psychology and Social Psychology*, 6(3), 313-21.

Mishra, G. and Verma, S. (1999). "Introduction: Concerns in the Study of Stress and Health", in Mishra, G. (ed.), *Psychological Perspectives on Stress and Health* (pp. 25-36), New Delhi: Concept Publishing Company Pvt. Ltd.

Moss-Morris, R., Petrie, K.J. and Weinman, J. (1996). "Functioning in Chronic Fatigue Syndrome: Do Illness Perceptions Play a Regulatory Role?", *British Journal of Health Psychology*, 1(1), 15-25.

Moss-Morris, R., Weinman, J., Petrie, K.J., Horne, R., Cameron, L.D. and Buick, D. (2002). "The Revised Illness Perception Questionnaire (IPQ-R)", *Psychology and Health*, 17(1), 1-16.

Petrie, K.J. and Pennebaker, J.W. (2004). "Health-related Cognitions", in S. Sutton, A. Baum and M. Johnston (eds.), *The Sage Handbook of Health Psychology* (pp. 127-42), UK: Sage Publications.

Rau, H. and Williams, P. (2013). "Illness Behaviour", in M.D. Gellman and J.R. Turner (eds.), *Encyclopedia of Behavioural Medicine* (Vol. 3), New York: Springer.

Rutter, D.R. and Rutter, C.L. (2002). "Illness Representation, Coping and Outcome in Irritable Bowel Syndrome (IBS)", *British Journal of Health Psychology*, 7(4), 377-91.

Scharloo, M., Kaptein, A.A., Weinman, J., Hazes, J.M., Willems, L.N.A., Bergmank, W. and Rooijmans, H.G.M. (1998). "Illness Perceptions, Coping and Functioning in Patients with Rheumatoid Arthritis, Chronic Obstructive Pulmonary Disease and Psoriasis", *Journal of Psychosomatic Research*, 44(5), 573-85.

Sperry, L. (2008). *Treatment of Chronic Medical Conditions: Cognitive-Behavioural Therapy Strategies and Integrative Treatment Protocols*, USA: American Psychological Association.

Taylor, R.R. (2006). *Cognitive Behavioural Therapy for Chronic Illness and Disability*, USA: Springer.

Turk, D.C., Rudy, T.E. and Salovey, P. (1986). "Implicit Models of Illness", *Journal of Behavioural Medicine*, 9(5), 453-74.

Watanabe, N., Stewart, R., Jenkins, R., Bhugra, D.K. and Furukawa, T.A. (2007). "The Epidemiology of Chronic Fatigue, Physical Illness, and Symptoms of Common Mental Disorders: A Cross-Sectional Survey from the Second British National Survey of Psychiatric Morbidity", *Journal of Psychosomatic Research*, 64(4), 357-62.

Weinman, J., Petrie, K., Moss-Morris, R. and Horne, R. (1996). "The Illness Perception Questionnaire: A New Method for Assessing the Cognitive Representation of Illness", *Psychology & Health*, 11(3), 431-45.

Westbrook, D., Kennerley, H. and Kirk, J. (2011). "Basic Theory, Development and Current Status of CBT", in D. Westbrook, H. Kennerley, and J. Kirk, *An Introduction to Cognitive Behaviour Therapy* (2nd edition), (pp. 1-21), Britain: Sage Publications.

White, C.A. (2001). "Cognitive Behavioural Principles in Managing Chronic Disease", *Western Journal of Medicine*, 175(5), 338-48.

Whitmarsh, A., Koutantji, M. and Sidell, K. (2003). "Illness Perception, Mood and Coping in Predicting Attendance at Cardiac Rehabilitation", *British Journal of Health Psychology*, 8(2), 209-21.

Zeidner, M., Boekaerts, M. and Pintrich, P.R. (2000). "Self-regulation: Directions and Challenges for Future Research", in M. Boekaerts, P.R. Pintrich and M. Zeidner (eds.), *Handbook of Self-Regulation* (pp. 749-68), San Diego, CA: Academic Press.

SECTION II

Health Care and Health Initiatives

5

Alternative Systems of Health Care and National Health Missions: Treading with Care

A.K. Sharma

Modern medicine has worldwide helped in raising life expectancy and overall health standards, though the relative role played by this factor in overall improvement in public health is not well established. Moreover, for a long time social scientists and practitioners have looked at bio-medical model of health quite critically. To them scientific practices may also be seen as magical, inadequate, disempowering and promoting a non-humanistic worldview. India has had a long tradition of alternative and complementary medicine systems. This explains why right from its inception National Rural Health Mission (NRHM), the health project of Government of India has accorded important role to alternative system of health care. Way back in March, 1995 Ministry of Health and Family Welfare created the Department of Indian Systems of Medicine and Homoeopathy (ISM&H). This was re-named as Department of Ayurveda, Yoga and Naturopathy, Unani, Siddha and Homoeopathy (AYUSH) in November, 2003. Even earlier, the National Health Policy (NHP) 1983 had committed to AYUSH for "simpler and gentler therapies for improving the quality of life and avoiding iatrogenic problems" (National Policy on Indian Systems of Medicine and Homoeopathy, n.d.). The aim was laudable: to provide focussed attention to development of education and research in indigenous system which were still in practice among people of India. The Department was expected to lay emphasis on upgradation of "educational standards, quality control and standardization of drugs, improving the availability of medicinal plant material, research and development and awareness generation about the efficacy of the systems domestically and internationally" (Department of AYUSH, 2013). In the Twelfth Five Year Plan an increased amount of budget has been allocated to AYUSH. Inclusion of urban health in the National Health Mission has further stressed the alternative systems (Planning Commission, 2013, pp. 39-40). Recently, by amending the Maharashtra Medical Practitioners Act, 1961, the Maharashtra Government has allowed Homoeopathic, Ayurvedic and Yunani practitioners to prescribe Allopathic drugs and perform minor surgeries such as cataract, hydrocele, appendix, vasectomy, hysterectomy, etc. on the grounds that (a) these things are taught in MS/MD courses in Homoeopathic, Ayurvedic and Yunani courses; (b) this would improve the reach of medical services in rural areas where there is a shortage of doctors; and (c) they are already prescribing Allopathic medicines (Shukla, 2014).

Ironically, there has been inadequate scientific, evidence based research on therapeutic aspects of AYUSH and on managerial issues involved in integration of scientific and alternative systems. Some pertinent issues are: To what extent are AYUSH effective in curing diseases some of which are of modern origin? What are their contraindications? What training do the AYUSH practitioners require to share responsibility under NHM? The Twelfth Five Year Plan document notes that the medical doctors are wary of AYUSH which are based on traditional belief systems and customary practices. This chapter argues that there is a need for exercising caution in adopting AYUSH simply for pragmatic reasons. AYUSH are rooted in paradigms different from that underlying the scientific medicine. In the framework of science, which is risky to be abandoned by a secular and progressive nation state, only those medicines need to be promoted which are found to be based on scientific bio-chemical principles; mere clinical support or experimental findings in favour of AYUSH would not be enough for making them part of the National Health Policy. There are several possible dysfunctions of inclusion of AYUSH in the NHP: (a) legitimating less tested and poor quality health services among the rural poor and other vulnerable sections of society; (b) a general attitude of permissiveness and often promotion of magic and blind faith in traditional practices doing harm to people in the long run; (c) lending selective support to religious and superstitious practices associated with such practices; (d) rejection of health inequality hypothesis; and (e) partial or full withdrawal of state services from the remote areas.

In this context, the choice between (or combination of) scientific medicine and alternative systems, goes beyond the instrumental rational choice and raises serious questions about life and living. The social scientists working in the field of health need to be critical of health policy and not merely play a supporting role to health policy and programmes.

Crisis of Paradigm

It is now an accepted idea in philosophy of science that during the normal times nobody talks about paradigms because all members of the profession use the same paradigm. However, debate on paradigm starts when the existing paradigm cannot take care of the newly observed anomalies. This idea applies to health system also. For a long time biomedical model of health was the dominant perspective on health: sociologists who worked in the field of health used Durkheimian (or Parsonian) functional perspective, though in a liberal perspective Illich criticized the medicalization of health as leading to iatrogenesis — cultural dependence on medicine and its personal and social harms (Illich 1993). In a recent publication Banerjee (2009) has shown how globalization, Government policies and capitalist interests interact with definitions of health and illness, commoditization of health, position of practitioners, pharmacological practices, and health delivery. Attempts have been made by Marxists and other critics of biomedical model to examine class inequalities in health both outside and in India, abandoning the biomedical model of health (Yadavendu, 2001). This challenge to the functional perspective has come from those sociologists and others who stress that the concept of health is socially constructed.

In the field of medicine, the struggle for control over knowledge, its application by professionals/healers, and the role of the state in ensuring equity in health involve numerous ethical conflicts (Qader, 2003). Thus, the subject of health can be contextualized and made subjective. This leads to promotion of overlapping and multiple perspectives. To some extent the recent concern about inclusion of AYUSH is the product of the realization of inadequacy, lack of affordability, inaccessibility and contradictions of 'scientific medicine'. But this has also a potential for uncritical and disinterested acceptance of AYUSH. In this chapter we will explore the alternative perspectives on health and illness. The ideas developed here require a more systematic examination by experts however. There is also a need for empirical examination of beliefs held by people in remote and peripheral areas not so much under the influence of Westernization. The new ideas require to be situated in the current debate on processes and power in health policy in the developing countries (Walt, 2000). According to Touraine (2000), the medicine is unable to treat serious illnesses such as cancer and AIDS and this situation is giving rise to public debates over the relationship between young people and education, or between curing the illness and caring for the patient.

Apology of AYUSH

The development of biopsychosocial model of health has renewed interest in alternative or complementary care approaches. It is claimed that if the goal is to treat the 'whole person' the evidence-based scientific medicine may be combined with the alternative approaches including acupressure, acupuncture, massage, chiropractic, herbal therapies, homoeopathy, yoga, meditation, etc. (Grochowski, 2014). In the West both pull factors and push factors, i.e. attractiveness of the alternative models and more and more known adverse effects of orthodox medicine have attracted patients towards alternative systems of medicine. These factors also include the idea that complementary treatments are "more natural, effective, relaxing, sensible and that one could take an active part in it"; "specific failure of orthodox medicine to bring them relief"; "poor communication between patients and orthodox medicine practitioners"; and "easy availability and cost-effectiveness of alternative medicines"; which has increasingly drawn people towards alternative therapies (Vincent and Furnham, 2001).

After studying the Kung approach to healing in Africa, Katz (2001) avers that most diseases are self-limiting and they heal on their own. In the cultures of developing world people believe that the traditional healing practices such as dance cure the disease. Similar factors are at work in India. But that alone does not explain India's secular democratic state's interest in AYUSH. To us there are two main reasons for promotion of AYUSH in India. One reason is the failure of the modern medicine to ensure universal health, and the other is the promise of health by integrating well established traditional practices and the indigenous medical knowledge system widely in use. Countries like China have already benefitted from this approach. In India the collective outcome of state, medicine, and business processes has failed to provide required services to all classes, regions, social groups, and women. The cost of modern medicine for most people is exorbitant. There are also iatrogenic conditions. There are new afflictions which seem to be impossible to cure. There are also several lifestyle diseases where modern medicine seems to fail at the present level of knowledge and power. Moreover, it is more vivid than it was in the heyday of the modern medicine that in the scientific medicine the relationship between doctor and patients is very unequal and disempowering to patients. In remote areas people are also going for medical pluralism due to inadequate facilities of modern medicine. This is the context in which people are looking for alternatives. Obviously, the alternatives do not come from the vacuum or from a completely alien world as the alternatives will have to be supported by and anchored in the pre-existing social representations. AYUSH systems provide a hope.

In addition, there are several other reasons why state got attracted to AYUSH:

- supplementing manpower at the lower levels for service delivery and various health campaigns in some of which expert knowledge of the field is not required;
- low cost of diagnosis and treatment;
- consistency with the value system of people; and
- effects of pressure groups (religious groups, associations of traditional practitioners, business interests).

There is a need for sociological examination of the health policy in India. Using the distinction made between *sociology* of medicine and *sociology* in medicine by Robert Strauss (Hafferty and Castellani, 2007), it may be said that there is a need for the development of *sociology* of medicine in India, which could offer a sociological critique of medical practices making them sociologically more reflective. It has to be different from the *sociology* in medicine which has remained in supportive role by focussing more on epidemiological and organizational issues. The task of examining conflicting perspectives in pluralistic milieus is fraught with danger, but certainly there is a need for reflexive interventions.

Historical Perspective of Integration of AYUSH in the General Health Policy

The earlier usage for AYUSH was ISM. The National Health Policy (NHP) 1983 referred to importance of promoting Indian systems of medicine (ISM), and integrating them with the modern medicines. ISM included Ayurveda, Siddha, Yoga, and Yunani systems of medicine, but discarded magical, home based and traditional healing practices. Among them Ayurveda, Siddha, and Yoga are of Indian origin and Yunani system came to India with entry of Islam centuries ago; it too has become part of Indian health practices among both Hindus and Muslims.

There are many similarities between Ayurveda and Yunani practices. It is notable that the National Health Policy (NHP) 1983 (n.d.) committed to AYUSH to provide for the "simpler and gentler therapies for improving the quality of life and avoiding iatrogenic problems". To quote:

> Complementary and Alternative Medicine or Traditional Medicine is rapidly growing worldwide. In India also, there is resurgence of interest in Indian Systems of Medicine. People are becoming concerned about the adverse effects of chemical based drugs and the escalating costs of conventional health care. Longer life expectancy and lifestyle related problems have brought with them an increased risk of developing chronic, debilitating diseases such as heart disease, cancer, diabetes and mental disorders. Although new treatments and technologies for dealing with them are plentiful, nonetheless more and more patients are now looking for simpler, gentler therapies for improving the quality of life and avoiding iatrogenic problems.

In 1999, the Central Council for Health and Family Welfare recommended that there should be at least one practitioner of ISM at every health centre. The policy on Ayurveda goes further and includes in its ambit promotion of medical tourism. To quote from the National Policy on Indian Systems of Medicine and Homoeopathy-2002 (n.d.):

> The interest in our systems overseas for gentler and plant based treatment has been growing rapidly. More than that, certain therapies are becoming extremely popular and tourists/visitors come to India for such therapies like *Panchkarma* and *Yoga*. Medical tourism not only popularises our system but offers good avenue for foreign exchange earnings. Little has been done to create a chain of *Panchkarma* Centres and establish centres of excellence for *yoga* therapy, meditation and teaching.

Till the Eighth Five Year Plan Indian systems of medicine and homoeopathy were proposed to be used for strengthening primary health system, filling the gaps in rural areas, and promoting family planning. It got an encouragement during the Ninth Five Year Plan 1997-2002 when the Volume 2 of the Plan document included an independent section (3.6) on ISM under health (Chapter 3). To quote:

> The Indian Systems of Medicine and Homoeopathy consist of Ayurveda, Siddha, Unani and Homoeopathy, and therapies such as

Yoga and Naturopathy. Some of these systems are indigenous and others have over the years become a part of Indian tradition. It is estimated that there are over 6 lakh ISM and H practitioners in the country. Many of them work in remote rural and urban slum areas and thus, could play an important role in improving the quality and outreach of health care. These practitioners are close to the community, not only in the geographical sense but in terms of cultural and social ethos. The cost of care is affordable and hence, these systems have wide acceptance among all segments of the population. The National Health Policy visualized an important role for the ISM and H practitioners in the delivery of health services. Measures to popularize and develop Indian Systems of Medicine and Homoeopathy have been vigorously pursued during the Eighth Plan. In order to give focussed attention to the development and optimal utilization of ISM and H for the health care of the population, a separate Department for ISM and H was set-up in 1995.

The Plan suggested the following approaches (Planning Commission, 1997):

1. improve quality of primary, secondary and tertiary care in ISM and H;
2. invest in human resource development for ISM and H, so that, there is a marked improvement in the quality of services provided by these practitioners;
3. preserve and promote cultivation of medicinal herbs and plants;
4. complete the Pharmacopoeia for all systems of ISM and H; drawing up a list of essential drugs belonging to these systems;
5. encourage Good Manufacturing Practices (GMP) and ensure quality control of drugs; and
6. promote research and development (R and D) especially on new drug formulations, clinical trial of promising drugs through strengthening of the Central Research Councils and coordination with other research agencies. Special emphasis will be laid on encouraging research aimed at improving ISM and H inputs in National Health Programmes.

National Policy on Indian Systems of Medicine and Homoeopathy-2002 is an exhaustive document dealing with all aspects of ISM including infrastructure, research, regulation, industry, pharmacological and pharmacognostical studies, herbal plants, finances and education. In

2007, the Ministry of Health and Family Welfare, Government of India, published the first *Ayurvedic Pharmacopoeia of India*. Centre for Research Planning and Action (CFRPA), New Delhi, Institute for Research in Medical Statistics (IRMS), Indian Council of Medical Research (ICMR) and ORG-MARG have conducted studies of demand for ISM&H services and support promotion of indigenous systems. Central Council for Research in Yoga and Naturopathy organized a "National Workshop on Management of Diabetes and Hypertension" on 29th and 30th of April, 2002 in New Delhi. Efforts are also made to draw attention of the world to importance of ISM&H. Department of ISM&H organized a presentation-*cum*-exhibition on Ayurveda and Yoga on 15th May, 2002 for delegates to World Health Assembly in Geneva. At several institutes and colleges medical researchers are conducting research on chemical structures of herbal compounds and screening of herbs for their claimed activities.

Looking at the vast potential for ISM products industry has also taken a keen interest in producing and distributing Indian medicines. However, the revival of ISM&H is selective: it accepts and promotes the magical aspects of curative health practices, but stigmatizes the basic principles on which Indian systems are based. Adams (2002) has highlighted the same plight of Tibetan medicine. There are few takers of the philosophical framework in which ISM is rooted. Thus, the products of ISM are alienated from the philosophy of health and philosophy of life as part of the indigenous knowledge and promoted to benefit the new ISM industry. This has alienated and disempowered the traditional practitioners and traditional knowledge systems retaining that part which fits the modern system of health knowledge and health delivery.

Government is using AYUSH to meet the unmet needs in different fields of medical services: To quote from the Twelfth Five Year Plan (Planning Commission, 2013, p. 30):

> AYUSH doctors, wherever feasible, would be given SBA, RCH and IMNCI training and their services will be used in meeting unmet needs. This will increase the availability of trained human resource for better outreach of child and maternal health services.

This is true that many AYUSH doctors can be trained and used in various medical campaigns, but same is the case with graduates in bio-sciences and with unregistered medical practitioners. Can we not involve the unregistered medical practitioners in the programme? They have the trust of people and they are anyway approached first for health services.

There are legal, technical and ethical issues, however. The following long quote reveals the Government thinking on the matter (Planning Commission, 2013, p. 38):

> There are two prerequisites before this can be done — first by amendment of the legal framework to authorize the practice of modern medicine for primary care by practitioners of Indian Systems of Medicine; and secondly by supplementing skills of AYUSH graduates by imparting training in modern Medicine through bridge courses. High professional standards of eligibility for, and qualifying in the bridge courses should be laid down, so that, the quality of such primary care integrated physicians remains high. States like Tamil Nadu and recently Maharashtra have shown the lead in this regard. Associations of Allopathic practitioners are generally opposed to AYUSH practitioners being allowed to prescribe Allopathic medicines; they will have to be persuaded to yield in the national interest of serving the masses, particularly the rural population and the urban poor. Suitably trained, AYUSH graduates can provide primary health care, and help fill in the human resource gaps in rural areas.

AYUSH is also supported for its role in geriatrics. The Twelfth Five Year Plan says that geriatrics and therapies in restoration and rejuvenation in old age, and metabolic and lifestyle diseases like diabetes and hypertension, and treatment for drug-abuse (de-addiction) can benefit from AYUSH (Planning Commission, 2013, pp. 40-41).

Philosophic Foundations of AYUSH

AYUSH includes several, and often conflicting systems. In this chapter we take Ayurveda as the representative of alternative systems included under AYUSH. This is the most promoted component of it. However, more detailed analysis of alternative systems is needed than provided here. In the mainstream, biomedical practices health is defined more in terms of public health and, therefore, in terms of indicators of health such as morbidity and mortality rates. When sociologists, demographers, or public health experts deal with health issues they are looking for data on gestational age, birth weights, crude death rate, infant mortality rate, maternal mortality ratio, life expectancy, knowledge of HIV/AIDS, institutional deliveries, couple protection rate, etc. (IIPS, 2001). In the Western perspective, health consciousness entails medicalization. It refers to "the extension of the range of social phenomena mediated by the concept of health and illness, often focusing on the importance of that process for understanding the social control of deviance" (Yadavendu, 2001). There is seldom an attempt to define health as a value or quality of life. NHP and NHRM produce the latest figures on health indicators and including health inequality with respect to gender, wealth, community and urban-rural residence. To biomedical practitioners health is basically a state of absence of illness although the World Health Organization (WHO) definition of health declares that health is a state of well-being and not merely the absence of disease. In this perspective even when public health experts show interest in indigenous knowledge it is only to counter superstitions, intervene in current practices, or evolve an optimum strategy for health delivery so as to improve the health indicators and indices. However, of late a debate has started on defining the social dimensions of health which entails exploring the subjective meanings attached to health, and social representations.

There is now a resurgent interest in research on mapping of local knowledge, differential rationalities involved in treatment, pattern of communication between providers and community, nature of community participation and relationship between culture and needs and resources of the community. It points out towards the process of de-differentiation and a conceptual link between medical and health terminologies and people's concepts (used for reasoning, diagnosis and treatment). Frank (1995) says that ill people recognize that "more is involved in their experiences than the medical story can tell". Sushma Swaraj, as the Health and Family Welfare Minister at the Centre, enunciated need for promoting marital fidelity as part of holistic approach to fight AIDS and gave the slogans of restraint and abstinence (Gupta, 2003; Jain, 2003). As mentioned above, the WHO defines health as a state of complete physical, mental, and social well-being and not merely the absence of disease or infirmity. In the new context of ageing the indicators of health include ability to perform all the daily activities without difficulty (Ogawa, Retherford & Saito, 2003). This approach warns against the biomedical model of health that defines health in a purely physical sense and assumes that promotion of health is a matter that requires understanding and use of science of body.

This critique of bio-medical model often paves the way for a theoretical eulogy of the AYUSH. Among various components of AYUSH, Ayurveda is one of the oldest systems of medicine developed in India. Vedas and Vedic literature provide several references to illness and medicines. *Rig Veda* contains verses on the nature of health and disease and discusses the concept of the three *doshas* (*vata*, *pitta*, and *kapha*). The verses of *Sama Veda* pray Somadeva and *Somarasa*. *Somarasa* was some sacred extract obtained from plants and herbs. The songs of *Sama Veda* are devoted to Soma to earn food, physical strength, long life, progeny, welfare, victory and bliss (Acharya, 1996). It was called the soul of *yajna* (sacrifice). Without Soma sacrifice is not possible, says Veda. *Soma* makes one fearless. It is present in all living beings, air and earth. In *Sama Veda*, the term *aushadhi* (medicine) is used for invigorating principle of vegetation. It was equally available to all social divisions. Another text, called the *Atharva Veda*, lists the eight divisions of Ayurveda: internal medicine, surgery of head and neck, ophthalmology and otorinolaryngology, surgery, toxicology, psychiatry, pediatrics, gerontology or science of rejuvenation, and the science of fertility. *Sushruta Samhita* and *Charaka Samhita* are two famous medical textbooks which are compilations and interpretations of Vedic texts. *Sushruta Samhita* provides a good outline of surgical techniques, the *Charaka Samhita* of internal medicine.

Ayurveda has been defined in various ways. Some are as follows (Ayurvedwebline, 2003): (a) by which liveliness is present; (b) by which one can get long life (*Ayu*); by which one can get knowledge of life; and which generates attitude to think on *Ayu* (life).

Ayurveda is divided into eight branches: *Shalya*, *Shalakya*, *Kaya Chikitsa*, *Bhutavidya*, *Kaumarbhritya*, *Agadatantra*, *Rasayanatantra*, *Vajikaranatantra*. Ayurveda is meant for two main purposes: rescue from disease; and to maintain good health. In India the traditional slogan '*dharmarthakamamokshanamarogyam mulamuttamam*' conveys that health is the root of all ends of life, *dharma, artha, kama* and *moksha*. In the first chapter of *Chhandogyopanishad* the story of *Ushashti* who accepts used *urad* from an elephant raiser, but not water, illustrates that to save life even deviance from norms is permitted. In the fourth part of *Taittiriyopanishad* also there is a prayer for body. In Chapter 12 of *Atharva Veda,* there are prayers for *aushadhis* (medicines). Here medicines are seen as mother and are believed to be responsible for removing thirst, hunger and diseases (Book Ten of *Srimad Bhagavata Mahapurana* enumerates six waves of existence, viz. hunger and thirst, grief and delusions, old age and death). These medicines are meant for countering bodily diseases which are caused by various factors such as sins associated with oath, playing in water, sin against Yama, curse of gods, etc. In the Vedic tradition medicines are believed to be living in heaven. When they come to earth; the person in whose body they mix cannot be destroyed and diseases do not attack him. In seventy fourth *Sarga* of Valmiki's *Ramayana* (*Yudha Kanda*) there are direct references to four medicines: *mrit sanjivini, vishalya karani, suvarnakarni*, and *sandhani*. Their smell gave a new lease of life to warriors who were injured in the war including Lord Rama and his brother Lakshmana. They lived on the hill Rishyamukha in Himalayas. It may be noted that on the one hand *Ramayana* talks about force that Hanuman applied on them to bring them to the battlefield near Lanka for the benefit of people, and on the other hand they were returned back to their abode in Himalaya with respect. No contradiction is seen between force used to bring them to earth for the treatment of people and respect for them and their place. Written in Hindi Tulsidasa's *Ramacharitmanas* a is less mythical about medicines; it accepts the importance of medicines for body but stresses that one can be happy only through cleaning of mind.

What is interesting is that medicines were worshipped not only because they eliminated diseases, but because they also turned long time enemies into followers. The aim of the Vedic prayers was to make all cells of the body blissful and this included fortune, morality, and existence with subjects (Chapter 20 of *Atharva Veda*). Those who followed Vedas had a holistic thinking.

In *Durgasaptashati* the devotee asks for *saubhagyam, arogyam* and *parmam sukham* (fortune, health and extreme happiness). *Shrimadbhagavadgita* uses six words for health (Das, 2001; Prabhupada, 1987), viz. *aayu, sattva, bala, arogya, sukh*, and *priti* which mean continuity of life, patience of mind, physical strength, absence of disease, happiness, and love. They depend on one's *svabhava*, i.e. natural inclinations of self (which are classified into *sattviki, rajasi* and *tamasi*) and food. In the Indian system of thought *svasthya* (health) means existing in *atma* self. *Svasthya* can also be considered as the state of happiness and ill health means living under control of diseases.

Ayurveda defines disease as anything that produces pain. It may be physical, mental, accidental or natural (such as hunger and thirst that are experienced daily). This system classifies all causes of diseases into three classes, namely *karmaja, doshaja*, and *ubhayaja*. Among them only *doshaja* diseases can be cured by medicines. *Karmaja* diseases are the result of wrong actions; they require recitation of name (of God), penance, *anushthana*, etc. *Ubhayaja* are the mixture of *doshaja* and *karmaja* diseases. According to Charaka, in the final analysis all diseases (manifestly caused by *vata, pitta* or *kapha*, are caused by *manovikriti*, i.e. the strain of mind (Vyas, 2001). *Uttarkanda* of *Ramacharitmanasa* describes five causes of diseases, viz. *kala, karma, guna, dosha* and *svabhava*, all of which can be removed by blessings of Lord Rama. Gandhiji, the father of the nation, too believed in the therapeutic value of reciting the name of Ram.

In one of the clearest exposition of Ayurvedic principles Vishnudas (2001) says that a disease has two causes: *aadhija* and *anadhija* (or *adhibhautika*). The former includes *saar* or *adhidaivika*, i.e. diseases caused by past actions, and general, i.e. diseases caused by psychosomatic reasons; they are due to internal reasons. The latter include all diseases caused by external factors such as drowning or diseases caused by germs (cholera, gastrointestinal, dysentery, all kinds of fevers). *Anadhija* diseases may be cured by medicines, but even they can be cured through spiritual interventions. No wonder that the *Kaliyuga* (the contemporary age of darkness) which is dominated by *tamas* has the life expectancy of 100 years only (Gautam, 1982). In *Sata Yuga* (age of Truth) in which people follow *dharma* (virtue) the life expectancy was 400 years. It reduces to 300 in *Treta* and 200 in *Dvapara* because of proportionate reduction in *dharma* in these ages.

For Indian seers, a person was believed to be having five bodies: *annamaya kosh* (physical body), *pranamaya kosh* (etheric body), *manomaya kosh* (mental body), *vigyanmaya kosh* (intellectual body), and *anandamaya kosh* (casual body). The interventions at various levels are: (a) activities at the level of physical body — *neti, dhauti, kapalbhati, tratak, nauli, vasti*, relaxation and exercises, *yogasanas*, and medicines of various types; (b) activities at the level of etheric body — *pranayama*, walking, breathing exercises, mountaineering, *prana vidya,* and *mantra vidya*; (c) activities at the level of mental body — meditation, concentration, recitation, *bhajana, mantrochchar,* and *yoga nidra*; (d) ativities at the level of intellectual body — study of *Vedas* and *Upanishads*, religious literature, meditation, concentration, *vipasyana*, altruistic acts, and bliss; and (e) activities at the level of casual body — *samadhi*, liberation, peace, bliss, and *sat-chit-anand*.

According to Ayurveda:

> *Samadosha samagnischa samadhatu malakriya prasanna atma mana svastha iti abhidhiyate.*
>
> (Having a balanced state of *doshas*, *agni* (digestive fire), *dhatus* (tissues) and normal functioning of *mala* (waste products), cheerful state of *atman* (soul), sensory organs, mind are the symptoms of healthy life.)

There is a direct reference to *svasthya* (health) in *Tattva Kaumudi Samhita*. It says: *svasth iti rajastamovritikalushaya budhyaasambhinna*, i.e. health means absence of contact with intellect polluted by *rajas* and *tamas* tendencies. In another reference to health thirteenth stanza of *Shvetashvetropanishad* says that the early achievement of *Yoga* is health; it is characterized by subjective feeling of lightness, absence of any type of disease, end of attachment to objects of desire, radiance of the body, sweetness of speech, good odour from body, and reduction in urine and stool.

In Indian tradition body is supposed to be embodiment of sufferings. At the body level it is impossible to remove sufferings for all and permanently (Aranya, 1987). One's mind and body are greatly the fruits of *karma* (in the sense in which a mango tree will bear mango fruits only, watering of tree and manures cannot basically change the nature of fruits). Interventions at the body level (breathing exercises and medicines) may temporarily and to a limited extent weaken the external causes of diseases but cannot make one healthy. *Niyati* (i.e. all internal causes which force one to engage in a certain action) the nature of self are two important determinants of health or misery. It is very important to understand that what one does in a state of ill-health or health determines the future state of health and happiness. Thus, a temporary state of ill-health may lead to better health in the future or a good health may lead to illness. It depends on the nature of self.

Yoga differs from Ayurveda in emphasis on bodily postures, meditation, concentration and spirituality. Yunani system was developed in Greece and introduced in India through Arabs. According to this system disease is a natural process and the role of a *hakim* (physician) is to assist the natural forces of the body in recovering from disease. This system got popularity through patronage of rulers of Delhi. In the British period, it suffered a setback due to withdrawal of the state patronage but it remained popular among masses. Its method of diagnosis of a disease through examination of pulse (along with blood, urine and stool) made it a quite attractive medicine system. Homoeopathy is based on a radical philosophy of similarity. According to it, a medicine can treat all those symptoms which will appear if the medicine is injected in a normal body. It also believes that by reducing the concentration of medicine its power can be enhanced many times.

The issue is: what does the National Health Policy have to say on the principles on which alternative and supplementary medicine systems of health are based? Obviously, the science does not accept the experiential, traditional systems based on beliefs and practices, but lacking in scientific evidence. How do they reconcile with the scientific or biomedical representations? Now that *Yoga* has got recognition from the United Nations (UN) there may be more incentive to conduct scientific experiments on physical impacts of *Yoga* processes. Yet, it is unthinkable to combine Yoga with modern values and life.

Mismatch with Science

From a sympathetic perspective, Indian/Ayurvedic approach to health and illness was holistic. It focussed on intervention at all levels — physical, mental and spiritual. It also assumed that due to their past deeds different individuals are at different levels of movement and are, therefore, constitutionally different. Even for the same diseases they may require different interventions. Spiritual considerations are deeply interwoven with Ayurvedic pharmacopeia as metaphysical and spiritual factors are believed to be at the root of all interventions. This view rejects the scientific perspective as western, alien, and based merely on study of body and body processes, thus discarding the mental and the spiritual.

The new approach to AYUSH, linked more to the demand of global and national capitalist industry (Banerjee, 2009), ignores this fact. The new approach has alienated a large number of Ayurvedic practitioners and the needs of the people.

There are also other issues. About 3.2 per cent of the health budget released during the Eleventh Five Year Plan was released for AYUSH and a similar proportion of allocation (3.3%) is planned during the Twelfth Five Year Plan. But the Twelfth Five Year Plan accepts that the medical doctors have some resistance in accepting AYUSH in the programme. The Plan document states: "Though considerable progress has been made in documenting identity and quality standards of herbal medicines, scientific validation of AYUSH principles, remedies and therapies has not progressed" (Planning Commission, 2013). A basic issue in the new approach is that the AYUSH have to seek legitimacy from science of modern medicine.

The selective revival of Indian medicines is taking place in a context in which it sheds its spiritual substratum. Most of the time quick researches are testing the herbs and other medicines statistically with scant attention to Indian understanding of body or western standards of molecular biology or quantum physics. In other words, magic (experimental connection) is accepted and indigenous theory is abandoned. This attempt is unlikely to succeed and the Indian medicines are unlikely to win the

Western game. With little support to identification of herbs, felling of forests, changes in environmental quality and new morbidity patterns, the ISM may be left either to play a subordinate role to Western medicine or may die a natural death. With accredited drugs produced by major pharmacies it has not remained a poor man's medicine also any more. Appreciation of traditional medicine makes greater sense when it is combined with traditional thought categories of Ayurveda. In this context, the remark once made by Gandhi is notable. He said that he would oppose even naturopathy if it makes the Indians dependent on wisdom from outside.

It is quite problematical that on the one hand there is a stress on a standardized approach to diseases and on the other hand Ayurveda believes in differences in essential nature of individuals and soul. According to Bode (2008) Ayurveda is closely linked with religion, culture and nationalism. To quote:

> Unlike biomedicine, Ayurveda has not distanced itself completely from aspects of life that we have learned to call 'religious' and 'magical'. Depending upon the audience and the locality, different aspects of Ayurveda's aetiology are highlighted. For example, at pharmacological conferences and in government publications positivism rules and the laboratory becomes the favoured site for the production of ayurvedic knowledge. . . . In some clinical settings religious aspects are prominent and on other occasions such as the centenary of the Arya Vaidya Sala, Ayurveda was celebrated as India's national medicine expressing the superiority of Indian culture.

For G.M. Foundation (2003) in Ayurveda treatment is contextual and personalized:

> In the Ayurvedic view, an imbalance between the *doshas* produces a condition called *vikriti*, a Sanskrit word that means 'deviated from nature'. *Vikriti* results from an overexpression of one or two *doshas* (usually the dominant *dosha*) and a diminished expression of the other *dosha*. This imbalance can be caused by eating the wrong foods, chronic mental stress, physical overexertion, negative emotions, or poor sleeping habits, and will eventually lead to the development of disease, obesity and/or mental disorders. As a result, to prevent disease, each individual must maintain the *doshas* in, or restore them to, their proper balance.

Selective revival of ISM focuses on the magical part. Several institutes in the country are researching on benefits of herbs on different diseases. This includes studying chemical properties of various herbs known for their treatment of certain diseases. Yet, this ignores the fact that according to ISM health is inseparably linked with life. In the Indian perspective, the relationship between the healer and people is what may be called 'multiple monopsonic' (Harvey, Quilley & Beynon, 2002) in which the sick is fully empowered. He is not objectified. Modern medicine involves entry into market but market is not conducive to philosophy of ISM. This rejection of ISM at the fundamental level and acceptance of its magical power is not conducive to creative application of the ISM.

Dysfunctions of AYUSH in the Present Set-up

In the present framework of service delivery, there are several possible dysfunctions of inclusion of AYUSH in the NHP:

(a) legitimation of less tested and poor quality health services among the rural poor and other vulnerable sections of society;
(b) permissiveness and often promotion of magic and blind faith in traditional practices doing harm to people in the long run;
(c) lending support to spiritual, religious and superstitious practices associated with Ayurveda;
(d) rejection of health inequality hypothesis; and
(e) often a basis of withdrawal of state from the remote areas.

At the moment there is a lack of consensus in the scientific community regarding what AYUSH remedy cures a particular disease and in what quantity. The drugs available in the market lack standardization. In most cases in the name of AYUSH competence of practitioner, training, and knowledge are compromised. Advertisement through media is a major source of affecting people ideas not all of whom can make a difference between advertisements and scientific truths. It is widely accepted that the AYUSH practitioners are allowed to prescribe Allopathic medicines in primary health services (after clearing bridge courses). Moreover, since the traditional practices combine religion, magic, herbal, astrological and many other types of practices, it becomes difficult to separate the effective part of AYUSH from other non-scientific practices and their practitioners. Acceptance of AYUSH in the official programme can lend credence to many superstitious and unfounded practices. By including AYUSH in NHM for remote, tribal and vulnerable areas a myth of universal health is unduly created.

The issue of evidence is contested. Both scientific medicine and alternative systems claim that they are evidence-based. However, the meaning of evidence is different in the two systems. The scientific medicine is based not only on principles of empirical/experimental evidence, generalization and universality of causes and remedies it is also based on recent advances in molecular biology, bio-chemistry, etc. From the scientific point of view diseases are part of genes or body and the causes and cures are universal: one does not necessarily have to look for spiritual or psychological dispositions to treat a physical symptom. Contrary to this, the AYUSH is based mostly on experimental trials and statistical generalizations. In the postmodern age media has become an important part of legitimacy processes. Along with official protection to AYUSH when media also links with the business interests to promote specific drugs by specific companies only, the traditional practice of Ayurveda and the interests of the common people suffer. They have to make choices. The questions are: On what basis do they make choices? Governments have hidden their limitations of planning, distribution channels, and manpower and financial shortages by including AYUSH in the service delivery. Religious leaders gain by supporting them to fight for their cultural and religious authority. Drug manufacturers gain by getting more clients, particularly from the dissatisfied users of modern medicine by stressing permanent cure and absence of side effects. Media gains by showing long sponsored programmes posing as though they are for informative and welfare oriented programmes (quite often without clearly exhibiting that they are advertisements or sponsored programmes). People also suffer and masses waste money while certain forms of knowledge and legitimations are produced in different networks which seek support from the doxa or the common belief systems.

The mismatch between scientific and AYUSH perspectives can even harm the health programme. During situation analysis of HIV and AIDS in Lalitpur district of UP we came across cases in which village homoeopathic doctors propagated the view that Government and Allopathic doctors have created a myth that HIV cannot be cured. They said that homoeopathy has cure for HIV and they cured hundreds of cases of sexually transmitted infection every year quite successfully. To justify their claim, they argued that homoeopathy does not follow the "scientific" classification system but focuses on symptoms, and is based on improving body's response to harmful outside agents.

Conclusion

Exploring Ayurveda, one of the components of AYUSH, this chapter argues that the Indian systems of medicine (e.g. Ayurveda) are rooted in divergent philosophical frameworks, which have increasingly become marginal, although the therapeutic part of these systems is promoted and validated. This is doing immense harm to the value system of the AYUSH and its inclusion in the NHM is ornamental and inadequate. There is a need to critique the manner of integration of scientific approach with AYUSH, and subject AYUSH to scientific scrutiny before it is made a notable part of the state programme. The present approach of convenience is not good for equity, quality and accessibility of health services or for real promotion of AYUSH. There is a need to understand the psychological and spiritual connection of physical health, which has been a matter of changing perspectives (Kaplan, 2005). There is a strong, considered view that alternative and complementary medicines may be used as the best placebos along with evidence based medicine (Kiresuk and Trachtenberg, 2005), but the discourse of AYUSH also has a value for providing a critique of modern, scientific epistemology.

REFERENCES

Acharya, Sri Ram Sharma (1996). *Samaveda Samhita*, Haridwar: Brahmavarchas, Shantikunj, verses 331, 820, 828, 331.

Adams, V. (2002). "Randomized Controlled Crime: Postcolonial Sciences in Alternative Medicine Research", *Social Studies of Science*, 32 (5-6), 659-90.

Aranya, Srimat Swamy Hariharanand (1987) *Patanjal Yoga Darshan*, New Delhi: Motilal Banarasidass, 534-61.

Ayurvedwebline (2003). Retrieved from: http://www.ayurvedwebline.com/ayurved/ayur_script.asp

Banerjee, M. (2009). *Power, Knowledge, Medicine: Ayurvedic Pharamaceuticals at Home and in the World*, New Delhi: Orient Blackswan Private Limited.

Bhattacharya, R. (1989). *Sankhya Tattva Kaumudi* (p. 343), New Delhi: Motilal Banarasidass.

Bode, M. (2008). *Taking Traditional Knowledge to the Market: The Modern Image of the Ayurvedic and Unani Industry 1980-2000* (p. 181), Hyderabad: Orient Longman Private Limited.

Das, R. (2001). Vastavik Arogya, *Kalyan: Arogya Ank*, Jan. and Feb. (pp. 116-18), Gorakhpur: Gita Press.

Department of AYUSH (2013). Retrieved from: http://indianmedicine.nic.in/

Frank, A. (1995). *The Wounded Storyteller: Body, Illness, and Ethics*, Chicago: The University of Chicago Press. Retrieved from: http://www.horsesenseatwork.com/psl/pages/postmoderndefined4.html

Gautam, C. (1982). *Manusmriti*, Sanskriti Sansthan (p. 23), Ved Nagar: Kwaja Kutub, Bareilly, U.P.

George Mateljan Foundation (2003). Retrieved from: http://www.whfoods.com/genpage.php?tname=diet&dbid=12#principles

Goswami, C.L. and M.A. Sastri (1982). *Srimad Bhagavata Mahapurana* (with Sanskrit text and English translation), Part-II. Gorakhpur: Gita Press, 1377.

Goyandka, H. (1982). *Ishadi Nau Upanishad* (pp. 281, 375), Gorakhpur: Gita Press.

Grochowski, J.R. (2014). *Families and Health* (pp. 28-29), Los Angeles: Sage Publications.

Gupta, M. (2003). "Family Focus in AIDS Ads", *The Telegraph*, Kolkata, April 12.

Hafferty, F.W. and Castellani B. (2007). "Medical Sociology", in Bryant, Clifton D. and Peck, Dennis L. (eds.), *21st Century Sociology: A Reference Handbook*, UK: Sage Publications.

Hare-Mustin, R.T. and Jeanne, M. (1988). "The Meaning of Difference", *American Psychologist*, 43(6), 455-64.

Harvey, M., Quilley, S. and Beynon, H. (2002). *Exploring the Tomato*, Edward Elgar.

Illich, I. (1993). *The Epidemics of Modern Medicine*, Retrieved from: http://www.soilandhealth.org/03sov/0303critic/030313illich/Frame.Illich.Ch1.html

International Institute of Population Sciences (2001). *Reproductive and Child Health Project: Rapid Household Survey (Phase I & II)*, Mumbai: IIPS.

Jain, K. (2003). "ABC of AIDS: Action, Better Health & Condoms", *The Times of India*, Lucknow, 4 June.

Katz, R. (2001). "The Kung Approach to Healing", in Matcha, Duane A. (ed.), *Readings in Medical Sociology* (pp. 318-31), Boston: Allyn and Bacon.

Kaplan, H.I. (2005). "History of Psychosomatic Medicine", in Sadock, Benjamin J. and Sadock, Virginia A. (eds.), *Comprehensive Textbook of Psychiatry*, Vol. II, Philadelphia: Lippincott Williams & Wilkins, 2105-12.

Kiresuk, T.J. and Trachtenberg, A. (2005). "Alternative and Complementary Health Practices", in Benjamin J. Sadock and Virginia A. Sadock (eds.), *Comprehensive Textbook of Psychiatry*, Vol. II (2406-26), Philadelphia: Lippincott Williams & Wilkins.

Ministry of Health and Family Welfare, *National Policy on Indian Systems of Medicine & Homoeopathy-2002* (n.d.), Retrieved from: http://india.gov.in/national-policy-indian-systems-medicine-homoeopathy-ayush

Ministry of Health and Family Welfare. (2007). *The Ayurvedic Pharmacopoeia of India, Part-II (Formulations): Vol. I*, Retrieved from: http://www.ccras.nic.in/PharmacopoeialWork/Links/Compfom/AyurvedicFarmocopia.pdf

National Policy on Indian Systems of Medicine & Homoeopathy-2002 (n.d.). Retrieved from: http://indianmedicine.nic.in/writereaddata/linkimages/7870046089-Ayush%20%20n%20policy%20ISM%20and%20H%20Homeopathy.pdf

Ogawa, N., Retherford, R.D. and Saito, Y. (2003). "Caring for the Elderly and Holding Down a Job: How are Women Coping in Japan?" *Asia-Pacific Population & Policy*, 65 (April), 1-4.

Planning Commission (1997). "Indian System of Medicine and Homoeopathy", *Ninth Five Year Plan (1997-2002): Volume-2*, Planning Commission, New Delhi. Retrieved from: http://planningcommission.nic.in/plans/planrel/fiveyr/welcome.html

Planning Commission (2013). *Twelfth Five Year Plan (2012-2017)*: Volume III, Social Sectors (p. 8). New Delhi: Planning Commission.

Prabhupad, A.C. Bhaktivedanta Swamy (1987). *Shrimadbhagavadgita: Yatharupa* (pp. 554-55), Bhaktivedanta Book Trust.

Qader, Imrana (2003). "Ethics and Medical Care in a Globalising World: Some Reflections", in Sen, Kasturi (ed.), *Restructuring Health Services: Changing Contexts & Comparative Perspectives* (pp. 53-64), London: Zed Books.

Saffron Soul (2003). http://www.saffronsoul.com/usr/ayur1.asp, 15 June.

Satel, Sally (2000). *PC, M.D.: How Political Correctness is Corrupting Medicine*, New York: Basic Books.

Sharma, A.K. (2003). *Perspectives on Health, Illness and Well-Being: An Agenda for Future Research*, National Seminar on Social Dimensions of Health, Centre for Behavioural and Cognitive Sciences, Allahabad University, April 10-12.

Sharma, S.R. (1981). *Yajurveda*, Bareilly: Sanskriti Sansthan.

Shukla, S. (2014). "Now, Unani, Ayurvedia Practitioners can Prescribe Allopathy Medicines", *The Indian Express* (p. 5), Lucknow: National Network, Lucknow edition, Saturday, 1 March, 2014.

Touraine, A. (2000). *Can We Live Together? Equality and Difference*, UK: Polity Press.

Vincent, C. and Furnham, A. (2001). "Why Do Patients Turn to Complementary Medicine? An Empirical Study", in Duane A. Matcha (ed.), *Readings in Medical Sociology* (pp. 309-18), Boston: Allyn and Bacon.

Vishnudas, V. (2001). *Vyadhi aur unki Aikatmika Chikitsa, Kalyan: Arogya Ank*, Jan. and Feb. (pp. 494-96), Gorakhpur, Gita Press.

Vyas, K. (2001). "Manasayurveda Parichaya", *Kalyan: Arogya Ank*, Jan. and Feb. (pp. 126-28), Gorakhpur, Gita Press.

Walt, G. (2002). *Health Policy: An Introduction to Process and Power* (pp. 11-33), London, Zed Books.

Yadavendu, V.K. (2001). "Social Construction of Health: Changing Paradigms", *Economic and Political Weekly*, July 21, 2784-95.

6

Financing Health Care in India
Reforms and Challenges

Dharitri Panda

Health is now globally recognized as a basic human right (Gottret & Schieber, 2006) and the Millennium Development Goals (MDG) declared by UN has elaborated on health priorities. The United Nations Millennium Declaration signed in September, 2000 commits world leaders to combat poverty, hunger, diseases, illiteracy, environmental degradation, and discrimination against women. India is also one of the 191 signatories to the declaration. Out of eight MDGs, the health related MDGs are three that are directly devoted to health. They are MDG 4-6:

4: to reduce child mortality
5: to improve maternal mortality
6: to combat HIV/AIDS, malaria and other diseases.

All the above MDGs are interdependent. Further, all the MDGs influence overall health status of the nation and improvement in public health would help in achieving the health and other MDGs.

It is clear that the MDGs cannot be achieved without huge infusion of funds, improving health infrastructure and ensuring equitable access to effective health interventions. The ultimate goals of health system reforms are to improve health outcomes, provide financial protection and ensure consumer satisfaction. How they can achieve them in a given time framework is a serious challenge before the developing countries. It must be recognized that there is no single road for achieving these goals as each country's social, economic, political, demographic and epidemiological context shall determine the road to health reforms. It is an uphill task for the developing countries which account for 84 per cent of the global population and 90 per cent of the global disease burden but only 12 per cent of global health spending (Gottrett & Schieber, 2006). The shift in demographics (high but declining rates of population growth and increasing life expectancy along with epidemiological transition, i.e. shift from communicable to non-communicable diseases) will increase the burden on health financing in the low income countries. This stresses the need to explore the methods and strategies of health financing.

I. Functions and Models of Health Financing

Health financing is concerned about three functions: how societies collect revenues and allocate to health, how they manage the revenues to pool health risks equitably and efficiently, and how they purchase services for health care are. According to Gottrett & Schieber, there are three basic principles of Public Health Financing:

Principle 1: Raise enough revenues to provide individuals with a basic package of essential services and financial protection against catastrophic medical expenses caused by illness and injury in an equitable, efficient and sustainable manner.

Principle 2: Manage these revenues to pool health risks equitably and efficiently.

Principle 3: Ensure the purchase of health services in ways that are allocatively and technically efficient.

Though each country tries to follow these principles, but the path is rather rough for resource starving, low income countries. There are five models of implementing the above principles. Although they are the dominant models of health financing, but generally each country makes use of a combination of two or more models.

(1) National Health Service system or State funded health systems (NHS/SHS).
(2) Social Health Insurance (SHI).
(3) Community Based Health Insurance (CBHI).
(4) Private, voluntary Health Insurance (PHI).
(5) Direct purchases by consumers — commonly known as Out of Pocket (OOP) spending.

In the National Health Service systems the primary funding is from general revenues, i.e. the taxation system. They aim to provide medical coverage to the country's entire population popularly known as universal coverage and their services are delivered through a network of public providers. UK is the best example of application of the National Health Service model. Most developed countries have a robust state funded health system. However, in such systems reliance on state budgets makes health financing vulnerable to the vicissitude of annual budget priorities and changes in political priorities.

Social Health Insurance (SHI) systems are characterized by independent or quasi-independent insurance funds, a reliance on mandatory earmarked payroll contributions and a clear link between these contributions and right to defined package of health benefits. The payroll base of much of the funding of social health insurance system insulates them from budgetary negotiations that may subject the national health system to more variable fund. Yet social health insurance systems may not be adequate to fully fund health care costs and government may have to infuse more funds to subsidize the health care costs of the poor and vulnerable sections of society. However, Social Health Insurance systems are easier to administer in countries with large formal sector, with defined payroll contribution and with a large urban sector. Some of the countries where the model of Social Health Insurance is followed are: France, Germany, Switzerland and Netherland.

The Community Based Health Insurance (CBHI) Schemes can be broadly defined as not for profit prepayment plans for health care that are controlled by a community that has voluntary membership. Most Community Based Health Insurance Schemes operate according to core social values and cover beneficiaries which are excluded from other health coverage. However, this caters to small communities and generally complements other forms of health financing.

Private Health Insurance (PHI) is paid for by non-income based premiums which entitle the holder to a defined package of health benefits. Either the employer pays the premium or the individual pays the premium. Primary Health Insurance can be primary — as main source of coverage for a population or sub-population like in USA or complementary, i.e. covering cost sharing under public programme or supplementing for services not covered by the public programme. Private/voluntary health insurance has a risk pooling mechanism. However, it has limits as it may not be affordable by the poor who may get excluded from the health care. Countries like USA have supplemented voluntary health insurance with Medicare and Medicaid to provide health care to the senior citizens (above 65) and poor but the health insurance market is so powerful that any intended liberalization of health care as proposed by President Barrack Obama has run into steep hurdles so much so that US Federal Government went on partial shut down for days together in September-October 2013.

Out of pocket spending is the last form where the individual or consumer makes direct purchase of health care. Out of pocket expenditures are defined as any direct outlay including gratuities or in kind contributions that households make for services and goods from doctors, pharmacists, medical supply vendors and others.

II. Health Spending and Its Impact on Health Indicators

The information about nature and sources of health spending are useful in developing sound policies. Health economists use certain indicators for studying the effectiveness of different policies and for improving financing health care. The main economic indicators are: Gross Domestic Product (GDP), GDP per capita, the per capita health spending, total health spending as a share of GDP, the private share of total health spending, the percentage of private spending out of pocket, and the share of total health spending through external assistance (Gottrett & Schiber, 2006).

It has been seen that high income countries spend an average of more than 9 per cent of GDP on health while middle income countries spend between 5 to 6 per cent of GDP on health. Due to paucity of resources and conflicting demands on them low income countries spend less than 5 per cent of GDP on health. It has also been observed that in low income countries there is a high percentage of out of pocket spending. Statistically, in low income countries out of pocket spending accounts for more than 90 per cent of private spending and more than 60 per cent of total health spending. High out of pocket spending in a country denotes lack of risk pooling and potential inequity in health financing.

The public share of total health spending is a measure of how actively Governments intervene to ensure the financing of basic health and personal health services, protect the poor and facilitate risk pooling through public programmes. The WHO also brings out the statistics annually on health spending. Table 6.1 shows an analysis of data for a few selected countries including India. They cover countries at various levels of development based on Human Development Index (HDI). Among them USA and UK are very highly developed countries; Brazil and Sri Lanka are highly developed countries; China, Ghana, and India are at medium level of development; Bangladesh, Pakistan, and Nepal are at low level of development (Human Development Report 2013).

Table 6.1 shows that most highly developed countries invest more than 9 per cent of GDP on health and more than 45 per cent out of total spending is by Government. The case of low income countries is different. The majority of spending in these countries is from private expenditure. Pakistan seems to be an exception. Though Pakistan is spending only 1 per cent of GDP on health, its public expenditure on health in 2010 is 76.6 per cent. Here only 23.4 per cent of expenditure on health is by private means. It may be noted that although Pakistan is spending only 1 per cent of GDP on health its health indicators are quite good. Out of pocket spending in low income countries is above 85 per cent which is not a healthy indicator as this shows that the poor have to spend a lot on health expenditure despite their limited ability to pay. High out of pocket spending also hinders allocative efficiency and financial protection efforts (Gottrett & Schieber, 2006).

If we see the impact of health spending on the health indicators we shall be able to gauge its importance. Table 6.1 indicates that with increased health spending there is improvement in the mortality rates. Developed countries spend more on health than developing countries and this is reflected in the better health indicators in these countries. The surprising result is that in USA though the other indicators have improved there is some increase in the maternal mortality rate. Bangladesh and Sri Lanka have done remarkably well in all indicators despite decreased Government spending and this could be attributed to efficiency in spending. India has done quite well in all the indicators and there has been an overall positive impact of its improved public spending on health indicators.

III. Status of Health in India

At present, India's health care system consists of a mix of public and private sector providers of health services. The public sector is characterized by a three-tier system: primary or village level; secondary or district level; and tertiary or speciality level. This network of health care facilities provides free or very low cost health services. There is also an expansive private health care sector, covering the entire spectrum from individual doctors and clinics to general hospitals and super speciality hospitals and is becoming a hub for medical tourism for African and other South Asian countries.

Table 6.1: Health Expenditure in Selected Countries and Impact on Health Indicator

Country	*HDI Index*	*Total Exp. on Health as % of GDP*	*Gen. Govt. Exp. on Health as % of Total Exp. on Health*	*Pvt. Exp. on Health as % of Total Exp. on Health*	*OOP Spending*	*MDG — 4 Child under 5 Mortality Rate (Probability)*	*MDG — 5 Maternal Mortality Ratio (per 100000)*	*MDG — 6 Specific Mortality Rate (per 100000) HIV/AIDS*
	2013	*2010*	*2010*	*2010*	*2010*	*2011*	*2010*	*2011*
USA	3	17.6	48.2	51.8	22.7	8	21	6.5
UK	26	9.6	83.2	16.8	53.1	5	12	0.8
Brazil	85	9.0	47.0	53.0	57.8	16	56	No Information
Sri Lanka	92	3.5	45.6	54.4	81.9	12	35	1.2
China	101	5.0	54.3	45.7	77.2	15	92	21
Ghana	135	5.2	58.2	41.8	66.7	78	350	61
India	136	3.7	28.2	71.8	86.0	61	200	No information
Bangladesh	146	3.7	36.5	63.5	96.6	46	240	0.2
Pakistan	146	1.0	76.6	23.4	No Information	72	260	2.7
Nepal	157	5.1	37.4	62.6	90.4	48	170	1.5

Sources: *World Health Statistics*, 2013, accessed from www.who.int

Quantity of Healthcare

Through the Tenth Five Year Plan special efforts have been underway to improve the public health care system in India. Despite this health care services are woefully inadequate in both quantity and quality. At the start of Eleventh Plan, the number of doctors per lakh of population was only 45 whereas desirable number is 85 per lakh of population. Similarly, the number of nurses and Auxiliary Nurses and Midwifes (ANMs) available was 75 per lakh population whereas the desirable number is 255. The overall shortage is further distorted by a wide geographical variation with rural areas being poorly served. As of March 2012, total number of all facilities functioning in the country was 30,969 as shown in Table 6.2 which is quite inadequate to cater to the whole population of the country.

Table 6.2: Facilities Functioning — 24 × 7 as on March 2012

	Facilities that are Considered 24 × 7 Level of Function in					
	Total Created Facilities in India	*India*	*High Focus — Non-NE*	*High Focus — NE*	*Non-High Focus — Large*	*Non-High Focus — Small & UT*
APHCs + PHCs + others	25,121	9,709	2,835	1,008	5,811	55
CHC	4,809	4,266	1,948	200	2,068	50
Above CHC - below district level	1,039	1,039	222	54	764	1
Total	**30,969**	**15,014**	**5,005**	**1,262**	**8,641**	**106**

Source: NRHM State-wise Progress as on March, 2012, NRHM in the Eleventh Plan (NHSRC Publication).

Quality of Healthcare

As regards quality of services, the public health services has been characterized by overcrowding, absenteeism, lack of professionalism, lack of motivation and lack of accountability. A study conducted by the Programme and Evaluation Unit (PEU) of Planning Commission assessed quality of health care delivery in rural health services under NRHM based on health visit details, distance travelled to centre, length of wait at centre, availability of free medicines, attended to by which member of medical staff and patient satisfaction. Results showed that patients in Rajasthan travelled on an average of 6.3 km to reach nearest health centre followed by Uttar Pradesh (5.9 km), Bihar (4.7 km) and Andhra

Pradesh (3.8 km).This could be either due to absence of public health facility in closer proximity or because the particular service was not available in facility closer to their residence. As per length of wait to be attended, Bihar had the longest wait (138 mts) followed by Uttar Pradesh (97 mts), Andhra Pradesh (85 mts) and Rajasthan (21 mts). Further, it turned out that across states between 58 to 75 per cent of patients were attended to by paramedical staff rather than medical officers, which could indicate either shortage of medical officers or absenteeism. As regards negative experience, Bihar reported 61 per cent negative experience followed by Uttar Pradesh (43%), Rajasthan (35%) and Andhra Pradesh (32%). The major reasons cited were lack of medicines, staff absenteeism, long wait and corruption. As regards patient satisfaction, Andhra Pradesh recorded the highest patient satisfaction (75%) followed by Uttar Pradesh (49%), Rajasthan (39%) and Bihar (23%) (Gill, 2009).

Outcomes

The health indicators reflect that India is still way behind in achieving the MDG targets. The Twelfth Plan document of Planning Commission shows that while there has been a decline of 5.8 per cent per year in the Maternal Mortality Ratio (MMR) from 2004-06 to 2007-09, it is well short of the target of 100 as shown in Table 6.2. Only few states like Kerala (81), Tamil Nadu (97) and Maharashtra (104) have achieved the MDG target.

Assam has shown the greatest improvement between 2005 and 2008, but despite a drop of 90 maternal deaths per 1,00,000 live births, it still has the highest MMR of 390 per live births. The states that have a MMR higher than national average account for 68 per cent of the total maternal deaths. These States are Odisha, Bihar, Jharkhand, Madhya Pradesh, Chhattisgarh, Rajasthan, Uttar Pradesh, Uttarakhand and Assam (NRHM in the Eleventh Five Year Plan by NHSRC).

The Infant Mortality Rate (IMR), another important indicator of health, was at 44 in year 2011 (Table 6.3) and though it witnessed an improvement and fell by 5 per cent per year from 2006-2011, but again this was short of target. Fifteen States and Union Territories have attained the NRHM goal of 30 per 1000 live births (SRS-2011) while 20 States and Union Territories are still behind this target. However, the heartening thing is that the data reveals an accelerated decline in infant and child mortality, particularly in rural areas. This could be attributed to improved access to health care that resulted from National Rural Health Mission (NRHM — Eleventh Five Year Plan).

The Total Fertility Rate (TFR), which is considered to be an indicator of both fertility level and health, declined from 2.8 to 2.5 (2006-2010), but fell short of the target of 2.1 (the replacement level fertility) as shown in Table 6.3. The Sample Registration Scheme (SRS) Bulletin 2012 reveals that 10 States have achieved TFR of 2.1 while some States like Chhattisgarh (2.8), Jharkhand (3.0), Rajasthan (3.1), Madhya Pradesh (3.2), Uttarakhand (3.5) and Bihar (3.7) are way above the target figure (i.e., 2.1).

IV. Health Spending in India

In India, the models of financing health care are the taxation funded public health service, the private network and the health insurance sector which are both in private and public sector. As health is in the state list in charter of duties between Federal Government and State Governments, the expenditure on health is mostly borne by State Government with almost a 67-33 per cent spending by States and Centre respectively. One major cause of such a low level of health services in the public network has been the low level of public spending on health. The National Health Accounts of 2004-05, state that the total expenditure on health care in India taking public, private and household out of pocket expenditure was about 4.25 per cent of GDP. The public expenditure on health was 19.67 per cent of total health expenditure; the private sector spent 78.05 per cent; and the external flows were 2.28 per cent. External flows are funding from multilateral donors such as World Bank, ADB, DFID, GAVI, etc. The WHO report, *World Health Statistics 2013*, states that the total health spending has reduced to 3.7 per cent of GDP in 2010 and the public expenditure on health has increased to 28.2 per cent of total health spending and the private expenditure has decreased to 71.8 per cent of total health spending. The out of pocket expenditure is still substantially high at 86 per cent.

As discussed above, the public expenditure on health in India is one of the lowest in ten selected countries. Data from the National Sample Survey Organization (NSSO) indicate that between 1986-87 and 2004, the diseases not treated due to financial reason have increased from 15 to 28 per cent — rural areas (Rao & Chaudhury, 2012). NSSO also reports that outpatient treatment account for nearly three fourths of out of pocket expenditure by household which would include cost of drugs and consultations. India is also going through both demographic transition (reduction in mortality followed by reduction in fertility) and epidemiological transition (transition from communicable to non-communicable diseases) which also affects the health care costs. With rising life expectancy, the population is vulnerable to chronic non-communicable diseases and has to bear the dual burden of disease. A WHO report in 2008 states that in India, Communicable Diseases form 37 per cent, Non-Communicable Diseases form 53 per cent while injuries form 10 per cent of the disease burden (Planning Commission, Twelfth Plan Document, Vol. III).

Table 6.3: Eleventh Plan Monitorable Goals and Achievements

Sl.No.	*Eleventh Plan Monitorable Target*	*Baseline Level*	*Recent Status*
1.	Reducing Maternal Mortality Ratio (MMR) to 100 per 100000 live births	254 (SRS, 2004-06)	212 (SRS, 2007-09)
2.	Reducing Infant Mortality Rate (IMR) to 30 per 1000 live births	57 (SRS, 2006)	44 (SRS, 2011)
3.	Reducing Total Fertility Rate (TFR) to 2.1	2.8 (SRS, 2006)	2.5 (SRS, 2010)
4.	Reducing malnutrition among children of age group 0-3 to half its level	40.4 (NFHS, 2005-06)	No recent data available
5.	Reducing anaemia among women and girls by 50%	55.3 (NFHS, 2005-06)	No recent data available
6.	Raising the sex ratio for age group 0-6 to 935	927 (Census, 2001)	914 (Census, 2001)

Source: Twelfth Five Year Plan (2012-17), Planning Commission, Vol. III.

Table 6.4 shows that there is a great disparity in terms of public expenditure on health. This is bound to have an impact on the health infrastructure and the mortality rates. Rao and Chaudhury report that in 2008-09, the level of public spending on health in Bihar was less than one third of the level of Kerala and Tamil Nadu — the top two states in terms of health spending. Moreover, the difference between the per capita public spending in the top three States (Kerala, Tamil Nadu and Punjab) and bottom three States (Bihar, Madhya Pradesh and Odisha) have increased during last two decades leading to a divergence between the two categories of States. The public expenditure on health is positively correlated with income levels by States and their fiscal space. In its broadest sense, fiscal space can be defined as the availability of budgetary room that allows a Government to provide resources for desired purpose without any prejudice to the sustainability of a Government's financial position (Heller, 2005). Thus, States that are on the growth path to improve their GDP and have better governance and tax administration structures have more fiscal space to spend more on health. Central

Government transfer of funds to the States through the NRHM and other Centrally-sponsored schemes have improved the public spending on health during the Eleventh Plan period onwards. States with low expenditure on health are also the States with low per capita GSDP and some of the poorest health indicators and infrastructure in country as shown in Table 6.4. Madhya Pradesh and Odisha, the two States with worst IMR in the country, have the worse access to health infrastructure and professionals than Kerala and Tamil Nadu, the two best States in country in terms of health indicators (Rao, 2005).

Table 6.4: Per Capita Public Expenditure on Health in 14 Major States

(*Figures in Rupees*)

	Per Capita Health Expenditure		*Per Capita NSDP*
	1993-94	*2008-09*	*2008-09*
Andhra Pradesh	75	402	40,902
Bihar	53	166*	13,663
Gujarat	82	320	49,251
Haryana	80	364	68,614
Karnataka	85	405	41,513
Kerala	100	507	49,316
Madhya Pradesh	81	214*	21,648
Maharashtra	86	351	54,867
Odisha	58	303	29,464
Punjab	110	348	52,879
Rajasthan	84	405	27,001
Tamil Nadu	98	421	45,058
Uttar Pradesh	70	269*	18,710
West Bengal	73	292	36,322
Standard Deviation	**15.3**	**89.1**	
Mean	**81.1**	**340.5**	

Source: Health Care Financing Reform in India by Govind Rao and Mita Chaudhury, NIPFP, New Delhi (2012) accessed from www.nipfp.org

V. Health Reforms in India

Health system has five aspects or knobs that interact with each other and influence its basic nature and direction (i) financial (tax, user fees, out of pocket expenditure insurance); (ii) payment systems (providers are paid salary per service rendered, capitation); (iii) organizational (manner in which the delivery systems are organized and structured; (iv) legal (regulatory frameworks); and (v) social (access to health information advertising (Hsaio, 2000).

The evolution of Indian health system can be categorized into three distinct phases (Rao, 2005):

Phase 1 (1947-83)

When the country became independent, life expectancy was low and population was growing at more than 1 per cent rate per year. People were poor with low purchasing power and the burden of communicable diseases was very high. Thus, the early health policy was based on two principles (i) that none should be denied care for want of ability to pay; and (ii) and that it was the State's responsibility to provide health care to people. This phase saw the establishment of the public health system of India, setting-up centres of excellence like AIIMS, eradication of small-pox and plague, containment of malaria and cholera, halving of MMR and reduction in IMR among other developments. The focus was also on small family norm and family planning.

Phase 2 (1983-2000)

During this phase the first National Health Policy of 1983 articulated the need to encourage private initiative in health care service delivery. It also attempted to expand access to publicly funded comprehensive primary health at the same time. This phase witnessed an expansion of health facilities for providing primary health care in rural areas and implementation of national health programmes for diseases control under vertically designed and centrally monitored structures such as the malaria to tuberculosis (TB) control programme of the Central Government. This period also saw an infusion of funds from donors for specific programmes which made an impact on general health scenario. Guinea worm was eradicated, leprosy was eliminated except in 70 districts, TB cure rate was improved drastically and polio cases decreased from 29,709 to 100. However, there were serious omissions in public health policy (Rao, 2005).

(i) The private sector was encouraged to spend funds on health without adequate regulation and accreditation process.
(ii) There was absence of surveillance and epidemiological surveys.
(iii) Advantage was not taken of 73rd and 74th Constitutional amendments for decentralizing programme implementation to local bodies.
(iv) Research and development was neglected.
(v) Lack of concerted investment in developing the critical mass of required skills and human resources.

Phase 3 (Post-2000-2005)

During the third phase the health programme in India witnessed the following:

(i) A desire to utilize private sector resources for addressing public health goals.
(ii) Liberalizing of the insurance sector to include private insurers to provide new avenues for health financing.
(iii) Redefining the role of State from being a provider to financier of health services as well.

The beginning of this phase saw a virtual breakdown of the public health system. There was decrease in utilization of public facilities for outpatient care from 26 to 19 per cent, decrease in access to free care from 19 to 10 per cent and increase in out of pocket expenditure to almost 90 per cent. Alarmed at the mortality rates, and rise in certain diseases, Ministry of Health brought forth the National Population Policy (2000), the National Health Policy (2002) and the AYUSH Policy (2000) and declared an intention to increase public investment in health to 2-3 per cent of the GDP. India also signed the MDG declaration of the UN. However, in spite of declaration, public investment in health did not substantially increase resulting in continuing poor health infrastructure, inadequate provision of critical inputs such as drugs, equipments and diagnostics and low critical mass of human resources. Thus, policy interventions lacked a focus, were not based on hard evidence and had weak institutional capacity to translate policy into action (Rao, 2005).

Phase 4 (2005-2012) (11th Five Year Plan)

The fourth phase of health reforms took place with initiation of the National Rural Health Mission which kick started in 2005. Realizing the need to infuse more funds for health strengthening and for architectural correction, the Central Government introduced the National Rural Health Mission (NRHM) in a mission mode approach. To quote the background paper issued by Planning Commission to Twelfth Five Year Plan process for health sector:

> "NRHM was conceptualized in response to what were perceived as systemic flaws in the health system namely, the lack of a holistic approach, absence of linkages with collateral health determinants,

gross shortage of infrastructure and human resources, lack of community ownership and accountability, non-integration of vertical disease control programmes, inadequate responsiveness to community needs and lack of financial resources."

The key components of NRHM were to augment financial, infrastructure and human resources in the States, integrate the vertically run disease control programmes under one overarching umbrella, and to bring about community participation and involve the local bodies in monitoring and planning. Further, the approach was to make a targeted intervention by dividing States into focus States — those with weak health indicators and non-focus States — those with better health indicators.

During this phase there was a positive impact on disease prevalence. Detection and treatment of TB substantially improved, there was a 29.67 per cent reduction in reported malaria cases and 32 States and Union Territories eliminated leprosy and no new polio cases were reported in 2012-13. The critical mass of human resources was augmented and role of the ASHA (Accredited Social Health Activist) has been laudable. However, the outcomes reflect that while there have been improvements in all indicators except juvenile sex ratio; the goals are still way ahead. The NRHM certainly has had a positive impact and succeeded in putting back the issue of public health at the top of government agenda (Hussain, 2011). It also put pressure on the State Governments to divert resources to the health sector as under NRHM the State Governments have to share the total funding pattern. There was marginal increase in public health expenditure from 0.9 to 1.04 per cent of the GDP. The direct fund flow from Centre to the State autonomous societies ensured that funding reached the implementation agencies faster. Also innovative schemes such as the conditional cash transfers in schemes such as Janani Suraksha Yojana and Janani Shishu Suraksha Yojana proved to be successful instruments in improving safe institutional deliveries.

However, according to Hussain, the goals and targets of NRHM were overambitious, particularly in a period of less than a decade and did not adequately take into account the complexity of Indian rural society characterized by gender disparities, and divided on lines of caste, class, religion, politics and poor governance. This is particularly true for the focus States. The focus States were Bihar, Chhattisgarh, Jharkhand, Himachal Pradesh, Jammu & Kashmir, Madhya Pradesh, Odisha and Uttarakhand. All the eight States of North-East such as

Arunachal Pradesh, Assam, Manipur, Tripura, Meghalaya, Mizoram, Nagaland and Sikkim were also given focus States status. The focus States were states with poor health indicators such as MMR, IMR and TFR.

While an important objective of NRHM was to increase public health spending to 3 per cent of GDP it increased only up to 1.04 per cent of GDP. Table 6.5 reflects the allocation and spending by the Central Ministry of Health & Family Welfare which clearly shows that while allocation by Planning Commission was ₹ 1,25,923 crore in Eleventh Plan, the actual releases by Finance Ministry was ₹ 87,460 crore which was only 69 per cent of the allocation.

Thus, the point in consideration is that while funding for both Central and State Governments have increased but it was not enough to achieve the MDG targets even in the Twelfth Plan as seen in Table 6.3. The overall fiscal deficit in the country and the worsening macro economic situation has led to reduction of budgetary releases in all the three plans from the Tenth Plan to Twelfth plan periods from the indicative Plan approvals given by Planning Commission.

Table 6.5: Allocation and Spending by Ministry of Health in Eleventh Plan

(Figures in ₹ crore)

Department	*Eleventh Plan Allocation*	*Eleventh Plan Release*	*Eleventh Plan Expenditure*	*% Expenditure to Release*
HFW	1,25,923	87,460	83,407	95.4
Of which under				
NRHM	89,478	68,064	66,127	97.2
AYUSH	3,988	3,083	2,994	97.1
DHR	4,496	1,938	1,870	96.5
AIDS Control	5,728	1,500	1,305	87.0
Total	**1,40,135**	**93,981**	**89,576**	**95.3**

Source: Twelfth Plan Document (Planning Commission), Vol. III.

A review of funds flow under NRHM over last seven years shows that the Central Government has made a total release of ₹ 66,560 crore for the explicit purpose of financing state plans to strengthen public health services. This includes release of funds for disease control programmes and Reproductive and Child Health schemes (RCH) (NHSRC Report). Tables 6.6, 6.7 and 6.8 show allocation, releases and expenditure and unspent balances by states.

The states with better health indicators were non-focus states which were Andhra Pradesh, Goa, Gujarat, Haryana, Karnataka, Kerala,

Maharashtra, Punjab, Tamil Nadu and West Bengal. Tables 6.6, 6.7 and 6.8 show that in the initial years of NRHM, expenditure on health was low and absorption capacity was also low but in the latter years the expenditure picked up. The MIS report is not showing the releases under State share thereby distorting the expenditure patterns and the unspent balances. The large unspent balances from 2005-06 to 2009-10 show that the states were struggling to utilize the funds released to them. Further, due to a longer gestation period of infrastructure works in capital expenditure, the utilization of funds picked up only after 2008-09. NRHM evaluation studies have shown that the transfer to States through an independent society route and through electronic mode improved the funds transfer right up to the health facility to village level. Better governed institutions have shown better utilization of fund. The NHSRC Report published by Ministry of Health and Family Welfare lists the factors that led to better absorption of funds in latter years of NRHM.

(i) Better financial management in terms of electronic transfer and use of accounting software to monitor expenditure and releases;
(ii) Decentralization both in decision-making and funds transfer directly to the state health societies;
(iii) Stronger management structures by setting up of Performance Management Units (PMUs); and
(iv) Human Resource Development both in terms of augmentation of human resources and capacity-building.

Table 6.6: Allocation, Releases and Expenditure for High Focus States Other than North-East States

(Figures in ₹ crore)

Year	*Total State-wise Allocation under NRHM from Centre*	*Amount Released by GoI (Central Share)*	*Expenditure by States**	*Unspent Amount*
2005-06	2,285.89	2,207.54	1,618.47	589.08
2006-07	3,362.45	2,766.15	2,226.51	1,128.72
2007-08	4,390.43	3,926.22	3,385.46	1,669.47
2008-09	4,937.22	4,926.29	5,060.12	1,535.65
2009-10	5,515.76	5,257.05	6,349.97	442.73
2010-11	6,199.58	6,542.93	8,253.04	–1,267.38
2011-12	6,930.43	6,649.68	7,289.04	–1,906.75
2012-13	8,172.15	6,483.17	8,546.69	–4,559.34
Grand Total	**41,793.89**	**38,759.03**	**42,729.29**	**–2367.82**

* Expenditure reported is out of releases from both Central and State share of funds.
Source: MIS dt. 31/03/2013, accessed from www.nrhm.gov.in

Table 6.7: Allocation, Releases and Expenditure for High Focus States of North-East

(*Figures in ₹ crore*)

Year	*Total State-wise Allocation for Centre*	*Total Releases under NRHM*	*Total Expenditure Reported by States**	*Unspent Amount*
2005-06	405.35	311.44	190.32	121.12
2006-07	801.81	624.08	388.43	356.76
2007-08	1,008.79	929.69	820.12	466.33
2008-09	1,022.68	935.87	1,100.61	301.59
2009-10	1,414.66	1,294.02	1,208.86	386.75
2010-11	1,445.41	1,186.02	1,630.28	–57.51
2011-12	1,388.31	1,301.34	1,610.92	–367.08
2012-13	1,724.92	1,318.42	1,728.87	–898.64
Grand Total	**9,211.92**	**7,900.88**	**8,678.41**	**309.33**

* Expenditure is out of releases from both Central and State share of funds.
Source: MIS dt. 31/03/2013, accessed from www.nrhm.gov.in

Table 6.8: Allocation, Releases and Expenditures for Non-high Focus States

(*Figures in ₹ crore*)

Year	*Total State-wise Allocation under NRHM*	*Total State-wise Releases*	*Total Expenditure Reported by States**	*Unspent Balance*
2005-06	1,893.51	1,866.58	1,354.55	512.03
2006-07	2,754.05	2,319.00	1,846.93	984.10
2007-08	3,517.24	3,568.05	2,727.27	1,824.87
2008-09	4,093.26	3,633.23	4,313.72	1,144.39
2009-10	4,481.75	4,801.57	5,528.67	417.29
2010-11	5,085.19	4,982.82	6,081.78	–681.67
2011-12	5,735.18	5,911.00	6,617.20	–1,387.79
2012-13	6,599.10	5,879.96	7,137.31	–3,157.17
Total	**34,159.28**	**32,962.29**	**35,607.43**	**–343.96**

* Expenditure reported is out of releases from both Central and State share of funds.
Source: MIS dt. 31/03/2013, accessed from www.nrhm.gov.in

However, the poor performers brought the whole system back as they could not provide the utilization certificates on time. The focus States could not bring in efficient systems of governance and corruption led to massive malpractices especially in Uttar Pradesh, as reported by the Comptroller and Auditor General (CAG).

Clearly, the answers lie in improving the governance and efficiency in spending, differential financing based on results rather than set norms, improving the financial management systems with adequate and trained personnel, accounting and auditing systems based on latest technology in order to check leakages and malpractices, improving the flexibility of funding along with accountability and increased funding for focus States and North-Eastern States after taking into consideration State specific requirements and fiscal situation of States rather than an uniform pattern of funding. For example, the focus States are also the States which are under fiscal stress and therefore are under tremendous pressure to allocate the increased State share during Twelfth Plan under the modified Central Share funding pattern. In the first phase of NRHM in the Eleventh Plan the shares of funding between Centre and States was 85-15 per cent while in the Twelfth Plan the share of states has increased to 25 per cent and that of Centre has reduced to 75 per cent for all States except North East & J&K who are to be funded by 90-10 Central-share allocation.

In the Twelfth Plan, the Federal Government has launched the National Health Mission (NHM) that would cover all villages and towns in the country. The objective of NHM would be to extend the operation of the mission all over the country and promote universal access to a continuation of cashless health services from primary to tertiary care to population living in both rural and urban areas particularly those residing in urban slums. The scheme for the urban poor would be National Urban Health Mission (NUHM) and its estimated cost for 5 years is ₹ 22,507 crore with the Central Government share of ₹ 16,955 crore. Centre-State funding pattern would be 75-25 per cent except for North-East State, Jammu & Kashmir, and Himachal Pradesh where it would be 90-10 per cent. The releases under NUHM though conceptualized in 2011 started only in 2013-14.

Universal Coverage

A high level Expert Group set-up the Planning Commission for Twelfth Plan had recommended that Government should increase public expenditure on health from the current level of 1.2 per cent of the GDP to at least 2.5 per cent by the end of the Twelfth Plan to at least 3 per cent of the GDP by 2022. General taxation should be used as the principal source of health care financing, and not levying sector specific taxes. Specific purpose transfers should be introduced to equalize the levels of per capita public spending on health across different States. A National Health Package should be developed as part of the entitlement of every citizen so as to provide essential health services at different levels of the health care delivery system to all the needy people. (Planning

Commission, Twelfth Plan 2012-17). However, the Twelfth Plan Document does not set a clear-cut road map for ensuring universal coverage.

VI. Financial Protection

Another model of health financing in India is through the mechanism of health insurance. The health insurance sector today is characterized by the Private Health Insurance (PHI) and the government approved health insurance schemes. While insurance schemes ensure risk pooling, the Private Health Insurance (PHI) caters mostly to the middle and upper segments of society as the premium are quite high and inevitably the poor are left out who have to spend from out of pocket during illness. Further, the private insurance does not cover Out Patient Department (OPD) costs and drugs and therefore this could be a major flaw in the design of insurance as a survey shows that drugs and OPD form majority of the out of pocket expenditure. Currently, any form of insurance including the Central Government Health Scheme (CGHS), Employees State Insurance Scheme (ESIS), other Government sponsored schemes and private health insurance together cover approximately 302 million individuals, i.e. only 25 per cent of Indian population in 2010. Out of this the Rashtriya Swasthya Bima Yojana (RSBY) shares a substantial coverage (79.45 million), all other Government sponsored schemes 167.55 million and private health insurance 55 million. Till 2007, India was witness to three programmes, the PHI, the CGHS and the ESIS. However, since 2007, it is now swamped with plethora of insurance programmes like RSBY (launched by Ministry of Labour in 2008, Government of India) and State sponsored schemes like Rajiv Aarogyasri Scheme (Andhra Pradesh), Kalaignar (Tamil Nadu), Vajapayee Aarogyasri (Karnataka), and Yeshasvini (Karnataka).

While health insurance is supposed to be a sustainable mode of financing as premiums are paid by individuals (in PHI) or through payroll contributions (both by employer and employee in social health insurance), in India the insurance schemes are mostly funded by the Government (either by Central or State). Therefore, the coverage and financing of the schemes depend on the fiscal space of the Governments and their tax revenues. Thus, the financial sustainability of the Government sponsored schemes which are mostly for the poor is a major concern for all stakeholders. However, these schemes have certainly contributed to improve the access to health care by the poor and to reduce out of pocket spending and improve the quotient of equity. The RSBY is one of the important reforms launched by the Central

Government. It is designed to provide health insurance coverage up to ₹ 30,000 for Below Poverty Line (BPL) families for hospitalization. This is intended to cover the informal sector workers. Pre-existing conditions are covered from day one and there is no age limit. Coverage extends to five members of family and they need to pay only ₹ 30 as registration fee with the premium being paid by the Central (75%) and State Governments (25%) (90-10 in North-East, Himachal Pradesh and Jammu & Kashmir). Every beneficiary family is issued a smart card and the empanelled hospitals are IT enabled to ensure smooth flow of data regarding service utilization. The beneficiary has choice of public as well as private hospitals for cashless treatment. The RSBY has been extended to street vendors, *beedi* workers, domestic workers, Mahatma Gandhi National Rural Employment Guarantee Act (MNREGA) beneficiaries and other construction workers. The scheme is currently implemented in 24 States/UTs and about 3.3 crore families have been covered as on date and 43 lakh persons have availed hospitalization under this scheme till November, 2012 (Twelfth Plan 2012-17 Planning Commission).

Under RSBY, a package of services has been defined which also cover common hospitalization expenses. Yet, the RSBY also suffer from some shortcomings. They include high transaction costs due to insurance intermediaries, inability to control provider induced demand, and lack of coverage for primary health and outpatient care and drug costs which is a high component in out of pocket spending. Inadequate primary care then leads to cost escalation as the patient has to go for costlier secondary or tertiary level of treatment. The RSBY also does not take into account specific State variations in disease profiles and health needs. A study of RSBY (Naryana, 2010) revealed that enrolment of poor in its third year of operation in 2010 did not show any sign of reaching all poor by 2012. Only Kerala showed positive results largely due to its political commitment. The inadequate coverage of insurance schemes of both private and public could be also attributed to limited public awareness. It also shows that the insurance mechanism as a mode of financing has not been very successful in providing financial protection and there is need to review the plethora of insurance schemes and probably bring them under one umbrella and redesign the models, so that, they are more useful to the public.

VII. Health Research Financing

There is very limited literature available to analyze the level of health research financing in India. In Table 6.9, an analysis of the expenditure by the Department of Health Research reveals the insignificant amount of public spending on health research today. The plan outlays from 2008-09 show that it varied between ₹ 420 crore to ₹ 726 crore, 2013-14 for a department which conducted health research for a population of over a billion people.

Table 6.9: Health Spending: Department of Health Research

(Figures in ₹ crore)

Year	*Health Research*									*% Utili-zation wrt RE*
	BE			*RE*			*Actual Expenditure*			
	Plan	*Non-Plan*	*Total*	*Plan*	*Non-Plan*	*Total*	*Plan*	*Non-Plan*	*Total*	
2008-09	420.00	111.75	531.75	420.00	147.00	567.00	390.56	174.00	564.56	99.57
2009-10	420.00	186.00	606.00	400.00	200.00	600.00	399.90	184.07	583.97	97.33
2010-11	500.00	160.00	660.00	530.00	160.00	690.00	515.12	159.90	675.02	97.83
2011-12	600.00	171.00	771.00	588.26	182.00	770.26	564.50	181.93	746.43	96.91
2012-13	660.00	248.00	908.00	464.00	861.00	725.00	460.31	260.13	720.44	99.37
2013-14	726.00	282.00	1008.00							

Source: Ministry of Health and Family Welfare.

While the Central Government created a separate department of health research only in 2008, the Indian Council of Medical Research (ICMR) is a 100 year old medical research body and is the largest publicly funded body in health research. India roughly spends only about 2 per cent out of the total health spending by Ministry of Health and Family Welfare on health research — whereas in comparison federal funding for health research totalled about $39.5 billion in 2011 in USA. Thus, there is a strong case to increase public spending in health research along with health care spending as not only does advances in medical research help in improving health care, investment in health research is also a catalyst in economic growth as it leads to new business in diagnostics, equipments and helps in generation of employment. Health research helps in innovations in diagnostics, drug discoveries and advancements in equipments which go a long way to promote public health.

VIII. Challenges and Way Forward

This chapter based on research from secondary data has outlined the concept of health financing, health spending in the world and its impact on the health indicators and the status of health in India, its policies and the recent reforms in the health scenario and shows that health financing in India is facing several challenges. They are continued under investment in public health spending; high fiscal deficit and limited fiscal space;

inefficient health spending; unregulated private sector; inadequate financial protection; and competing political priorities. The analysis shows that public health spending is a very important factor in improving the health status of the population, especially in a developing country where a significant proportion of the population lives below the poverty line.

Principle 1 of public health financing suggests that there is a need to "raise enough revenues to provide individuals with a basic package of essential services and financial protection against catastrophic medical expenses caused by illness and injury in an equitable, efficient and sustainable manner". India today is a mixed bag as far as delivery of health services is concerned. A dominant private health network, a weak public health system, with an insignificant private health insurance sector, has made India realize that public health spending has to improve to at least 3 per cent of the GDP from 1.2 per cent of the GDP today. For that, additional fiscal space is required. Today at 15.5 per cent tax to GDP ratio, India has one of the lowest taxes to GDP ratio in the world. So, the first challenge is to find additional fiscal space and with competing demands such as food security, education and MNREGA, reference this is certainly an issue. Whether or not, the Central Government and State Governments allocate the desired amount of funds to health shall depend much on the socio-political environment. While, through its various centrally sponsored schemes and State schemes and reform initiatives, India has embarked upon an ambitious path to improve health infrastructure, it must now have a twenty year road map with a clear cut vision and political commitment to generate and allocate sufficient funds to health sector so as to achieve the MDG targets. It may be worthwhile to introduce earmarked taxes such as health cess to generate more resources and improve the tax administration to generate more direct taxes.

On issues of universal coverage with basic package of essential health services, it is still in recommendation stage and has not been implemented yet. Through CGHS, ESIS and RSBY and a few other state sponsored schemes only a quarter of population are somewhat accessible to affordable health care. The high out of pocket expenditure of more than 80 per cent reflect the lack of equity in health care. Thus, there is a strong case in increasing public health spending and bringing about universal coverage as it would protect both poor and non-poor households from financial impact of unanticipated health shocks. However, it is essential to work out the financial implications of universal coverage and plan out a roadmap so as to ensure sufficient and regular supply of funds to ensure fiscal sustainability.

Principle 2 of public health financing states that these revenues need to be managed by pooling health risks equitably and efficiently.

Principle 3 states that health services need to be provided in ways that are allocatively and technically efficient.

It is seen that mere provision of funds and health expenditure does not directly impact health indicators. What matters is how it is spent. Thus, both quantity and quality of health spending matter. Even though Bangladesh and Sri Lanka are spending less on health, their mortality rates are much lower than that of India which could be due to efficiency in spending. What is needed, therefore, is to increase the efficiency in spending. For this, overall improvement is required in governance and organizational structure, monitoring of spending by setting up of oversight committees and a proper framework of concurrent evaluation on a systematic and regular basis. There is a need to leverage information technology in fund transfers, strong MIS systems, auditing and accounting, and to develop the human resources and enhance capacity building. Along with it, an adequate vigilance structure is required to prevent leakages and malpractices and a strong regulatory structure to monitor the private sector.

The private health insurance sector and state sponsored health insurance have reached only a few. The wide plethora of insurance schemes that exist, need to be reviewed and brought under one umbrella, provided the States agree thereby leveraging on the efficiencies of each scheme. The deficiency of such schemes are that they do not cater to primary care and do not include cost of drugs and consultations as they cover only hospitalization expenses while studies have shown that bulk of (Out of Pocket) OOP treatment consists of drugs and OPD treatment. Therefore, the insurance schemes are not easily accepted by the public. There is a need to redesign the schemes accordingly. Further, the state sponsored schemes such as RSBY can be extended to the non-poor by taking contributions from them for a defined package. By this, the fiscal sustainability can be enhanced and also the health risks can be pooled more efficiently. Another important issue is that there is lack of awareness about the insurance schemes for which there is a need for improving the socio-behaviour communication aspect in 'spreading health information'.

The administrative and regulatory structures also need to be reviewed. While NRHM did envisage decentralized decision-making to local bodies, the participation of local bodies is still marginal. The programme management units in both administrative and financial matters have to be strengthened as with introduction of the Urban Health Missions, the health societies will get and spend more funds. Thus, these structures need to be evaluated to ensure that there are adequate personnel who have been trained well to utilize funds efficiently. Further, strong Project Management Units (PMUs) are needed to monitor effective implementation and there is a strong framework of monitoring and concurred evaluation of the implement.

In order to increase technical efficiency, the interventions have to be targeted both in terms of geography and the kind of goals they are expected to serve. At present in NRHM, funds are provided to all States — focus, non-focus and North-East States. It is more expedient to pool the resources and focus on States where it is required the most rather than spread the resources thinly. A targeted approach both in States and districts where health indicators are worst would bring in more results rather than trying to do everything and everywhere and achieving less. The marginal effect of additional health spending (of a Rupee) in EAG States would be higher than that spent in non-EAG States. Further, the incentive based schemes or result based financing need to be developed to motivate State Governments to achieve desired outcomes and to target the interventions properly.

Finally, needless to say no reform is possible without community participation and political commitment which need to be factored into any design for health reforms.

Disclaimer: The article reflects my personal viewpoint and is not related to my official position.

REFERENCES

Gill, K. (2009). A Primary Evaluation of Service Delivery under the National Rural Health Mission — Findings from a Study in Andhra Pradesh, Uttar Pradesh, Bihar and Rajasthan. Working Paper No. 1/2009-PEO, Planning Commission of India. Retrieved on August 16, 2014, from http://planningcommission.nic.in/reports/wrkpapers/wrkp_1_09.pdf

Gottret, P. and Schieber, G. (2006). *Health Financing Revisited: A Practitioner's Guide*, Washington DC.: World Bank.

Hussain, Z. (2011). "Health of the National Rural Health Mission", *Economic and Political Weekly*, 46(4), 53-60.

Human Development Report. (2013). Retrieved from http://hdr.undp.org/en/2013-report

MIS Reports of March. (2012). Retrieved from http://www.nrhm.gov.in

Narayana, D. (2010). "Review of the Rashtriya Swasthya Bima Yojana", *Economic and Political Weekly*, 45(29), 13-18.

NRHM in the Eleventh Five Year Plan. (2007-2012). *National Health System Resources Centre*, New Delhi. Retrieved 2013, from file:///C:/Users/Nidhi/Downloads/NRHM%20Eleventh%20Five%20Year%20Plan.pdf

Planning Commission of India, Government of India. (2013). *Twelfth Five Year Plan: Social Sectors (2012-2017)*, (Vol. III), New Delhi: Sage Publications.

Rao, G.M., and Chaudhury, M. (2012). "Health Care Financing Reforms in India", *National Institute of Public Finance & Policy*, Working Paper no. 2012-100. Retrieved from http://www.nipfp.org.in/media/medialibrary/2013/04/wp_2012_100.pdf

Rao, S. (2005). *Financing and Delivery of Health Care Services in India*, National Commission on Macroeconomics & Health, Ministry of Health & Family Welfare, Government of India, New Delhi. Retrieved from: http://www.who.int/macrohealth/action/Background%20Papers%20report.pdf

Reddy, K.S., Selvaraj, S., Rao, K.D., Chokshi, M., Kumar, P., Arora, V., Bhokare, S. and Ganguly, I. (2011). *A Critical Assessment of the Existing Health Insurance Models in India*. Retrieved from http://planningcommission.nic.in/reports/sereport/ser/ser_heal1305.pdf

Report of the Working Group on National Rural Health Mission (NRHM) for the Twelfth Five Year Plan (2012-2017). Retrieved from http://planningcommission.gov.in/aboutus/committee/wrkgrp12/health/WG_1NRHM.pdf

Siva Kumar, A.K., *et al.* (2011). "Financing Health Care for All: Challenges and Opportunities", *The Lancet*, 377(9766), 668-79.

U.S. Investment in Health Research (2011). *Are We Willing to Relinquish on Global Leadership*. Retrieved from: http://www.researchamerica.org/sites/default/files/uploads/healthdollar11.pdf

World Health Organization. (2013). *World Health Statistics 2013*. Retrieved from http://www.who.int/gho/publications/world_health_statistics/EN_WHS2013_Full.pdf

7

Disease, Illness and Health Care
A Sociological Conceptualization of the Indian Experience

Mohammad Akram

India has a large burden of communicable and non-communicable diseases. There is a need for effective treatment of diseases and illness conditions for improving life expectancy. Here, treatment refers to the interventions made to regain the state of well-being or health from a state of illness and sickness. It needs to be emphasized that curative treatment (medicinal as well as surgical) is seldom offered without the individual's or the community's cognizance of the occurrence of disease through the illness or sickness roles. Globally, different systems of treatment have existed for long. The modern bio-medical system of clinical care has made significant impact on combating the causation and spread of diseases, correcting the complications, and prolonging life. There are other medicine systems grounded in different principles, developed at different periods of time in different parts of world. They are generally known as traditional medicines. In India, medicinal pluralism exists because people have a wide acceptance of different systems of medicine. Among them Ayurvedic, Unani, Siddha and Homoeopathy are the formally (and also officially) recognized systems of medicine besides the Allopathic system. Further, folk medicines, faith healing, household medicine are also the popular forms of treatment. However, any system of medicine or treatment is effective only when supplemented by Basic Health Goods (BHGs) like food, nutrition, potable drinking water, hygiene and sanitation and favourable Social Determinants (SDs) like education, awareness, income, inclusive society, etc. These factors not only have curative role, but also have a potential for prevention of diseases.

The impact of the curative medical care varies from culture to culture even in case of application of same medicines because of the differential availability of the BHGs and SDs. The Western system of Allopathic medicine is very successful in industrialized countries not only because of the medicinal value but also because of the positive role of BHGs, SDs and environment. In the developing countries, the poor availability and accessibility of BHGs and SDs are the biggest challenges in combating diseases and ensuring medical and health care. The developed world has almost controlled the conventional communicable diseases (such as cholera, diarrhoea, etc.) which transmit from an agent to a human. This is made possible because of the availability of potable water, hygiene, and sanitation which together combat the spread of most of communicable diseases. On the other hand, in a country like India, in the absence of the nutrition, proper diet, safe drinking water, sanitation, education, etc. communicable diseases are still the largest killer.

Medical care largely depends on clinical care. Medical care is curative as well as preventive. Immunization and vaccinations are the very important preventive interventions for combating the occurrence and prevalence of disease. The public health systems of the developed countries largely depend on the preventive as well as curative courses of the medical care systems. The BHGs and SDs supplement the medical interventions and get the desired results closest to the optimum level. However, health care is a broad term and includes the medical care as well as the BHGs and SDs as per the Alma Ata Declaration of 1978. We find the most basic definition of 'health care' in the Alma Ata Declaration (1978) on 'primary health care' (PHC) which says: primary health care includes at least (i) education concerning prevailing health problems and the methods of preventing and controlling them; (ii) promotion of food supply and proper nutrition; (iii) an adequate supply of safe water and basic sanitation; (iv) maternal and child health care, including family planning; (v) immunization against the major infectious diseases; (vi) prevention and control of locally endemic disease; (vii) appropriate treatment of common disease and injuries; and (viii) provision of essential drugs.

It is notable that health care and medical care are not synonymous. The medical care is primarily clinical care (as prescribed by different systems of medicines) whereas the health care is much broader and includes all the associated quality of life factors like food, nutrition, potable drinking water, hygiene and sanitation and also the favourable social determinants like education, awareness, income level, inclusive society, etc. along with the medical care. However, the dominance of the bio-medical system of medicine often creates discourses which build up impressions in which 'medical care' and 'health care' are used interchangeably. Official policies, literature, discourses, directives and even common sense understanding, in India, often get trapped in a 'design' which promotes using the two phrases synonymously.

The problem of health and disease in India is caused not only because of scarcity of medical care but also because of the persisting and even enlarging gaps between 'health care' and 'medical care'. Most of the BHGs (like nutrition, potable water, and sanitation) and SDs (like education, health awareness, and good income), the two integral components of health care, are often not adequately available to the majority of the masses. They are ignored to the extent that they are yet to be included in the health care agenda. This gap between the medical care and health care in the academic arena is reflected through the gap between the 'bio-medical approach' and the 'social determinants' approach. However, even the social determinants approach does not take into consideration the BHGs in a comprehensive way. Further, even within the medical care framework, 'disease', 'illness' and 'sickness' are different 'states' and need to be understood separately. Medical care comes into focus only when the state of disease gets translated to illness and further recognized as sickness. Among the masses when the disease fails to get the recognition of sickness, people remain in a state of 'illness doubt' and the larger impact, at the societal level, is a state of 'health illusion' rather than health. Thus, an exploration of the various conceptual nuances is imminent to contextualize health and disease scenario in India.

Disease, Illness, Sickness and Health

Oxford English Dictionary defines *disease* as "a condition of the body or some part or organ of the body in which its functions are disrupted or deranged". Webster's Dictionary defines *disease* as "a condition in which body health is impaired, a departure from the normal state of health, an alteration of the human body interrupting the performance of vital functions". Disease is a departure from the state of health. Health is a state of well-being. Disease is a state of not being well or being unwell. The notion of wellness is cultural and hence disease is also cultural. According to Cockerham and Ritchey (1997: 34), "disease is considered an adverse physical state consisting of a physiological dysfunction within an individual, as compared to an illness (psychological awareness of a disease) or a sickness (a social state)". For the bio-medical approach, disease is a state of bio-physical dysfunction or infirmity within an individual. It is a phenomenon characterized by altered functioning of a body as a biological organism. The World Health Organization (WHO) has defined health, but not disease. The WHO definition of health states: "health is a state of complete physical, mental, social and spiritual well-being and not merely an absence of disease or infirmity". Disease is also multidimensional and may refer to different states of being, but the complete well-being. Disease may refer to a state of malfunctioning, overfunctioning, underfunctioning or non-functioning of one or more organs or mechanisms of the body or in the perceived understanding of the functioning of the body with a larger cognizance that the alteration may take place instantly, intermittently, continuously or even simultaneously. From a sociological point of view, disease is considered as a social phenomenon, occurring in all societies and defined and fought in terms of the particular forces prevalent in the society.

Illness, on the other hand, is a subjective phenomenon, pertaining to an individual's awareness of having a disease, symptoms and pain and having an altered state of his/her perceptions of himself/herself. Thus, interpretations of illness and wellness are both objective and subjective depending upon the larger understanding of biological, physiological, psychological, social, medico-technological and cultural factors. Illness is transformed into sickness when the condition of the ill person becomes socially known through announcement by the affected person, observations by significant others or professional diagnosis. Unlike illness, the amount of sickness varies widely from society to society and reflects the perceptions and responses of society at that point of time.

Kleinman (1988) suggests that disease is a biophysical event and the prime concern of medical practitioners, whereas illness "refers to how the sick person and members of the family or wider social network perceive, live with and respond to symptoms and disability" (1988, p. 3). Dingwall argues that there is no such thing as 'essential illness', rather, illness is construed through the meanings and interpretations that are accorded to certain categories of experience and "there is no necessary relationship to any biological happening" (1976, p. 26). For Giddens (2006), illness has both personal and public dimensions. When we become ill, not only do we experience pain, discomfort, confusion and other challenges, but others are affected as well. Hence, Sarah Nettleton concludes, "rather than simply observing illness behaviour, sociologists must endeavour to understand illness action. The former refers to the way people behave given the presence of symptoms, whilst the latter focusses on how people make sense of and interpret their illness experience and, crucially, what it means to them" (1995, p. 78).

Mechanic and Volkart (1960) identified four dimensions of illness that influenced the decision to seek medical help: (1) the frequency with which the illness occurs in a given population; (2) the familiarity of the symptoms; (3) the predictability of the outcome of the illness; and (4) the amount of threat and loss that is likely to result from the illness. Mechanic (1978) has identified few other factors also relating to illness that influence help-seeking behaviour. These include the visibility of the symptoms, the perceived present and future seriousness of the symptoms, the extent to which symptoms disrupt social activities, the frequency of symptoms, and interpretations of the cause of symptoms, and availability of treatment. In addition, Mechanic recognized that the impact that illness had on those caring for the patient was an important determinant of illness behaviour.

Zola (1972) identified five factors which initiate a person into consulting the doctor. First, there is the occurrence of an interpersonal crisis, such as the death of a known person from a related symptom/ disease. Second, a perceived interference with social or personal relations in which the symptoms start to have an impact on the person's social life. Third, a sanctioning by which family members or friends agree to seek medical help and thereby agree that there is a need to go to the doctor. Fourth factor is a perceived interference with vocational or physical activity. Finally, there is the temporalizing of symptoms, where a time limit is placed on the illness. People will often say that they will consult the doctor if the symptom has not gone within a given time frame. Although the decision to consult the doctor is shaped by the type of illness and a person's individual and social circumstances, it is unusual for a person to seek medical help without first discussing their symptoms with at least one other person (Gabe, Bury and Elson, 2004). Zola (1973) also saw the ability to cope with symptoms as an important determinant of illness behaviour. Zola suggested that rather than consulting when they are most sick, people often consult when their ability to accommodate symptoms breaks down. The following sections present the approaches to health and illness in the biomedical and sociological models.

Biomedical Model of Disease and Health

The biomedical model of disease finds its origin in the post-industrial era of growth of scientific knowledge and regards disease as the consequence of certain malfunctions of the human body. The *biomedical model of disease is based on certain assumptions like:* disease is an organic condition; disease is caused by some 'agent' which is defined as a substance, living or non-living, or a force, tangible or intangible, the excessive presence or relative lack of which may initiate or perpetuate a disease process; disease is a temporary organic state that can be eradicated — cured — by medical intervention; disease is experienced by a sick individual, who then becomes the object of treatment; disease is treated after the symptoms appear — the application of medicine is a reactive healing process; medical specialists possess 'expert knowledge' and prescribe the only valid treatment of disease; and, disease is treated in a medical environment — a surgery or a hospital — away from the site where the symptoms first appeared.

According to Park (2009), a disease may have a single agent, a number of independent alternative agents, or a complex of two or more factors whose combined presence is essential for the development of disease. The disease agents may be classified into different groups like biological, nutrient, physical, chemical, mechanical and social. Biological agents are the living agents of disease, namely, viruses, fungi, bacteria, protozoa, and metazoan which exhibit certain 'host-related' biological properties such as (i) infective — the ability of an infectious agent to invade and multiply in a host, (ii) pathogenicity — the ability to induce clinically apparent illness, and (iii) virulence — the proportion of clinical cases resulting in severe clinical manifestations. Nutrient agents are the agents present in food like fats, proteins, carbohydrates, vitamins, minerals, water, etc. A deficiency of the intake of such nutrient elements may result in nutritional disorders like Protein Energy Malnutrition (PEM), anaemia, goitre, obesity, and vitamin deficiencies. Physical agents like heat, cold, humidity, pressure, radiation, electricity, sound, etc. may cause disease in cases of excessive exposure. Chemical agents are endogenous as well as exogenous. The endogenous chemicals may be produced in the body as a result of derangement of function, e.g. urea (uraemia), serum bilirubin (jaundice), ketones (ketosis), uric acid (gout), calcium carbonate (kidney stones), etc., and the exogenous chemicals arise outside human host, for example, drugs, allergens, metals, fumes, dust, gases, and insecticides which may be acquired by inhalation, ingestion, or inoculation. Mechanical agents activate during exposure to chronic friction and other mechanical forces and may result in crushing, tearing, sprains, dislocations, and even death. Social agents are related to quality of life and unhealthy practices like poverty, malnutrition, deprivation, stress, social isolation, smoking, abuse of drugs and alcohol, etc.

Sociological Understanding of Disease and Health

Health and well-being has always been a basic human need. Societies have always created mechanisms and discourses for responding to the physical, mental or social conditioning of its members. The concepts of health, disease and treatment are related to the social structures of communities. Every culture, irrespective of its simplicity or complexity, has its own system of beliefs and practices concerning health and disease, and evolves its own system of treatment to combat disease (Akram, 2007). Definitions and conceptualization of health also vary among various social groups within a society. Moreover, different accounts of health are drawn according to social circumstances (Nettleton, 2006). Thus, sociologists have looked at health from a more holistic perspective though they are quite divided into functionalist, Marxist and symbolic interactionist groups. Sociologists show how diseases could be differently understood, treated and experienced by demonstrating how disease is produced out of social organization and not merely by the nature, biology, or individual lifestyle choices (White, 2002). A functional definition of health treats health as the ability of a person to participate in normal social roles. Parsons believed that illness is dysfunctional for both individual and the larger society (Kendall, 2011). According to Parsons, the sick role exempts the patient from routine activities for a period of time and assumes that the individual will seek appropriate medical attention and get well as soon as possible. Physicians are empowered to determine who may enter the sick role and when patients are ready to exit it. For this, they are certified by the society to be 'gatekeepers' of the sick role. Parsonian sociology emphasizes the role of medicine in maintaining social harmony.

Marxist approach emphasizes the causal role of class in the production, distribution and treatment of disease. For Marxist writers, in a capitalist society medicine reflects the characteristics of capitalism. Medicine is profit-oriented and reproduces the class structure within the medical profession itself. It emphasizes the social, economic, and political forces that affect health, disease and the health delivery system. Marxist theorists are interested in issues related to unequal accessibility of health care facilities; power relationships between doctors and other health care workers; critique of the dominance of the medical model of health care; and the role of profit in the health care system (Kendall, 2011).

Symbolic interaction perspective focuses on how health, health care, and illness conditions are influenced by meanings, definitions, and labels and how such meanings are learned through interaction with others, and through media messages and portrays (Knox, 2008). According to McNeill (1990), symbolic interactionists believe that individuals actively construct understandings of themselves using the evidence that comes from their interaction with others. Some of these interactions may lead them to understand themselves as healthy. In contrast to biomedical and social positivist researchers, interactionists tend to focus on the more subjective aspects of health. Among post-modern writers, Foucault highlights the social role of medical knowledge in controlling populations, and like Parsons he emphasizes the diffused nature of power relationships in modern society. Also, like Parsons, he sees the professions, especially the helping professions, playing a key role in inducing individuals to comply with 'normal' social roles. For Foucault, modern societies are systems of organized surveillance with the catch being that individuals conduct the surveillance on themselves, having internalized 'professional' models of what is appropriate behaviour (White, 2002).

Ecologists, psychologists and anthropologists also have an alternative conception of health. According to them the biomedical approach which dominated the medical thought till the end of nineteenth century and is based on the 'germ theory of disease', views health as an 'absence of diseases'. This approach almost ignores the role of environmental, psychological and other socio-cultural factors in defining health. The ecological approach views health as a dynamic equilibrium between man and his environment. For them, disease is maladjustment of the human organism to environment. The psychological approach states that health is not only related to the body but also to the mind and especially to the attitude of the individual. The socio-cultural approach considers health as a product of the social and community structure (Advani and Akram, 2007).

Health Rights and Capabilities

The Universal Declaration of Human Rights stated in Article 25: "Everyone has the right to a standard of living adequate for the health and well-being of himself and his family. . ." (United Nations, 1948). The Preamble to the World Health Organization (WHO) constitution affirms that it is one of the fundamental rights of every human being to enjoy the highest attainable standards of health. Article 21 of the Constitution of India also identifies health as an integral aspect of human life (Desai, 2007). Health is human being's natural condition; health is his/her birth right. It is the result of living in accordance with natural laws pertaining to the body, mind, and environment. These laws relate to fresh air, sunlight, diet, exercise, rest and relaxation, sleep, cleanliness, right attitude of mind, good habits, and above all lifestyle. Improving health status of the citizens is one of the most important goals of all the modern welfare governments. The Alma Ata Declaration made in 1978 has set the target of achieving the goal of "health for all" by 2000. The target could not be achieved within the stipulated time period. This eventually gave way to the world agreement on the Millennium Development Goals to be attained in a phased manner.

According to Sen (2006), health contributes to a person's basic capability to function. Capability, in turn, refers to the freedom of persons or groups to promote or achieve things which they consider valuable (Alkire, 2003). Health is the most basic requirement for every individual. Denial of health is not only denial of 'good life-chance'; it is also a denial of fairness and justice. Sen regards functioning as doings and beings which create a better conceptual space to examine social welfare than utility or opulence. Sen is known for his immense contribution to the capabilities approach, a new paradigm for policy debate on human development which inspired the creation of the UN's Human Development Index.

According to Peter (2006), Sen's capability approach, provides a useful alternative for accessing health problems in society. Sen regards good health as an example of functioning. Peter, however, points out that it is more favourable to use health as a capability or a subset of capability because of the fact that health itself is composed of various functionings such as ability to move around, not being tired and others. Sen leaves it open which functionings are to be included while accessing a particular social situation. Sen stresses that in each case, this will require a process of selecting a relevant functioning and weighing its relative importance. Seeing health as a capability or a subset of capability requires a process that involves value judgements and which is subjected to political contestation. Thus, according to Peter, the process of defining health and determining what counts as health, and what as another type of social problems, cannot be solved by the health specialists alone, but depends on other aspects of social institutions, and may change over time (Akram and Beg, 2014).

Disease, Morbidity and Health Situation in India

The Annual Report to the People on Health (Ministry of Health and Family Welfare, 2010) examines the progress made in the health sector in the post-Independence era in India. There are wide divides in the achievements in terms of life expectancy, child survival and maternal mortality across the states. There are inequities based on rural urban divide, gender and caste. There are wide differentials in terms of health, income and education indices. The Human Development Index (HDI)[1] is a reflection of the composite values of the Health Index,[2] Income Index[3] and Education Index.[4] Among all Indian states Kerala is the best performing state in terms of education, health and income indices and has the highest Human Development Index.

Life expectancy is considered to be the most commonly used indicator of health. In India life expectancy at birth has more than doubled in the last sixty years. It increased from around 30 years at the time of Independence to over 66.9 years in 2006-10. But the wide variance in performance across states is of special concern. While in Kerala, a new born child is expected to live for 74.5 years, in States like Assam, Madhya Pradesh, Odisha, and Uttar Pradesh a new born child is expected to live for 62-64 years only. Overall, India's life expectancy is lower than the global average of 67.5 years. Table 7.1 exhibits the state-wise variations in life expectancy and a few other indicators of health.

India's Infant Mortality Rate (IMR) too has shown a steady decline, from 129 deaths per 1,000 live births in 1971 to 50 in 2009. Yet, the disparity between urban and rural areas is very high as urban IMR is 34 as compared to the rural IMR of 55. Widespread disparities are also visible among various social categories in India. The IMR per 1000 live births, for the period 2005-06, among Scheduled Castes (SCs), Scheduled Tribes (STs), Other Backward Classes (OBCs), and Others is 66.4, 62.1, 56.6 and 48.9, respectively (IIPS, 2007). Maternal health is a key indicator of women's health and status. Maternal Mortality Ratio (MMR) measures number of women aged 15-49 years dying due to maternal causes per 1,00,000 live births. India had a MMR of 460 in 1984 which declined to 212 deaths per 1,00,000 live births in 2007-2009. However, a great disparity is visible among the states even in MMR as Kerala and Tamil Nadu report low MMR of 81 and 97 respectively whereas other States, viz. Assam (390), Madhya Pradesh (269), Odisha (258), Rajasthan (318) and Uttar Pradesh (359) (Registrar General of India-SRS estimates for 2007-09) have a high MMR.

Table 7.1: HDI and its Various Components in Ten States of India

Sl. No.	*States*	*Health Index*	*Income Index*	*Education Index*	*HDI*	*Incidence of poverty*	*Percentage of women with Any Anaemia*	*IMR*	*Percentage of live birth at home*	*Maternal Mortality Ratio*	*Life Expectancy at birth*	*Percentage of households without Latrine*	*Percentage of households by source of drinking: Tap*	*Percentage of households by source of drinking: Tube-well/ Hand-Pump*
		2008	*2007-8*	*2007-8*	*2007-8*	*2004-5*	*2005-6*	*2009*	*2005-6*	*2007-9*	*2006-10*	*2008-9*	*2008-9*	*2008-9*
Five poorly performing states starting from bottom to top in terms of Health Index 2008														
1.	Assam	0.407	0.288	0.553	0.444	19.7	69.5	61	77.5	390	62.2	12.1	9.8	62.6
2.	Madhya Pradesh	0.430	0.173	0.522	0.375	38.3	56.0	67	73.5	269	62.9	70.2	23.4	61.5
3.	Odisha	0.450	0.139	0.499	0.362	46.4	61.2	65	63.8	258	63.5	78.7	15.0	65.2
4.	Uttar Pradesh	0.473	0.175	0.492	0.380	32.8	49.9	63	79.3	359	64.2	42.5	12.2	83.4
5.	Bihar	0.563	0.127	0.409	0.367	41.4	67.4	52	79.7	261	66.9	74.1	4.1	90.9
Five best performing states starting from bottom to top in terms of Health Index 2008														
1.	Tamil Nadu	0.637	0.355	0.719	0.570	22.5	53.2	28	12.1	97	69.1	46.6	84.6	7.2
2.	Maharashtra	0.650	0.351	0.715	0.572	30.7	48.4	31	35.1	104	69.5	36.4	71.1	14.5
3.	West Bengal	0.650	0.252	0.575	0.492	24.7	63.2	33	57.7	145	69.5	32.4	24.0	69.7
4.	Punjab	0.667	0.495	0.654	0.605	8.4	38.0	38	48.6	172	70.0	24.0	54.2	44.8
5.	Kerala	0.817	0.629	0.924	0.790	15.0	32.8	12	0.6	81	74.5	4.3	22.6	3.0
	All India	**0.563**	**0.271**	**0.568**	**0.467**	**27.5**	**55.3**	**50**	**61.1**	**212**	**66.9**	**49.2**	**43.1**	**43.7**

Sources: Various tables in *India Human Development Report 2011* (2011).

Between the two — communicable and non-communicable diseases — India witnesses a higher burden of communicable diseases. Communicable diseases transmit from one person or agent to another. Of the 9.2 million cases of tuberculosis (TB) that occur in the world every year, nearly 1.9 million are in India. Thus, India accounts for one-fifth of the global TB cases. Further, experts estimate that about 2.5 million persons have HIV infection in India, world's third highest. More than 1.5 million persons are infected with Malaria every year. Diseases such as dengue and chikungunya have emerged in different parts of India, and a population of over 300 million is at risk of getting acute encephalitis syndrome/Japanese encephalitis. One-third of the global cases infected with filaria also live in India. Nearly half of leprosy cases detected in the world in 2008 were detected in India. More than 300 million episodes of acute diarrhoea occur every year in India in children younger than 5 years of age (MOHFW, 2010).

Regarding the burden of non-communicable diseases (NCDs), it is estimated that NCDs are the major cause of death worldwide, killing more than 36 million in 2008. Cardiovascular diseases were responsible for 48 per cent of such deaths, cancers for 21 per cent, chronic respiratory diseases for 12 per cent and diabetes for 3 per cent. One of the findings shows that men and women in low-income countries are around three times more likely to die of NCDs before 60 years than in high-income countries (Planning Commission, 2011). These differential outcomes in health indicators are obvious indication of perpetuating health inequalities. WHO had estimated that, in 2008, over 5.2 million people in India, died of non-communicable diseases (NCDs) such as cardiovascular diseases, stroke, diabetes and cancer (Sinha, 2011; WHO, 2011). NCDs accounted for 53 per cent of all deaths. Among men, 38 per cent of the deaths due to NCDs occurred under 60 years, and among women 32 per cent of the deaths due to NCDs occurred under 60 years. Cardiovascular diseases accounted for 24 per cent of all deaths. Cancers, respiratory disease, diabetes and other NCDs accounted for 6 per cent, 11 per cent, 2 per cent and 10 per cent respectively.

NFHS-3 (IIPS, 2007) has produced rich and reliable data on many aspects of mother and child health. It shows that almost one out of every five women in India did not receive any antenatal care for their last birth in the five years preceding the survey. The utilization of antenatal care services differed greatly by state. Nine indicators of antenatal care were considered. Kerala and Tamil Nadu each ranked highest on four of the nine indicators, but Arunachal Pradesh, Nagaland, Uttar Pradesh,

Jharkhand, and Rajasthan performed poorly on most of the indicators. Compared with Tamil Nadu, for example, where 96 per cent of mothers had three or more antenatal care visits, only 17 per cent of mothers in Bihar and 27 per cent in Uttar Pradesh had three or more visits. This shows that the record of antenatal care in some states is quite dismal. It is also found that in India as a whole, mothers of only 15 per cent of births received all of the required components of antenatal care. This indicator ranges from a high of 64 per cent in Kerala and 56 per cent in Goa to a low of only 2 per cent in Nagaland and 4 per cent in Uttar Pradesh. Kerala, followed closely by Goa, also outperformed all other states in terms of delivery care, with nearly all deliveries taking place in medical institutions and a similarly high percentage of deliveries assisted by a health professional. Other states that performed almost as poorly as Uttar Pradesh and Nagaland on all the required components of antenatal care indicators include Bihar, Arunachal Pradesh, Madhya Pradesh, Jharkhand, Meghalaya, Rajasthan, and Mizoram, where only 6-9 per cent of women received the recommended components of antenatal care.

Public Health and Health System in India

The Health Survey and Development Committee, also known as the Bhore Committee (1946), was appointed in 1943 and submitted its report in 1946 (before India got Independence in 1947). This report is considered as the backbone of India's health planning and programmes. It laid emphasis on integration of curative and preventive medicines at all levels. It suggested development of one Primary Health Centre (PHC), manned by two doctors, one nurse, four public health nurses, four midwives, four trained dais, two sanitary inspectors, two health assistants, one pharmacist and fifteen other class IV employees, for a population of 40,000, and a secondary health centre, to provide support to PHC, and to coordinate and supervise their functioning. But the model recommended by the committee was never implemented in totality. On the basis of the recommendation of the various committees (Mudaliar Committee, Chadda Committee, Mukherji Committee, Jugalwalla Committee, Kartar Singh Committee, etc.), national/international directives, and health policies, a specific health structure has developed in India. A large number of specific disease control programmes (such as National Malaria Control Programme, National Leprosy Eradication Programme, National Tuberculosis Control Programme, National Cancer Control Programme, etc.) were designed and implemented as vertical programmes to address the specific diseases, and these vertical programmes rather than an integrated health programme became the core of health structure in India.

In the Constitution of India health is defined as a State subject, though the Centre plays an important role as regulator, advisor and resource provider. The Government is obligated to provide health care to every citizen of India. The health sector in India is characterized by: (i) a Government sector that provides publicly financed and managed curative and preventive health services from primary to tertiary level, throughout the country and free of cost to the consumer (these account for about 18 per cent of the overall health spending and 0.9 per cent of the GDP), and (ii) a fee-levying private sector that plays a dominant role in the provision of individual curative care through ambulatory services and accounts for about 82 per cent of the overall health expenditure and 4.2 per cent of the GDP. The provision of health care by the public sector is a responsibility shared by State, Central, and local Governments, although it is effectively a State responsibility in terms of service delivery (See, Advani and Akram, 2007).

The organization of health care services in the country extends from the national level to village level. At the national level health services are organized by the Union Ministry of Health and Family Welfare. The Ministry has three departments, namely, Health; Family Welfare; and, Indian System of Medicine and Homoeopathy (ISM & H). At the State level health services are organized by the Department of Health and Family Welfare, headed by a Minister. At the grassroots level, health care facilities are available in the form of Community Health Centre (CHC), Primary Health Centre (PHC), and Sub-Centre (SC). One CHC is established for every 80,000 to 1,20,000 population, and this centre provides the basic speciality services in general medicine, paediatrics, surgery, obstetrics, and gynaecology. Further down, there is one PHC covering about 30,000 (20,000 in hilly, desert, and difficult terrains) or more population. Each PHC has one medical officer, two health assistants — one male and one female — and supported by health workers and staff. The most peripheral health facility is the Sub-Centre (SC) manned by one male and one female multi-purpose health worker for a population of 5,000 in plains and 3,000 in hilly and tribal areas (For a detailed discussion, see Akram 2014).

Challenges in the Medical Care and Health System

India had its first National Health Policy (NHP) in 1983 and before it only vertical health programmes existed which focussed on control and treatment of various infectious diseases. Besides this, family planning and population control programmes were implemented to arrest rising growth of population of India. Health was never seen in a holistic perspective and the focus of health programmes remained on clinical treatment of 'diseases'. The second National Health Policy (2002) came in the aftermath of Millennium Development Goals (MDGs). The Centrally sponsored, National Rural Health Mission (NRHM) was launched in 2005 (NRHM, 2005) to ensure participation of the local self-government institutions at village panchayat level in a participatory manner. This has produced mixed results. There are several challenges in the health system. Some of these are discussed below.

(a) *Limited Reach and Scope of Primary Health Care*

Primary health care is the backbone of the health system in India. The Alma Ata Declaration (1978) has given a very comprehensive definition of primary health care (as discussed earlier). However, most of the elements suggested for primary health care seldom find any mention in the structuring of 'Primary Health Centres (PHCs)' in India. According to the declaration, primary health care includes awareness about health problems and the methods of preventing and controlling them. Factors like food supply and proper nutrition, safe water and basic sanitation, maternal and child health care, prevention and control of locally endemic disease, appropriate treatment of common disease and injuries, and, provision of essential drugs are also included but less emphasized in practice. PHCs focus mostly on treatment of common diseases and injuries, immunization, and provision of essential drugs. If we go back to the Bhore Committee Report submitted in 1946, we find that many of the radical suggestions made by the committee have never been implemented. The PHCs in India have adopted only the clinical aspects from the Alma Ata's definition of primary health care; education about prevailing health problems, food supply and nutrition, adequate supply of safe water and basic sanitation, etc. remained beyond the purview of PHCs. Further, the PHCs are understaffed and in majority of States suffer from the problem of absenteeism and lack of physical resources.

(b) *Lack of Infrastructure*

Lack of health care infrastructure is a major problem in India. The shortfall in health infrastructure as per 2011 population in various States of India is presented in Table 7.2. At the level of Sub-Centres, Bihar

Table 7.2: Shortfall in Health Infrastructure as per 2011 Population (Provisional) in India (as on March, 2012)

Sl. No.	State/UT	Total Population in Rural Areas	Sub-Centres				PHCs				CHCs			
			R	P	S	% Shortfall	R	P	S	% Shortfall	R	P	S	% Shortfall
1.	Andhra Pradesh	5,63,11,788	12,283	12,522	*	*	2,004	1,624	380	19	501	281	220	44
2.	Assam[3]	2,67,80,516	5,841	4,604	1,237	21	953	975	*	*	238	109	129	54
3.	Bihar	92,075,028	18,533	9,696	8,837	48	3,083	1,863	1,220	40	770	70	700	91
4.	Gujarat[4]	3,46,70,817	9,156	7,274	1,882	21	1,433	1,158	275	19	358	318	40	11
5.	Haryana[4]	1,65,31,493	4,159	2,520	1,639	39	657	447	210	32	164	109	55	34
6.	Jammu & Kashmir[1]	91,34,820	3,044	1,907	1,137	37	456	396	60	13	114	84	30	26
7.	Jharkhand	2,50,36,946	6,043	3,958	2,085	35	964	330	634	66	241	188	53	22
8.	Kerala	1,74,55,506	3,525	4,575	*	*	586	809	*	*	146	217	*	*
9.	Madhya Pradesh	5,25,37,899	12,314	8,869	3,445	28	1,977	1,156	821	42	494	333	161	33
10.	Maharashtra	6,15,45,441	13,410	10,580	2,830	21	2,189	1,811	378	17	547	363	184	34
11.	Odisha	3,49,51,234	8,136	6,688	1,448	18	1,308	1,226	82	6	327	377	*	*
12.	Punjab	1,73,16,800	3,463	2,951	512	15	577	449	128	22	144	132	12	8
13.	Rajasthan[4]	5,15,40,236	15,172	11,487	3,685	24	2,326	1,528	798	34	581	382	199	34
14.	Tamil Nadu[2]	3,71,89,229	7,555	8,706	*	*	1,254	1,227	27	2	313	385	*	*
15.	Uttarakhand	70,25,583	2,341	1,848	493	21	351	257	94	27	87	59	28	32
16.	Uttar Pradesh	15,51,11,022	31,037	20,521	10,516	34	5,172	3,692	1,480	29	1,293	515	778	60
17.	West Bengal[2]	6,22,13,676	13,186	10,356	2,830	21	2,166	909	1,257	58	541	348	193	36
	India	**83,30,87,662**	**1,89,094**	**1,48,366**	**43,776**	**23**	**30,565**	**24,049**	**7,954**	**26**	**7,631**	**4,833**	**3,044**	**40**

R : Required; P : In Position; S : Shortfall; * : Surplus

(*Contd.*)

Table 7.2 (*Contd.*)

Notes: The requirement is calculated using the prescribed norms on the basis of provisional rural population from Census, 2011 and estimated rural tribal population in 2011 using % of tribal population out of rural population in 2001. All India shortfall is derived by adding state-wise figures of shortfall ignoring the existing surplus in some of the states.

1. As the entire State is included under Hill Area Development Programme, the total rural population of the State is taken as in the Tribal/Hilly/Desert areas.
2. The rural population of districts included under the Hill Area Development Programme has been added in the rural population under Tribal/Hilly/Desert areas.
3. The two districts in Assam, namely North Cachar and Karbi Anglong are included in the list of districts under Hill Area Development Programme. However, as these two districts are having more than 50 per cent tribal population, no change is made in the rural population under Tribal/Hilly/Desert Areas.
4. The rural population of districts included under the Desert Development Programme (DDP) also added in the rural population under Tribal/Hilly/Desert areas.

Source: Rural Health Statistics in India 2012. www.mohfw.nic.in/shawfile.php?lid=2279

shows a huge shortfall of 48 per cent. Haryana, Jammu & Kashmir and Jharkhand are other States with massive shortfall. Kerala, Tamil Nadu and Andhra Pradesh are three States with surplus number of Sub-Centres. We have seen that these States with surplus Sub-Centres perform very well in terms of health index (Table 7.1). Further, at the level of Primary Health Centres, States like Jharkhand and West Bengal reflect huge shortfall. Even Bihar, Madhya Pradesh and Rajasthan show massive shortfall. Primary Health Centres are the backbone of health care delivery system in India. At the level of Community Health Centres, States like Bihar and Uttar Pradesh show shortfall of 91 per cent and 60 per cent respectively. These figures suggest that these facilities are almost non-existent in these States.

(c) *Lack of Health Professionals*

Table 7.3 shows the situation related to availability of male health workers in various States of India. Table 7.3 reflects the vacant positions at the level of Sub-Centres and also computes the shortfalls. The States like Uttar Pradesh, Andhra Pradesh, West Bengal, Maharashtra, Karnataka, etc. show that huge number of vacant positions exist at the level of Sub-Centres. Further, these States also reflect huge shortfalls in terms of availability of male health workers also. States like Uttar Pradesh, Bihar, Madhya Pradesh and Rajasthan present huge shortfalls in terms of their population. Thus, the poor performance of these States in health outcome can be appropriately explained by the huge vacant positions and shortfalls in terms of availability of health workers at the grassroots levels.

Table 7.3: Shortfall of Health Worker [Male] at Sub-Centres

Sl. No.	State/UT	Required[1] [R]	Sanctioned [S]	In Position [P]	Vacant [S-P]	Shortfall [R-P]
1.	Andhra Pradesh	12,522	7,601	4,608	2,993	7,914
2.	Assam	4,604	NA	2,386	NA	2,218
3.	Bihar#	9,696	2,135	1,074	1,061	8,622
4.	Chhattisgarh	5,111	4,784	2,514	2,270	2,597
5.	Goa	205	150	137	13	68
6.	Gujarat#	7,274	7,239	4,874	2,365	2,400
7.	Haryana	2,520	NA	1,682	NA	838
8.	Himachal Pradesh	2,065	2,008	1,183	825	882
9.	Jammu & Kashmir	1,907	1,907	541	1,366	1,366
10.	Jharkhand	3,958	NA	957	NA	3,001
11.	Karnataka	8,871	5,853	3,148	2,705	5,723
12.	Kerala#	4,575	1,399	1,285	114	3,290
13.	Madhya Pradesh	8,869	5,300	3,733	1,567	5,136
14.	Maharashtra#	10,580	10,579	6,665	3,914	3,915
15.	Meghalaya+	397	84	133	*	264
16.	Nagaland#	396	276	234	42	162
17.	Odisha	6,688	4,729	3,827	902	2,861
18.	Punjab	2,951	2,858	1,694	1,164	1,257
19.	Rajasthan	11,487	2,217	1,592	625	9,895
20.	Tamil Nadu	8,706	2,896	1,266	1,630	7,440
21.	Tripura	719	NA	543	NA	176
22.	Uttarakhand	1,848	920	184	736	1,664
23.	Uttar Pradesh	20,521	9,080	1,729	7,351	18,792
24.	West Bengal#	10,356	9,457	4,478	4,979	5,878

Notes: # Data for 2011 repeated.
+ Data for 2010 repeated.
NA Not Available.
* Surplus. All India figures for Vacancy and Shortfall are the totals of State-wise Vacancy and Shortfall ignoring surplus in some States/UTs.

1. One per each existing Sub-Centre.
2. For calculating the overall percentages of vacancy and shortfall, the States/UTs for which manpower position is not available, may be excluded.

Source: RHS 2012, p. 55 (As on March, 2012).

(d) *Policy Shift and Privatization*

The policy shifts in last two decades favour privatization of healthcare services in India. It has also paved the path of health tourism for the health consumers coming from abroad. But the policies are almost silent on broadening the base or the scope of public health facilities at the national level. On the other hand, despite tall claims, the total fund allocation for implementing the various health programmes is dismal.

For policy to be effective, it is desirable that health financing is so adequate to reduce the overall out-of-pocket (OoP) expenditure on health care, and protect against financial catastrophe related to health care. The global standard related to the 'desirable' limit of OoP to protect people from financial catastrophe is less than 15 per cent of total health spending. In contrast, in India, the OoP is to the tune of 71 per cent of total health spending (Ministry of Health and Family Welfare, 2010). The per capita public health spending is low in India, being among the five lowest in the world. Consequently, 3.2 per cent Indians fall below the poverty line because of high medical bills. Further, about 70 per cent of Indians spend their entire income on health care and purchasing drugs, according to the WHO (Sinha, 2011).

It is also important to note here that the out-of-pocket expenditure on health care forms a major barrier to health seeking in India. According to the National Sample Survey Organization (NSSO), the year 2004 saw 28 per cent of ailments in rural areas go untreated due to financial reasons — up from 15 per cent in 1995-96. Similarly, in urban areas, 20 per cent of ailments were untreated due to financial reasons — up from 10 per cent in 1995-96 (Ministry of Health and Family Welfare, 2010). However, the Government has not done much to make the funds available to the needy. Responding to the initiative of WHO to find new means and ways for coverage of health needs of people, Government of India constituted a High Level Expert Group (HLEG) in 2010 to evolve a new model of Universal Health Coverage (UHC) for providing universal accessibility and affordability of health care for all (HLEG, 2011). But the practices at the grassroots level are far from the theory.

(e) *Limited Budgetary Allocation*

Limited budgetary allocation from the Central and State Governments is a big hurdle. In developed countries, Government health spending is more than 5 per cent of the GDP (Norway — 6.9% of GDP, USA — 6.2% of GDP, etc.). Even in developed Asian countries excluding India, the average health spending is around 3 per cent of the GDP (Government Health Expenditure in India: A Benchmark Study, 2006). India, which is currently seen as an economic powerhouse and one of the success stories of global economic growth in the past decade, has government health expenditure amounting to less than 1 per cent of GDP (Mukhta, 2011). Further, this ratio is not only low from the international standard but over the years it has been declining. The low spending on health and the dominance of private sources of financing lead to public health problems in India (Sodani, 2007). It may be noted that the proportion of public spending on health in India is low, partly because India has a rather low per capita income, but also because of the low percentage of public spending on health. This shows that the Government of India accords relatively low priority that to the health sector (High Level Expert Group, 2011) (for details on health expenditure also see, Khanday and Akram, 2013).

(f) *Over-medicalization*

Medicalization is a multidimensional issue and refers to several things: identifying new medical territories; increasing medical hegemony and gaze; and, pharmaceuticizing the food and drinks, etc. (Ballard and Elston, 2005; Lowenberg, and Davis, 1994). Medicalization of health budget caused substantial proportions of the health budgets to go on expanding subsidized medical training, public sector employment for medical graduates, and high-end tertiary medical services — all of which benefit the middle class more and detract from the provision of public and primary health services. One of the consequences of over-medicalization, in India, is that the field of 'primary health care' becomes narrow. One further variant of overmedicalization in India is allocation of much of the budgetary allocations meant for health to medical functions. Health is often used (selectively and consciously) as synonymously with medical. In all such situations, all other social and environmental dimensions of health are relegated to the background. Consequently, the very important health components, like the Basic Health Goods (BHGs) become victim of medical (say, financial) negligence and 'overlooking'.

(g) *Narrowing of Public Health*

The notion of primary health care is supposed to rest upon the system of 'public health'. The Expert Committee of the WHO has defined *public health* as the "science and art of preventing diseases, prolonging life and promoting mental and physical health and efficiency through organized community efforts for the sanitation of the environment, the control of communicable infection, the education of the individual's personal hygiene, the organization of medical and nursing services for early diagnosis and preventive treatment of disease, the development of the social machinery to ensure to every individual a standard of living, adequate for the maintenance of health and so organizing these benefits as to enable every citizen to realize his birth right of health and longevity" (WHO, 1952). Looked at from this perspective, public health in India is in a dilapidated condition. The high rate of prevalence of communicable diseases is a testimony of it. There is no formal identifiable structure for promoting public health in India and the existing institutions are getting diluted. The creation of the Public Health Foundation of India (PHFI) is more cosmetic than structural (because of lack of supporting infrastructure and undefined target/resource base). No specific budget is earmarked for various requirements under public health. Water, sanitation, food, nutrition, adulteration, etc. are not seen from a comprehensive public health perspective. With the increasing medicalization of health structures and stress on curative treatment, public health services are gradually relegated to the background. Reviewing the state of public health in India Das Gupta (2005) found several conditions and factors responsible for poor state of public health in India. Some of these conditions reflect the limits of public health in contemporary India and most of its States.

(h) *Health Coverage in India*

The High Level Expert Group (HLEG) constituted in 2010 for suggesting the model of Universal Health Coverage (UHC) for India talked about financing; resource generation; ensuring access to essential drugs, vaccines and medical technology; and, allowing participation of private for-profit sectors in delivery of health care in India but was almost silent on what is meant by 'universal coverage'. The Central Government is yet to start any viable health coverage programme that can benefit the vulnerable and marginalized sections of society at all-India level. Only a few States have started some programmes to meet specific needs of the vulnerable groups. Even in such programmes, the amount covered is very less and cannot meet out the high cost of private medical care. Universal health coverage in India cannot be completely attained only through insurance policies because a large number of diseases are acute but recurrent. Health insurance is a more viable institution for meeting out the expenditure required in treatment of non-communicable diseases. Initially, the government laid Terms of References (ToR) said nothing about the social determinants of health and these were included on the insistence of some members later (HLEG, 2010). Above all, the ToRs completely ignored that WHO had suggested an equitable coverage and not an equal coverage to all. An equitable coverage is the right means to address the problems of health inequality that India is increasingly realizing (Akram, 2012).

(i) *Policy Deficits and Implementation Deficits*

Many of the States in India have a lackadaisical approach towards making universal availability of primary health care and BHGs. The practice of denying primary health care and BHGs to the population or a part of it or even gradual withdrawal from it is denial of health chance and it can conveniently be termed as 'dehealthism' (Akram, 2012). 'Dehealthism' when not promoted by the State but caused by its apathy and ignorance may be termed as 'ahealthism'. Any group, community or state practicing dehealthism or ahealthism can't achieve the goal of health for all, no matter how much medicalization is promoted. Often, dehealthism or ahealthism is a result of wilful undermedicalization. The very ambitious policy initiative of Government of India, NRHM, has missed the importance of sanitation, potable water and nutrition as health enabling factors. The Village Health, Sanitation and Nutrition Committees which are responsible for promoting nutrition, sanitation, and quality of drinking water are simply performing some token services at the village level because each of them needs a major economic investment. It gives the impression that health policies and plans in India are designed and regulated in a way that BHGs are becoming victim of 'medical neglecting'. 'Overmedicalization of health', 'privatization of health care', and 'pharmaceuticization of health behaviour' are the dominant trends of Indian health scenario promoting dehealthism.

The underachievement of various development plans and programmes and the wastage and pilferage of the resources are 'bureaucratically managed' by blaming the people for their cultural poverty and illiteracy (povertism). Also, the poorly designed public health institutions are further degraded by 'medical absenteeism'. In place of blaming the health organization and governance (for example, absenteeism among medical professionals) health problems are as attributed to people's traditionalism and lack of preference for institutional care. Further, blaming illiteracy as the cause of prevalence of communicable disease among rural or urban poor is also a part of the larger mechanism of blaming people for inadequate institution building, improper policy making, inefficient programme implementation, unprofessional and *ad hoc* target making. The bureaucratic managers divert all the issues of negligence, absenteeism and discrimination through capitalizing povertism (*see*, Akram, 2012).

Medical managers and vested interests are playing dominant role in redesigning the public domains of 'health care' and 'health coverage' as 'medical care' and 'medical coverage'. The cumulative and compounding negative consequences of 'medical neglecting', targetism, povertism, absenteeism and 'overmedicalism' are manifested in continuous perpetuation of prevalence of communicable disease in India. Even globalization and market forces, in different forms and facades, advocate dehealthism for promoting private interests through invisible networking. The World Bank through its various publications and recommendations has argued for strengthening of private health care with the state shifting its role from being a provider to controller and regulator of services and their quality (Qadeer, 2011). Needless to say, the global agencies dictate 'terms of reference' to the Government for constitution of commissions which will work for promoting their interests. The adoption of managerial or techno-managerial approaches and strategies in policy and planning making serves the interests of various such invisible agencies (Sivaramakrishnan, 2012).

Resource Deprivation and Quality of Life

While the term 'quality' implies the degree of excellence of a characteristic, quality of life means different things to different people (Carr, Higginson and Robinson, 2003). According to the WHO's Quality of Life Group's (WHOQOLG) definition, it refers to ". . . individuals' perception of their position in life in the context of the culture and value systems in which they live and in relation to their goals, expectations, and standards and concerns. It is a broad-ranging concept affected in a complex way by the person's physical health, psychological state, level of independence, social relationships, and their relationships to salient features of their environment" (WHO, 1993). It is also a concept that is dependent on the perceptions of individuals. Research has cast doubt on the power of objective variables alone in predicting quality of life ratings, especially in view of the paradox of well-being (Mroczek and Kolarz, 1998).

Quality of life is a collection of interacting objective and subjective dimensions. Thus, it is a dynamic concept; values and self-evaluations of life may change over time in response to life and health events and experiences. Each area of quality of life can also have knock on effects on the others. Quality of life is a multidimensional concept and its parts affect each other as well as the sum. For the most part quality of life denotes bunches of *qualities* of life, bunches that can be ordered on the basis of two distinctions. The first distinction is between *opportunities* for a good life and the *outcomes* of life. A second difference is between *external* and *inner* qualities. Quality of life necessitates certain basic resources. In a situation of resource deprivation, not only the subjective perception, but also the objective quality of living environment gets down. The states of illness and sickness (as discussed earlier) depend a lot on the perceptions of the individual and the group about the state of disease. And hence, the prevailing quality of life perceptions and the resource bases play very important role in deciding the operationalization of the treatment and care. Some of the important quality of life factors which play an important role in deciding the nature of intervention (from treatment to health care) in the trajectory of health-disease-illness-sickness-treatment-health are discussed here.

(a) *Nutrition and Food Security*

More than a fourth of the world's hungry are Indians. "As per the WHO's standards, 40 per cent of Indian children under the age of 3 are underweight, 45 per cent are stunted and 23 per cent have wasting" (HLEG 2011:278). Malnutrition itself is the result of several other determinants that have extended and extenuating lifetime impact on the health and well-being of women and their children (Jose and Navaneetham, 2010). Even economically developed states — Gujarat, Maharashtra, Andhra Pradesh and Karnataka — have high level of food insecurity (United Nations World Food Programme, 2008). Further, the focus of India's current nutrition programmes has been on supplementary nutrition and preschool education for 4-6 year olds, belying the need to focus adequately on the first 2 years of a child's life — critical to prevent undernutrition and its sequelae (Paul, *et al.*, 2011). The High Level Expert Group Report (2011) acknowledges that even as breastfeeding should be advocated as a universal practice up to at least six months of the infant's age, the circumstances that govern the life of a poor working mother (who has access to neither maternity leave nor a nearby crèche) must be borne in mind. In urban areas, the decline in food insecurity between 2000 and 2006 has been by a margin of only 0.4 per cent, out of step with the 6 per cent growth rate in the same period. Nutrition is a social determinant of health and is itself influenced by many other social determinants. Vertical programmes will, therefore, not provide complete or lasting solutions.

(b) *Water and Sanitation*

There is a clear correlation between inadequate and poor quality of water or sanitation and health. The High Level Expert Group Report (2011) also refers to a study of urban poor communities in Mumbai which found that water-related diseases accounted for almost a third of all diseases among adults, and almost two-thirds of all diseases among children. Another study in five Indian States found a negative correlation between the provision of household toilets and community level prevalence of communicable diseases including cholera, typhoid/enteric disease, diarrhoea/vomiting, hepatitis, nematodal infections as well as malaria and dengue. A 2002 Planning Commission report expressed alarm over the "rather extensive presence" of fluoride and arsenic in Indian drinking water, which is associated with a number of cancers (of the skin, lungs, kidneys, and bladder). According to the Water and Sanitation Programme, the cost per Disability Adjusted Life Year (DALY) of poor sanitation in urban areas is estimated at ₹ 5,400 (HLEGR, 2011). Another major finding is that use of improved facilities is strongly correlated with sanitation related knowledge and hygiene-promotion attitudes.

(c) *Social Exclusion*

Social exclusion in India is commonly defined in terms of gender, caste and community. In rural India, women are three times more likely than men to go without treatment for long-term ailments, a trend that persists even amongst the non-poor. When treatment is sought, significantly smaller sums of money are spent on treatment of women than on men (HLEG, R. 2011). Provisional data from the 2011 Census suggests that gender inequity is a persistent and worsening phenomenon in India, occurring throughout the life-cycle: a 13 point decline in the male-female sex ratio from 927 females per 1,000 males in 2001 to 914 females per 1,000 males in 2011 suggests that as more families are having fewer children, gendering of sex composition is rising. Girls that survive till adolescence must navigate situations of both wanton neglect and unwanted attention: a study of backward districts in 12 Indian States is found that 88 per cent of adolescent girls were undernourished while almost two-thirds (64.6%) reported some form of sexual abuse (HLEGR, 2011).

Apart from gender, social status is also associated with systemic neglect and poor health. Caste and social stratification in India determine health, education, employment, social, and economic outcomes. For example, Indians in the lowest socio-economic stratum presently experience cardiovascular disease in greater proportions than those in higher strata. National Sample Survey Data (NSSD) reveal that, controlling for a number of determinants (such as gender, residence in a forward or backward State, urban or rural areas, living conditions, and socio-economic status), the mean age of death was 5-7 years lower among Scheduled Tribes (ST) and Scheduled Castes (SC) and 6-9 years lower among Muslims in comparison to Hindus.

Data for Kerala for the year 2006 suggests that even in a State with good health outcomes, the odds of reporting poor health are 88 per cent higher among ST/SC and 73 per cent higher among Other Backward Classes (OBC) women as compared to forward castes (HLEG, R. 2011). The gravity of caste-based social exclusion is seeing recognition in the incorporation of this indicator in the 2011 Census. The health of tribal populations is also of particular concern. The National Family Health Survey (IIPS, 2007) found a complete lack of treatment for diarrhoea for over a third of respondents from Scheduled Tribes (36.3%), as compared to 27.6 per cent among Scheduled Castes, 28.2 per cent among Other Backward Castes, and less than a quarter among the rest of the Indian population (23.8%). Multiple studies have found that tribal children face the greatest incidence of malnutrition in India, particularly in the States of Jharkhand, Bihar, Madhya Pradesh, Chhattisgarh, Odisha, and West Bengal. There are significant inter-state differences in health indicators as discussed earlier.

(d) *Work (in) Security, Occupational Health and Disasters*

Globalization and the concomitant casualization of labour have resulted in the growth of informal economies that account for 93 per cent of the Indian workforce. Migrant workers are among the poorest and most exploited, performing low level, unskilled and hazardous work. This population faces significant disease burden including musculoskeletal injuries, chronic obstructive lung diseases, toxic chemical exposure and poisoning and noise-induced hearing loss. Rapid urbanization has spurred concentration of services and industries in cities, at times making them epicentres of protracted public health disasters, like the 1984 methyl-isocyanate leak in Bhopal. In rare cases, like the plague in Surat, Social Determinants of Health crises have catalyzed reforms in sanitation and health services. Civil conflict is also associated with poor health: political combatants and refugees in Chhattisgarh face epidemic like situations of malnutrition, malaria, and other communicable diseases.

Health Illusion and Illness Doubts

The conditions of 'disease' prevailing among vulnerable groups in India, very often, are not getting the social recognition of state of 'sickness' or 'illness' and hence, the state ignores or misses the required intervention of treatment through 'medical and health care intervention'. Several factors like socio-cultural patterns, political economy constraints and medico-pathological indifferences play important role in this. Lack of optimum public facilities and absence of quality of life factors often mitigate the differences between the 'symptoms and pains' of pathological conditions of 'disease' and social conditions of 'resource deprivation' creating 'illness doubts' and 'health illusions' within the overall understanding of illness and health care discourses. Although there is lack of comprehensive data on morbidity in terms of the social background of the concerned persons, data provided by National Council of Applied Economic Research (NCAER) can be used for a better understanding of the issue. The data was collected by NCAER from a rural sample of 33,230 households drawn from 16 States and the survey was conducted between January and May 1994. The survey was commissioned by the Planning Commission and financed by a consortium of international organizations such as UNDP, UNICEF, UNFPA, CIDA/ IDRC (*see* India: Human Development Report — A Profile of Indian States in the 1990s).

An analysis of the data on Short Duration Morbidity Prevalence Rate (MPR-SD) and Point Prevalence Rate for Major Morbidity (PPR-MM) among the Age Group 15-34 against the Household Income Groups compiled by NCAER for the year 1994 helps us to understand the larger trajectory of disease-illness-sickness-health care. Incidences of diarrhoea, cough and cold, and unspecified fevers during a 30-day reference period preceding the date of survey were considered as constituting short duration morbidity. The MPR-SD for all-India worked out to 122 per 1000 population for the 30-day reference period. For estimating the Point Prevalence Rate for Major Morbidity (PPR-MM), the medication of any of the family members in a household for chronic or major illness (such as epilepsy, heart disease, hypertension, tuberculosis, diabetes, mental disorders, and leprosy) was taken into account. The survey enabled estimation of the all-India Point Prevalence Rate for all ages and all types of major morbidity and worked out to be 4,578 per lakh population. Table 7.4 presents these data to make a comparison between States. It is noteworthy that the prevalence of both MPR-SD and PPR-MM is adjusted for per thousand populations.

Table 7.4: Prevalence Rate (Per Thousand Population) of Short Duration Morbidity among Age Group 15-34 Years by States

Sl. No.	*State*	*Household Income Groups (₹ per year)*				
		Up to 20,000	*20,001-40,000*	*40,001-62,000*	*Above 62,000*	*All Groups*
1.	Uttar Pradesh	57	50	52	43	53
2.	Madhya Pradesh	124	115	108	100	117
3.	Odisha	94	90	75	76	91
4.	Rajasthan	76	65	65	54	69
5.	West Bengal	139	92	85	55	119
6.	Maharashtra	65	42	45	48	54
7.	Bihar	78	71	55	67	73
8.	Tamil Nadu	134	141	113	136	135
9.	Kerala	56	42	6	14	41

Source: India: Human Development Report — A Profile of Indian States in the 1990s.

Table 7.5: Prevalence Rate (Per Thousand Population) of Major Morbidity among Age Group 15-34 Years by States

Sl. No.	*State*	*Household Income Groups (₹ per year)*				
		Up to 20,000	*20,001-40,000*	*40,001-62,000*	*Above 62,000*	*All Groups*
1.	Uttar Pradesh	20	29	29	29	25
2.	Madhya Pradesh	23	29	21	25	25
3.	Odisha	28	35	27	40	30
4.	Rajasthan	17	16	24	38	20
5.	West Bengal	36	44	43	33	38
6.	Maharashtra	26	9	17	17	19
7.	Bihar	29	25	1	19	25
8.	Tamil Nadu	33	42	43	26	36
9.	Kerala	37	25	10	6	26

Source: India: Human Development Report — A Profile of Indian States in the 1990s.

The figures given in Table 7.4 reflect that the instances of MPR-SD are decreasing with the increasing household income levels in most of the states. It suggests that in the lower income households, the prevalence of short duration morbidities is high. As the level of income is increasing, the prevalence is largely decreasing. It should be noted here that the short duration diseases like diarrhoea, cough and cold, and unspecified fevers are largely symptomatic and easily identifiable. Hence, the instances of diseases are easily diagnosed and the households (or the individuals suffering from such morbidities).

However, the trend is almost reverse in about the prevalence of PPR-MM in some of the poor performing States (Table 7.5). The data on PPR-MM reflect the identified cases of chronic or major illness (such as epilepsy, heart disease, hypertension, tuberculosis, diabetes, mental disorders, and leprosy) for which some medication is going on. In several States — Uttar Pradesh, Madhya Pradesh, Odisha, Rajasthan, West Bengal and Tamil Nadu — the instances of PPR-MM increase with the increasing income level of the household. Keeping in mind the overall health situation of these States, it is unlikely that the cases of PPR-MM will be actually low in the lower income groups and high in the higher income groups. The trend is very different in a State like Kerala, where the instances of PPR-MM are decreasing with the increasing income level. Thus, a possible explanation is that among the poor, the cases of PPR-MM go undiagnosed and unreported. The most important causes of such unreported morbidities are the prevalence of conditions of 'health illusion' and 'illness doubts'. In the lower income groups, the cases of PPR-MM often go untreated and under diagnosed. A situation in which disease is prevalent and suffering is realized but sickness is not recognized because of lack of diagnosis or failure of social capital is a state of 'illness doubt'. Persistence of illness doubt over a long period of time and failure in obtaining health care for treatment of the problem gives a pseudo feeling of being healthy. This pseudo feeling of being healthy despite persistence of ailment is a state of 'health illusion'. An important reason for prevalence of state of 'health illusion' is the fact that pains and suffering of such morbidities are not much different from the pains and sufferings of resource deprivations.

Conclusion

The popular grand narrative on disease (largely the bio-medical approach) ignores the social construction of states of illness and sickness. Similarly, the narratives on 'medical care' largely ignore 'health care' components. In the absence of macro-level health care variables (the BHGs like food and nutrition, potable drinking water, hygiene and sanitation) and favourable SDs (education, income, electricity, inclusive policy, etc.), the diseases hardly get the cognizance of illness and sickness and hence, remain far away from possible interventions through clinical care or other treatment and health care. The official discourse on health care is constrained by the absence of BHGs and SDs. Thus, a habitus is built which is more disease friendly than health friendly and people living within those conditions develop social worlds which fail to make a distinction between a pathological condition and a resource deprivation condition. Lack of appropriate social capital needed for making health care intervention perpetuates the situation. The health programmes are constructed without taking into consideration the actual objective conditions of the pain and infirmity and fail to make a dent on the poverty and the lifestyle compulsions. Lack of sanitation, food adulteration and poor quality of drinking water, important determinants of disease (both communicable and non-communicable), diminish the differences between 'health' and 'health illusion'. The poor intervention made by the Government agencies in developing the public facilities (say health care) fail to create appropriate public spheres which is very important for the poor, marginalized and vulnerable groups in a welfare society as it promises to deliver public goods. Under the existing conditions, there is hardly any distinction between the 'public' and 'private' spheres for these social categories.

Despite more than six decades of planned development, even the medical facilities in most of the poor performing States are scanty. We have already seen the criminal negligence in providing the basic health care infrastructure and manpower. Shortfall of medical staff and absenteeism of the existing staff have reduced the existing medical facilities to mere symbolism. The larger government interventions for ensuring health for all, in many of the States are still confined to only medicalized interventions. The National Rural Health Mission, introduced in 2005 as an architectural correction for the health initiatives, still lack in providing the necessary impetus in the desired direction. The health policies, at a larger level, do not respond to the health needs of the population in the poor performing States. The sanitation needs are undefined, food adulteration is uncontrolled, safe drinking water is unmentioned and nutrition is unimagined. There is no space for basic health goods in health policies and programmes. The use of insecticides and pesticides in agriculture is uncontrolled and unregulated. The pollution level of the industries is unchecked. The garbage producing urban spaces are going unnoticed. The groundwater is getting polluted day-by-day. The lack of medical attention is very obvious. This medical indifference is pathetic.

The chapter can be concluded saying that several conditions like lack of public health facilities, social discriminations and marginalization, medical indifference, overmedicalization of limited medical interventions through corporatization, profit orientations of private and corporate sectors and bureaucratic managerialism create the disease-friendly 'habitus' and 'social worlds' for the vulnerable and distance them from the interventions of health care. Illness doubts prevail along with the sickness. The state of health is being encountered by the state of health illusion. Under these conditions, the poorly designed health programmes and policies and their deficient implementations make the contributions of limited health care facilities insignificant. The health needs of the deprived and the vulnerable categories remain unaddressed. Health inequality is growing. The government is promoting medical tourism for all those who can afford to pay and leaving the rest to go for further impoverishment. Unfortunately, the principle of distributive justice is yet to be actualized in the domain of health care in India.

NOTES

1. HDI = 1/3 (Health index + Education Index + Income index).
2. The Health Index is computed using life expectancy at birth for the years 2000 and 2008. The IHDR (2011) has used the SRS, Report of the Technical Group on Population Projections 2001-26 as data source for projected levels of life expectancy at birth.
3. The Income Index is computed as the per capita consumption expenditure adjusted for inflation and inequality (Gini coefficient). The data sources for computing Income Index is NSS 1999-2000 and 2007-2008.
4. The Education Index is a weighted average of literacy and adjusted mean years of schooling. It is defined as: Education index = 1/3 (literacy index) + 2/3 (adjusted mean years of schooling index) where Literacy Index = Literacy rate of population (aged 7+).

REFERENCES

Advani, M. and Akram, M. (2007). "Health Concerns in India", in M. Akram (ed.), *Health Dynamics and Marginalized Communities* (pp. 3-26), Jaipur: Rawat Publications.

Akram, M. (2007). "Introduction", in M. Akram (ed.), *Health Dynamics and Marginalized Communities* (pp. 9-20), Jaipur: Rawat Publications.

Akram, M. (2012). "Looking Beyond the Universal Health Coverage: Health Inequality, Medicalism and Dehealthism in India", *Public Health Research*, 2(6), 221-28.

Akram, M. (2014). *Sociology of Health*, Jaipur: Rawat Publications.

Akram, M. and Beg, S.R. (2014). "Health Inequalities in India and the Challenges before Social Transformation", in I. Modi (ed.), *Polity, Civil Society, Development and Agrarian Issues*, Jaipur: Rawat Publications.

Alkire, S. (2003). *Valuing Freedoms: Sen's Capability Approach and Poverty Reduction*, New Delhi: Oxford University Press.

Ballard, K. and Elston, M. (2005). "Medicalization: A Multi-dimensional Concept", *Social Theory and Health*, 3, 228-41.

Bhore Committee Report (1946). Retrieved from: http://www.nhp.gov.in/sites/default/files/pdf/Bhore_Committee_Report_VOL-1.pdf

Carr, A.J., Higginson, I.J. and Robinson, P.G. (2003). *Quality of Life*, London: BMJ Books.

Cockerham, W.C. and Ritchey, F.J. (1997). *Dictionary of Medical Sociology*, London: Greenwood Press.

Das Gupta, M. (2005). "Public Health in India: An Overview", *World Bank Policy Research Working Paper 3787*, The World Bank, December 2005.

Desai, M. (2007). "Judicial Responses to Health Care", in M. Akram (ed.), *Health Dynamics and Marginalized Communities* (pp. 27-37), Jaipur: Rawat Publications.

Dingwall, R. (1976). *Aspects of Illness*, London: Martin Robertson.

Economic Research Foundation (2006). *Government Health Expenditure in India: A Benchmark Study*, New Delhi: Mac Arthur Foundation.

Gabe, J. Bury, M. and Elson, M. (2004). *Key Concepts in Medical Sociology*, London: Sage Publications.

Giddens, A. (2006). *Sociology* (5th ed.), Cambridge: Polity Press.

High Level Expert Group Report on Universal Health Coverage (2011). Instituted by the Planning Commission of India. Retrieved from: http://planningcommission.nic.in/reports/genrep/rep_uhc0812.pdf

India Human Development Report 2011: Towards Social Inclusion (2011), Institute of Applied Manpower Research, Planning Commission, Government of India, Oxford University Press, New Delhi.

International Institute for Population Sciences (IIPS) and Macro International (2007). *National Family Health Survey (NFHS-3), 2005-06: India*, Vol. I, Mumbai: IIPS.

Jose, S. and Navaneetham, K. (2010). "Social Infrastructure and Women's Undernutrition", *Economic and Political Weekly*, 45(13), 83-89.

Kendall, D. (2011). *Sociology in Our Times* (8th edition), Wadsworth: Cengage Learning.

Khanday, Z.A. and Akram, M. (2013). "A Study of Health Structure and Health Expenditure Patterns in Anantnag District of Jammu & Kashmir", *International Journal of Social and Behavioural Sciences*, 1(2), 065-076.

Kleinman, A. (1988). *The Illness Narratives: Suffering, Healing and the Human Condition*, New York: Basic Books.

Knox, D. (2008). *Understanding Social Problem*, USA: Wordsworth Cengage.

Lowenberg, J.S. and Davis, F. (1994). "Beyond Medicalization-demedicalization: The Case of Holistic Health", *Sociology of Health and Illness*, 16(5), 579-99.

McNeill, P. (1990). *Health*, London: Routledge Publications.

Mechanic, D. (1978). *Medical Sociology*, New York: The Free Press.

Ministry of Health and Family Welfare, Government of India. (2010). NHRM: Meeting People's Health Needs in Partnership with States, the Journey so far 2005-10, New Delhi: MoHFW, GoI.

Mroczek, D.K. and Kolarz, C.M. (1998). "The Effect of Age on Positive and Negative Affect: A Developmental Perspective on Happiness", *Journal of Personality and Social Psychology*, 75, 1333-49.

Mukhta, S.A. (2011). "Financing Healthcare in India", Budget, *Yojana*, pp. 46-51.

National Rural Health Mission (NRHM). (2005). Retrieved from: http://mohfw.nic.in/NRHM/Documents/5_Years_NRHM_Final.pdf

Nettleton, S. (2006). *The Sociology of Health and Illness*, Cambridge: Polity Press.

Park, K. (2005). *Park's Text Book of Preventive and Social Medicine*, Jabalpur: M/s. Banarsidas Bhanot Publishers.

Paul, V.K., Sachdev H.S., Mavalankar D., Ramachandran, P., Sankar, M.J., Bhandari, N., Sreenivas, V., Sundararaman, T., Govil, D., Osrin, D. and Kirkwood, B. (2011). "Reproductive Health, and Child Health and Nutrition in India: Meeting the Challenge", *The Lancet*, 377(9762), 332-49, DOI: 10.1016/S01406736(10)61492-4.

Peter, F. (2006). "Health Equity and Social Justice", in S. Anand, F. Peter and A. Sen (eds.), *Public Health, Ethics and Equity*, New Delhi: Oxford University Press.

Planning Commission, Government of India (2011). *Report of the Working Group on Disease Burden for the Twelfth Five Year Plan*, WG- 3(1): Communicable Diseases, No. 2(6)2010-H&FW. Retrieved from: http://planningcommission.nic.in/aboutus/committee/wrkgrp12/health/WG_3_1communicable.pdf

Qadeer, I. (2011). *Public Health in India: Critical Reflections*, New Delhi: Daanish Books.

Sen, A. (2006). "Why Health Equity?" in S. Anand, F. Peter and A. Sen (eds.), *Public Health, Ethics and Equity* (pp. 21-33), New Delhi: Oxford University Press.

Shariff, A.S. (1999). *India — Human Development Report: A Profile of Indian States in the 1990s*, New Delhi: Oxford University Press.

Sinha, K. (2011, September 17). "Non-communicable Diseases Claimed 53 per cent Lives in India in 2008", *The Times of India*. Retrieved from: http://timesofindia.indiatimes.com/india/Non-communicable-diseases-claimed-53-lives-in-India-in-2008/articleshow/10013021.cms?referral=PM

Sivaramakrishnan, A. (2012). *Public Policy and Citizenship: Battling Managerialism in India*, New Delhi: Sage.

Sodani, P.R. (2007). "Health Seeking Behaviour and Health Expenditure in Tribal Areas of Rajasthan", in M. Akram (ed.), *Health Dynamics and Marginalized Communities* (pp. 251-65), Jaipur: Rawat Publications.

The Declaration of Alma-Ata (1978). Retrieved from: http://www.who.int/social_determinants/tools/multimedia/alma_ata/en/

United Nations (1948). *Documents*. Retrieved from: http://www.un.org/en/documents/udhr/

United Nations World Food Programme (2008). M.S. Swaminathan Research Foundation, *Report on the State of Food Insecurity in Rural India*, Chennai: Nagaraj and Company Private Limited.

White, K. (2002). *An Introduction to the Sociology of Health and Illness*, London: Sage.

WHO (1952). *Report of Expert Committee on Public Health Administration*, WHO/SEARO.

WHO (1993). *Instrument* (WHOQOL), Geneva: WHO.

WHO (2011). *Non-communicable Diseases Country Profiles 2011*. Retrieved from: http://whqlibdoc.who.int/publications/2011/9789241502283_eng.pdf

Zola, I.K. (1972). "Medicine as An Institution of Social Control", *The Sociological Review*, 20, 487-504.

8

Psychoneuroimmunology
Implications for Health and Immune System

Soumi Awasthy, Dinika Anand, Gurpreet Kaur and *Lilly Ganju*

The relationship between the mind and body has been a matter of much debate and study for human kind since ancient times. The intertwined nature of the mind and body is a well established and accepted fact today. Contemporary wisdom and literature has clearly shifted the singular focus from eating well, exercise, and managing stress in order to stay fit and healthy and equal emphasis is now laid on the thought processes, thinking patterns, attitudes and attribution styles. The vast body of research in the domain of psychoneuroimmunology (PNI) is also responsible for changing people's ideas about health and well being.

Psychoneuroimmunology is the field of study investigating the link between multidirectional communication among the thought processes, nervous system including endocrine system, and the immune system and also the implications of these linkages for physical health. Many researchers have tried to explore the biological link between the nervous system and immune system (Bulloch & Pomeranz, 1984; Cabanac, 1931 & Bulloch, 1985). Literature exploring and validating the multi-directional communication between bodily systems is of value for almost every profession ranging from doctors to trainers to teachers. In one sense, the domain of PNI can help answer questions ranging from why certain people fall sick more often, or how does a right handed person learn to work with the left hand after a traumatic injury, or why do different children in a class learn the same chapter at a different pace.

This chapter attempts to bring together literature in the field of PNI which elucidates connections between the immune, endocrine and nervous system. The synthesis of literature dwelling upon psychological correlates of health and well-being paves the way for a better understanding of human behaviour. This review endeavours to further expound some of the intervention techniques like relaxation training, meditation and hypnosis which foster positive health and functioning. Essentially, this review aims to familiarize the reader with different ways in which intertwined functioning of body systems manifests itself in our day-to-day functioning and the implications of the same for our health, behaviour and functioning. The first section delves into questions of how our thoughts, unconscious desires, feelings, personality factors and attitudes are shaped by and shape the processes of the immune system and endocrine system. Interventions like meditation, hypnosis and relaxation training are discussed in the second section which highlights the ways in which our understanding of the multidirectional communication between mind and body is beneficial. In sum, the aim is to help acquaint the reader to the factors and techniques that can be facilitative in promoting good health.

The landmark article "Emotions, Immunity and Disease: A Speculative Theoretical Integration" published by Solomon *et al.*, in 1964 has served as a beacon in the domain of PNI. Solomon opines that PNI explains the integration of one's thoughts and emotions with health and immune system. In simple terms psycho stands for psychology, neuro stands for nervous system and immunology stands for immune system (Ader, *et al.*, 2001). PNI unites three classically separated sciences of neuroscience, immunology and endocrinology.

Psychoneuroimmunology emerged in the neurosciences in the late 1970s to early 1980s and has extended its influence to the fields of psychology, psychiatry, endocrinology, physiology, and the biomedical research community. But it is only after 1990s that research has been carried out explaining the dynamics of this subject. Traditionally immune system was believed to be independent and self-regulatory from rest of the body but contemporary research on PNI had made these views less legitimate. The legitimacy of this view is questioned by researches on stress responses, immune system functioning, psychological factors and the processes underlying medical conditions (see reviews by Herbert & Cohen, 1993; O'Leary, 1990; Segerstrom & Miller, 2004).

Psychological Correlates of Health and Well-being

The domain of PNI makes inroads into links between the various psychological factors and how they imprint our health and immune system. Psychological factors range from our thought processes at one end to ways in which stress affects the functioning of the bodily systems at the other end. The practices that evolve from the research in PNI explain that the functioning of the human body, one's personality, environmental factors like presence or absence of stress, living conditions and emotions are all intertwined.

One area of inquiry in PNI explores the ways and mediums through which attribution styles, thinking patters and processes impact physiological functioning. This domain of inquiry gives credence to the belief system that positive thinking acts as an aid to drug and treatment response, recovery and recuperation process. Conditioning and training of the immune system has also been studied in the domain of PNI. The mind-body link is the basis of most research in this domain which was initially explored through the work of Ader and Cohen (1982). Another way in which psychological factors influence immune and physiological functioning is through our underlying schemas and thought patterns which act as adjuncts to conscious thinking. Personality factors like introversion-extroversion, coping styles, optimism, resilience and problem solving styles are also known to shape and alter the body's response to various situations. In sum, an individual's thoughts, response patterns, attribution styles, unconscious schemas, disposition and personality collectively exert an influence on the physiological and immune system response to any situation. The discussion in the following pages is directed towards highlighting this very aspect of human functioning. The chapter draws upon PNI research that gives importance to associations between the immune system and psychological, emotional and environmental factors.

Thought Patterns and Immune Functioning

The field of PNI is rich with research studies that emphasize the links between one's thought patterns, attribution styles and ruminations and immune functioning. Many scholars have linked together stressful events, negative thinking and immune functioning together in their work. There is a vast body of literature that indicates that when individuals engage in negative thinking or are experiencing higher levels of negative emotions, their immunity is also compromised.

In our daily lives also, situations that evoke negative or unpleasant thoughts are often accompanied by sense of physical fatigue, tiredness and burn-out. The imprint of the psychological strain is seen on the physiological functioning and we find ourselves drained out, tired and fatigued. Research evidence in this direction comes from Cohen and

Herbert (1996) who found that stressful events and negative thinking alter immunity as they have an impact on behaviour and neuro-endocrine responses.

Our mood, feelings, health and well-being are basically all spokes of the same wheel and thus imbalance in any one is bound to have impact on others. The link between feeling low or depressed and being sick is an accepted fact today. In the same vein, research has also highlighted the role of patient's emotional health and illness response in impacting the drug and disease factors. As an illustration, Byrnes, *et al.* (1998), in a study of HIV+ women with HPV infection found that greater pessimism was found to be strongly related to lower natural killer cell cytotoxicity (NKCC) and T cytotoxic/suppressor cell (CD8+CD3+) percentage in addition to CD4+ cell due to HIV infection itself. NK cells and T cells are both lymphocytes which are known to play critical role in cell mediated immunity and thus the authors concluded that pessimism may thus be associated with immune decrements and possibly poorer control over HPV infection and increased risk for future promotion of cervical dysplasia to invasive cervical cancer. Segerstrom, Taylor, Kemeny, and Fahey (1998) also found that optimism was associated with better mood, higher numbers of helper T cells, and natural killer cells. In their research, mood was found to partially account for the optimism and helper T cell relationship.

The impact of one's context in terms of work problems and chronic interpersonal difficulties with family or friends also increases the likelihood of developing symptoms of cold after exposure to flu virus. Data suggests that positive emotional state lowers the risk of developing clinical cold symptoms (Cohen, *et al.*, 1998; & Cohen, Doyle, Turner, Alper, & Skoner, 2003).

Thomsen, *et al.* (2004), conducted a study testing the association between rumination, *i.e.* negative, recurrent thoughts with immune parameters and health care utilization. The sample comprised of 196 young subjects (20 to 35 years) and 314 elderly subjects (70 to 85 years) who were made to complete questionnaire measures of rumination, sadness, and subjective sleep quality. Immune measures included leukocyte counts, lymphocyte subsets, natural killer cell activity, and T-cell proliferation. Contacts with primary care physicians were registered for 1 year through central registers. Rumination displayed a positive association with total leukocyte count, total lymphocyte count, and number of B-cells among the elderly, and this was not mediated by sadness or subjective sleep quality. Rumination was also positively associated with number of telephone consultations during the follow-up for the elderly, and this was partly mediated by sadness and subjective sleep quality. No significant associations were found for the young participants. The study clearly shows that negative thoughts may be detrimental to health, independent of negative affect.

Thus, the interrelationships between one's thought patterns, attribution styles, and ways of thinking about day-to-day life situations at one end and the corresponding functioning of our immune and physiological systems are evidenced in a number of contemporary researches. Scientists and healthcare practitioners are increasingly using the wisdom gathered from research to for directing treatment practices and find ways to better manage daily life situations like managing exam stress, interview anxiety, professional pressures and so on.

Classical Conditioning and Immune Functioning

Current trends and wisdom in the domain of brain research with patients and healthy subjects is increasingly pointing towards brain and neural plasticity. In the field of immunity research, the possibility of training the immune system and also some aspects of our physical health and well-being was discussed initially through conditioning studies (Ader, Cohen & Felten, 1995). Barrett (1993) further explored through his work linkages between the immune system and the mind. In one such illustrative study, conditioning procedures with rats were used and pairing was done between sweetened water and a drug causing nausea. Rats were seen to develop a taste aversion to the sweetened water. To a surprise, many animals even died because the drug used weakened their immune system by destroying the white blood cells (Ader & Cohen, 1975). On similar lines, research has been done to see the effect of cancer treatments like chemotherapy on one's disease (Benoist, *et al.*, 2005; Simmonds, 2000). Though there are studies showing that conditioning weakens the immune system (Bovjberg, 1991) in case of cancer patients but there are some studies which illustrate positive results of conditioning on the immune system also (MacQueen, Marshall, Perdue, Siegel & Bienenstock, 1989; BuskeKirschbaum, Kirschbaum, Stierle, Lehnert & Hellhammer, 1992, & BuskeKirschbaum, Kirschbaum, Stierle, Jabaij, & Hellhammer, 1994; Madden, *et al.*, 2001).

There is tremendous potential and clinical relevance of classical conditioning of immune functions and disease outcome in various cases of chronic inflammatory diseases, organ transplant survival or tumour development. This has been illustrated through animal studies that have shown delay in tumour growth and corresponding increase in lifespan of organism after transplantation of T-cell lymphomas through conditioned immune response (Ghanta, Hiramoto, Solvason, Soong, & Hiramoto, 1990; Ghanta, Hiramoto, Soong, Miller, & Hiramoto, 1993). All these animal studies and experiments are a critical source of information and knowledge on the role of conditioning.

Conditioning of the immune system opens vast possibilities for disease management in case of patients with autoimmune disorders and allergy disorders. Research has shown that conditioning of the immune system can help individual patients reduce their dependence on medication as illustrated by Olness and Ader (1992). The research findings regarding conditioned pharmaco-therapeutic effects on animals with autoimmune disease were applied on human subjects with autoimmune problems. In the conditioning process, they paired the therapy with cod liver oil and rose perfume monthly for 3 months and then reduced the therapeutic substance to a frequency of once every other month. It was found that the dosage of medicine was halved for the conditioning group with marked clinical improvement (Ader & Cohen, 1982). Evidence in support of conditioning also comes from asthma studies linking the use of accessory muscles, gasping, coughing and other such behaviours with conditioning (Exton, *et al.*, 1999).

Sometimes conditioning can lead to immune-stimulation which comes through a shift towards cellular immunity (mediated by cytotoxic T-lymphocytes and NK cells) from humoral immunity (mediated by antibody producing B-lymphocytes) with an increase in phagocytic activity and memory cell production thereby increasing resistance towards increased risk of infection or disease. Thus, animal studies and experiments conducted on human subjects have repeatedly demonstrated that the sympathetic nervous system plays an integral role in effecting conditioned immune-modulation in both animals and healthy humans.

Unconscious Reservoir and Immune Functioning

Individual's unconscious storehouse plays a significant role in shaping one's thought processes, leading to endocrine and immunological functioning. Unconscious mind, in the form of repressed desires, past experiences, values, beliefs and attitudes guide and monitor our perception. Ray (2004) and others researched that thoughts, feelings, beliefs, and hopes translate to chemical and electrical activity in the nerve cells of our brains (O'Donnell, Brydon, Wright, & Steptoe, 2008). Personality and cognitive factors affect our physiology, including the immune system (Heyman, 1989). Daily environmental stimuli, whether social or physical, are interpreted not only by conscious thoughts, perceptions, and beliefs in the "higher" centers of the brain, but also affect "lower", unconscious areas. The physiological activity further affects somatic and visceral responses that may also modulate immune system mechanisms, which are interlinked through various receptors, cytokines, chemokines, NK cells, etc. and establish the bi-directionality of the feedback mechanism existing between the immune system and the physiology.

The mechanism of placebo is also related to one's unconscious state. Patient's belief system about his own curative abilities imbibed in unconscious mind stimulates the required changes in immune systems that intercede healing. Placebo effects are the best way to describe that thoughts affect health making a patient's belief the healing force. This is, in essence, the nature of the placebo effect, such that placebos are often referred to as the doctor residing within the individual. It is basically an individual's belief or unconscious thinking that particular medicine or procedure will have a healing effect. Thus, placebo not only demonstrates the reality of psychosomatic healing, but it also demonstrates the extent of the mind's power in effecting it.

Research in the field of PNI also explores how covert emotional content also impacts our physical health and well-being. Positive thoughts, feelings and emotion states are associated with favourable changes in the immune system while their negative counterparts are associated with increasing the tendency towards illness and infirmity. One proverb, reads "pleasant words are a honeycomb, sweet to the soul and healing to the bones". Positive thinking is multifaceted incorporating emotions like joy, contentment, hope and gratitude that produce modifications in people's thoughts, actions, and physiological responses, through huge impact on neurological pathways and biochemical composition in the brain and body (Fredrickson & Branigan, 2005). Positive emotions facilitate the immune system, whereas negative emotions correlate with a weakened immune system.

Research evidence for the role of positive and negative thinking at a conscious or unconscious level has been provided by many different studies. Most of these studies indicate how positive thought processes can be linked with better health and immunity fortifying features while negative affect and thought is easily linked with poor health outcomes. Zorilla, *et al.* (2001), showed that depression and stressors have an effect on immunity. Positive thinking affects health and healing directly through physiological systems. Rossi (1986) found that positive attitudes and emotions can affect the biochemistry of the body to enable personal healing.

Positive thoughts originate from the left prefrontal cortex and promote homoeostatic physiology and inhibit stress and adaptive physiology, whereas negative thoughts initiate from the right prefrontal cortex and promote stress and adaptive physiology and inhibit homoeostatic physiology (Chestnut, 2005). Research supports that positive emotions, optimism, and social support, weakens psychological hyper responsiveness and/or reduce adverse clinical event rates (Rozanski & Kubzansky, 2005).

Positivity facilitates creativity which further promotes creation of individual's resources, such as physical and intellectual resources, or social and psychological resources. And these resources function as reserves for dealing with stressful events (Fredrickson, 2004). One study was conducted investigating emotional style and susceptibility to the common cold. The study found that increased positive emotional style was associated with lower risk of developing a cold, as well as reporting fewer unfounded symptoms (Cohen, Doyle, Turner, Alper, & Skoner, 2003).

In addition to the research mentioned, our attitudes are also believed to play a role in alterations in individual's mental and physical health. For example, attitude like trust which gets developed during childhood is associated with stress hormones. It is widely known that infants with affectionate and kind upbringing show lower stress hormone responses as compared to those who are not brought up gently and tenderly. Thus, the enmeshed nature of physiological, immune and thought processes is further strengthened.

Personality Characteristics and Immune Functioning

The impact of our personality characteristics and traits like use of different coping styles ranging from problem solving to escape or avoidance focussed to our decision making styles, anger, aggression, support seeking impact functioning of the immune and the endocrine system. Literature available shows that personality traits and attributes shape the patterns of responding and reacting to situations, and the relationship between behavioural response patterns and immune system has been well documented. In essence, links between personality factors and immune function is one of the most robust findings in psychoneuroimmunology, spanning diverse populations and stressors (Uchino, Cacioppo, & Kiecolt-Glaser, 1996).

The amount of emotional and psychological support an individual has bears imprint on the way the individual responds to stressors and negative events as well. The presence of caring, supportive friends and family members act as buffers and helps us in coping with challenging events with more positivity and optimism. Research in this direction has found that low perceived emotional support is associated with a more rapid decline in CD4T-cells, an important marker of the progression of HIV infection (Theorell, Blomkvist, Jonsson, Schulman, Berntorp, & Stigendal, 1995). Similarly, better natural killer (NK) cell activity in breast cancer patients is related to high quality emotional support from a spouse, perceived social support from the patient's physician, and actively seeking social support as a coping strategy (Levy, Herberman, Whiteside, Sanzo, Lee, & Kirkwood, 1990). Further evidence in this direction was found by Shea, Burton, & Girgis, (1993) who found that subjects classified as repressors of negative affect (low absorption/low neuroticism), or extreme expressers of negative affect (high absorption/high neuroticism), showed lower immune responses than other group of subjects.

The relationship between personality factors and immunity has also been explored by studying patients of brain tumour, lung cancer, Alzheimer's disease and so on. In one such study the relationship between the Big Five factors of personality and immune regulation as indicated by Lymphocyte counts was investigated. The researchers noted parameters of B-cells which are involved in the manufacturing of antibodies against antigens as well as NK cells which play an analogous role to that of cytotoxic T-cells in vertebrate adaptive immune response. The results demonstrated that the model using the Big Five factors as predictors of Lymphocyte counts is significant in predicting the variance in NK and B-cell counts and among the Big Five traits, agreeableness showed the strongest predictive function (Ozura, Ihan, & Musek, 2012).

Personality characteristics, such as academic achievement, motivation and aggression have been associated with immunological alterations as well. Aggression, operationalized using DSM-III-R anti-social personality disorder symptoms, was positively associated with T- and B-cell numbers in male military personnel, and this effect was found to be independent of testosterone level, age, health status or behaviours (Granger, Booth & Johnson, 2000).

The implications of research linking personality characteristics and immune functioning are vast and multifaceted. At a basic level, understanding how our apprehension before a big exam can make us more prone to catching a cold or falling sick with the flu can help individuals achieve better control over their behaviour and thereby save themselves and those around, from these unnecessary bouts of illnesses. The more complex implications pertain to the way specific personality traits like optimism, hopefulness and so on are linked to individual's response to illness, trauma and disease.

Acute physiological stress also influences mucosal activity. Salivary Immunogoblin A (IgA) has been found to increase in response to active laboratory work, examination stress and mental arithmetic (Carroll, Ring, Shrimpton, Evans, & Willemsen, 1996; Willemsen, *et al.*, 1998; Ring, Carroll, Willemsen, Cooke & Ferraro, 1999; Ring, *et al.*, 2000; Willemsen, Ring, McKeever, & Carroll, 2000; Bosch, *et al.*, 2001). The cold pressor has been associated with decreased IgA when measured during the tasks. The rapidity of IgA response to stress suggests sympathetic nervous system involvement. These studies further suggest that cellular mucosal immune responses are regulated differently under stressful situations.

Stress and Immune Functioning

Stress is a complex term which is today understood as a multilayered and multifaceted phenomenon. The way each of us experiences, understands and copes up with stress also varies greatly. The human body's response to stress involves responses at physiological, psychological as well as emotional level. The immune system's response to stress involves a complex cascade of events in which catecholamines, glucocorticoids, endorphins and other neuropeptides play a vital role (Croiset, Heijnen, Veldhuis, de Wied & Ballieux, 1987). Many researchers have demonstrated a close relationship between depression and the magnitude of immune changes (Irwin, Daniels, Bloom, Smith, & Weiner, 1987; Glaser, *et al.*, 1990; Kiecolt-Glaser, Dura, Speicher, Trask, & Glaser, 1991; Irwin, Lacher, & Caldwell, 1992).

Natural calamities like earthquakes and floods which are a source of considerable stress and worry have also been associated with significant modulation of the immune response (Benight, *et al.*, 1997; Segerstrom, Kemeny & Fahey, 1998; Solomon, Segerstrom, Grohr, Kemeny & Fahey, 1997). Independent studies link acute psychological stressors to leukocytosis, increased CD8/CD4 ratios, increased natural killer cell cytotoxicity (NKCC) and reduced proliferative response to mitogen (Owen & Steptoe, 2003).

Our endocrine system is the central gateway that impacts health as stress and depression can provoke the release of pituitary and adrenal hormones. Rabin (1999) also discussed the role of the endocrine system as a gateway that impacts health and well-being. Different kinds of stressors can substantially elevate stress hormones, like catecholamines and cortisol, and these hormones have multiple immunomodulatory effects (Glaser & Kiecolt-Glaser, 1994). Distressed individuals are more likely to have habits that may put them at greater risks for physical disorders as well as have immunological and endocronological consequences (Kiecolt-Glaser & Glaser, 1988).

Stress *via* activation of the Sympathetic Adrenal Medullary axis (SAM) and Hypothalamic Pituitary Adrenal axis (HPA) modulates the immune system. The autonomic nervous system and hormones of the neuroendocrine complex directly modulate the immune system whereas the immune system sends signals to the neuro-endocrine complex *via* cytokines (Besedovsky & Sorkin, 1977; Besedovsky, del Ray, Sorkin, Lotz & Schwulera, 1985; Khansari, Murgo & Faith, 1990). Almost all immune cells have receptors for various hormones like corticosteroid (CORT), ACTH, β-endorphin, catecholamines, vasopressin, prolactive, etc. (Besedovsky & Rey, 1996). There are also direct innervations of lymphoid argaus like spleen and thymus by the sympathetic branch of catecholamines on lymphoid tissues (Bellinger, *et al.*, 1990; Khansari, Murgo & Faith, 1990; Glaser & Kiecolt-Glaser, 2005). Besedovsky, del Ray, Sorkin, Dinarello (1986) demonstrate that an antigenic immune response could activate the HPA. Human monocyte derived ILI given to mice and rats, stimulated the synthesis of CRH from hypothamamus leading to an increase in plasma levels of ATCH and CORT. This overall signalling occurs through receptors, chemokins, cytokins and this close networking.

Interaction of Cytokines with Other Systems

The neuroendocrine and immune systems play a major role in adaptation. Any stressor or threat to the stability of the internal milieu is counteracted by responses of the organism: 'the adaptive response'. The effectors of these responses are the corticotrophin releasing hormone (CRH) and locus cerulus noradrenaline (LC-NA)/autonomic (sympathetic) neurons of the hypothalamus and brainstem, which regulate the peripheral activities of the HPA axis and the systemic/adrenomedullary Sympathetic Nervous System (SNS) respectively. Activation of the HPA axis SLC-NA/autonomic system results in systemic elevation of glucocorticoides and catecholamines (CAS) respectively) which act in concert to maintain the steady state or homeostasis. Any immune challenge that threatens the stability of the internal milieu can be regulated as a stressor. The past two decades have provided the evidence that certain cytokines, especially tumour neurosis factor (TNF-α), IL 1, IL6 and Leukaemia Inhibitory Factors (LIF) activate the stress system *in vivo*. Moreover, cytokines, either alone or in conjunction with components of the stress system and the classic stress hormones induce fever, sleepiness, fatigue, loss of appetite and decreased libido and activate the hepatic synthesis of acute phase. These changes as referred as 'sickness behaviour' and acute phase response stress that is associated with an immune challenge is called an immune or inflammatory stress and like other forms of stress is coordinated by the central stress system and its peripheral arms.

Structural changes in the brain due to depression and chronic stress such as decrease in weight of the thymus gland (Dohmus & Metz, 1991), ventricular enlargement and hippocampus atrophy (Duman, Henninger & Nessler, 1997) have also been reported. There is anatomical evidence also proving the communication between the nervous system and the immune system. For example, damage to the hypothalamus and cerebral hemisphere is related to the damage of immune system (Cross, Markesbery, Brooks & Roszman, 1980). The contribution of pro-inflammatory cytokines to these structural changes was also noted by Leonard and Myint (2009).

The deep seated impact of stress on our health is also evidenced in studies which assess recovery of patients post-surgery and incidence of infection and surgery related complications in patients who showed signs of negative affect, worry or stress before the surgery. In one such study, authors found that higher reported psychological stress before surgery was linked with slower rates of wound repair and recovery in patients. The authors also noted that key mechanisms for recovery namely the inflammatory response and matrix degradation processes were adversely impacted in patients who reported higher levels of worry pre- and post-surgery (Broadbent, Petrie, Alley, & Booth, 2003). The findings highlight ways in which better recovery protocols for surgery patients can be created as well as better treatment models generated.

Traumatic life events demand a high amount of energy and investment in terms of resources both physical and emotional. They force us into situations of extreme stress and place extreme demands on our physiological systems also. There is evidence that these events prime the inflammatory response system causing it to react more rapidly to subsequent life stressors at one end and the increased inflammation levels acting like causal factors in many chronic disorders at the other end (Kendall-Tackett, 2009). Traumatic events are believed to cause dysregulation of sympathetic nervous system as well as the HPA axis, thereby leading to higher probability of serious and life-threatening illnesses as reported widely in literature (Roger, Neo, Chua, Cheak, & Anselm, 2010). Similar findings are reported by Mann (2003), who suggests that the short-term expression of stress activated cytokines may be an adaptive response to stress, whereas long-term expression of these molecules is maladaptive as it may produce cardiac decompensation.

Interventions for Positive Health: Lessons from Psychoneuroimmunology

The preceding pages create a compelling case for ways in which the physiological, immunological and endocrine systems can be affected, modulated and positively shaped by the psychological, emotional and environmental factors. One can infer that positively altering the processes of the immunological, neurological and endocrine pathways can be beneficial for our health and well being. In this light, the following pages are dedicated to a discussion of ways in which these systems can be positively altered and affected. The researches discussed in the following pages deliberates over intervention methods like relaxation, meditation and hypnosis to name a few that can help to positively improve health and well-being.

Meditation and Positive Health

Evidence pointing towards the potential benefits of meditation and mindfulness for mental and physical health and well-being has been growing steadily in the past few years. Impact of meditation practices on immunity, physiological pathways, and the neuro-endocrine system has also been reported in many studies (Taylor, 1995; Carlson, Speca, Patel & Goodey, 2003; Davidson, Kabat-Zinn, Schumacher & Rosenkranz, 2003; Hidderley & Holt, 2004; Carlson, Speca, Patel & Faris, 2007; Ospina, *et al.*, 2007; & Tang, *et al.*, 2007).

Meditation and mindfulness practices are widely believed to be beneficial for patients with chronic illnesses today. The value of these practices stems from their ability to impact thought processes, attribution patterns and perceptual styles of individuals. Evidence for the positive effects of meditation practices in case of people dealing with illnesses like cancer comes from studies like that of Carlson, Ursuliak, Goodey, Angen, and Speca (2001). The authors assessed the effects of participation in a mindfulness meditation-based stress reduction programme on mood disturbance and symptoms of stress in cancer outpatients immediately and at 6 months of programme completion. It was found that participation in the programme was effective in decreasing mood disturbance and stress symptoms in patients with a wide variety of cancer diagnoses, stages of illness, and educational background, and with disparate ages (Carlson, Ursuliak, Goodey, Angen, & Speca, 2001).

Mindfulness meditation is found to increase the production of antibodies after vaccination as reported by Davidson, Kabat-Zinn, Schumacher & Rosenkranz (2003) who conducted a study on a group of participants receiving influenza vaccination. Tang, *et al.* (2007), also reported reduced cortisol responses to a 3-minute mental arithmetic stressor after training in integrative meditation. Similarly, in a study where early stage cancer patients were trained in Mindfulness-Based Stress Reduction, the participants showed decreases in monocyte numbers as well as decreased stimulated production of interferon-gamma and interleukin (IL)-10 (Carlson, Speca, Patel, & Faris, 2007).

Researchers are also exploring possibilities of changes in the activation patterns in the different brain regions as a result of practice of meditation and mindfulness. An illustrative study in this regard investigated the effects of an 8-week clinical training programme in mindfulness meditation on brain and immune function. Significant changes in anterior activation asymmetry as a function of meditation training were demonstrated. The findings indicated increases in relative left-sided anterior activation that are associated with reductions in anxiety and negative affect and increases in positive affect (Davidson, Kabat-Zinn, Schumacher, & Rosenkranz, 2003). Correspondingly, another research found that brief exposure to compassion meditation training also affects activity in stress-relevant brain areas such as anterior cingulate and amygdala (Lutz, Brefczynski-Lewis, Johnstone, & Davidson, 2008).

These research findings have opened an entire new area of inquiry and investigation for the scientists and healthcare practitioners because of surmounting evidence that innate immune inflammatory signalling pathways are implicated in the pathogenesis of vascular disease (Willerson & Ridker, 2004), cancer (Aggarwal, Shishodia, Sandur, Pandey & Sethi, 2006; Hiratsuka, Watanabe, Aburatani & Maru, 2006), diabetes (Pradhan, Manson, Rifai, Buring & Ridker, 2001) and neurodegenerative conditions (Perry, Cunningham & Holmes, 2007).

Meditation and mindfulness training are increasingly established as powerful tools for strengthening our brain. There is evidence favouring meditation as a tool for neural pathway regeneration, strengthening of existing neural pathways, sharpening of intellect, boosting immunity and so on. Meditation practices are known to bolster the immune system against harmful disease causing viruses and bacteria and evidence for this comes from research as much from folk wisdom when one looks at the sages and saints. The link between meditation practices and immunity is being researched and studied for patients of chronic illnesses and the area offers potential scope for research and application also. Understanding ways of immune-modulation through meditation can help bolster the fidelity of alternative and adjunct therapies in patients of chronic illnesses.

Cognitive Behaviour Training and Positive Health

Intervention research linking cognitive behaviour training and immune system responses has shown that altering the thought patterns and attribution styles of patients and healthy controls has positive health benefits as well. The body of literature using Cognitive Behaviour Training (CBT) based practices for creating positive health benefits or facilitating drug response in patients has significantly increased in the recent years. This line of research has marked significance for patients suffering from chronic illnesses like cancer because a positive approach and benefit finding attitude is critical for their life contexts.

In this regard, Cognitive Behavioural Stress Management (CBSM) training has been used to aid and facilitate the coping and treatment experience of many patients with cancer and other chronic illnesses. In case of illnesses like cancer, CBSM interventions play an important role because they promote benefit finding approaches in the patients and caregiver. Essentially, as the patients are dealing with chronic illnesses so a change in their attribution style helps them by facilitating positive mood and positivity towards the situation. Improved lymphocyte proliferation and cellular immune function has also been documented (McGregor, *et al.*, 2004).

Cognitively-Based Compassion Training (CBCT) is a type of contemplative practice that teaches active contemplation of loving-kindness, empathy and compassion towards loved ones, strangers, and enemies (Ozawa-de Silva & Dodson-Lavelle 2011; and Ozawa-de Silva, Dodson-Lavelle, Raison & Negi, 2012). Building on basic mindfulness practice, CBCT employs a variety of cognitive restructuring and affect generating practices with the long-term goal of developing equanimity of mind that fosters acceptance and understanding of others (Salzberg, 2002). Pace, *et al.* (2009, 2010), note that CBCT provides multi-level benefit of providing an immediate and effective stress management and coping technique as well as its impact on physiological functioning leading to additional health-relevant benefits.

The advantage of CBCT was also reported in a study wherein youth from foster care were trained in the use of CBCT. Participants reported specific instances of using CBCT strategies to regulate emotion, manage stress or to respond more compassionately towards others and qualitative results also showed that the participants found the training useful for dealing with daily life stressors. The training was positively evaluated by the majority of this population of at risk adolescents and most reported they would recommend it to a friend (Reddy, *et al.*, 2013).

Hypnosis and Positive Health

Hypnosis is defined as a state in which there is a "weakening of the generalised reality orientation" (Shor, 1959) and habitual mental functioning is in some way modified by the hypnotic process (Carrese, 1993). Early research on hypnosis and the immune system mostly involved injection of the same antigen in both arms with hypnotic instructions to differentially decrease the reaction in one arm, while increasing the allergic reaction in the other. However, the findings of these researches were mostly inconclusive with some studies showing significant differences in responsiveness between arms (Zachariae, Bjerring, & Arendt-Nielsen, 1989; Zachariae & Bjerring, 1990) and some reporting no difference (Beahrs, Harris, & Hilgard, 1970; Locke, *et al.*, 1987) as well.

The use of hypnosis as a technique for immune modulation and altering the physiological responses allows doctors, healthcare practitioners and nurses to seek ways of managing the pain, allergy, fear, anxiety and phobia related symptoms of their patients that does not necessarily involve conventional drug and pharmaco-therapies. The inception of this idea can perhaps be traced to the classic 1937 study by Clarkson. The author described the effect of hypnosis on an 18-year-old girl with asthma and an allergic reaction to egg. In the condition of 30 minutes of hypnosis with repeated suggestion for no allergic reaction to occur, no allergic response to egg presentation was observed.

Similar studies have illustrated that hypnosis is found to buffer the effects of stress on immune functions in medical students at exam time, and the comparison of self-hypnosis with and without immune imagery confirmed advantages to targeted imagery for both immune function and mood, and importantly, fewer winter viral infections in a study published by Gruzelier in 2002 (Clarkson, 1937).

Olness, Culbert, and Uden (1989) conducted a prospective, controlled study examining the effect of self-hypnosis on sIgA in saliva. Fifty-seven children were randomly assigned to either: (a) self-hypnosis (group A); (b) self-hypnosis with specific suggestion to increase saliva immunoglobulins (group B); and (C) an attention (no-treatment) control group (group C). The final results showed that only the participants who were given specific suggestion to increase salivary immunoglobulins demonstrated an increase in salivary sIgA amongst all the groups.

The beneficial nature of hypnosis in buffering the effects of stress has also been demonstrated by many researchers. Fewer instances of viral infections and common infections have been reported by participants in a number of similar studies (Gluzelier, 2002). These researches basically help create a case for focussing attention on the role that methods like hypnosis, guided imagery and so on can play in modulating the immune system. The studies are particularly useful for treatment of patients with chronic illnesses wherein alternative techniques for treatment and disease management are explored frequently.

Relaxation and Positive Health

Glaser (1994) is considered as a pioneer for investigating the links between stress, personal relationships and immune function through her work in the field of psychoneuroimmunology. She provided the first evidence of the possibility of behavioural interventions playing a role in immune regulation in a study wherein participants were divided among the treatment condition of relaxation training, social contact and no intervention. The immune enhancement noticed in the participants receiving relaxation training set the ball rolling for use of behavioural interventions.

In contemporary research, the impact of relaxation training on immune system is measured by studying leukocytes, total immunoglobulin levels and cellular functions. Also, the salivation response is seen as a marker of the impact of relaxation training in many studies as the level of immunoglobulin-A in the saliva has been found to be sensitive to relaxation training (Dillon, Minchoff & Baker, 1985; Valdimarsdottir & Stone, 1997).

Relaxation exercises and training have been documented to be useful for achieving positive health outcomes like anger management, controlling negative emotional responses and emotional outbursts at one end to even helping manage asthma symptoms. In an illustrative study, Castes, *et al.* (1999), examined the effect of a 6-month psychosocial intervention (PSI) on immunity and health outcomes among children with asthma. Youth were made to engage in relaxation sessions and had supervised relaxation practice every weekday and were encouraged to use relaxation when they anticipated an asthma episode. At the end of the study, youth in the intervention group showed a greater reduction in IgE responses to allergen than control children, as well as other immune changes (e.g. an increase in NK cells) that were not observed in the control group. Furthermore, youth in the intervention group had fewer asthma attacks and improved pulmonary function during the intervention compared to 6 months prior to it; no such changes occurred in the control group.

Contemporary research documents the impact of relaxation training through investigations assessing the impact of biofeedback-assisted training studies. Biofeedback training is today established to have tremendous benefits for reducing the stress and anxiety levels of individuals and for helping people manage their fear and anxiety related symptoms. In one such study, Kern-Buell, McGrady, Conran, and Nelson (2000) investigated the impact of biofeedback-assisted relaxation on arousal level, asthma symptomatology, pulmonary function, and immunity. Relaxation training entailed autogenic relaxation, deep breathing training, and progressive muscle relaxation, with four of the sessions involving biofeedback. The findings indicated decreased forehead muscle tension, reduced asthma severity, reduced medication use, and improved pulmonary function among treatment participants relative to controls.

Conclusion

This chapter endeavoured to create a foundation on which the associations between the immune, neurological and endocrine functioning of the body can be synthesized to evolve and develop ways to better manage and care for people in case of illnesses as well as stressful and traumatic events. The second goal of this chapter was to present research findings that establish the implications of psychoneuroimmunology research for day-to-day lives. The research discussed in the preceding pages shows that psychological, physiological and emotional factors are all intertwined and psychoneuroimmunology helps integrate these three together. Implications of these findings can help us manage many aspects of our life.

While an attempt has been made to present a comprehensive and detailed review of the literature in the field, it is not within the realms of this chapter to discuss every facet and aspect of the field of psychoneuroimmunology. In sum, the vast body of past, current and developing research in psychoneuroimmunology has clearly directed scientists, researchers, practitioners and healthcare professionals to view human behaviour and performance within the context of the mind-body relationship. Further studies can help in better management of symptoms and disease features in case of cancer, stroke and trauma patients at one end and also help organizations and individuals better understand the impact of personality attributes, stress, anger, environmental factors and life events on behaviour and productivity.

REFERENCES

Ader, R. and Cohen, N. (1982). "Behaviourally Conditioned Immunosuppression and Murine Systemic Lupus Erythematosus", *Science*, 215, 1534-36.

Ader, R. and Cohen, N. (1975). "Behaviourally Conditioned Immunosuppression", *Psychosomatic Medicine*, 37, 333-40.

Ader, R., Cohen, N. and Felten, D. (1995). "Psychoneuroimmunology: Interactions between the Nervous System and the Immune System", *Lancet*, 345, 99-103.

Ader, R., Felten, D. and Cohen, N. (eds.) (2001). *Psychoneuroimmunology* (IIIrd ed.), San Diego: Academic Press.

Aggarwal, B.B., Shishodia, S., Sandur, S.K., Pandey, M.K. and Sethi, G. (2006). "Inflammation and Cancer: How Hot is the Link?" *Biochemical Pharmacology*, 72, 1605-21.

Barrett, S. (1993). "Psychoneuroimmunology — The Bridge Between Science and Spirit", in B.B. Kane, J. Millay and D. Brown (eds.), *Silver Threads: 25 Years of Parapsychology Research* (pp. 170-75), London: Praeger.

Beahrs, J., Harris, D. and Hilgard, E. (1970). "Failure to Alter Skin Inflammation by Hypnotic Suggestion in Five Subjects with Normal Skin Reactivity", *Psychosomatic Medicine*, 32, 627-31.

Bellinger, D., Lorton, D., Romano, T., Olschowka, J., Felten, S. and Felten, D. (1990). "Neuropeptide Innervation of Lymphoid Organs", *Annual Academy of Science*, 594, 17-33.

Benight, C.C., Antoni, M.H., Kilbourn, K., Ironson, G., Kumar, M.A., Fletcher, M.A., Redwine, L., Baum, A. and Schneiderman, N. (1997). "Coping Self-efficacy Buffers Psychological and Physiological Disturbances in HIV-infected Men following a Natural Disaster", *Health Psychology*, 16(3), 248-55.

Benoist, S., Paultrat, K., Mitry, E., Rougier, P., Penna, C. and Nordlinger, B. (2005). "Treatment Strategy for Patients with Colorectal Cancer and Synchronous Irresectable Liver Metastases", *The British Journal of Surgery*, 92(9), 1155-60.

Besedovsky, H. and Sorkin, E. (1977). "Network of Immune-neuroendocrine Interactions", *Clinical and Experimental Immunology*, 21(1), 1-12.

Besedovsky, H., Del Rey, A., Sorkin, E., Lotz, W. and Schwulera, U. (1985). "Lymphoid Cells Produce An Immunoregulatory Glucocorticoid Increasing Factor (GIF) Acting through the Pituitary Gland", *Clinical and Experimental Immunology*, 59(3), 622-28.

Besedovsky, H., Del Rey, A., Sorkin, E. and Dinarello, C. (1986). "Immunoregulatory Feedback between Interleukin-1 and Glucocorticoid Hormones", *Science*, 233, 652-54.

Besedovsky, H. and Del Rey, A. (1996). "Immune-neuro-endocrine Interactions: Facts and Hypotheses", *Endocrine Review*, 17, 64-102.

Bosch, J.A., de Geus, E.J., Kelder, A., Veerman, E.C., Hoogstraten, J. and Amerongen, A.V. (2001). "Differential Effects of Active *versus* Passive Coping on Secretory Immunity", *Psychophysiology*, 38, 836-46.

Bovjberg, D. (1991). "Psychoneuroimmunology: Implications for Oncology", *Cancer*, 67, 828-32.

Broadbent, E., Petrie, K., Alley, P. and Booth, R. (2003). "Psychological Stress Impairs Early wound Repair following Surgery", *Psychosomatic Medicine*, 65(5), 865-69.

Bulloch, K. and Pomerantz, W. (1984). "Autonomic Nervous System Innervation of Thymic-related Lymphoid Tissue in Wildtype and Nude Mice", *Journal of Comparative Neurology*, 228(1), 57-68.

Bulloch, P.K. (1985). "Neuroanatomy of Lymphoid Tissues: A Review", in R. Guillemin and *et al.* (eds.), *Neural Modulation of Immunity* (pp. 49-85), New York: Raven Press.

BuskeKirschbaum, A., Kirschbaum, C., Stierle, H., Lehnert, H. and Hellhammer, D. (1992). "Conditioned Increase of Natural Killer Cell Activity (NKCA) in Humans", *Psychosomatic Medicine*, 54, 123-32.

BuskeKirschbaum, A., Kirschbaum, C., Stierle, H., Jabaij, H. and Hellhammer, D. (1994). "Conditioned Manipulation of Natural Killer (NK) Cells in Humans Using a Discriminative Learning Protocol", *Biological Psychology*, 38, 143-55.

Byrnes, D., Antoni, M., Goodkin, K., Efantis-Potter, J., Asthana, D., Simon, T., Munnaj, J., Ironson, G. and Fletcher, M. (1998). "Stressful Events, Pessimism, Natural Killer Cell Cytotoxicity, and Cytotoxic/Suppressor T-cells in HIV+ Black Women at Risk for Cervical Cancer", *Psychosomatic Medicine*, 60(6), 714-22.

Cabanac, J. (1931). "Les Nerfs du Thymus", *Bullentin of Association of Anatomy*, 25, 92-100.

Carlson, L., Speca, M., Patel, K. and Faris, P. (2007). "One Year Pre-post Intervention Follow-up of Psychological, Immune, Endocrine and Blood Pressure Outcomes of Mindfulness-based Stress Education (MBSR) in Breast and Prostate Cancer Outpatients", *Brain, Behaviour, and Immunity*, 21, 1038-49.

Carlson, L., Speca, M., Patel, K. and Goodey, E. (2003). "Mindfulness-based Stress Reduction in Relation to Quality of Life, Mood, Symptoms of Stress, and Immune Parameters in Breast and Prostate Cancer Outpatients", *Psychosomatic Medicine*, 65, 571-81.

Carlson, L., Ursuliak, Z., Goodey, E., Angen, M. and Speca, M. (2001). "The Effects of a Mindfulness Meditation-based Stress Reduction Programme on Mood and Symptoms of Stress in Cancer Outpatients: 6 Month Follow-up", *Supportive Care in Cancer*, 9(2), 112-23.

Carrese, M. (1993). "The Paradox of the New Hypnosis", *Australian Journal of Clinical Hypnotherapy and Hypnosis*, 14, 31-40.

Carroll, D., Ring, C., Shrimpton, J., Evans, P. and Willemsen, G.F. (1996). "Secretory Immunoglobulin A and Cardiovascular Responses to Acute Psychological Challenge", *International Journal of Behavioural Medicine*, 3, 266-81.

Castes, M., Hagel, I., Palenque, M., Canelones, P., Corao, A. and Lynch, N.R. (1999). "Immunological Changes Associated with Clinical Improvement of Asthmatic Children Subjected to Psychosocial Intervention", *Brain, Behaviour and Immunity*, 13, 1-13.

Chestnut, J.L. (2005). *The Innate State of Mind and Emotional Hygiene*, Victoria, British Columbia: Global Self Health Corporation.

Clarkson, A.K. (1937). "The Nervous Factor in Juvenile Asthma", *The British Medical Journal*, 2, 845-50.

Cohen, S. and Herbert, T.B. (1996). "Health Psychology: Psychological Factors and Physical Disease from the Perspective of Human Psychoneuroimmunology", *Annual Review of Psychology*, 47, 113-42.

Cohen, S., Frank, E., Doyle, W., Skoner, D., Rabin, B. and Gwaltney, J.J. (1998). "Types of Stressors that Increase Susceptibility to the Common Cold in Healthy Adults", *Health Psychology*, 17(3), 214-23.

Cohen, S., Doyle, W.J., Turner, R.B., Alper, C.M. and Skoner, D.P. (2003). "Emotional Style and Susceptibility to the Common Cold", *Psychosomatic Medicine*, 65, 652-57.

Croiset, G., Heijnen, C., Veldhuis, H., de Wied, D. and Ballieux, R. (1987). "Modulation of the Immune Response by Emotional Stress", *Life Science*, 40, 775-82.

Cross, R., Markesbery, W., Brooks, W. and Roszman, T. (1980). "Hypothalamic-immune Interactions: The Acute Effect of Anterior Hypothalamic Lesions on the Immune Response", *Brain Research*, 196, 79-87.

Davidson, R.J., Kabat-Zinn, J., Schumacher, J. and Rosenkranz, M. (2003). "Alterations in Brain and Immune Function Produced by Mindfulness", *Psychosomatic Medicine*, 65, 564-70.

Dillon, K., Minchoff, B. and Baker, K. (1985). "Positive Emotional States and Enhancement of the Immune System", *International Journal of Psychiatry in Medicine*, 15(1), 13-18.

Dohmus, J. and Metz, A. (1991). "Stress Mechanisms of Immune Suppression", *Veterinary Immunology and Immunopathology*, 30(1), 89-109.

Duman, R., Henninger, G. and Nessler, E. (1997). "A Molecular and Cellular Theory of Depression", *Archives of General Psychiatry*, 54, 597-606.

Exton, M.S., Schult, M., Donath, S., Strubel, T., Bode, U., del Rey, A., Westermann, J. and Schedlowski, M. (1999). "Conditioned Immunosuppression Makes Subtherapeutic Cyclosporin Effective *via* Splenic Innervation", *American Journal of Physiology*, 276 (6 Pt 2), 1710-17.

Fredrickson, B. (2004). "The Broaden-and-build Theory of Positive Emotions", *Philosophical Transactions of the Royal Society of London*, 359(1449), 1367-78.

Fredrickson, B. and Branigan, C. (2005). "Positive Emotions Broaden the Scope of Attention and Thought-action Repertoires", *Cognition and Emotion*, 19(3), 313-32. Retrieved October 14, 2013, from http://www.logan.edu/mm/files/LRC/Senior-Research/2012-dec-2

Ghanta, V., Hiramoto, N.S., Solvason, H., Soong, S.J. and Hiramoto, R.N. (1990). "Conditioning: A New Approach to Immunotherapy", *Cancer Research 50*, 50, 4295-99.

Ghanta, V.K., Hiramoto, N.S., Soong, S.J., Miller, D.M. and Hiramoto, R.N. (1993). "A Multiple Modality Approach Combining the Effect of Conditioning with Adoptive Chemoimmunotherapy", *International Journal of Neuroscience*, 71, 251-65.

Glaser, R., Kennedy, S., Lafuse, W., Bonneau, R., Speicher, C., Hillhouse, J. and Kiecolt-Glaser, J. (1990). "Psychological Stress-induced Modulation of Interleukin 2 Receptor Gene Expression and Interleukin 2 Production in Peripheral Blood Leukocytes", *Archives of General Psychiatry*, 47(8), 707-12.

Glaser, R. and Kiecolt-Glaser (eds.) (1994). *Handbook of Human Stress and Immunity*, San Diego, California, USA: Academic Press.

Glaser, R. and Kiecolt-Glaser, J. (2005). "Stress-induced Immune Dysfunction: Implications for Health", *Nature Reviews Immunology*, 5(3), 243-51.

Granger, D., Booth, A. and Johnson, D. (2000). "Human Aggression and Enumerative Measures of Immunity", *Psychosomatic Medicine*, 62, 583-90.

Gruzelier, J. (2002). "A Review of the Impact of Hypnosis, Relaxation, Guided Imagery and Individual Differences on Aspects of Immunity and Health", *Stress*, 5(2), 147-63.

Herbert, T.B. and Cohen, S. (1993). "Stress and Immunity in Humans: A Meta-analytic Review", *Psychosomatic Medicine*, 55, 364-79.

Heyman, S.R. (1989). "Psychoneuroimmunology: Implication for Clinical Practice, Vol. 8" (pp. 5-13), in P.A. Keller and S.R. Heyman, *Innovations in Clinical Practice: A Source Book* (Vol. 8, pp. 5-13), Sarasota, FL, England: Professional Resource Exchange.

Hidderley, M. and Holt, M. (2004). "A Pilot Randomized Trial Assessing the Effects of Autogenic Training in Early Stage Cancer Patients in Relation to Psychological Status and Immune System Responses", *European Journal of Oncology Nursing*, 8, 61-65.

Hiratsuka, S., Watanabe, A., Aburatani, H. and Maru, Y. (2006). "Tumour-mediated Upregulation of Chemoattractants and Recruitment of Myeloid Cells Predetermines Lung Metastasis", *Nature Cell Biology*, 8, 1369-75.

Irwin, M., Daniels, M., Bloom, E.T., Smith, T.L. and Weiner, H. (1987). "Life Events, Depressive Symptoms, and Immune Function", *American Journal of Psychiatry*, 144, 437-41.

Irwin, M., Lacher, U. and Caldwell, C. (1992). "Depression and Reduced Natural Killer Cytotoxicity: A Longitudinal Study of Depressed Patients and Control Subjects", *Psychological Medicine*, 22, 1045-50.

Kendall-Tackett, K. (2009). "Psychological Trauma & Physical Health: A Psychoneuroimmunology Approach to Etiology of Negative Health Effects and Possible Interventions", *Psychological Trauma: Theory, Research, Practice, and Policy*, 1(1), 35-48.

Kern-Buell, C.L., McGrady, A.V., Conran, P.B. and Nelson, L.A. (2000). "Asthma Severity, Psychophysiological Indicators of Arousal, and Immune Function in Asthma Patients Undergoing Biofeedback-assisted Relaxation", *Applied Psychophysiology & Biofeedback*, 25, 79-91.

Khansari, D., Murgo, A. and Faith, R. (1990). "Effects of Stress on the Immune System", *Immunology Today*, 11(5), 170-75.

Kiecolt-Glaser, J.K. and Glaser, R. (1988). "Methodological Issues in Behavioural Immunology Research with Humans", *Brain, Behaviour, and Immunity*, 2, 67-78.

Kiecolt-Glaser, J.K., Dura, J.R., Speicher, C.E., Trask, O.J. and Glaser, R. (1991). "Spousal Caregivers of Dementia Victims: Longitudinal Changes in Immunity and Health", *Psychosomatic Medicine*, 53, 345-62.

Leonard, B.E. and Myint, A. (2009). "The Psychoneuroimmunology of Depression", *Human Psychopharmacology: Clinical and Experimental*, 24, 165-75. doi:10.1002/hup.1011

Levy, S., Herberman, R., Whiteside, T., Sanzo, K., Lee, J. and Kirkwood, J. (1990). "Perceived Social Support and Tumour Estrogen/ Progesterone Receptor Status as Predictors of Natural Killer Cell Activity in Breast Cancer Patients", *Psychosomatic Medicine*, 52, 73-85.

Locke, S.E., Ransil, B.J., Covino, N.A., Toczydolwski, J., Lohse, J.M., Dvorak, H.M., Arndt, K.A. and Franke, F.H. (1987). "Failure of Hypnotic Suggestion to Alter Immune Response to Delayed-type Hypersensitivity Antigens", *Annals of the New York Academy of Science*, 496, 745-49.

Lutz, A., Brefczynski-Lewis, J., Johnstone, T. and Davidson, R. (2008). "Regulation of the Neural Circuitry of Emotion by Compassion Meditation: Effects of Meditative Expertise", *PLoS One*, 3(3). doi:10.1371/journal.pone.0001897

MacQueen, G., Marshall, J., Perdue, M., Siegel, S. and Bienenstock, J. (1989). "Pavlovian Conditioning of Rat Mucosal Mast Cells to Secrete Rat Mast Cell Protease II", *Science*, 243(4887), 83-85.

Madden, K.S., Boehm, G.W., Lee, S.C., Grota, L.J., Cohen, N. and Ader, R. (2001). "Onetrial Conditioning of the Antibody Response to Hen Egg Lysozyme in Rats", *Journal of Neuroimmunology*, 113, 236-39.

Mann, D. (2003). "Stress-activated Cytokines and the Heart: From Adaptation to Maladaptation", *Annual Review of Physiology*, 65, 81-101.

McGregor, B., Antoni, M., Boyers, A., Alferi, S., Blomberg, B. and Carver, C. (2004). "Cognitive-behavioural Stress Management Increases Benefit Finding and Immune Function Among Women with Early-stage Breast Cancer", *Journal of Psychosomatic Research*, 56(1), 1-8.

O'Donnell, K., Brydon, L., Wright, C. and Steptoe, A. (2008). "Self-esteem Levels and Cardiovascular and Inflammatory Responses to Acute Stress", *Brain, Behaviour, and Immunity*, 22, 1241-47.

O'Leary, A. (1990). "Stress, Emotion, and Immune Function", *Psychological Bulletin*, 55, 364-79.

Olness, K. and Ader, R. (1992). "Conditioning as An Adjunct in the Pharmacotherapy of Lupus Erythematosus", *Journal of Developmental and Behavioural Pediatrics*, 13, 124-25.

Olness, K., Cuthbert, T. and Uden, D. (1989). "Self-regulation of Salivary Immunoglobulin A by Children", *Pediatrics*, 83, 66-71.

Ospina, M.B., Bond, K., Karkhaneh, M., Tjosvold, L., Vandermeer, B., Liang, Y., Bialy, L., Hooton, N., Buscemi, N., Dryden, N.P. and Klassen, T.P. (2007). "Meditation Practices for Health: State of the Research", *Evidence Report/Technology Assessment*, 155, 1-263.

Owen, N. and Steptoe, A. (2003). "Natural Killer Cell and Proinflammatory Cytokine Responses to Mental Stress: Associations with Heart Rate and Heart Rate Variability", *Biological Psychology*, 63, 101-15.

Ozawa-de Silva, B. and Dodson-Lavelle, B. (2011). "An Education of Heart and Mind: Practical and Theoretical Issues in Teaching Cognitive-based Compassion Training to Children", *Practical Matters*, I(4), 1-28.

Ozawa-de Silva, B., Dodson-Lavelle, B., Raison, C.L. and Negi, L. (2012). "Compassion and Ethics: Scientific and Practical Approaches to the Cultivation of Compassion as a Foundation for Ethical Subjectivity and Well-being", *The Journal of Healthcare, Sciences, and the Humanities*, 2, 145-64.

Ozura, A., Ihan, A. and Musek, J. (2012). "Can The Big Five Factors of Personality Predict Lymphocyte Counts?" *Psychiatria Danubina*, 24(1), 66-72.

Pace, T.V., Negi, L.T., Adame, D.D., Cole, S.P., Sivilli, T.I., Brown, T.D., Issa, M. J. and Raison, C.L. (2009). "Effect of Compassion Meditation on Neuroendocrine, Innate Immune and Behavioural Responses to Psychosocial Stress", *Psychoneuroendocrinology*, 34(1), 87-98.

Pace, T.W., Negi, L.T., Sivilli, T.I., Issa, M.J., Cole, S.P., Adame, D.D. and Raison, C. (2010). "Innate Immune, Neuroendocrine and Behavioural Responses to Psychosocial Stress do not Predict Subsequent Compassion Meditation Practice Time", *Psychoneuroendocrinology*, 35(2), 310-15.

Perry, V., Cunningham, C. and Holmes, C. (2007). "Systemic Infections and Inflammation Affect Chronic Neurodegeneration", *Nature Reviews Immunology*, 7, 161-67.

Pradhan, A., Manson, J., Rifai, N., Buring, J. and Ridker, P. (2001). "C-reactive Protein, Interleukin 6, and Risk of Developing Type 2 Diabetes Mellitus", *Journal of the American Medical Association*, 286, 327-34.

Rabin, B.S. (1999). *Stress, Immune Function, and Health: The Connection*, New York: Wiley-Liss & Sons.

Ray, O. (2004). "How the Mind Hurts and Heals the Body", *American Psychologist*, 59(1), 29-40.

Reddy, S., Negi, L., Dodson-Lavelle, B., Ozawa-de Silva, B., Pace, T. and Cole, S. (2013). "Cognitive-Based Compassion Training: A Promising Prevention Strategy for At-Risk Adolescents", *Journal of Child and Family Studies*, 22(2), 219-30. doi:10.1007/s10826-012-9571-7

Ring, C., Carroll, D., Willemsen, G., Cooke, J. and Ferraro, A. (1999). "Secretory Immunoglobulin A and Cardiovascular Activity during Mental Arithmetic and Paced Breathing", *Psychophysiology*, 36(5), 602-09.

Ring, C., Harrison, L.K., Winzer, A., Carroll, D., Drayson, M. and Kendall, M. (2000). "Secretory Immunoglobulin A and Cardiovascular Reactions to Mental Arithmetic, Cold", *Psychophysiology*, 37(5), 634-43.

Roger, C.H., Neo, L.F., Chua, A.N., Cheak, A.A. and Anselm, M. (2010). "Research on Psychoneuroimmunology: Does Stress Influence Immunity and Cause Coronary Artery Disease", *Annual Academy of Medicine,* Singapore, 39, 191-96.

Rossi, E. (1986). *The Psychobiology of Mind-Body Healing*, New York: Norton & Co. Inc.

Rozanski, A. and Kubzansky, K. (2005). "Psychologic Functioning and Physical Health: A Paradigm of Flexibility", *Psychosomatic Medicine*, 67(1), 47-53. Retrieved October 14, 2013, from http://www.logan.edu/mm/files/LRC/Senior-Research/2012-dec-24

Salzberg, S.L. (2002). *Lovingkindness: The Revolutionary Art of Happiness*, Boston, MA, USA: Shambala Publications Inc.

Segerstrom, S.C. and Miller, G.E. (2004). "Psychological Stress and the Human Immune System: A Meta-analytic Study of 30 Years of Inquiry", *Psychological Bulletin*, 130, 601-30.

Segerstrom, S., Taylor, S., Kemeny, M. and Fahey, J. (1998). "Optimism is Associated with Mood, Coping, and Immune Change in Response to Stress", *Journal of Personality & Social Psychology*, 74(6), 1646-55.

Shea, J., Burton, R. and Girgis, A. (1993). "Negative Affect, Absorption, and Immunity", *Physiology & Behaviour*, 53(3), 449-57.

Shor, R.E. (1959). "Hypnosis and the Concept of the Generalized Reality Orientation", *American Journal of Psychotherapy*, 13, 582-602.

Simmonds, P. (2000). "Palliative Chemotherapy for Advanced Colorectal Cancer: Systematic Review and Meta-Analysis", *British Medical Journal*, 321(7260), 531-35.

Solomon, G.F., Segerstrom, S.C., Grohr, P., Kemeny, M. and Fahey, J. (1997). "Shaking Up Immunity: Psychological and Immunologic Changes after a Natural Disaster". *Psychosomatic Medicine*, 59, 114-27.

Tang, Y., Ma, Y., Wang, J., Fan, Y., Feng, S., Lu, Q., Yu, Q., Sui, D., Rothbart, M.K., Fan, M. and Posner, M.I. (2007). "Short-term Meditation Training Improves Attention and Self-regulation", *Proceedings of the National Academy of Sciences of the United States of America*, 104, 17152-17156.

Taylor, D.N. (1995). "Effects of a Behavioural Stress Management Programme on Anxiety, Mood, Self-esteem and T-cell Count in HIV Positive Men", *Psychological Reports*, 76, 451-57.

Theorell, T., Blomkvist, V., Jonsson, H., Schulman, S., Berntorp, E. and Stigendal, L. (1995). "Social Support and the Development of Immune Function in Human Immunodeficiency Virus Infection", *Psychosomatic Medicine*, 57, 32-36.

Thomsen, D.K., Mehlsen, M.Y., Hokland, M., Viidik, A., Olesen, F., Avlund, K., Munk, K. and Zachariae, R. (2004). "Negative Thoughts and Health: Associations among Rumination, Immunity, and Health Care Utilization in a Young and Elderly Sample", *Psychosomatic Medicine*, 66(3), 363-71.

Uchino, B., Cacioppo, J. and Kiecolt-Glaser, J. (1996). "The Relationship between Social Support and physiological Processes: A Review with Emphasis on Underlying Mechanisms", *Psycholical Bulletin*, 119, 488-531.

Valdimarsdottir, H. and Stone, A. (1997). "Psychosocial Factors and Secretory Immunoglobulin A", *Critical Reviews in Oral Biology & Medicine*, 8, 461-74.

Willemsen, G., Ring, C., Carroll, D., Evans, P., Clow, A. and Hucklebridge, F. (1998). "Secretory Immunoglobulin A and Cardiovascular Reactions to Mental Arithmetic and Cold Pressor", *Psychophysiology*, 35(3), 252-59.

Willemsen, G., Ring, C., McKeever, S. and Carroll, D. (2000). "Secretory Immunoglobin A and Cardiovascular Activity during Mental Arithmetic: Effects of Task Difficulty and Task Order", *Biological Psychology*, 52(2), 127-41.

Willerson, J. and Ridker, P. (2004). "Inflammation as a Cardiovascular Risk Factor", *Circulation*, 109 (Suppl. I), 2-10.

Zachariae, R., Bjerring, P. and Arendt-Nielsen, L. (1989). "Modulation of Type I Immediate and Type IV Delayed Immunoreactivity Using Direct Suggestion and Guided Imagery during Hypnosis", *Allergy*, 44, 537-42.

Zachariae, R. and Bjerring, P. (1990). "The Effect of Hypnotically Induced Analgesia on Flare Reaction of the Cutaneous Histamine Prick Test", *Archives of Dermatological Research*, 282, 539-43.

Zorilla, E., Lubowsky, L., McKay, J., Rosenthal, R., Houldin, A., Tax, A., Mccorkle, R., Seligman, D.A. and Schmidt, K. (2001). "The Relationship of Depression and Stressors to Immunological Assays: A Meta-analytic Review", *Brain, Behaviour, and Immunity*, 15, 199-226.

SECTION III

Mental Health and Mental Illness

9

Mental Illness and Mental Health
Questions for Research

Arun K. Sharma

Studies of health make a distinction between physical health and mental health. Although there is a close connection between the two they refer to two different domains of health — one related to physical body, another to cognitive, emotional and spiritual. In the early Independence period the burden of infectious diseases was so high that State and National planning agencies focussed more on control of epidemics. Gradually, their attention shifted towards reproductive health and health inequality. Thus, physical health has been on the centre stage. Almost all the studies of health have focussed on mortality, morbidity, physical disabilities, behavioural change, and accidents and injuries and few studies have focussed on mental health. Thus, a discussion of mental health is practically absent in sociological literature in India despite the fact that a sizeable population is suffering from mental health problems. This chapter attempts to seek attention of social scientists to this emerging, though neglected, sub-field of sociology of health and raise a few questions regarding the role of social structure on mental health. Based on literature survey, certain issues regarding happiness and subjective well-being are also discussed. It may be noted that sociology of mental health is itself a rather new addition to various fields of sociology and it goes beyond mere empirical correlations between social structure and frequency of mental health disorders as it implicates body and knowledge in the larger discourses of power and politics.

What is Mental Health?

It has been found to be enormously difficult to define mental health or mental illness as there is no observable basis to distinguish between the two. A person gets identified when one is in dire need of help (i.e. on the basis of self-report of distress), on the basis of observed unpredictability of behaviour in a particular role (Davis, 1966), or judgement of the practitioners (Rosenhan, 1973). The majority of mental conditions are the result of one's social position and conflict of values but psychiatrists attribute them to one's personality or functioning of brain. The major issue in mental health is that the distressed persons and their families are stigmatized. In a recent paper Rogers and David (2011) have shown how both sociology and psychiatry — the two disciplines dealing with mental health issues — are concerned with three things: social psychiatry, stigma and psychoanalysis. Sociology is concerned more with social inequalities and the context of the construction of medical knowledge and uses empirical and theoretical approaches to explain mental disorders. Sociology is sociology of mental conditions and, therefore, it has a theoretical orientation focussing on critique of social conditions. For example, in a sociological perspective, Hamilton, *et al.* (1990), have shown that there is a link between employment condition and mental health. They have produced data to show the three categories of workers — the laid-off workers, would-be laid-off workers, and workers in secured employment — differ in rates of mental disorders. Psychiatry is more concerned with classification and treatment of various mental disorders. Thus, psychiatry has mainly a therapeutical orientation and is linked with clinical processes.

At this juncture we need to note that there are two sides of mental health: disorders and perfect health, though there are overlapping conditions. Disorders are easier to observe; perfect health is only an ideal. To quote the World Health Organization (WHO):

> Mental health refers to a broad array of activities directly or indirectly related to the mental well-being component included in the WHO's definition of health: "A state of complete physical, mental and social well-being, and not merely the absence of disease". It is related to the promotion of well-being, the prevention of mental disorders, and the treatment and rehabilitation of people affected by mental disorders. (WHO, 2014a)

Further,

> Mental health is not just the absence of mental disorder. It is defined as a state of well-being in which every individual realizes his or her

own potential, can cope with the normal stresses of life, can work productively and fruitfully, and is able to make a contribution to her or his community (WHO, 2014b).

The above definition focusses on realization of one's potential but the starting point is the absence of mental disorder. In view of this, three aspects of mental health interventions need to be discerned: the prevention of mental disorders; the treatment and rehabilitation of people suffering from mental disorders; and finally, the promotion of well-being. On each account there are formidable problems. In particular, the link between social structure and mental health is problematic. The following section shows how the social structure affects mental health.

Social Structure and Mental Health

Mental health issues have long been studied by psychologists and psychiatrists. It is now well established that stress leads to cardiovascular diseases, Alzheimer's and Parkinson's disorders, metabolic syndrome and diabetes, arthritis and pain disorders, cancer and suppression of immune system, obesity, head trauma concussion and depression which in turn is the major cause of addiction and anxiety (Anisman, 2014). In the recent past, sociologists have taken a keen interest in studying mental health, in relation to social institutions and social structure. However, depending on their theoretical perspectives they differ a lot in issues, approaches and methods. Marxist theorists were perhaps the first to demonstrate that the patterns of health (and that includes patterns of mental health) are closely associated with the forces of production and class relations. Parsonian sociologists focussed more on sick role as product of modern society. Foucault and Fourcauldian, post-modern, sociologists have taken greater interest in madness and how it is implicated with the genealogy of power. Providing a broad view of sociological research on this subject, Macionis and Plummer (2014) argue that the sociological explanation of mental problems uses one or more of the following four broad theories:

1. Social causation theories
2. Labelling theories
3. Constructionist theories
4. Structural realist theories

Social causation theory explains mental problems in terms of social and environmental causes such as war and unemployment. Labelling theory looks at ways in which in social interactions produce meanings and definitions leading to the label of someone being in a state of mental illness. Constructionist theory explains how power shapes language, science, and psychiatric workings of the idea of mental illness. It is based on the Foucauldian idea of genealogy of power and knowledge. Structural realist theories combine both the material conditions which produce mental illness in a specific context, and symbolic categories of illness so produced. Mental problems may also be seen as caused by various types of role conflicts. Weiss and Lonnquist (1996) divide these role conflicts into four categories: interpersonal conflict within role sets, i.e. conflict between persons in different roles; interrole conflict, i.e. conflict between two or more roles of the same person; role captivity, i.e. when a person is in a role in which expectations from the person are different from what one wants to do; and role restructuring, i.e. change in long established patterns (Weiss and Lonnquist, 1996).

With an eye on intervention some sociologists have also examined etiology, classification and treatment of mental disorders (Scheff, 2009). Sociologists claim that prevalence and severity of mental disorders are not randomly distributed among all classes of society and are rather concentrated in certain strata (Aneshensel, *et al.*, 2013). Social constructionist and structural approaches are needed to explain the identity of disorder in a society and explain the patterns of disorder, the latter being highly dependent on patterns of socio-psychological and material resources. At the fundamental level, mental disorders require a social definition as the symptoms are varyingly interpreted in different societies. In sociology of mental disorders, social structure and social conditions are found to be having a determined effect on the degree and nature of mental disorders (Davis, 1966; Hamilton, *et al.*, 1990; Weiss and Lonnquist, 1996; Rogers and Pilgrim, 2010) in the same way as they determine physical health.

Davis (1966) attributes mental disorders, e.g. neurosis, schizophrenia, alcoholic psychosis, phobias and anxiety to three types of conflicts: (a) "Ends may be incompatible because they are opposite in character"; (b) "Different ends may compete for scarce ends"; and (c) "Conflict may arise from too great a disparity between ends and means". For Davis, at the root of unfounded fear (phobia), fixed idea (obsession), oft repeated acts (compulsion) and anxieties (e.g. guilt-induced anxieties) there is always a social conflict and the mental disorders have a close association with type of society, class and urban ecology. Weiss and Lonnquist suggest that mental disorders are associated with social class and race, urban-rural residence, and marital status. The gender differences in mental disorders are, however, not so clear and depend on socialization. Such differences may occur from genetic inheritance, social stress and also from social selection (i.e. the hypothesis that ill persons may drift downwards in the social structure) (Weiss and Lonnquist, 1996). All this shows that prevention of mental disorders may require restructuring of some aspect of society.

Prevalence, Treatment and Rehabilitation

As said above, definition and identification of mental health disorders is a challenging task. The boundary between mental health and mental illness is fuzzy. Sometime or other, everyone suffers from stress and psychological conditions and may require help from others. Only when some people suffer from more intense problems for a long time, and require specialized care, they are considered to be suffering from mental illness. The examples of prolonged sufferings requiring care are: anxiety disorders, depression, alcohol or drug abuse, schizophrenia and anti-social personality disorders (Weiss and Lonnquist, 1996). As shown above, although mental disorders are caused by genetic or physiological reasons, environmental reasons or social reasons, the social reasons are the most important ones as they not only cause them but also define them. Therefore, all estimates are to be treated with caution and interpreted in a social context. To quote the World Health Organization (WHO, 2011): "The suicide rate for males is 12.2 per 1,00,000 population and for females is 9.1 per 1,00,000 population. In India, neuropsychiatric disorders are estimated to contribute to 11.6 per cent of the global burden of disease" (based on 2008 estimates of the WHO). Further, "According to a study conducted by the National Commission on Macroeconomics and Health in 2005, nearly 5 per cent of India's population suffers from common mental disorders, such as depression and anxiety" (DNA, 2013). The report suggests that overall 6-7 per cent of India's population suffers from mental disorders. To quote from *Annual Report to the People on Health* (December, 2011), (Ministry of Health and Family Welfare, 2011):

> The World Bank Report (1993) revealed that the Disability Adjusted Life Year (DALY) loss due to neuro-psychiatric disorder is much higher than diarrhoea, malaria, worm infestations and tubercuiosis if taken individually. Together these disorders account for 12 per cent of the Global Burden of Disease (GBD) and an analysis of

trends indicates this will increase to 15 per cent by 2020 (World Health Report, 2001). One in four families is likely to have at least one member with a behavioural or mental disorder (WHO, 2001). These families not only provide physical and emotional support, but also bear the negative impact of stigma and discrimination. Most of them (>90%) remain untreated. Poor awareness about symptoms of mental illness, myths and stigma related to it, lack of knowledge on the treatment availability and potential benefits of seeking treatment are important causes for the high treatment gap.

To quote from Introduction to the *Annual Reports 2012-13* of the Ministry of Health and Family Welfare (2013):

> It is estimated that 3 per cent of the population suffer from Severe Mental Disorders (SMD) and 10 per cent of the population from Common Mental Disorders (CMD). In line with global trends India looks towards moving away from a mental hospital based treatment protocol with a greater focus on community and home based care.

To quote WHO (2014a):

> Hackett, *et. al.* (1999), assessed 1403 children and found the prevalence of psychiatric disorders to be 9.4 per cent as per ICD-10. Psychiatric morbidity was associated with gender (male), socio-economic status (low), parental education (poor), attainment in school (impaired) and life events." (WHO, 2014a)

Further:

> A meta-analysis of 13 psychiatric epidemiological studies (*n* = 33 572) yielded an estimated prevalence rate of 5.8 per cent (Reddy & Chandrashekar, 1998). Organic psychosis (0.04%), alcohol/drug dependence (0.69%), schizophrenia (0.27%), affective disorders (1.23%), neurotic disorders (2.07%), mental retardation (0.69%) and epilepsy (0.44%) were commonly diagnosed. Psychiatric morbidity was associated with residence (urban), gender (females), age group (35-44 years), marital status (married/widowed/divorced), socioe-conomic status (lower) and family type (nuclear). Epilepsy and hysteria were significantly more common in rural communities. Nandi, *et al.* (2000), reported that psychiatric morbidity decreased from 11.7 to 10.5 per cent over 20 years in a rural setting.

While there is a lot of scope for Sociology in Health to help in the implementation of mental health programme there is a need for critical study of mental health knowledge and practices using Sociology of Health (Strauss, 1957) perspective. As the Global Health Indicators Report (WHO, 2014b) shows mental health facilities in South Asian countries are grossly neglected. In India, during 2006-2010, the number of psychiatrists per 10,000 population was less than 0.05 against the global average of 0.3. During the same period the number of psychiatric beds was 0.2 per 10,000 population (as against the global average of 2.5). This was about 35 times less than the number of hospital beds per 10,000 population (70). There are few facilities for treatment and rehabilitation of those suffering from severe mental disorders as only 0.06 per cent of the total health budget is spent on mental health (WHO, 2011). The number of mental hospitals per 1,00,000 population is only .004 and number of beds in mental hospitals is only 1.469 per 1,00,000 population. The facilities for outpatients (OPD services) in mental health hospital is 0.329 per 1,00,000 population and psychiatric beds in general populations is only 0.823 per 1,00,000 population. Although these data pertain to the Central Government only it may be said that the facilities for treatment and rehabilitation of mental health sufferers are inadequate. The data on treatment is not available and the only information in this regard is that admissions to mental health hospitals are 14.52 per 1,00,000 population; and most of those in mental hospitals (62%) have stayed in hospital for less than one year (WHO, 2011). The training of psychiatrists, medical doctors, nurses, psychologists, social workers, occupational therapists and other health workers is dismal and there are no data on informal human resources (family and user associations) and expenditures on medicines for mental and behavioural disorders.

WHO (u.d.) divides mental (Category E of causes of deaths) and neurological conditions (Category F) into 18 sub-categories, and reports mortality estimates (DALYs), separately for males and females, under each sub-category. The sub-categories are as follows:

Mental and behavioural disorders

1. Unipolar depressive disorders
2. Bipolar disorder
3. Schizophrenia
4. Alcohol use disorders
5. Drug use disorders
6. Anxiety disorders
7. Eating disorders

8. Pervasive developmental disorders
9. Childhood behavioural disorders
10. Idiopathic intellectual disability
11. Other mental and behavioural disorders

Neurological conditions

1. Alzheimer's disease and other dementias
2. Parkinson's disease
3. Epilepsy
4. Multiple sclerosis
5. Migraine
6. Non-migraine headache
7. Other neurological conditions

Statistical data show that among all the above causes of deaths in India, the numbers under epilepsy, alcohol and drugs are highest. There is a need for more data on prevalence of the above disorders and whether they are treated or not treated. It may be noted that about 70 per cent of the times epilepsy responds to treatment but nearly three-fourths of the affected people in the developing countries do not get the treatment, and suffer from stigma and discrimination (WHO, 2012).

Mental Health Policy in India

In India, health is a State subject but the Centre has a National Mental Health Programme (NMHP). This was implemented in 1982 (WHO, 2011). At present 123 districts are covered under District Mental Health Programme under this programme. In absence of an all-India survey little is known about the prevalence of mental health disorders in India. Yet, the prevalence seems to be quite substantial. It may be noted that till 2014 India did not have a mental health policy though plan for mental health existed for a long time and was revised in 2009.

In the post-Independence India a Mental Health Act (MHA) was passed in 1987 by the Parliament that came into existence in all States and Union Territories in 1993. This replaced the Indian Lunacy Act (ILA) of 1912. The time gap of 75 years between the two Acts explains how mental health was rather ignored by the health planners in India. It is notable that while the ILA, 1912 (RFHHA) aimed at segregation of mentally ill people for the protection of society, the MHA, 1987 aimed at protection of patients and their human rights (NIHFW, u.d.). The new Act changed the discourse on mental health. The term "nursing home asylum" was changed to "psychiatric hospital"; "lunatic" was changed to "mentally ill person"; "criminal lunatic" was changed to "mentally ill prisoner". Now, the psychiatric patients could go on "leave of absence" emphasizing the concept of community rehabilitation. Yet, the new Act has the problem that a person can be kept in psychiatric nursing hospital involuntarily on an application made by a relative or a friend of the ill person on his/her behalf. Such provisions have been used to granting divorce and can lead to harassment of women and old people. On 10 October 2014, first time, the Ministry of Health and Family Welfare (MoHFW, 2014) announced the National Mental Health Policy. The new policy includes the following values: equity, justice, integrated care, evidence based care, quality, participatory and rights based approach, governance and effective delivery, value base in all training and teaching programmes, and holistic approach. It recognizes the special needs of orphaned persons, children of persons with mental health problems, and elderly caregivers. The policy aims to provide health facilities with the involvement of persons with mental health problems and caregivers in grassroots level health programmes and various committees (Swasthya Gram Samiti, Rogi Kalyan Samiti).

Since, mental health was not a priority there are only small efforts to prevent mental disorders. Of course one reason behind this problem is that the causes of mental disorders are least understood and most disputed, and due to stigma there is also a less demand for mental health services. The new policy recognizes the importance of this when it proposes the following four research questions:

1. Ways of providing treatment in routine healthcare.
2. Causes of mental disorders in the Indian context.
3. Identifying effective treatment methods, including indigenous systems.
4. Deeper understanding of bio-psycho-social determinants.

Understanding Subjective Well-being

From the well-being perspective mental health promotion is a social issue (and to a lesser extent a counselling issue), and is not the same thing as clinical treatment of disorders. In this perspective mental health is defined as subjective well-being or happiness and this concept of mental health goes beyond mere absence of mental disorders. Thus, this side of mental health is even more social than the sociologized understandings of mental illness. This section reviews how social scientists measure, view and look at mental health as subjective well-being.

At the outset, to study something empirically is to measure it. Thus, measuring happiness is a new phenomenon in the West where most works on subjective well-being have been done. In the Western context, where happiness is one of the most researched topics, scales have been developed to measure to what extent a person is happy. Such measures are particularly needed if one wants to know to what extent happiness is dependent on demographic and socio-economic factors such as age, sex, marital status and economic characteristics. In addition, for study of level, causes, consequences and dynamics of happiness we have to have some psychometric measures of happiness which provide overall scores of happiness as well as scores of different dimensions of happiness. Several efforts have been made in this direction. As with any other psychometric scales, to construct a scale of happiness, first of all one needs to develop an inventory of items which may be used as proper measure of happiness. This can be done by using existing literature on the subject or by conducting qualitative studies of how people conceptualize happiness. Then appropriate scales such as Likert scale are developed to measure each item. Finally, the overall or unitary happiness score is obtained by taking a simple or weighted sum of all the items. At the end, researchers have to provide estimates of reliability and validity of the suggested scale. In other words, they have to tell us to what degree their results can be reproduced in further research and to what degree they are the exact measures.

Böckerman and Ilmakunnas (2006) used World Values Surveys measures of happiness based on a simple question: "Taking all things together, would you say you are 4 (very happy), 3 (quite happy), 2 (not very happy), or 1 (not at all happy)." Likewise life satisfaction is measured by asking the question: "All things considered, how satisfied are you with your life as a whole in these days?" Böckerman and Ilmakunnas used a scale from 1 to 10 for responses. Such scales provide overall measures of happiness without referring to any particular dimension of happiness. It is assumed that although their happiness may depend on a number of things, but people are able to think in terms of overall levels of happiness and communicate with others in those terms.

Lyubomirsky and Lepper (1999) developed a measure of subjective happiness and it was validated on more than two thousand seven hundred student participants in USA. Their scale consists of four items, each of which attempts to explore the subjective side of one's happiness. The four items are: (i) whether *in general* one considers himself/herself to happy person; (ii) whether compared to most of his/her peers one considers himself/herself to happy person; (iii) regardless of what is going on in life whether one considers himself/herself to happy person as some people are generally happy and try to get the most out of everything; (iv) to what extent is one happy considering the fact that some people are generally not very happy, although not depressed. This way of conceptualization looks at happiness as it relates to present condition, personality, and evaluation of life. While present condition are very much part of social structure in both absolute and relative sense, personality is based on individual's organization of different roles and it affects evaluation of life.

Oxford Happiness Questionnaire (OHQ) is more known of the scales of happiness. It was developed by Hills and Argyle in The Oxford Happiness Project, School of Psychology, Oxford Brookes University, Oxford, and used by Kelm of Appreciative Living LLC (http://happiness-survey.com/survey/, 2010). It has been derived from Oxford Happiness Inventory (OHI) which comprises 29 items, each involving the selection of one of the four options. The options for each item were different. OHQ uses the same items but single statement for each item which can be endorsed on a uniform six-point Likert scale. OHI/OHQ includes 29 statements for measuring happiness. The choices on a six-point scale vary from strongly disagree to strongly agree. The choices are: Strongly Disagree (1); Moderately Disagree (2); Slightly Disagree (3); Slightly Agree (4); Moderately Agree (5); and Strongly Agree (6). On the basis of respondent's choices an overall score is obtained by adding all 29 choice scores and dividing this by 29; certain negative statements are reverse coded, i.e. for them the scores would be: Strongly Disagree (6); Moderately Disagree (5); Slightly Disagree (4); Slightly Agree (3); Moderately Agree (2); and Strongly Agree (1). It is said about the score that the most unhappy person gets a "1" and the happiest person gets a "6". The average person scores slightly over 4.

The International Institute of Management is conducting a survey of happiness that asks the respondents to rate their satisfaction in seven areas: (1) Economic satisfaction (savings, debt and purchasing power); (2) Environmental satisfaction: (pollution, noise and traffic); (3) Workplace satisfaction (job satisfaction, motivation, ethics, conflict, etc.); (4) Physical health (severe illnesses, overweight, . .); (5) Mental health (usage of antidepressants, self-esteem, positive outlook. . .); (6) Social satisfaction [including family and relationship satisfaction] (domestic disputes, communication, support, sex, discrimination, safety, divorce rates, complaints of domestic conflicts and family lawsuits, public lawsuits, crime rates, etc.); (7) Political satisfaction (quality of local democracy, individual freedom, and foreign conflicts, etc.).

In addition, the following questions are also asked:

1. What are the top 10 positive things in your life?
   (Home, work, society, health, economic, politics and environment)
   (List up to 10 positives. Max 1000 character)
2. What are the top 10 challenges in your life?
   (Home, work, society, health, economic, politics and environment)
   (List up to 10 challenges. Max 1000 character)
3. What would you advise your government and business leaders?
   (Home, work, society, health, economic, politics and environment)
   (List up to 10 improvement recommendations. Max 1000 character)
4. What are the most influential (positive or negative) local or global governmental and non-governmental initiatives/projects?
   (Home, work, society, health, economic, politics and environment)
   (List up to 10 projects. Max 1000 character)

The purpose of this survey is stated to be as follows: "to provide a public policy white paper to world governments, NGOs and businesses to advise their leaders on current and emerging issues and share innovative solutions and best practices to improve your personal and professional lives". In this exercise seven areas, namely, home/family, work, society, physical and mental health, economy, political, and living environment are rated on a eleven-point scale from 0-10, with 0 being very dissatisfied, 5 being neutral, and 10 being very satisfied. In this case happiness is seen as a joint outcome of satisfaction with seven conditions: economic, environmental, workplace, health, mental health, social relationships, and political with equal weight attached to all. One may argue that the list is not complete or that happiness does not depend equally on all seven dimensions. Many things may be seen as missing. Moreover, the contribution of the different factors in making a person happy or unhappy may be different. For example, a one-point reduction in economic satisfaction may not be compensated by a one-point improvement in political satisfaction; a one-point improvement in economic satisfaction may improve the overall happiness by the same amount or less, or more, as a one-point improvement in political satisfaction.

In addition to surveys of happiness, The World Values Survey (WVS) also reveals a lot about values and happiness. These surveys have shifted the attention of researchers from who is happy to why are people happy and they explore the processes which affect subjective well-being (Diener, 2000). They also aim at exploring how people's values and beliefs change over time and what social and political impact they have. The WVS measures, monitors and analyzes the following: support for democracy, tolerance of foreigners and ethnic minorities, support for gender equality, the role of religion and changing levels of religiosity, the impact of globalization, attitudes toward the environment, work, family, politics, national identity, culture, diversity, insecurity, and subjective well-being.

In India ICMR-WHO Project (Shah, Parhee, Kumar, Khanna & Singh, 2005) has developed scales of subjective well-being (40 items) and community well-being (33 items) which have shown good factor and concurrent validity. The project has also developed scales to measure risk among children.

In 2008 World Map of happiness ranked Denmark as the happiest nation (Conger, 2011). The same year World Database of happiness ranked it second. The findings of the WVS show that initially as per capita income increases the survival and well-being measure increases at a rapid pace, and after attaining a certain level of per capita income it increases little and eventually stagnates. The relationship is, however mediated, by several factors such as extent of TV viewing (Bruni and Stanca, 2005). It is notable that the developing countries such as India which have a rather lower per capita income are not so poor in happiness. Does this mean that in India happiness is not defined primarily in economic terms, or does this mean that the economically developed countries have followed a path of development that has made people unhappy by giving rise to new forms of conflicts, stressors, and frustrations? If you argue that the economically developed countries have followed a path of development that has made people unhappy should India follow the same path of development and become unhappy? The gains of economic development seem to be neutralized by loss of happiness on other fronts.

Needless to say, the findings based on surveys of happiness and values have certain limitations. First of all, there is a lack of match between understanding of happiness and values between the laypersons and experts. Secondly, we are not so sure about reliability and validity of scales of happiness and values in different cultural settings. In case multiple items are used to measure happiness, there is a need to go for item analysis and check whether there are some items having too strong or too weak an effect on the overall scores. Thirdly, the meaning of or the factors of happiness may vary from one culture to another. Fourthly, the correlations between socio-economic factors and happiness reveal only macro-level relationships. It will be a folly to assume that the micro-level relationships are same as the macro-level relationships. Thus, if there is a strong positive relationship between income and happiness, it does not mean that all the rich people are happy. The macro-level correlations are certainly needed for policy making but they add little to theory making at the individual level. Lastly, there may be no relationship between percentage unhappy and threat to society. The threat may come from a small number of people, the intellectuals who can theorize human conditions and demonstrate the need and ways for change.

Thus, although important from policy and academic points of view, the happiness measurements add very little to our understanding of level and correlates of happiness. Such researches are important in their own rights but they need to be combined with the philosophical and speculative works on the subject. There is also a need to use qualitative methods such as narratives and participatory rapid (or relaxed) appraisal techniques to understand people's understanding of happiness and values. Through such researches we can know about happiness and its correlates more from people's perspective rather than experts' perspective. These researches can bridge the gap between purely positivistic research on the subject and the demands of the developing theory of happiness at the individual level. There is also a need to critique the well-being approach and how well-being is implicated in the larger dynamics of power and knowledge.

In the East, measurement of happiness seems to be a relatively less researched topic as the dominant view on mental health is that it is state of being free from known mental disorders. Bhutan is the only example where planning process has a direct concern with happiness. It has pursued the goal of Gross National Happiness (GNH) since 1972 (Johnston, 2010). Gross National Happiness Commission (GNHC) evaluates projects and policies based on 26 criteria which include culture, economic security, rights, gender equality, values and pollution (GNHC, 2011).

It needs to be stressed that mental disorders and happiness are not binary concepts and are also not fully dependent on each other. A person suffering from air travel phobia may enjoy a high degree of happiness if he has all the factors of happiness. Also lack of phobia or schizophrenia does not imply happiness as the two states are dependent on different facts. Yet, there are certain common social factors which shape both of them. While high level of trust, social capital, governance, equality of resources, and social security are likely to reduce mental illness and promote well-being, distrust, alienation, chaos, extreme inequality and insecurity may lead to higher incidence of mental illness and lower subjective well-being. More researches are needed to explore their social connections and link the two.

Combining Mental Disorders and Happiness and Research Issues in India

From an integral perspective proposed here, there is a need to develop an integrated approach to the two mental issues: mental disorders and subjective well-being. The two are the overlapping dimensions of mental health and both of them are determined by social structure and processes. The above discussion shows that the concept of mental health is far from being binary and two aspects of mental health — mental illness and subjective well-being or happiness — maintain some degree of independence. Sqheff (2009) uses the social status theory to distinguish between mental disorder and positive mental health which explains the duality of the mental health. To quote:

The following six criteria are among those most prominent:

1. Attitude towards one's self: self-esteem, correctness of self-conception, etc.
2. Growth, development, or self-actualization.
3. Integration of the self.
4. Autonomy; independence.
5. Adequacy of perception of reality.
6. Mastery of the environment.

These disparate and conflicting criteria of mental health would appear to be little related to ordinary notions of health, but rather formulations of what the various authors regard to be the highest values to which our society ought to aspire in shaping ourselves and our children. As such values, the concept of positive mental health comes very close to being what has been described as the status ideal.

Status ideals are, however, the product of society and social processes. Figure 9.1 hypothesizes the connection between society and personality on the one hand, and the mental disorders and subjective well-being on the other. The model assumes that the two aspects of mental health — illness and well-being — need not be seen as two poles along the same continuum but as two different aspects of mental health. Both of them interact with physical health and social roles, though the role of personality in shaping each of them cannot be overestimated. From a purely sociological point of view, even personality can be reduced to organization of roles in a normative set-up. The figure also implies that mental health is an important issue because it affects social health directly as well as through its impact on physical health and well-being. Social structure is shown as an exogenous variable and all others as endogenous variables.

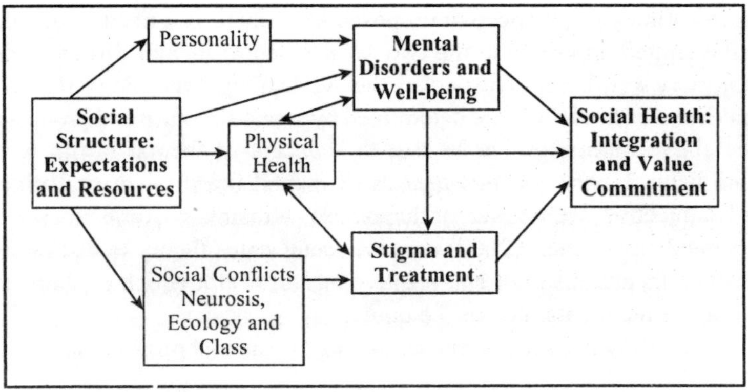

Figure 9.1: Social Structure and Mental Health

The model shown in Figure 9.1 implies that integration between individual and society is the key to mental illness and health. As such this is a very old proposition in sociology: in his famous study of suicide which paved the way for empirical sociology, Emile Durkheim posited that suicide, an extreme case of mental distress, is connected with the degree of social integration. Of course, society has its own laws of history; social transformation is not a thing that can be aimed at largely to produce good health. Therefore, though society determines the levels of mental illness and mental health it cannot be changed structurally to produce desired health outcomes with this as the main goal. Only some useful interventions can be planned by the health planners and civil society actors. The main contribution of understanding this link is twofold: (a) to sensitize health workers and psychiatrists to go beyond clinical conditions and understand health issues in local and global social contexts; and (b) to look for rehabilitation and institutional mechanisms to help the sufferers. There is one thing that can, however, easily be done at the social level and that is fighting against stigma. Countering stigma has helped in fighting against leprosy, HIV/AIDS and other health problems. It should be quite useful in identifying and solving mental health problems and promoting well-being.

In the above framework there is a need to do more research in the Indian social context. The major questions for research would be:

1. What are major mental health disorders in India?
2. What proportion of population is suffering from them?
3. What is the nature and role of stigma against mental disorders? What are successes and failures of interventions launched to fight against stigma?
4. What are social, demographic, environmental and individual determinants of them?
5. What is the degree of mental health inequality in India? How is it associated with socio-economic and political inequalities? Do gender, class and community affect mental health?
6. What are levels and determinants of happiness in India?
7. What are the consequences of economic reforms (withdrawal of state from health and greater reliance on lifestyle and agency) on well-being and mental health inequality?
8. What interventions are needed by state and civil society actors to normalize mental health conditions and provide services to the needy?

Conclusion

The above survey shows that mental health and well-being are multi-faceted and liminal concepts. They overlap as well as determine each other. Recent works in sociology of mental health have opened the wide array of windows into research on mental health from sociological perspective. They clearly demonstrate that mental disorders are associated with social class and race, urban-rural residence, and marital status. We need more literature on socio-cultural specificity and diversity, social tensions and conflict, to contribute to the emerging branch of mental health under the auspices of sociology of health. To be happy is to be economically satisfied, living in healthy environment, to be happy with work, absence of diseases, malnutrition and obesity, freedom from mental disorders, happy family and political emancipation. Mental illness may adversely affect happiness but so can any other social and environmental cause of subjective well-being. Also absence of mental illness does not mean happiness and mental disorder does not necessarily lead to unhappiness. Moreover, it is not possible for the state in the present times to intervene at all the levels of satisfactions, treatment and rehabilitation. In complex world of today both state and civil society have to work together for a perfect system in which all social needs of all citizens are satisfied, and in which no class of people remain under stress or develop distress. Both can help in building a society in which mental disorders are not stigmatized and sufferers can be made functional to the extent possible. The example of Bhutan can serve as guideline. Moreover, along with physical health, mental health services should become integrated part of primary, secondary and tertiary health services and become available to all.

REFERENCES

Aneshensel, C.S., Phelan, Jo C. and Bierman, A. (2013). "The Sociology of Mental Health: Surveying the Field", in Aneshensel, C.S., Phelan, Jo C. and Bierman, A. (eds.), *Handbook of the Sociology of Mental Health* (p. 10), New York: Springer.

Anisman, H. (2014). *An Introduction to Stress and Health*, London: Sage.

Böckerman, P. and Ilmakunnas, P. (2006). "Elusive Effects of Unemployment on Happiness", *Social Indicators Research*, 79(1), 159-69.

Bruni, L. and Stanca, L. (2005). *Income Aspirations, Television and Happiness: Evidence from the World Values Surveys*, Working Paper, Economics Department, Milan Bicocca University, Retrieved from: http://dipeco.economia.unimib.it/repec/pdf/mibwpaper89.pdf

Conger, C. (2009). *How do You Measure Happiness?* Retrieved from: http://science.howstuffworks.com/life/measure-happiness.htm

Davis, K. (1966). *Human Society*, New York: The Macmillan Company.

Diener, E.D. (2000). *Subjective Well-being*, Retrieved from: http://internal.psychology.illinois.edu/~broberts/Diener%202000.pdf

GNHC, Bhutan (2011). Retrieved from: http://www.gnhc.gov.bt/wp-content/uploads/2011/05/Policy-and-Project-Screening-Tools.pdf

Hamilton, *et al.* (1990), quoted in White, K. (2011). *An Introduction to Sociology of Health and Illness* (2nd ed). London: Sage.

Hills, P. and Argyle, M. (2002). "The Oxford Happiness Questionnaire: A Compact Scale for the Measurement of Psychological Well-being", *Personality and Individual Differences*, 33, 1073-82.

Inglehart, R. (1997). *Modernization and Post-modernization*, Princeton: Princeton University Press.

International Institute of Management (n.d.). Retrieved from: http://www.iim-edu.org/polls/grossnationalhappinesssurvey.htm

Johnston, P. (2010). "How Can we Measure Happiness?" *The Telegraph* (16 Nov.). Retrieved from: http://www.telegraph.co.uk/comment/columnists/philipjohnston/8136139/How-can-we-measure-happiness.html

Lyubomirsky, S. and Lepper, H.S. (1999). "A Measure of Subjective Happiness: Preliminary Reliability and Construct Validation", *Social Indicators Research*, 46, 137-55. Retrieved from: http://www.psychologytoday.com/files/attachments/496/subjective-happiness-scale.pdf

Macionis, J.J. and Plummer, K. (2014). *Sociology: A Global Introduction* (5th ed.), Noida, India: Prentice-Hall.

Ministry of Health and Family Welfare. (2011). *Annual Report to the People on Health* (December, 2011). Retrieved from: http://www.mohfw.nic.in/index1.php?lang=1&level=1&sublinkid=1724&lid=1616

Ministry of Health and Family Welfare (2013). *In Introduction to the Annual Reports 2012-13 of the Ministry of Health and Family Welfare (2013).* Retrieved from: http://mohfw.nic.in/index1.php?lang=1&level=2&sublinkid=3854&lid=2028

Ministry of Health and Family Welfare (2014). *National Mental Health Policy.* Retrieved from: http://mohfw.gov.in/index1.php?lang=1&level=2&sublinkid=4523&lid=2964

National Institute of Health and Family Welfare, u.d., *Mental Health Act 1987.* Retrieved from: http://nihfw.nic.in/ndc-nihfw/html/Legislations/MentalHealthAct.htm

Prabhakar, A. and Dubouis, K. (2013). *Finally, a National Survey on Mental Health Disorders in India*, Retrieved from DNA, http://www.dnaindia.com/health/report-finally-a-national-survey-on-mental-health-disorders-in-india-1848694

Read, Jen'nan G. and Gorman, B.K. (2011). "Gender and Health Revisited", in B.A. Pescosolido, J.K. Martin, J.D. McLeod and A. Rogers (eds.), *Handbook of the Sociology of Health*, Illness and Healing (pp. 411-29). New York: Springer.

Research Foundation of Hospital and Healthcare Administration (RFHHA), u.d., *Indian Lunacy Act 1912.* Retrieved from: http://www.rfhha.org/images/pdf/Hospital_Laws/Indian_lunacy_act_1912.pdf

Rogers, A. and David, P. (2010). *A Sociology: Mental Health and Illness*, 4th edition (pp. 12-19), Open University Press.

Rogers, A. and David, P. (2011). "Medical Sociology and Its Relationship to Other Disciplines: The Case of Mental Health and the Ambivalent Relationship between Sociology and Psychiatry", in Poscosolido, A. Bernice, Jack K. Martin, Jane D. McLeod, and A. Rogers (eds.), *Handbook of the Sociology of Health*, Illness and Healing (pp. 21-38), New York: Springer.

Rosenhan, D. (1973). "On Being Sane in Insane Places", *Science*, 179(4070), 250-58.

Scheff, T.J. (2009). *Being Mentally Ill: A Sociological Theory* (3rd ed.), Transaction USA: Aldine.

Shah, B., Parhee, R., Kumar, N., Khanna, T. and Singh, R. (2005). *Mental Health Research in India: Technical Monograph on ICMR Mental Health Studies.* Retrieved from: http://www.icmr.nic.in/publ/Mental%20Helth%20.pdf

Strauss, R. (1957). "The Nature and Status of Medical Sociology", *American Sociological Review*, 22(2), 200-04.

Weiss, G.L. and Lonnquist, L. (1996). *The Sociology of Health, Healing and Illness* (pp. 75-77), New Jersey: Prentice-Hall Inc.

World Health Organization (2004a). *Heath Topics: Mental Health.* Retrieved from: http://www.who.int/topics/mental_health/en/

World Health Organization (2004b). *Heath Topics: Mental Health.* Retrieved from: http://www.who.int/features/qa/62/en/

World Health Organization (2011). *Mental Health Atlas.* Retrieved from: http://www.who.int/mental_health/evidence/atlas/profiles/ind_mh_profile.pdf?ua=1.

World Health Organization (2012). *Epilepsy*. Retrieved from: http://www.who.int/mediacentre/factsheets/fs999/en/

World Health Organization (2014a). *Profiles Countries E-I*. Retrieved from: http://www.who.int/mental_health/evidence/mhatlas05/en/

World Health Organization (2014b). *Global Health Indicators*. Retrieved from: http://www.who.int/gho/publications/world_health_statistics/2014/en/

World Health Organization, u.d., *DALY Estimates 2000-2012: Health Statistics and Information Systems: Estimates for 2000-2012*. Retrieved from: http://www.who.int/healthinfo/global_burden_disease/estimates/en/index2.html

World Values Survey, http://www.worldvaluessurvey.org/ http://www.worldvaluessurvey.org/wvs/articles/folder_published/article_base_56

10

The Concept of Mental Illness, Healing Traditions, and Involvement of Families in Caring in the Indian Context: A Review

Bidisha Banerjee and *Shikha Dixit*

Conceptualizations and philosophical thoughts regarding illness contribute in development of explanatory models and beliefs of an individual regarding mental illness. Explanatory models of health and illness are the meaningful connections and shared beliefs that people share regarding a etiology of illness and health seeking behaviour (Kleinman, 1980). Explanatory models define the attitude and actions of family members towards the illness as well as the patients (Karp, 2001). The present chapter aims to discuss the concepts and understanding of mental illness, health care pluralisms, and role of families in psychiatric care in India. It can be observed from the following discussion that most studies in mental illness context have been conducted with patients' experiences as the focal point and family members' experiences got only a peripheral attention. Even though family plays an important role in psychiatric care in India, family members' voices are largely ignored in researches. Thus, this review aims to suggest some future research possibilities that would be able to address the family members' needs and suffering with their relatives' experiences.

This chapter has been divided into six major sections. In the first section, the philosophical thoughts, concepts of mental illness, and different healing traditions in India have been discussed. The second section describes the nature of psychiatric pluralism in India. In the third section, the role of families in psychiatric care is discussed. The fourth and fifth sections are devoted to survey of Indian studies on care giving and explanatory models. The chapter ends with a conclusion that comprises of the major observations from the review and future directions for caring research in India.

Indian Philosophical Thoughts about Self and Conceptualization of Mental Illness

Culture in India is a multifaceted phenomenon (Sinha & Kumar, 2004). Cultural diversity, varied languages, religions, and geographical variations characterize India. There exist 4639 ethnic communities in India (Gangadharan & Shankar, 2009). Within this diversity, however, there exist similarities amongst cultures and ethnic groups. Therefore, the culture in India is known as "unity in diversity" (Khandelwal, Jhingan, Ramesh, Gupta, & Srivastava, 2004; p. 128). Like other South Asian countries, India is also recognized for its pluralistic health care system and its age-old healing traditions (Patel, Sumathipala, Khan, Thapa, & Rahman, 2007; Obeyesekere, 1977; Bhattacharyya, 1983; Leslie, 1980; Weiss, *et al.*, 1986). Along with biomedicine, Ayurvedic, Siddha, Unnani, Tibetan, Homoeopathic and folk healing traditions coexist in India. Among these, Ayurveda and Siddha are the traditional Indian healing systems. Each of these healing systems has its own ontology and epistemology (philosophical understanding) and conceptualizations of illness. The Indian philosophy also has a distinct explanation of self and body. These philosophical understandings contributed in construction of beliefs and explanations regarding illness. In the following sub-sections, the Indian concept of self, classical health care system and conceptualization of mental illness, and the contemporary mental health care system have been discussed.

The Concept of Self in Indian Philosophy

The Indian philosophical systems are mostly based on the knowledge of *Upaniṣads* and *Vedas*. The "self" is known as the "subtle body" (Kakar, 1982). The constituent parts of the subtle body include the following — "*buddhi*" (intellect and cosmic intelligence), "*ahaṁkarā*" or "I-ness" (the unique aspect of individual which distinguish an individual from others), "*manasa*" or "*manas*"[1] (to some extent signifies, but not similar as mind, and resides in human heart), the "*indrias*" (five sensory organs, and the related motor organs involved in speech, handling, walking, evacuation, and reproduction), and the "*tanmātrās*" (the subtle matter or potential energies, such as sound, touch, colour, taste, and smell) (Kakar, 1982, p. 239).The knowledge of self —

> . . . lies beyond the senses, the mind, and the intellect; its essence cannot be seen with the eyes or captured by the mind or by words, for the Self is not observable and locatable within physical bodies; it is disembodied, hence everywhere like space (Paranjpe, 1998; p. 118).

Health is a balance and coordination between the *manasa*, the self and the body, which are connected. The life is situated within the connection (Dasgupta, 1968; cited in Obeyesekere, 1977). *Manas* is filled with the three *guṇas* (qualities) such as, *sattva* (purity, light, intellect), *rajas* (passion and activity), and *tamas* (inertia or darkness) (Kakar, 1982, p. 244). *Manas* becomes active and dynamic through the activities of three *guṇas* or qualities. Each of these three qualities continuously tries to achieve the highest state within *manas* (Kakar, 1982, p. 244).

The Classical Health Care System and the Conceptualization of Mental Illness

The traditional or classical health care systems in India, Ayurveda and Sidhha, originated around 1200 A.D. (Greenough, 2003). According to Kakar (1982) "Ayurveda is the principle architect of the Indian view of the person and the body" (p. 224). The meaning of Ayurveda is the science of long and disease free life (Shamasundar, 2008, p. 141). The basic assumption of Ayurveda insists upon maintaining equilibrium of different elements and humours of the body (Obeyesekere, 1977).

Illness in general, and mental illness in particular has been understood in Ayurveda through imbalance in three fundamental principles: five *bhūtas* (wind, fire, earth, water, and ether); the three humours or *tridōṣa* (wind or *vāyu*, bile or *pitta*, and water as phlegm or *kapha*); and seven *dhātus* or body components (juice, blood, flesh, fat, bone, marrows, and semen) (Obeyesekere, 1977).

There are different theories of causation of mental illness in Ayurveda:

1. Mental illness occurs when the equilibrium of the three humours (wind, bile, and water) gets disturbed and when there is a problem in proper functioning of heart due to malfunction of ducts (*sirā*) and other channels (*dhamani*) that carry the humours and body components (*dhātus*). This indicates the somato-psychic nature of the causes of mental illness (Obeyesekere, 1977).

2. The balance controls *manas* and disequilibrium of *rajas* and *tamas* (excitation and disturbance) can lead to mental illness. *Rajas* and *tamas* are recognized as the mental humours of *manas* (Kakar, 1982, p. 244).
3. Disturbance or impairment of functions of *manas*,[1] is another reason for causation of mental illness (Kakar, 1982, Obeyesekere, 1977).

There are other three types of mental illnesses described in Ayurveda. The classification has been done according to the origin of the illness and the nature of manifestations of symptoms. First, there are some diseases that have originated in mind and manifestation of the symptoms are mental, such as *unmāda* (madness or severe mental illness). *Unmāda* covers most of the psychotic disorders, impulse neurosis, and obsessions. Second, there are some diseases that originate in mind but manifestation of symptoms occurs physically. For example, "epilepsy (*apasmāra*), hysterical fits (*apatantraka*), diarrhoea caused by grief and fear (*sokaja* and *bhayātisāra*), insomnia (*nidrānāsa*), "fever from grief and sexual desire" (*sokaja* and *kamajajvara*). Third, there are also some diseases that originate physically, but symptoms manifestation happens mentally, such as *attatvabhinivesa* or "certain delusional states", and *mada* or "alcohol or drug intoxication" (Kakar, 1982, pp. 242-43).

Unmāda has also been classified according to the disequilibrium in the humours, such as, "*vatounmāda*" (due to exaggeration of *vāyu* or wind), "*pittounmāda*" (due to exaggeration of *pitta* or bile), and "*kaphounmāda*" (due to excessive amount of *kapha* or phlegm) (Kapur, 1979, p. 28). On the other hand, *Unmāda* has been divided as *nija* and *āgantu* according to the origin of cause (inside or outside causes) by *Caraka Saṁhitā* and *Bhela Saṁhitā* (Weiss, *et al.*, 1986).

The internal causes of *Unmāda* are considered as the imbalance in humours or functions of *manasa*. Whereas, *Unmāda* due to the external or outside causes is regarded as supernatural interferences such as *bhūta, deva, gandharva, yakṣa* and *piśāca* (Weiss, *et al.*, 1986; Wagner, Duveen, Themel, & Verma, 1999; Kapur, 1979), the *Unmāda* due to external or supernatural causes depends on the following behaviours (Weiss, *et al.*, 1986): when the individual engages in inappropriate deeds such as, sexual activity during full moon or the new moon; eating foods that are forbidden; engaging in action that might offend gods, teachers, and elders; when the individual faces pressure and helplessness; and when the individual indulges in improper thinking and understanding.

According to Indian philosophy, a mentally healthy person —

> . . . attends to one's legitimate duties in personal, family, social and occupational areas fulfilling spiritual, affectional, and material needs of self and family in harmony among one's role functions, one's abilities and limitations, prevailing circumstances and righteous means with sincerity and honesty, hope and confidence, and contentment (Shamasundar, 2008; p. 140).

The metaphysical theories of the Indian philosophy are centred on the "*mokṣa-dharma-karma complex*" which is also known as the "liberation theory" (Kakar, 1982, p. 224). *Dharma* is known as the virtue or responsibility towards others and oneself. The Hindu philosophy provides four important goals of life, such as *dharma* (virtue), *artha* (material goods), *kāma* (sensual pleasure), and *mokṣha* (self-realization) (Kakar, 1982, p. 224). The goal of Ayurveda, the traditional healing system of India encompasses these goals (Kakar, 1982).

The practitioners of Ayurveda are known as *vaid* (Kakar, 1982; Kapur, 1979). Treatment of mental illness in Ayurveda mainly aims to re-establish the balance among the humours. There are various healing methods prescribed in Ayurveda, such as *yoga*, food restrictions, decoctions (using various indigenous herbs, oils), head pack, and *nasna* (draining of phlegm through the nose) (Obeyesekere, 1977; Kapur, 1979).

Another healing tradition, which originated in South India, and which shares similarities in fundamental concepts with Ayurveda is known as "*Sidhha*" (Somasundaram, 2009). *Sidhha* has its origin in mythology (Somasundaram, 2009) and it propagates the use of alchemy (Fabrega Jr., 2009). Other Indian healing traditions include folk healing, astrology, *tantra*, religious healing, and faith healing (Kakar, 1982). Other popular traditions are Unani system of medicine (origins in Arabic and Greek traditions), Tibetan medicines, homoeopathy (originated in Europe), etc.

Like Ayurvedic system, Indian folk healing tradition is also ancient and it has been mentioned in *Atharvaveda* (Wagner, *et al.*, 1999; Kapur, 1976; Nizamie & Goyal, 2010). Folk healing was suggested for treating illness or mental illness caused by supernatural entities (Weiss, *et al.*, 1986). There exist different types of folk healers who are experts of *bhūta-vidyā,* such as "*ojhā*" or "*ojhā-guṇi*" (Wanger, *et al.*, 1999), shamans, peers, and *tāntrics* (Kakar, 1982). These healers use different rituals and activities to heal their patients.

The Contemporary Mental Health Care Systems and Psychiatry in India

Before Independence in 1947, most people suffering from mental illness used to live in the community, and with the family (Murthy, 2011). There were religious healing places and shrines, which were known for keeping mental patients to heal them. Historical evidence suggests the presence of many therapeutic centres especially for mental patients at the reign of King Asoka and presence of asylums during the rule of Mohammad Khilji (Nizamie & Goyal, 2010). The British introduced psychiatry and mental asylums by establishing country's first mental hospital in Kolkata (previously known as Calcutta) in 1787 (Kumar, 2004; Thara, Padmavati, & Srinivasan, 2004). After that, many hospitals were established within the country for patients with mental illness (e.g. Mumbai, Chennai and other cities). After Independence, some remarkable developments happened in mental health care. Some of those are as follows: (a) initiative of involving families of the patients in the psychiatric care by Dr. Vidya Sagar in Amritsar; (b) establishing psychiatric wards in general hospitals to reduce stigma and spread awareness; (c) the development of community psychiatry by merging mental health services with general health care services in 1975; and (d) the formulation of the National Mental Health Programme (NMHP) in 1982 to propagate and spread the community psychiatry approach at national level (Murthy, 2011). Along with that, some non-governmental organizations (NGOs) also took initiatives to provide specialized mental health care in the community and villages (Thara, *et al.*, 2004).

At present, the mental health care in India is suffering from the scarcity of treatment facilities (such as hospitals and hospital beds), deficits in skilled professionals (mostly in rural areas), lack of awareness, lack of acceptance of biomedical care (mostly in rural areas), under utilization of health care services by the families and patients, and inadequate number of hospitals for long-term care (and proper infrastructures and management) (Murthy, 2010). However, to address the unmet need and challenges some initiatives were taken by the Government. This includes: (a) intervention by the National Human Rights Commission to address the rights of patients with mental illness; (b) opening of more psychiatric services in general hospitals; (c) a restructured NMHP with a budget of ₹ 130 crore; (d) inclusion of mental health in Eleventh Five Year Plan (2007-2013) with funding of ₹ 472.91 crore for manpower development, improving infrastructure and facilities in hospitals, and improving community mental health programme at district level, etc.; (e) some level of family support and human resource development; (f) legislation (e.g. Person With Disability Act or P.W.D. Act of 1995, and the Act of Narcotic Drugs and Psychotropic Substances or NDPS Act of 1985); (g) integrating traditional healing with biomedicine and providing a culturally sensitive care; (h) flourishing private sectors in psychiatry; and (i) increasing number of researches in this field (Murthy, 2010).

A collaborative study done in four centres in India (Bengaluru, Baroda, Kolkata, and Patiala) suggests the prevalence rate of severe mental illnesses (schizophrenia, mania, and depressive psychosis) is 9.4 per 1,000 population (Indian Council of Medical Research, 2005). According to the WHO report Mental Health Atlas (2005) there is 77 per cent deficit of psychiatrist (more than one-third of the population has 90 per cent deficit of psychiatrists) in India with some exceptions of Chandigarh, Delhi, Goa, and Puducherry. Less than 50 per cent deficits were reported in Kerala and Maharashtra only. This report also highlighted the similar inadequacy in case of psychologists, psychiatric social workers, and nurses in India. In addition to this, a recent reporting in *The Hindu* (a national daily newspaper) highlighted "acute shortage of mental health care professionals, including psychiatrists considering the high prevalence of mental health disorder" (Special Correspondent, 2013). However, there exists inconsistency in the estimates of prevalence rates of mental illness in India (Math, Chandrashekar, & Bhugra, 2007; Sarin & Jain, 2012). The estimates vary from 9.5 to 370 per 1,000 population (Math, *et al.*, 2007). Math, *et al.* (2007), criticized the research methods and lack of epidemiological studies in the area of common mental disorder in India.

Other than standard classifications of mental illnesses, studies from India have identified some specific mental illnesses among populations and they are included in international classification system (Jacob, 2010). Some of the examples are, the acute psychosis (brief psychotic episode caused by stressful situation; sub-classified as confusional, paranoid hallucinatory, schizo affective, and hysterical psychosis), and *dhāta* syndrome (culture bound syndrome; characterized by male patient's complain of semen loss, weakness, fatigue and other somatic symptoms) (Jacob, 2010). Other such illness is the "possession disorder" (included in ICD-10 under Trance and Possession Disorder as Dissociative Disorder Not Otherwise Specified or NOS) (Jacob, 2010).

Causes of mental illness in India are diverse, ranging from socio-economic conditions, urbanization, decrease in joint families and migration, unemployment and underachievement among men, natural and manmade disasters, and cumulative stressful lifestyle of Indian population. Moreover, as majority of Indian population still lives in rural areas and does not have required health care facilities and financial support, people seek treatment from various types of traditional and folk healers with whom they share explanatory models of illness and which are found to be affordable (Khandelwal, Jhingan, Ramesh, Gupta, & Srivastava, 2004). Thus, traditional healers have a major involvement in health care (Thara, Padmavati, & Srinivasan, 2004). Studies have also documented pluralistic health care beliefs and practices among people of India. In the following section health care pluralism and attitude towards mental illness are discussed with examples.

The Indian Mindset about Mental Illness: Research Evidence of Health Care Pluralism and Stigma in Mental Illness

Scholars have described the "Indian mindset" as pluralistic as well as collective (Sinha, *et al.*, 2010). According to Sinha, *et al.* (2010), the "core of the Indian mindset" is constituted by "discrepancy", "inconsistency", and "contradiction" (p. 3). Scholars have argued about the contradictory nature of Indian self by pointing out two discrete characteristics: On the one hand, Indian self is generally known as "collectivist". On the other hand, the philosophical description of Indian self highlights that, there exists a "well-protected secret self that contains highly individualistic thoughts, feelings and fantasies" (Roland, 1988, cited in Sinha & Kumar, 2004, p. 99). This contradiction and pluralism may be reflection in beliefs regarding aspects of life. The pluralistic beliefs and contradictory explanatory models are reflected in the widespread pluralistic health care practices in India, in physical as well as mental illness. This is documented through researches conducted in various parts of India among general and patient populations and healers.

Wagner, *et al.* (1999), explored "social representations of madness" in Northern India (Patna, Bihar). The aim of the research was to explore how common people in modernized Patna cope with the available pluralistic health care beliefs and practices that are contradictory in nature. They interviewed 19 men and 20 women from upper middle class, professional background, using a vignette. Using a social representation theoretical framework, they discussed the various explanations of mental illness given by participants with three themes. The first theme "family, norms, and adjustment" described the causes of mental illness as unfulfilled desires, fear, shock, psychic and physical pressure, and depression. Tension between social norms and fulfilment of desires, poverty, and unemployment were also cited by participants as causal factors. The second theme, "ideas of heredity and its moral threat to the family" described the attitude and beliefs of others (e.g. neighbours). The third theme described participants' "ideas of ghost or spirit possession". Regarding representations of healing and treatment, the authors discussed the conventional view of family as primary resource, holding to religious views, representing traditional healing as well as biomedical treatment, and ambivalence of choice among different methods of healing. One of the notable findings of this study was that though the participants denied authenticity of traditional healing or folk healing, they provided detailed description of such healing tradition. On the contrary, they failed to provide similar descriptions regarding the modern medicine in which they claimed to have faith.

A study was conducted by Chowdhuri, Chakraborty, and Weiss (2001) in three villages of two blocks of Sundarban Delta in West Bengal to identify local mental health problems and how some specific mental illnesses were understood and experienced in the community. The study used an ethnographic approach (first phase) which was followed by a cultural epidemiological survey (second phase; the local adaptations of Explanatory Models Interview Catalogue or EMIC was employed). According to the findings, the nature of the perceived threats by common people include changing environmental conditions and disruptions of ecosystems, alcohol abuse, adultery, availability of cash that may lead to unaccepted behaviour amongst youths, poverty and debt, community violence, intercaste and interreligious marriages, unemployment, political tensions, barrenness of women, birth of a female child, and dowry system. Involvements of local organizations (*samiti*) were mentioned as social support. The local health care system depends on Government services and NGOs. The study reported available treatment for general illnesses as being offered by the quacks, a few allopathic doctors, a number of homoeopathic doctors, and magico-religious healers or folk healers. Mental illness was reported to be having a lower priority as far as health is concerned, though "mental tension" was reported to be more pervasive among people. They can clearly differentiate between ideas of mental illness and mental tension. Mad people or those with severe mental illness (known as "*pāgla*" or "*pāgol*" in Bengali) were characterized as demonstrating nonsense talks, and hostile and aggressive behaviour. The causes of madness were identified as diet, possession, traumatic shock, and addiction of smoking cannabis (*gāñja*). Observation of help seeking behaviour revealed that people try each available source, such as *guṇins* and *ojhās* (folk healers), homoeopathic and allopathic doctors, and quacks.

Studies conducted with patient population also reported pluralistic explanatory models and treatment preferences. In a landmark ethno-psychiatric study on mental health pluralism in Bengal, Bhattacharyya (1983, 1986) interviewed patients and their families, mental health professionals (psychiatrists and psychoanalysts, Ayurvedic practitioners, folk healers and temple priests), and general population. She identified three kinds of pluralisms in Bengal: institutional, cognitive, and structural pluralism. The institutional pluralism denotes the existence of various healing traditions (including biomedicine), and multiple theories of illness and health, treatment, and treating personnel. Pluralism at cognitive level denotes presence of different explanatory models of illness. The author delineated three conceptual frameworks which explain *paglami* (mental illness); the ghost possession (*bhutebhor*); sorcery (*tuk*); and the *tridoṣa* theory of Ayurveda. "Shock" (mental shock), was cited often as the reason for mental illness by general population. Other explanations include mourning, grief, worries, sorrow, poverty or insufficiency, and mental conflicts (1986, p. 127). The author identified "frustrations" regarding not getting the desired goals as a key factor. Also, there exist discrepancies or "conflicting perspectives" between patients' and practitioners' understanding of illness, which results in structural pluralism. The author stressed that the presence of diverging perspectives among patients (cognitive pluralism) and psychiatrists (institutional pluralism) creates "a distinctive structure of the psychiatric domain" (1983, p. 950).

Mark Nichter (1981) identified the "idioms of distress" among *Havik Brahmin* women of South Karnataka. The commonly used idiom among these women was "food". Women expressed their distress through food-serving styles, weight loss, fasting, and poisoning (suspicion of poisoning). Amongst others, they also mentioned obsession and ambivalence regarding maintaining purity and cleanliness, illness idioms (such as, beliefs in multiple healing systems, such as Allopathy, Astrology, Homoeopathy, Ayurveda, exorcism, spirit possession, and combinations of these), supernatural causes of illness (e.g. evil eye and spirit possession), and *bhakti* or expression of devotion. Moreover, the author observed that somatization of distress was used as a common idiom among the participants.

Kapur (1975, 1979) observed the pattern of mental health care in a village located between Mumbai and Cape Comorin (western coast of

India) by conducting three separate studies. The first study investigated the conceptual frameworks of traditional healers and modern doctors. The study identified four types of healers: *vaids, mantrawādis, patris*, and practitioners of modern medicine in the village. The study informed "confusing explanatory models" among folk healers. The study revealed that popularity and reputation of healers determined the choice of healer by the patients and their families. The modern doctors were observed to be having poor training and were found prescribing minor and major tranquilizers arbitrarily. The second study was conducted to observe the attitudes of 354 randomly selected adult members of the village (three communities) regarding preferences of healers or doctors for four unambiguous psychiatric symptoms — fits with convulsions, delusion of possession, excitement, and social withdrawal. The study revealed that consultation with doctor was preferred for all the illnesses except "possession". The preference for doctor by women participants was observed in case of excitement and withdrawal. However, this study reported no relationship between age, education, and income with choice of healers. Finally, a population survey was conducted to elicit information from individuals with one or more symptoms regarding consultation of any healers. The study observed that a statistically significant relationship exists between number of symptoms and consultations; majority of the population consulted both doctors and traditional healers, and a greater proportion of women participants reported to be having consultation with doctors than male participants.

Weiss, *et al.* (1986, 1988), observed that causal explanations of mental illness ranges from humoral imbalance (heat in the head or loss of *dhāta*, i.e. semen; blood rushing to the head), psychosocial stress (mental shock), due to performing some socially unacceptable activities (violation of social and religious taboos), and biomedical causes (however, those who reported these causes could not explain them further). These studies also reported the help seeking by the patients from medical doctors, *ojhās, fakirs, maulānas, pujāris, puṇḍits*, etc.

Saravanan, Jacob, Johnson, Prince, and Bhugra (2007) used SEMI along with other instruments (the Brief Psychiatric rating scale or BPRS and Global Assessment of Functioning or GAF) to elicit explanatory models and associated clinical variables among first episode psychotic populations (131 patients) in Vellore, Tamil Nadu (South India). In this study, 70 per cent of the patients reported supernatural causes (spiritual and mystical factors) responsible for their illness. Twenty two per cent of patients showed "multiple model of illness". Beliefs and knowledge of biomedicine were found to be significantly related to higher score on insight scale. Further analysis identified three precipitating factors related to supernatural belief model, such as gender (female), low education, and visit to traditional healers. High level of insight was related to belief in biomedicine. However, this finding contradicts the earlier finding of lack of significant relationship between age, education, and income with choice of healers (Kapur, 1975).

Consultation with religious healers prior to seeking biomedical help is common in India. A study conducted among psychiatric patients in Tamil Nadu (South India) reported that 43 per cent of the patients consulted some religious healers before seeking biomedical help (Campion & Bhugra, 1997). Later, in a continuation of the earlier study Campion and Bhugra (1998) interviewed ten healers from different religious background (Hindus, Muslims, and Christians). This study reported the presence of pluralistic explanatory models amongst the healers and use of "pluralistic holistic approach" in treatment. Some healers in this study also could recognize mental illness requiring professional attention and referred patients to the professionals.

Shankar, Saravanan, and Jacob (2006) studied traditional and faith healers and their patients to understand their explanatory models in the context of common mental illness (CMI) in Vellore, Tamil Nadu (South India). Focus group discussions, in-depth interviews, vignettes, and key informants' interviews were used to elicit data. The traditional and faith healers were reported to hold various causal beliefs about CMIs. However, the healers did not recognize presence of any illness condition in the vignettes shown to them; they recognized the possible causes responsible for such conditions, such as family problems, alcoholism, spiritual factors, evil spirits, and witchcraft. The healers also revealed that sometimes they referred some patients who do not respond to their treatment, to the medical doctors. Majority of the patients presented their problems through cognitive and psychological symptoms (e.g. excessive worries and paying too much attention). One-third of the patients reported somatic complains. A significant number of patients expressed their belief in *karma*, and a few of them reported black magic. Seeking religious healing and having religious beliefs is also reported in studies conducted in other countries (Dein & Sembhi, 2001; Bhui, Bhugra, & Goldberg, 2002).

Thus, the tendency of consulting multiple healers indicates that Indian people try out all the possibilities available to them that can "fit" to their situation and explanatory models (Halliburton, 2004). Halliburton

(2004) conducted a study in Kerala (South India) to describe the experiences of patients with mental illness and healing methods applied by three kinds of healing practices available in Kerala (Ayurvedic, Allopathic, and religious healing at a Hindu temple, a Muslim mosque, and a Christian church). A follow-up interview was conducted after six to nine months of the first interview to see the changes in the illness conditions (improvement or decline) perceived by the patients and families. The results indicated that most of the therapies are effective at some level, availability of different therapies effect the care, and families and patients try all available therapies and continue the one which suits the patients and families most. However, Quack (2013) has argued, in his ethnographic study with psychiatrists and their patients (families and communities) in North India, that the tendency of taking multiple consultations among patients and families is governed by the desire and hope of getting cured.

Stigma associated with mental illness in India has also been explored. It has been reported that patients with psychological symptoms suffer more from stigma than patients with somatic symptoms (Raguram, *et al.*, 1996; cited in Jadhav, Littlewood, Ryder, Chakraborty, & Jain, 2007; Weiss, Jadhav, Raguram, Vounatsou, & Littlewood, 2001). Jadhav, *et al.* (2007), observed that there is higher stigma against mental illness in rural areas as compared to urban areas. Their study was conducted in Kanpur, Kolkata, and Assam. However, they also found that rural people showed tolerant behaviour towards neighbours suffering from mental illness; there is less secrecy about mental illness; and there is higher expectation of return to the community after recovery. Contrary to this, urban population showed open-minded attitude towards mental illness (respondents from Kolkata), but also expressed their hesitation to work with individuals with mental illness.

Thus, from the review it can be observed that pluralism in mental health care exists in India in terms of social representation of mental illness, attribution of causes, expression of illness, and help seeking or treatment choices. The pluralistic belief was observed among common people as well as people who were suffering from mental illness and their relatives. Stigma related to mental illness is also present in society. However, role of families of the patients who play an important role in health care, right from recognizing the illness, to decision-making about treatment choices, and rehabilitation and further treatment needs to be fully explored.

The next section deals with the role of Indian families in mental health care.

Role of Family in Mental Health Care in India

Research suggests that over 90 per cent of the persons suffering from schizophrenia live with their families (Sharma, Murthy, Agarwal, & Wilkinson, 1998) and there are inadequate welfare facilities or benefits for the patients and their families in India (Murthy, 2011). The data suggest a number of things, such as lack of mental health care facilities, lack of Government support, and most importantly the primary dependence of patients on their family (Avasthi, 2010; Thara, 2004). Due to insufficient health care infrastructure in India, relatives' involvement in mental health care has also been encouraged by psychiatrists and other mental health professionals (Shankar & Rao, 2005). On the other hand, three cross-national studies conducted by World Health Organization (WHO) have highlighted better outcome of dealing with schizophrenia in developing countries, such as India (e.g. WHO — the International Pilot Studies on Schizophrenia or IPSS; the Determinants of Outcome of Severe Mental Disorders or DOSMeD; and the International Study of Schizophrenia or ISoS; cited in Avasthi, 2010, p.115). Similar findings have been documented by other studies such as a comparative study of first episode psychosis in Montreal, Canada and Chennai (India) by Iyer, Mangala, Thara, & Malla (2010) and a comparative study of people with schizophrenia from Liverpool, England and Bengaluru (India) by Sharma, *et al.*, 1998. A 20 years longitudinal study by Thara (2004) also reported a relatively better prognosis among schizophrenic patients in India. In addition to these, a multicentred five years follow-up study conducted in India, demonstrated a strong association between good outcome of schizophrenic patients and attitude of the key relatives (Verghese, *et al.*, 1990). All these studies highlight the effective involvement of the families in caring for the relatives suffering from mental illness (Avasthi, 2010).

The active participation of family members in mental health care in India has been documented in literature (Nunley, 1998; Sethi, 1989; Sharma, *et al.*, 1998; Iyer, *et al.*, 2010; Shankar & Rao, 2005; Chakrabarti, 2011; Avasthi, 2010). Nunley (1998), in his ethnographic study conducted in North India (Lucknow and Varanasi), has described how an Indian family got involved in mental health care. He described that one or more relatives or friends of the patient accompanied almost all the patients. They participated in choosing the treatment appropriate for the patient, explaining the illness behaviour or symptoms of the patient to the psychiatrists, understanding the related information from the psychiatrists, taking major decision regarding treatment and medication, and taking prescription of medicine from the psychiatrists. Other than these, families of patients often accompany the ill relatives in inpatient admission. Some major psychiatric hospitals in India have provisions for family members to stay with the patients. Generally, the responsibility of the family members begins with recognizing the illness. This is followed by other acts such as, choosing the appropriate treatment and taking the relative to the outpatient unit, keeping medical records, deciding over the admissions, managing financial expenditures, helping medical staffs in taking care of patients, overall management of illness, staying with the patient, if needed (in case of patient admission), reporting the behaviour of the patient, monitoring and giving medication, handling the patients in the difficult times, and handling the discharge and continuing the treatment. Kakar (1982) has commented on help seeking behaviour in the context of mental illness in India. He stated that therapy "is generally a family and collective affair, the therapist very often has to listen to the family members of the patient recount their version of the illness before he gets a direct access to the patients" (Kakar, 1982, p. 43).

Generally, family serves three main functions. They are: biological, psychological, social and cultural (Sethi, 1989). Family also influences the personality development of the members (Chopra, 1984). "Traditionally, Indian families are joint families"[2] (Uberoi, 2003) and recognized for "strong bonds of emotional attachment, interpersonal relationships and considerable social and economic support" (Sethi, 1989; p. 24). A traditional joint family in India provides needed support to the distressed members and the responsibility of care is shared between all members of the family. In fact, the patient does not have control over his/her treatment choice or illness related aspects. However, due to rapid changes in socio-economic scenario, industrialization, urbanization, and migration from rural to urban places, joint families are getting fragmented into small nuclear families (Chopra, 1984; Nunley, 1998; Avasthy, 2010; Shankar, 1994). In this transitional phase, Gore (1968) has given the concept of "functional jointedness", which implies that, though the joint families in India have been fragmented and members do not live in the same house, they maintain good and supportive relations with each other (cited in Shankar, 1994).

Empirical evidence suggests that there exists a relationship between family structure (joint *vs.* nuclear) and family location or domicile (rural *vs.* urban) and different psychiatric disorders (Chopra, 1984; Sharma, Sethi, & Bhiman, 1984; Sethi, & Manchanda, 1978). According to available studies, patients from rural areas, where most families are traditional, joint families are better adjusted than the urban families, which are mostly nuclear in structure. These studies also reported that urban nuclear families are more susceptible to psychiatric disorders than the rural joint families. On the contrary, Dube (1970) and Thacore, *et al.* (1971, 1975), observed that psychiatric problems are more prevalent in joint families. Carstairs and Kapur (1976) did not observe any significant relationship between family structure and mental illness (cited in Chopra, 1984; p. 338). Janardhana, Shravya, Naidu, Saraswathy, and Seshan, (2011) explored the load of caregiving in 200 families with mental illness in Andhra Pradesh to observe the gender differences in caregiving. By using an interview schedule, they interviewed 101 men and 100 women carers who are from rural areas. Women were identified as the main caregivers. In addition to this, the authors also observed differences of caring engagements among male and female patients.

However, involvement of families in mental health care serves some important purposes. Firstly, the active participation in this process makes the relatives aware about the illness and related aspects; secondly, it provides necessary information and training regarding care and handling relapse situations; thirdly, it increases acceptance of the afflicted person at home and in society; fourthly, afflicted persons can adjust better if a relative stays with them throughout the cure; fifthly, with the paucity of psychiatric health care facilities, involvement of families saves the time and labour of the medical staff; and finally, this involvement also works as an important means for spreading awareness and reduction of social stigma related to mental illness. The relatives who were once involved in the care can go back to the locality and can identify others and persuade the others to take medical help in future (Verghese, 1988; Shankar & Rao, 2005; Nunley, 1998).

The family members who take care of the afflicted relative bear the whole responsibility of treatment and related needs. As a consequence, these caregivers are likely to experience the burden and stress of caregiving during the course of the illness. Scholars in this field expressed concerns, and suggested interventions and psycho education programmes that can facilitate family members to deal with the adverse situation more effectively (Shankar, 1994; Chakrabarti, 2011). The next section deals with the caregiving experiences in mental illness.

Caring Experiences of Family Members in the Context of Mental Illness: Burden, Coping, and Quality of Life

Studies have observed burden of care among relatives in the context of severe mental illness, such as schizophrenia, and affective disorder (Rammohan, Rao, & Subbakrishna, 2002; Prafulla, Murthy, & Ramaprasad, 2010; Chakrabarti, Raj, Kulhara, Avasthi, & Verma, 1995; Roychaudhuri, Mondal, Boral, & Bhattacharyya, 1995; Thomas, Kumar, Verma, Sinha, & Andrade, 2004; Creado, Parkar, & Kamath, 2006; Vikas, Avasthi, & Sharan, 2011), and in the context of neurotic disorders, such as dysthymic disorder, generalized anxiety disorder, and obsessive compulsive disorders (Chakrabarti, Kulhara, & Verma, 1996). A study by Chakrabarty, *et al.* (1996), reported less subjective burden among family members of neurotic patients. The authors explained this finding in terms of an attitude of tolerance towards family members. Somewhat similar observations were made by a cross-cultural study conducted by Talwar and Matheiken (2010). The authors observed less perceived burden among carers of schizophrenia patients in India than carers from Malaysia. They also reported that the perceived difficulties among Indians cover financial management, relationships in the family, and well-being and health. Comparative studies observed significantly higher burden (objective as well as subjective) experienced in the context of schizophrenia than affective disorder (Chakrabarti, *et al.*, 1995; Roychaudhuri, *et al.*, 1995) and obsessive compulsive disorder (OCD) (Thomas, *et al.*, 2004). Comparison between depression (affective disorder) and OCD revealed that higher burden is experienced in depression while relatives of patients diagnosed with OCD had a relatively better quality of life (Vikas, *et al.*, 2011). A study conducted by Srivastava, Bhatia, Sharma, Rajender, and Kumar (2010) reported poorer QOL among the bipolar patients and caregivers compared to the healthy controls. On the other hand, some studies have explored positive appraisal of caregiving in schizophrenia and affective disorder (Roychaudhuri, *et al.*, 1995; Aggarwal, Avasthi, Kumar, & Grover, 2011; Grover, *et al.*, 2012). However, Grover, *et al.* (2012), observed presence of negative as well as positive appraisal among caregivers of bipolar disorder and schizophrenia, with more negative appraisal among caregivers of schizophrenia. Aggarwal, *et al.* (2011), reported that educational level of caregivers, adopted coping strategies, and available social support affect the final appraisal of caregiving.

Studies have observed use of emotion-focussed coping strategies amongst relatives of persons with schizophrenia and bipolar disorders

(Chandrasekaran, Sivaprakash, & Jayestri, 2002; Nehra, Chakrabarti, Kulhara, & Sharma, 2005; Rammohan, *et al.*, 2002). Chandrasekaran and his colleagues (2002) observed use of "resignation" as emotion focussed coping strategy among 44 relatives of schizophrenic patients along with "failure to maintain social contacts" and "not seeking illness related information". The study also reported that expression of resignation by relatives had adverse effect on the patients' level of motivation, and develops negative symptoms amongst the patients. This study also found a significant correlation between resignation and family burden. This implies that resignation is not a very useful coping strategy for relatives of mental patients. Nehra, *et al.* (2005), studied caregiver coping among bipolar disorder and schizophrenia. They reported that relatives used both adaptive and non-adaptive coping strategies, such as consulting doctors, talking to family and friends, and help seeking. Other strategies such as collusion and cognitive avoidant coping were used by the caregivers in both illness contexts. Frequency of coercion and avoidant coping strategies were more common among carers of schizophrenia. Patients' level of dysfunction, gender, and caregivers' neuroticism were found to be having a significant influence on the coping patterns of relatives. Rammohan, *et al.* (2002), reported use of denial as coping strategy among parents of persons with schizophrenia. The use of denial as coping strategy induced higher level of burden among caregivers. Moreover, negative distraction strategies, such as use of alcohol or drugs, were more prominent amongst spouses of the patient. On the other hand, gender differences in use of coping strategies have been observed by Nehra, *et al.* (2005), and Kumar, Rani, Jain, and Mohanty (2010). Nehra, *et al.* (2005), observed that problem focussed coping strategies were significantly more likely to be used by female caregivers, compared to their male counterparts in the context of both schizophrenia and bipolar disorder. A significant association was also observed between seeking social support and female caregivers in the context of schizophrenia. Kumar, *et al.* (2010), reported that in male spouses, Emotion Focussed — Acceptance/Redefinition coping was a significant predictor of burden, whereas, Emotion Focussed — religion/faith and Problem Focussed — Problem Solving coping was significant predictor of burden among female spouses. The female spouses were found to be using more emotion focussed — religion/faith coping strategies.

Studies have also identified predictors of burden among carers of mental illness. Rammohan, *et al.* (2002), observed that patients' age, education level, and level of functioning and coping strategies used by caregivers (denial) were significant predictors of burden of care. Chakrabarti, *et al.* (1996), also reported patients' dysfunction as a predictor of burden along with the "longer duration of illness". Kumar, *et al.* (2010), observed that coping mechanism could be significant predictors of burden on spouses in the context of chronic schizophrenia. The authors also observed gender differences in experience of burden among carers, where female carers experience more burden than the male carers. Roychaudhury, *et al.* (1995), observed that age (young age), gender (male), income (low), and employment status (unemployment) of patients (schizophrenic) predict the level of burden (higher) among carers.

Studies have been conducted to observe family influence on course and severity of schizophrenia (Trivedi, Chaturvedi, Sethi, & Saxena, 1983), and (Deshpande, *et al.*, 2004). Based on the emotional expressiveness (EE) concept, Trivedi, *et al.* (1983), measured family members' attitude by administering "Attitude Questionnaire" (Sethi, *et al.*, 1982). The authors observed that in case of "relapsed or continuously ill patients" relatives used more comments that are critical, showed hostility and dissatisfaction, warmth and emotional overinvolvement. On the other hand, a cross-cultural study by Deshpande, *et al.* (2004), on a sample of affected sibling pairs compared influence of family on course and severity of schizophrenia among caregivers in United States and India. The authors did not find any significant cross-cultural variation in data.

The needs of patients and caregivers have been studied by Kulhara, *et al.* (2010). The most common needs expressed by both caregivers and patients are need for welfare benefits. In addition to this, patients also expressed need in terms of psychotic symptoms, psychological distress, information regarding condition and money. The caregivers expressed a need for relief from psychological distress, money, company, and intimate relationships. Another study by Prafulla, *et al.* (2010), reported that families cited their needs in areas of rehabilitation of the afflicted relative (support for the family, employment and occupation, psychosocial attitude modifications, and skill training).

There is a dearth of qualitative studies from India to explore caregiving experiences and coping mechanisms (Ganguly, Chadda, & Singh, 2010). In one of the very few studies on this issue, Ganguly, *et al.* (2010), explored the burden and coping mechanisms among carers in the context of schizophrenia and bipolar disorder. The authors conducted several Focus Group Discussions (FGDs) with carers over a period of one year. The observation of experience of burden by carers has been made in the areas of family functioning, social interactions, finance, and health. Uses of multiple coping strategies by the carers were also reported. According to the results, carers reported development of compassion in caring, hoping for a better future, developing faith in God, participation in religious practices, and helping others who are in a similar situation.

Most qualitative studies in India were conducted to explore the cultural impact, explanatory models of illness, religious and indigenous healing, and stigma in mental illness taking a culture-centric approach. The approach enables the researcher to uncover the inside view or EMIC perspective of the experience in a certain context. This approach encourages the discursive and dialogic engagement with the participant and this engagement enables the researchers and the participants to have a co-construction of reality rather than researcher's one sided construction. This dialogic engagement can be claimed to be self-reflexive and non-hierarchical in nature (Dutta & Basu, 2007). It may be emphasized that to understand the cultural context of psychiatric illness, studies should take into account the subjective experiences of patients and families. Culture and subjective experiences of patients and families are regarded as the two sides of cultural dimension of psychiatric disorders (Corin, Thara, & Padmavati, 2005). In order to understand the subjective experiences of families and patients, the cultural dimensions of psychiatric illness should be taken into account. The following section examines the culture-centric studies that have taken into consideration the family members' accounts of mental illness.

Explanatory Models of Patients and Family Members

Several studies had been conducted with culture-centric perspective in India in the context of mental illness. However, most of these studies have taken both patients' as well as relatives' accounts, though patients get more attention or central attention in these studies. Few studies have been conducted from caregivers' perspectives.

Corin, *et al.* (2005), conducted a comparative study of patients and the family members (pair-wise) regarding experiences and understanding of mental illness in Chennai, South India. The study observed similarities in reporting of symptoms, and causal attributions, between patients and families. This suggests that there was an empathic relationship between patients and their families that explained the observed convergence in reporting of symptoms. Relatives identified "aggressiveness and withdrawal" behaviours as core symptoms, and negative experiences (grief, loss, etc.) were reported as the causes of illness. Both patients and families frequently cited supernatural, psychological, and psychobiological causes. In some cases, however, a divergence in narratives among patients and relatives was also observed, and this was the indication of family conflict.

Banerjee and Roy (1998) studied 83 families of people suffering from schizophrenia from the outpatient unit of a teaching hospital in Kolkata, West Bengal to elicit the determinants and patterns of help seeking behaviour by using a proforma based on EMIC. The study identified indigenous explanatory models as one of the important predictors of nature of help seeking behaviour among participants. Observation of belief in supernatural causes and consultations of folk healers (e.g. *ojhā, baddi, guṇin, pīr*) was common among the participants. The study further revealed that, those who believe in supernatural causes of mental illness went first to the folk healers for consultation.

Beliefs of families regarding causes of mental illness, seeking social support and attitude towards sick relatives have also investigated by Srinivasan and Thara (2001) in Chennai, Tamil Nadu (South India). The authors interviewed 254 families of schizophrenic patients (who were receiving treatment in outpatient services of a well-known NGO) regarding the causal beliefs of illness. The frequently mentioned cause of the illness was "psychosocial stress" (84%), followed by "personality defect in adjustment" (23%), "heredity" (11%), "brain dysfunctions" (8%), "cause not known", "supernatural cause" (6%), and "fate/God's will" (1%). The study also examined the predictors of causal attribution; it revealed statistically significant sex differences in causal attribution ("cause not known" was more often cited for male patients and "heredity" was more often cited for female patients). The other reported predictors include education (of patient and informants), duration of illness, and nature of relationship with patients. However, the authors mentioned that the causal attributions made by relatives were subject to change with time and progress (from acute state to chronic state).

Seeking religious healing and temple healing is a common practice among families with mentally ill relatives in India (Raguram, Venkateswaran, Ramakrishna & Weiss, 2002). Raguram, *et al.* (2002), conducted an ethnographic study at the Muthusamy temple in Velayuthampalayampudur village of Dindigul district of Tamil Nadu (South India) over three months from June to August in 2000. The researchers elicited historical background of the temple, patient's experiences, and relatives' view on the illness with the help of EMIC. Along with this, the researchers also investigated the impressions of the subjects, perceived changes of course of illness of relatives during the stay in the temple, and level of satisfaction of treatment outcome. The illnesses reported in this study ranged from paranoid schizophrenia, delusional disorders, and bipolar disorder with recent manic episode. The results of this study highlighted the effectiveness of the temple healing. The effectiveness of the healing was observed by noticing reduction of some brief psychiatric rating score (nearly 20%), and family members' perception of improvement in illness conditions of patients. The researchers lent support to the theory that temple healing and residency in temple explains the improvement in psychotic symptoms of the patients without any pharmacological interventions. Moreover, the study also highlighted the accessibility and influence of local culture in healing processes.

Another study was conducted by Padmavati, Thara, and Corin (2005) to understand the reasons behind seeking help from religious sites by patients and families in India. The study was conducted at religious healing sites (three Muslim Darghas at Kovalam, Yerwadi and Nagoor, and two Hindu temples at Sholingur and Hanumanthapuram) in Tamil Nadu, South India. 26 participants (families and patients) were interviewed (in-depth interviews) regarding onset of illness, course, significant events, explanations of perceived abnormal behaviour, experiences with treatment, and most importantly reasons behind choosing a specific healing practice. Majority of the caregivers were women (mother or wife). Thematic analysis was employed for the analysis. The study revealed that, majority of participants cited supernatural causes (such as, evil spirits, planetary positions, and the *karmas* of previous life). Family members of those who were recovering discussed the healing choices. About help seeking decision, majority of the respondents reported the significant others' (e.g. who had personal experiences, priests, astrologers, faith healers, and elders in the family) intervention in the choice of religious sites. A very interesting finding of this study was that the choices of healing centres were made without considering the religion by birth. Moreover, families stayed with the patients for longer periods even at the cost of job and other serious engagements. The study concluded the efficacy of the religious healing and the pluralistic help seeking behaviour in India.

Bhana (1986) compared patients' and family members' (n = 86) experiences with indigenous healers and biomedical doctors by conducting interviews about patients' perceptions regarding mental illness, experiences, treatment, and diagnosis by indigenous healers and doctors at an outpatient unit in India. The study reported that, among patients and families there was a tendency to consult more than one healer. Regarding illness understanding, the author observed that most participants, who consulted indigenous healers, had little insight about their illness and described their condition as "nerves" or "worry", with attribution to "unknown" factors or other psychosocial factors such as marital problems, academic problems, death, injury/operation/and drugs. Out of 86, only six had cited supernatural cause responsible for their condition. The indigenous healers attributed the cause of mental illness either to "evil eye"/"tricked" or to unknown factors. Moreover, it has been observed that, patients or families who went to the indigenous healers were those who were more aware about the biomedical (psychiatric) diagnosis. However, the study revealed that relatively more number of patients believed in efficacy of doctors' treatments compared to indigenous healers. Thus, this explains why they shifted to present day biomedical treatment from indigenous healing.

To understand local perception of psychosis, Saravanan, *et al.* (2008), conducted Focus Group Discussions (FGDs) with relatives of patients with psychosis, with members of the community, and with recovered patients in Vellore, South India. According to the participants, indigenous healing can be regarded as complementary to biomedicine. The families of patients expressed need for support from the mental health professionals and community to deal with the stigma attached to mental illness. The community members expressed negative views regarding mental illness. The study revealed the presence of multiple explanatory models (biomedical and indigenous) and help seeking from both indigenous healers and biomedical doctors among participants.

Charles, Manoranjitham, and Jacob (2007) studied subjective relationship between experiences of stigma and beliefs related to mental illness among schizophrenic patients and their relatives in Vellore, South India. Short Explanatory Model Interview (SEMI) was administered along with Consumer Experiences of Stigma Questionnaire (CESQ), Family Views of Stigma Questionnaire, and Positive and Negative Syndrome Scale (PANSS) to different participants. It was observed that majority of patients and relatives held contradictory and multiple explanatory models. Most of the patients also consulted traditional healers. 60 per cent of the patients and 54 per cent of the relatives cited at least one non-biomedical causal belief. However, almost all the patients and relatives had expressed that the illness can be cured by the doctors (95% patients and 99% relatives). The correlation between the stigma scores of patients and relatives were found to be statistically significant. Factors associated with stigma against the mentally ill people were found to be many: sex of the patient (male), attribution of illness to *karma* or evil spirits (considered to be less stigmatizing), disease model of illness, the total number of causal models, the total number of non-medical causal beliefs, visiting traditional healing places for cure, total family stigma scores, and relatives' perceived stigma against the patient. Significant relationship were observed between stigma scores of relatives with gender of the caregivers (male), literacy, domicile (rural), beliefs of *karma*, and total patients' score on stigma. It was also noted that most of the relatives and patients attributed the cause of the illness to the *karma*, which is considered to be less stigmatizing in Indian culture. The authors highlighted that, the patients' and families' explanatory models could be the reason behind the increased stigma; or the patients and families employ explanatory models as an adaptive mechanism for lessening the stigma associated to mental illness. The authors conclude that beliefs about the illness can play a mitigating as well as an aggravating role in stigma.

In India, a few studies have been conducted to see the professional caregivers' attitudes towards mental illness. Pandey, Saddichha, & Kumar (2008) conducted a quantitative study to investigate attitudes of psychiatric ward attendants ($n = 100$; 50 male and 50 female) of Central Institute of Psychiatry, in Ranchi (Jharkhand). General attendants, chosen by guardians of the patients were used as a control group. CAMI (a scale developed by Taylor, Dear, and Hall, 1979) was used for measuring "attitudes towards mentally ill". The authors observed that psychiatric ward attendants showed more positive attitudes towards mental illness than did the general attendants. Moreover, more favourable attitudes were revealed by the older attendants, more educated attendants, and those attendants who had known the patients for longer duration. Joel, *et al.* (2003), studied explanatory models of psychosis among 80 community mental health workers in rural South India by administering SEMI. It was noted that, majority of community health workers failed to recognize the chronic psychosis as a disease condition. The study further revealed that, the community health workers held indigenous explanatory models and attributed the cause of psychosis to black magic, evil spirits, and poverty. They also expressed a low confidence to the efficacy of biomedical treatments.

The above review of available studies shows that most studies have been done from patients' perspectives and caregivers accounts were added as a supporting data. Most studies are context specific and could not be generalized for a larger population. As family members are an important part in the health care system, more studies are needed to address their issues, understand their experiences and meaning they assign to their caregiving role.

Conclusion: Main Observations and Research Issues

The present chapter provides a review of literature on family caregiving in the context of mental illness in India. It aimed at providing a historical development of mental illness care in India. The Indian philosophical understanding of illness and mental illness along with healing traditions, and development of present day psychiatry has been discussed. The second section demonstrates the existence of pluralistic mental health care system. In the third section, the role of families in psychiatric care has been discussed and researches suggest that Indian family plays an important role in mental health care. In the next section, some examples of studies of caregiving experiences in Indian context have been discussed. The fifth section was devoted to the discussion about studies conducted with explanatory models framework in India. Care was taken to provide review of the relevant studies.

In sum, Indian families hold an important position in mental health care and take all the major decisions and initiatives regarding treatment. Because of greater involvement in care, family members are expected to respond to the illness demands of their ill relatives. They have to endure the difficult situations and manage the overall distressing episodes along with their other commitments. Studies have been done mostly from patients' perspective to understand their needs and care related aspects; less attention has been given to the subjective experiences of family members. However, some studies have included the family members' voices, but they did it to get an understanding of the patients' problem or needs. Thus, the voices of the family members have not sufficiently been represented in literature in the Indian context. Ignoring the family caregivers' experiences could be detrimental in developing effective intervention programmes for caregivers in future.

Studies that have been conducted to explore the burden of care and its relationship with coping do not generally explore the subjective experiences of caregivers. Burden centred studies can capture the measurable or explicit aspect of caregiving experiences and produce facts and figures on duress and its management, but they cannot define caregivers' subjective experiences, which are not amenable to measurements and inventories. To understand the inner experiences of caregiving it is imperative to go beyond the burden of care concepts and adopt a different research approach that would be capable of capturing subjective experiences of family members. This also establishes the need for the qualitative methodology.

India is a plural, multi-ethnic society, and in India different healing traditions are harmoniously juxtaposed. The availability of various healing systems also influences the families' decisions and initiatives for care. It also influences upon the beliefs and understanding that people have about illness. To understand family caregivers' beliefs and understanding of mental illness more culture-centric studies are needed.

Most studies that have explored the explanatory models of the patients and families in India have been conducted with a presumption that decision regarding treatment choices depends only on the individuals' explanatory models of illness. Quack (2013) argued that these studies could not answer the confused mind set regarding causation of mental illness and treatment choices. He mentioned that, there were family members who did not have any idea about the cause of the mental illness and therefore, they tried whatever treatment was available to them including folk healing. Folk healing is a popular tradition in India and is still preferred by many Indians. In addition, they were also taking psychiatric help. Therefore, there is a need to address this situation where people have multiple beliefs and practices in health care.

Moreover, the present review revealed that most studies in caring have been conducted in the severe mental illness context, mostly in schizophrenia and manic depressive disorder and only a few have considered common mental illness. Therefore, there exists a gap in literature as the caring experiences in common mental illnesses were less explored and voices of the carers were underrepresented.

Most studies in caregiving whether conducted in India or outside India have predominantly represented only one key caregiver's voice (Barer & Johnson, 1990). Very few studies have considered taking multiple stakeholders' views, such as the accompanying relatives and others (neighbours, friends), professionals and other staff as well as traditional healers.

In the Indian setting, large differences exist amongst Southern, Northern, Eastern, and Western parts of India in cultural practices, health practices, language, food intake, rituals and so on. The review suggests that most of these culture-centric studies have been conducted in Southern and Northern part of India and very few studies conducted in Eastern parts. Very few studies have been done in other parts of India. The Southern and Northern India does not represent India as a whole nor do the findings of studies conducted in these parts (Patel, 2001). Thus, more studies need to be conducted beyond the boundary of some specific areas of India.

NOTES

1. *Manas* performs four functions, such as, (a) "*indriabhigraha*": "activation, direction, and coordination of the sensory and motor organs"; (b) "*svasyanigraha*": "self-regulation"; (c) "*uha*": "reasoning"; and (d) "*vicāra*": "deliberation, judgement and discrimination" (Kakar, 1982, p. 244).
2. Traditional Joint families in India are characterized as "matrilineal and patriarchal", comprised of a family head (mostly a male), who is the seniormost in the family, his wife, children, younger brothers and their wives and children and often other relatives. The major discussions and responsibilities are taken by the family head and the family functions as a unit. The family members are united and have "deep sense of solidarity" which in turn develops as "a measure of social security to its members". Therefore, at the time of distress of a member or members the whole family come together and faces the distress along with the affected person. Every member in the family is culturally assigned to some specific roles and is expected to fulfil that role in their life (Chopra, 1984).

REFERENCES

Aggarwal, M., Avasthi, A., Kumar, S. and Grover, S. (2011). "Experience of Caregiving in Schizophrenia: A Study from India", *International Journal of Social Psychiatry*, 57(3), 224-36.

Avasthi, A. (2010). "Preserve and Strengthen Family to Promote Mental Health", *Indian Journal of Psychiatry*, 52(1), 113-26.

Banerjee, G. and Roy, S. (1998). "Determinants of Help-seeking Behaviour of Families of Schizophrenic Patients Attending a Teaching Hospital in India: An Indigenous Explanatory Model", *International Journal of Social Psychiatry*, 44(3), 199-214.

Bhana, K. (1986). "Indian Indigenous Healers", *SAMJ*, 70, 221-23.

Bhattacharyya, D.P. (1983). "Psychiatric Pluralism in Bengal, India", *Social Science & Medicine*, 17(14), 947-56.

Bhattacharyya, D.P. (1986). *Paglami: Ethnopsychiatric Knowledge in Bengal*, New York: Foreign and Comparative Studies/South Asian Series, No. 11, Maxwell School of Citizenship and Public Affairs, Syracause University.

Bhui, K., Bhugra, D. and Goldberg, D. (2002). "Causal Explanations of Distress and General Practitioners' Assessments of Common Mental Disorder among Punjabi and English Attendees", *Social Psychiatry and Psychiatric Epidemiology*, 37, 38-45.

Campion, J. and Bhugra, D. (1997). "Experiences of Religious Healing in Psychiatric Patients in South India", *Social Psychiatry and Psychiatric Epidemiology*, 32, 215-21.

Campion, J. and Bhugra, D. (1998). "Religious and Indigenous Treatment of Mental Illness in South India — A Descriptive Study", *Mental Health, Religion & Culture*, 1(1), 21-29.

Chakrabarti, S. (2011). "Family Interventions in Schizophrenia: Issues of Relevance for Asian Countries", *World Journal of Psychiatry*, 1(1), 4-7.

Chakrabarti, S., Kulhara, P. and Verma, S.K. (1996). "Family Burden of Neurosis: Extent and Determinants", *Hong Kong Journal of Psychiatry*, 6(1), 23-28.

Chakrabarti, S., Raj, L., Kulhara, P., Avasthi, A. and Verma, S. K. (1995). "Comparison of Extent and Pattern of Family Burden in Affective Disorders and Schizophrenia", *Indian Journal of Psychiatry*, 37(3), 105-12.

Chandrasekaran, R., Sivaprakash, B. and Jayestri, S.R. (2002). "Coping Strategies of the Relatives of Schizophrenic Patients", *Indian Journal of Psychiatry*, 44(1), 9-13.

Charles, H., Manoranjitham, S.D. and Jacob, K.S. (2007). "Stigma and Explanatory Models among People with Schizophrenia and their Relatives in Vellore, South India", *International Journal of Social Psychiatry*, 53(4), 325-32.

Chopra, H.D. (1984). "Family Structure, Dynamics and Psychiatric Disorder in India", *Indian Journal of Psychiatry*, 26(4), 335-42.

Chowdhuri, A.N., Chakraborty, A.K. and Weiss, M.G. (2001). "Community Mental Health and Concepts of Mental Illness in the Sundarban Delta of West Bengal, India", *Anthropology & Medicine*, 8(1), 109-29.

Corin, E., Thara, R. and Padmavati, R. (2005). "Shadows of Culture in Psychosis in South India: A Methodological Exploration and Illustration", *International Review of Psychiatry*, 17(2), 75-81.

Correspondent, S. (2013, January 14). "Acute Shortage of Mental Health Care Staff in India", *The Hindu*, New Delhi, India.

Creado, D.A., Parkar, S.R. and Kamath, R.M. (2006). "A Comparison of the Level of Functioning in Chronic Schizophrenia with Coping and Burden in Caregivers", *Indian Journal of Psychiatry*, 48, 27-33.

Dein, S. and Sembhi, S. (2001). "The Use of Traditional Healing in South Asian Psychiatric Patients in U.K.: Interactions Between Professionals and Folk Psychiatries", *Transcultural Psychiatry*, 38(2), 243-57.

Deshpande, S., Bhatia, T., Wood, J., Brar, J.S., Thelma, B.K., Ganguli, R., Day, R., Gottesman, I.I. and Nimgaonkar, V.L. (2004). "Evaluation of Familial Influences on the Course and Severity of Schizophrenia among U.S. and Indian Cases", *Social Psychiatry and Psychiatric Epidemiology*, 39, 369-74.

Dutta, M.J. and Basu, A. (2007). "Health among Men in Rural Bengal: Exploring Meaning through a Culture-centred Approach", *Qualitative Health Research*, 17-48, 38-48.

Fabrega Jr., H. (2009). *History of Mental Illness in India: A Cultural Psychiatry Retrospective*, Delhi: Motilal Banarasidass Publishers Private Limited.

Gangadharan, G.G. and Shankar, D. (2009). "Medical Pluralism — The Challenges Ahead", *Indian Journal of Traditional Knowledge*, 8(2), 181-84.

Ganguly, K.K., Chadda, R.K. and Singh, T.B. (2010). "Caregiver Burden and Coping in Schizophrenia and Bipolar Disorder: A Qualitative Study", *American Journal of Psychiatric Rehabilitation*, 13(2), 126-42.

Greenough, P. (2003). "The Social and Cultural Framework of Health and Disease in India", in V. Das and V. Das (ed.), *The Oxford India Companion to Sociology and Social Anthropology* (Vol. 1, pp. 303-25), New Delhi: Oxford University Press.

Grover, S., Chakrabarti, S., Aggarwal, M., Avasthi, A., Kulhara, P., Sharma, S., *et al.* (2012). "Comparative Study of the Experience of Caregiving in Bipolar Affective Disorder and Schizophrenia", *International Journal of Social Psychiatry*, 58(6), 614-22.

Halliburton, M. (2004). "Finding a Fit: Psychiatric Pluralism in South India and Its Implications for WHO Studies of Mental Disorder", *Transcultural Psychiatry*, 41(1), 80-98.

Indian Council of Medical Research (2005). "Collaborative Study on Severe Mental Morbidity", *Mental Health Research in India*, New Delhi, India: Division of Non-communicable Diseases, Indian Council of Medical Research.

Iyer, S.N., Mangala, R., Thara, R. and Malla, A.K. (2010). "Preliminary Findings from a Study of First-episode Psychosis in Montreal, Canada and Chennai, India: Comparison of Outcomes", *Schizophrenia Research*, 121, 227-33.

Jacob, K.S. (2010). "Indian Psychiatry and Classification of Psychiatric Disorders", *Indian Journal of Psychiatry*, 52, S104-S109.

Jadhav, S., Littlewood, R., Ryder, A.G., Chakraborty, A. and Jain, S. (2007). "Stigmatization of Severe Mental Illness in India: Against the Simple Industrialization Hypothesis", *Indian Journal of Psychiatry*, 49(3), 189-94.

Janardhana, N., Shravya, R., Naidu, D.M., Saraswathy, L. and Seshan, V. (2011). "Giving Care to Men and Women with Mental Illness", *Indian Journal of Gender Studies*, 18(3), 405-24.

Joel, D., Sathyaseelan, M., Jayakaran, R., Vijayakumar, C., Muthurathnam, S. and Jacob, K.S. (2003). "Explanatory Models of Psychosis among Community Health Workers in South India", *Acta Psychiatr Scand*, 108, 66-69.

Kakar, S. (1982). *Shamans, Mystics and Doctors: A Psychological Inquiry into India and Its Healing Traditions*, Chicago: The University of Chicago Press.

Kapur, R.L. (1975). "Mental Health Care in Rural India: A Study of Existing Patterns and their Implications for Future Policy", *The British Journal of Psychiatry*, 127, 286-93.

Kapur, R.L. (1979). "The Role of Traditional Healers in Mental Health Care in Rural India", *Social Science & Medicine*, 13(B), 27-31.

Khandelwal, S.K., Jhingan, H.P., Ramesh, S., Gupta, R.K. and Srivastava, V.K. (2004). "India: Mental Health Country Profile", *International Review of Psychiatry*, 16(1-2), 126-41.

Kleinman, A. (1980). *Patients and Healers in the Context of Culture*, Los Angeles: University of California Press.

Kulhara, P., Avasthi, A., Grover, S., Sharan, P., Sharma, P., Malhotra, S., *et al.* (2010). "Needs of Indian Schizophrenia Patients: An Exploratory Study from India", *Social Psychiatry and Psychiatric Epidemiology*, 45(8), 809-18.

Kumar, A. (2004). "History of Mental Health Services in India", *Journal of Personality and Clinical Studies*, 20, 171-80.

Kumar, S., Rani, U., Jain, A. and Mohanty, S. (2010). "Coping with Spousal Burden in Chronic Schizophrenia", *Indian Journal of Social Science Researches*, 7(1), 90-94.

Leslie, C. (1980). "Medical Pluralism in World Perspective [1]", *Social Science & Medicine*, 14B, 191-95.

Math, S.B., Chandrashekar, C.R. and Bhugra, D. (2007). "Psychiatric Epidemiology in India", *Indian Journal of Medical Research*, 126, 183-92.

Misra, G. (2010). "The Cultural Construction of Self and Emotion: Implications for Well-being", in R. Schwarzer and P.A. Frensch (eds.), *Personality, Human Development, and Culture: International Perspectives* (Vol. 2, pp. 95-112).

Murthy, S.R. (2011). "Mental Health Initiatives in India (1947-2010)", *The National Medical Journal of India*, 24(2), 98-107.

Nehra, R., Chakrabarti, S., Kulhara, P. and Sharma, R. (2005). "Caregiver-coping in Bipolar Disorder and Schizophrenia", *Social Psychiatry and Psychiatric Epidemiology*, 40(4), 329-36.

Nichter, M. (1981). "Idioms of Distress: Alternatives in the Expression of Psychological Distress: A Case Study from South India", *Culture, Medicine and Psychiatry*, 5, 379-408.

Nizamie, H.S. and Goyal, N. (2010). "History of Psychiatry in India", *Indian Journal of Psychiatry*, 52, S7-S12.

Nunley, M. (1998). "The Involvement of Families in Indian Psychiatry", *Culture, Medicine and Psychiatry*, 22, 317-53.

Obeyesekere, G. (1977). "The Theory and Practice of Psychological Medicine in the Ayurvedic Tradition", *Culture, Medicine and Psychiatry*, 1, 155-81.

Padmavati, R., Thara, R. and Corin, E. (2005). "A Qualitative Study of Religious Practices by Chronic Mentally Ill and their Caregivers in South India", *International Journal of Social Psychiatry*, 51(2), 139-49.

Pandey, V., Saddichha, S. and Kumar, R. (2008). "Attitudes of Ward Attendants Towards Mental Illness: Comparisons and Predictors", *International Journal of Social Psychiatry*, 54(5), 469-78.

Paranjpe, A.C. (1998). *Self and Identity in Modern Psychology and Indian Thought*, New York: Plenum Press.

Patel, V. (2001). "Cultural Factors and International Epidemiology", *British Medical Bulletin*, 57, 33-45.

Patel, V. and Kleinman, A. (2003). "Poverty and Common Mental Disorders in Developing Countries", *Bulletin of the World Health Organization*, 81(8), 609-15.

Patel, V., Sumathipala, A., Khan, M.M., Thapa, S.B. and Rahman, O. (2007). "South Asian Region", in K. Bhui, D. Bhugra, K. Bhui and D. Bhugra (eds.), *Culture and Mental Health: A Comprehensive Textbook* (pp. 212-24), London: Hodder Arnold.

Prafulla, S., Murthy, S.K. and Ramaprasad, D. (2010). "Family Burden and Rehabilitation Need of Beneficiaries of a Rural Mental Health Camp in a Southern State of India", *International Journal of Psychosocial Rehabilitation*, 15(2), 5-11.

Prevos, P. (2002, April 9th). *The Self in Indian Philosophy*. Retrieved June 9th, 2011, from prevos.net/humanities/philosophy/self

Quack, J. (2013). "'What do I know?' Scholastic Fallacies and Pragmatic Religiosity in Mental Health-seeking Behaviour in India", *Mental Health, Religion & Culture*, 16(4), 403-18.

Raguram, R., Venkateswaran, A., Ramakrishna, J. and Weiss, M.G. (2002). "Traditional Community Resources for Mental Health: A Report of Temple Healing from India", *BMJ*, 325, 38-40.

Rammohan, A., Rao, K. and Subbakrishna, D.K. (2002). "Burden and Coping in Caregivers of Persons with Schizophrenia", *Indian Journal of Psychiatry*, 44(3), 220-27.

Roychaudhuri, J., Mondal, D., Boral, A. and Bhattacharya, D. (1995). "Family Burden among Long-term Psychiatric Patients", *Indian Journal of Psychiatry*, 37(2), 81-85.

Saravanan, B., Jacob, K.S., Deepak, M.G., Prince, M., David, A.S. and Bhugra, D. (2008). "Perceptions about Psychosis and Psychiatric Services: A Qualitative Study from Vellore, India", *Social Psychiatry and Psychiatric Epidemiology*, 43, 231-38.

Saravanan, B., Jacob, K.S., Johnson, S., Prince, M. and Bhugra, D. (2007). "Belief Models in First Episode Schizophrenia in South India", *Social Psychiatry and Psychiatric Epidemiology*, 42, 446-51.

Sarin, A. and Jain, S. (2012). "The Census of India and the Mentally Ill", *Indian Journal of Psychiatry*, 54(1), 32-36.

Sethi, B.B. (1989). "Family as a Potent Therapeutic Force", *Indian Journal of Psychiatry*, 31(1), 22-80.

Sethi, B.B. and Manchanda, R. (1978). "Family Structure and Psychiatric Disorder", *Indian Journal of Psychiatry*, 20, 283-88.

Shamasundar, C. (2008). "Relevance of Ancient Indian Wisdom to Modern Mental Health — A Few Examples", *Indian Journal of Psychiatry*, 50(2), 138-43.

Shankar, J. and Muthuswamy, S.S. (2007). "Support Needs of Family Caregivers of People Who Experience Mental Illness and the Role of Mental Health Services", *Families in Society: The Journal of Contemporary Social Services*, 88(2), 302-10.

Shankar, R. (1994). "Interventions with Families of People with Schizophrenia in India", *New Directions for Mental Health Services*, (62), 79-88.

Shankar, R. and Rao, K. (2005). "From Burden to Empowerment: The Journey of Family Caregivers in India", in N. Sartorius, J. Leff, J.J. Lopez-Ibor, M. Maj and A. Okasha (eds.), *Families and Mental Disorders*, England: Wiley.

Shankar, R.B., Saravanan, B. and Jacob, K.S. (2006). "Explanatory Models of Common Mental Disorders among Traditional Healers and their Patients in Rural South India", *International Journal of Social Psychiatry*, 52(3), 221-33.

Sharma, M., Sethi, B.B. and Bhiman, A. (1984). "Family Jointness, Social Interaction and Neuroses: A Rural Urban Comparison", *Indian Journal of Psychiatry*, 26(4), 357-63.

Sharma, V., Murthy, S., Agarwal, M. and Wilkinson, G. (1998). "Comparison of People with Schizophrenia from Liverpool, England and Sakalwara-Bengaluru, India", *International Journal of Social Psychiatry*, 44(3), 225-30.

Sinha, J.B. and Kumar, R. (2004). "Methodology for Understanding Indian Culture", *The Copenhagen Journal of Asian Studies*, 19, 89-104.

Sinha, J.B., Singh, S., Gupta, P., Srivastava, K.B., Sinha, R.B., Srivastava, S., *et al.* (2010). "An Exploration of the Indian Mindset", *Psychological Studies*, 55(1), 3-17.

Somasundaram, O. (2009). "Medical, Literate, and Cultural Approaches to Mental Disorders in Tamil Nadu", in B. Sebastia and B. Sebastia (ed.), *Restoring Mental Health in India: Pluralistic Therapies and Concepts* (pp. 27-47), New Delhi: Oxford University Press.

Srinivasan, T.N. and Thara, R. (2001). "Beliefs about Causation of Schizophrenia: Do Indian Families Believe in Supernatural Causes?" *Social Psychiatry and Psychiatric Epidemiology*, 36, 134-40.

Srivastava, S., Bhatia, M.S., Sharma, V., Rajender, G. and Kumar, P. (2010). "Health — Related Quality of Life in Bipolar Disorder Patients and their Caregivers", *International Journal of Mental Health*, 39(4), 3-15.

Thara, R. (2004). "Twenty Year Course of Schizophrenia: The Madras Longitudinal Study", *Canadian Journal of Psychiatry*, 49(8), 564-69.

Thara, R., Padmavati, R. and Srinivasan, T.N. (2004). "Focus on Psychiatry in India", *British Journal of Psychiatry*, 184, 366-73.

Thomas, J.K., Kumar, S.P., Verma, A.N., Sinha, V.K. and Andrade, C. (2004). "Psychosocial Dysfunction and Family Burden in Schizophrenia and Obsessive Compulsive Disorder", *Indian Journal of Psychiatry*, 46(3), 238-43.

Trivedi, J.K., Chaturvedi, P.K., Sethi, B.B. and Saxena, N.K. (1983). "A Study of Attitudes of Key Relatives of Schizophrenic Patients", *Indian Journal of Psychiatry*, 25(4), 264-68.

Uberoi, P. (2003). "The Family in India: Beyond the Nuclear *versus* Joint Debate", in *The Oxford India Companion to Sociology and Social Anthropology* (Vol. 2). (V. Das, ed.) New Delhi: Oxford University Press.

Verghese, A. (1988). "Family Participation in Mental Health Care — The Vellore Experiment", *Indian Journal of Psychiatry*, 30(2), 117-21.

Verghese, A., Dube, K.C., John, J.K., Kumar, N., Nandi, D.N., Parhee, R., Rajkumar, S., Richard, J., Sarada, M.M., Sethi, B.B. and Trivedi, J.K. (1990). "Factors Associated with the Course and Outcome of Schizophrenia a Multicentred Follow-up Study: Result of Five Year Follow-up", *Indian Journal of Psychiatry*, 32(2), 211-16.

Vikas, A., Avasthi, A. and Sharan, P. (2011). "Psychological Impact of Obsessive Compulsive Disorder on Patients and their Caregivers: A Comparative Study with Depressive Disorder", *International Journal of Social Psychiatry*, 57(1), 45-56.

Wagner, W., Duveen, G., Themel, M. and Verma, J. (1999). "The Modernization of Tradition: Thinking About Madness in Patna, India", *Culture & Psychology*, 5(4), 413-45.

Weiss, M.G., Desai, A., Jadhav, S., Gupta, L., Channabasavanna, S.M. and Doongaji, D.R., *et al.* (1988). "Houmoral Concepts of Mental Illness in India", *Social Science & Medicine*, 27(5), 471-77.

Weiss, M.G., Jadhav, S., Raguram, R., Vounatsou, P. and Littlewood, R. (2001). "Psychiatric Stigma Across Cultures: Local Validation in Bengaluru and London", *Anthropology & Medicine*, 8(1), 71-87.

Weiss, M.G., Sharma, S.D., Gaur, R.K., Sharma, J.S., Desai, A. and Doongaji, D.R. (1986). "Traditional Concepts of Mental Disorder among Indian Psychiatric Patients: Preliminary Report of Work in Progress", *Social Science and Medicine*, 23(4), 379-86.

11

A Qualitative Exploration of Social Representations of Mental Health, Mental Illness and Health seeking behaviour in the Urban Middle Class Indians

Alankrita Maurya and *Shikha Dixit*

Research in the area of health psychology has highlighted the role of psychosocial and cultural factors in defining health and illness. The term illness involves a wide array of factors ranging from the illness experience to the expression of illness in a given context. While describing health and illness, Spector (1996) comments,

> Health and illness can be interpreted and explained in terms of personal experience and expectations. We can define our own health or illness, and determine what these states mean to us in our daily lives. We learn from our own cultural and ethnic backgrounds how to be healthy, how to recognize illness, and how to be ill (p. 65).

In order to have deeper understanding of health and illness it is important to look at the psychosocial and cultural explanations associated to it. This involves the way people understand illness and respond to the illness conditions. Emphasizing the relevance of the psychosocial explanations of health and illness Kleinman (1980), comments that the socially organized response towards illness constitutes an important part of the health care system. Response to illness is structured by the social context and the meanings that are held by the lay people. According to Kleinman (1980): "It is the lay, non-professional, non-specialist, popular culture arena in which illness is first defined and health care activities initiated" (p. 50).

The present chapter describes a qualitative study that employed the social representations theory to explore the lay meanings of mental health and mental illness. Social representations are the commonsense knowledge that are created and developed in the social world of everyday life, or the consensual universe for understanding the everyday reality (Moscovici, 1984). Social representations are formed through the exchange of conversations, experiences, beliefs, value system, attitudes, traditions, and behaviour in a particular socio-cultural context. Social representations can be seen as groups of associated ideas and images, which rather than being static, change and evolve over time and situations (Moscovici, 1988).

The social representations theory helps to understand how lay people make sense of health and illness. Herzlich (1973) did a pioneering study on social representations of health and illness and found that lay meanings of health and illness are rooted in psychosocial contexts. Researchers (Flick, 1998a, 1998b, 1998c, 2000; Joffe, 1998; Joffe & Bettega, 2003) have made attempts to explore social representations of physical health and illness and found that the commonsense connotations of health and illness held complex psychosocial explanations. In the Western context, exploration of mental illness using the social representation framework has been done by Zani, 1993, 1995; Petrillo, 1996, Morant, 1998, Foster, 2001 and the social representations of madness has been explored by De Rosa, 1987 and Jodelet, 1991. Exploration of lay meanings of mental health and mental illness in the Indian context from the social representations perspective has received little attention and only a few studies have been conducted. Dixit (2005) has explored the social representations of mental illness among educated youth and Maurya and Dixit (2008) have studied the social representations of mental health and illness among middle class Indians. A study done by Wagner, Duveen, Themel and Verma (1999) was conducted to explore the social representations of madness. The results of study by Wagner, *et al.*, revealed that people held polymorphic representations of madness.

Mental illness is a complex phenomenon. The socio-cultural explanations of mental health and illness focusses upon group based symbolic understandings and communication regarding mental health issues. The social representations theory can be applied to explore how socio-cultural factors influence health related thoughts and actions. The present study thus aimed to explore the lay meanings of mental health and mental illness among the urban middle class Indians using the social representations framework.

Objectives

The present study aimed to explore the social representations of mental health and mental illness in the urban middle class Indians. This study is an extension of the larger study done by the authors of the present study. The larger study aimed at obtaining the core themes of social representations of mental health and illness. The secondary aim was to develop a rating task to obtain the latent structure of social representations using quantitative techniques. The results of the study revealed the core dimensions of mental health and mental illness. To further understand the meanings of these representations the present qualitative study was formulated. In order to fulfil this aim an attempt was made to understand the role of psychosocial factors in determining mental illness; reasons behind stereotypes attached to mental illness; stigmatization and blame towards mentally ill; health seeking behaviour in mental illness; and measures for creating awareness about mental health and illness.

Method

Participants

Two groups were formed for the focussed group discussions, with six participants in each group. The first group comprised of three male and three female participants. The second group comprised of four female and two male participants. The age range of the participants was between 25 to 55 years. All participants belonged to the urban middle class background. The socio-economic status was measured in terms of annual family income as defined by NCAER (National Council for Applied Economic Research Report, 2006). All participants had completed the education of graduation level. Informed consent (verbal) was taken for willingly participating in the focussed group interview.

Measures

A semi-structured open-ended interview schedule was designed for the study which has been provided in Appendix A. The core themes that evolved from the larger study formed the basis of designing the semi-structured questionnaire for the in-depth qualitative exploration.

Procedure

The participants in the focus groups were provided a brief introduction about the theme and motives of the discussion before beginning the session. Consent to record the interview was also taken from all the participants. The focus groups progressed with the research questions as presented by the interviewer. The interview session was closed after all the questions were discussed by the participants. The participants were thanked for their cooperation in conducting the study.

Data Analysis

Data analysis involved applying qualitative content analysis following Ditcher's 'Concept Book Approach' as described by Mostyn (1985).

Findings

The present section reports the core themes derived from the qualitative content analysis of the two focussed groups. Some of the quotes of the participants have been mentioned anonymously. An attempt was made to identify consensus as well as disagreements in the representations of the participants. Points of disagreements also provide important information and play a vital role in identification of issues that need to be addressed further. The focus group discussions were conducted in Hindi since it was the mother-tongue of the participants. Responses of the participants were transcribed and then translated in English.

Defining of Mental Illness: The Core Themes

Stigmas Attached to Mental Illness

According to the participants there existed many stigmas against the mentally ill people. Participants believed that these stigmas were deep-rooted in the society and were difficult to change. According to the participants, labelling of a person as mentally ill led to a stigmatized image.

1. "Mental illness has been hyped by people in society. If a person suffers from a mild disorder then also people label him as mentally ill. This creates negativity in people and prohibits the sufferer from discussing their mental health problems."
2. "Mental illness is a matter of shame and people. Unless anyone close is affected, people do not feel concerned."

Behavioural Problems in Mental Illness

According to the participants, mentally ill people displayed abnormal behaviour.

1. "A mentally ill person shows repetitive behaviour and can be unpredictable."

According to the participants, in some cases of mental illness the behavioural symptoms were not present all the time. Such category included mentally ill people who suffered from illness episodes that occur at any time and could not be predicted.

2. "The abnormality in the behaviour is not present always. It is not certain when it will occur."

Mental Illness is Difficult to Recognize

The participants felt that due to lack of physical symptoms it was difficult to detect a mental problem at early stage.

1. "Most of the abnormal people are physically fit, but their cognitive functioning is impaired. Abnormalities can be seen in the behaviour of a person suffering from mental illness. Since, the symptoms of abnormality are visible in extreme conditions, it is therefore difficult to identify a person suffering from mild mental disorders."

The participants expressed that it was difficult to identify mental health problems at an early stage. As a result of this, the process of referral also got delayed.

2. "Family members and close people like spouse, friends, and relatives of the person suffering from any kind of mental illness can recognize some changes in behaviour of the person. A close observation of the mentally ill person displays changes in behaviour pattern which is different from normal."

Impairment in the Cognitive Functioning

According to the participants, mental illness was characterized by impairment in the cognitive functions essential to lead a normal life. The impairment included disorganization of thoughts and lack of ability to take decisions in life.

1. "Mentally ill people are not organized and their thoughts are scattered. They also cannot express themselves clearly and find it difficult to connect with normal people."

Biological Factors Causing Mental Illness

Some of the participants expressed that mental illness could be due to genetic factors or chemical imbalance in the body. However, the participants expressed that the psycho-social factors were more important than the biomedical factors.

1. "Some people have a history of mental illness in their family so it can pass from parents to children."
2. "Any chemical imbalance in body also could lead to mental health problems."
3. "Mental illness is primarily due to psychosocial reasons. Therefore, attempts should be made to deal with these problems taking a non-medical approach."

Deviation from the Norms of the Society

According to the participants, every person had some abnormality. The extent of deviation determines the level of abnormality. The participants expressed that mentally ill people were deviants who violated the norms of the society.

1. "Everybody has some degree of abnormality. The extent of deviation is important in classifying a person as mentally ill. Any kind of deviation from the norms of the society is abnormal. If people violate the norms of the society and do something undesirable they can be classified as mentally ill."
2. "Homosexuals are deviants. However, we do not know whether they are normal or abnormal."

Distinctions were made by the participants in classifying people as mentally ill and people who adopted alternative ways rather than conforming to the existent norms. This category of people included scientists and artists. Such people could not be considered as mentally ill according to the participants. However, they were also not perceived as other normal people. This difference in the representation can be understood from the following quote.

3. "Many of the scientists and artists are also different from normal people. However, they cannot be classified as mentally ill. Though, such people are lost in their own world and at times their behaviour seems bizarre, they have excellent knowledge about their fields."

Substance Abuse as Mental Illness

Participants expressed that people who consumed liquor and displayed aggressive behaviour could be considered as suffering from some kind of mental problem.

1. "I think that even drinking is also a kind of mental illness. Indulgence in drinking creates problems for them by affecting their health and also for other specially the family members."

Psychosocial Contexts Leading to Mental Illness

The participants expressed different psychosocial factors that could lead to mental illness.

Family Problems

Family pressures and expectations were considered to be major causes of stress for people. The restrictions in family were also considered to be responsible for creating stress in children.

1. "There are conflicts in thoughts among the family members which often lead to disturbance in family. It is very difficult to convince family members; when any member of the family takes a decision that is opposed to the wishes of other members in family; there is a constant tension in the family."

The participants believed that the change in the structure of family had led to change in the relationship between people. In the joint family system, people could share their problems with either parents, or other elder members. However, due to an increase in the trend of the nuclear family system, the support provided by the family members was lost. As a result, people could not release the stress in their lives. The participants however, also commented on the problems associated to the joint family system.

2. "The nuclear families have added to mental health problems. Earlier there were many people in the joint family to listen to grievances. The present situation has changed a lot these days and no one has time for anyone even in the family. Thus, the stress that could be released by talking to members in the family does not happen anymore."

3. "Yes, it is true that there are benefits of a nuclear family; there is more freedom and no decisions are imposed from elders, but at the same time people feel isolated and lonely."
4. "Dislocation from the family to distant places for better education and employment is also a major cause of increasing mental health problems."

Participants expressed that staying away from family members also caused stress in people. According to the participants, people moved out to metro cities and went abroad for the advancement of their career. This dislocation .from the family had many problems associated with it. Many people cannot cope with the demanding and fast paced life of the cities and the fact that there is no one to share their feelings of isolation and sadness. This results in the accumulation of stress that leads to mental health problems in people.

Work Related Problems

The participants expressed that stress related to work place was also responsible for mental health problems.

1. "Due to increase in competition in work field people face so many stresses. Sometimes people work hard but do not get due returns. At times someone else takes the credit of one's hard work. This leads to frustrations. Many people find it difficult to adjust to such situations."

Relationship Problems

According to the participants, tensions in relationships could also create mental illness.

1. "Relationship problems also cause mental problems. There could be tension between husband and wife; girlfriend and boyfriend; mother-in-law and daughter-in-law.

Imposed Pressure and Unrealistic Expectations Lead to Frustrations in Life

The participants expressed that unnecessary pressure in life was a common cause of mental illness.

1. "There are various kinds of pressures that cause mental illness. People feel pressurized from family, society and unrealistic

personal ambitions also create problems. Parents pressurize their children to perform well in exams. A highly rewarding career and being successful in life in comparison to other people are major pressures in people's life."

Failures in life are not taken in the right perspective these days by the youth. According to the participants, there was an increase in the suicidal cases because of this.

2. "People have become very impulsive these days. Failure in life could at times result in an extreme step to end one's life."

Compulsive Thinking as a Cause of Mental Illness

Thinking too much about any issue was also considered as cause of stress. The participants expressed that everybody faces stressful situation in life but when a person is not able to come back to normal state he faces mental problems.

1. "Due to tension and stress people have sleepless nights. They think too much about things and are not able to sleep due to constant stress which leads to mental illness."

Loss of Control Over One's Emotion

The participants expressed that loss of control over emotions led to mental imbalance. Situations such as death of a dear one could lead to loss of control over oneself and over one's emotions. Such emotional situations if not handled properly could lead to psychological problems.

1. "There can be many stressful situations in life when a person loses control over oneself. Many people are unable to handle their emotions in negative circumstances, e.g. death of someone in family, divorce with spouse, or break-up of any close relationship."

Negative Childhood Experiences

According to some participants, the negative experiences from past and traumatic experiences of childhood were also important factors that could contribute to mental health problems in people.

1. "Childhood experiences could be related to some kind of suppressed feelings. Many people are not able to do what they

want as their desires are curbed by elders in the family, and at times by situations."

2. "There are many incidences of child abuse which the child does not understand. However, when that child grows up as an adult he/she realizes that something wrong had happened in past. This can be a traumatic feeling and many a times it remains latent. However, the person could show some kind of mental problems in future."

Stigmatization and Negative Portrayal of Mental Illness

Avoidance

According to the participants, people avoided any discussion about mental illness problems. Even if someone in the family suffered from any kind of mental illness, there was a reluctance to admit the problem in public. The perception of stigma led people to avoid seeking help as it could reveal the illness. Some of the quotes of the participants reflect the stigmatized behaviour of people towards mental illness:

1. "Various types of stigmas are attached to mental illness. People suffering from mental illness and their family members are also stigmatized. People generally do not want to maintain relationship with them and avoid them. People also do not wish to marry the brother or sister of a person suffering from mental illness. Social distance and social exclusion is an important component of mental illness."
2. "Mentally ill people are aggressive and violent. They harm people and can be dangerous at times."

Blaming Mentally Ill People for their Mental Illness

The participants expressed that mentally ill people are responsible for their illness.

1. "Mentally ill people are responsible for their condition. Mentally ill people are unproductive, cannot work with efficiency and are dependent on others for survival."

Lack of Sympathy Towards the Mentally Ill

Another important observation from the focussed groups was that people did not show any sort of sympathy towards a mentally ill person. This lack of sympathy results due to the stigmatic reaction of blaming mentally ill for their condition. The participants also felt that due to lack of physical symptoms, mentally ill people were not considered to be suffering from any illness. The comment of a participant given below explains the reason behind lack of sympathetic attitude towards the mentally ill people.

1. "People do not show any sympathy towards the mentally ill as no physical impairment is visible to people. People have sympathy towards people suffering from physical illness because the source of ailment is known, that is any particular body organ is affected. But in case of mental illness, people attribute the cause to the person himself/herself."

Isolation and Individuation of the Mentally Ill

According to the participants, isolation was an important factor that could make the life of a mentally ill person worse. Such isolation is due to stigma towards mentally ill.

1. "Mentally ill people are left isolated and thus their recovery gets hampered. Mentally ill people need family and social support in order to deal with their problems."
2. "Mentally ill people are not provided proper care and they are condemned even by family members. The family members also do not understand their problem and feel irritated if someone shows symptoms that are not normal. Since, they do not have any awareness about mental illness; they do not give attention to problems. Thus, ignorance and not taking adequate steps makes the situation worse."

Defining of Mental Health: The Core Themes

The core themes of mental health have been discussed below along with the comments of the participants from the focussed groups.

Mental Health as Positive Health

The participants expressed the importance of positive attitude towards life. This involves facing all odds by adapting to situational demands important for maintaining mental health.

1. "Mental health means positive attitude, being happy, and having a capability to adjust to life situations. A mentally healthy

person can cope with all situations in life. Everyone faces ups and downs in life and only a mentally healthy and strong person can keep balance by adapting to difficult and demanding situations."

Self-organization and Mental Health

According to the participants, a mentally healthy person could express himself/herself, as well behaved, well organized, and completed tasks on time.

1. "How well people express themselves and how well behaved they are, is also important. People having mental health are well-organized people. They complete their work on time and do not leave things incomplete."

Social Norms and Mental Health

Mental health was also understood in terms of fulfilling one's duty. A mentally healthy person abides by the norms of the society and delivers his day-to-day duties. This can be understood from the comment given by one of the participants:

1. "A person who performs his due duties and behaves according to the norms of the society can be regarded as a mentally healthy person."

Spiritual Well-being as a State of Mental Health

According to the participants, mental health could be restored by getting involved in spiritual practices. Spiritual well being was considered to be an important feature of mental health.

1. "People adopt various means to attain mental health. Meditation and *yoga* are some of the ways that could help in maintenance of mental health."

Religion and Mental Health

The participants expressed that belief in God and involvement in religious practices provided mental strength to people.

1. "Belief in God and prayers help to maintain mental health. Through religious practices people gain mental strength to bear stress in life."

Health Seeking in Mental Illness

The participants expressed their awareness about mental health related facilities. However, due to stigma in society they feared to come forward to seek help.

Fear of Ostracism from the Society

According to the participants, the disclosure of mental illness restricted the social life and resulted in loss of prestige. The participants expressed that no one in the society wished to maintain relationship with a mentally ill person as he/she did not have any credibility.

1. "Once you go and seek help, people treat you as out of group. They treat the mentally ill person as different from normal, who should not be included in their group. The family, as well as the relatives of the mentally ill, are also not welcome in the social group. Thus, it becomes necessary to hide mental illness to the extent it is possible."

Inaccessibility of Mental Health Services

The participants expressed that the number of mental patients is on increase. Participants were of the opinion that in comparison to the increase in mental health problems the number of mental health professionals was very limited. Also, the high cost of treatment was beyond the reach of ordinary families.

1. "There are a few mental health specialists who can treat mental illness, but they are available only in metro cities. NGOs have made an effort to deal with mental illness; but these services are also limited to specific locations. There is an uneven distribution of services."

Lack of Supportive Environment

According to the participants, family and society could play a positive role in taking care of the mentally ill person. Without support from these sources rehabilitation of the mentally ill was difficult.

1. "People consider a mentally ill person to be unproductive and dependent. Such treatment from family and relatives weakens the hope for recovery. Mentally ill people face a lot of stress

due to their illness and the societal rejection worsens the problem further."

Measures Suggested for Creating Awareness about Mental Health and Mental Illness

Involvement of the Local Bodies

Various measures were suggested that involved participation of the local non-governmental organizations, schools and colleges in spreading information about mental health and mental illness.

1. "Local Non-Governmental Organizations (NGOs) are active only in certain regions. Thus, the distribution of services is not adequate. Such social organizations should spread the awareness message about mental health and illness at large."
2. "The concept of mental health and illness can be introduced in schools as part of the curriculum. Students should be given information about mental health and illness in the same manner as they are provided information about how to maintain physical health and hygiene. Teachers at school level can also contribute in identification of children with mental illness and special needs. The teacher should be given some training so that he/she is able to identify students at risk and can suggest for referrals."

Involvement of the Media

Various sources of media were acknowledged that could reform the negative representations of mental illness and could generate awareness about issues pertaining to mental illness. According to the participants cinema, television, radio, and newspapers could be helpful in creating awareness about mental health and illness.

1. "Media portrayal of mental illness needs a reformation. The negative representations generated by media about mental illness can be changed by providing appropriate information related to mental illness."
2. "Movies can promote representations of mental health and can try to reduce the negativity present in people. Instead of portraying mental health specialists as funny and crazy in movies, they can be represented as responsible people who could help mentally ill people to deal with their problems."

Creating Social Support

The participants suggested for a sympathetic behaviour towards the mentally ill person. According to the participants care, support, treatment and acceptance of mentally ill person by family and society could be helpful in recovery from mental illness. The participants expressed that the common people could be motivated to adopt a positive attitude towards the mentally ill by providing appropriate information.

Discussion

The present study focussed on in-depth exploration of social representations of mental health and mental illness in Indian urban middle class people. In this regard, an attempt was made to explore the role of psychosocial contexts contributing to mental illness, stigmatization of mentally ill, health seeking behaviour in mental illness, and measures to create awareness regarding mental health and mental illness. The results demonstrate that the meanings associated with mental health and illness is formulated within the psychosocial contexts relevant to people's lives. Interactions within these contexts generate these meanings and they are held collectively. A qualitative study by the authors of this chapter (Maurya & Dixit, 2008) explored the lay meanings of mental health and mental illness among 60 urban middle class people. The study also revealed that the lay meanings of mental health and mental illness were derived from the psychosocial contexts. Another study in the Indian context that reports similar psychosocial understanding of mental illness was conducted by Dixit (2005) on urban middle class youth. The study found that social representations of mental illness were structured in terms of social understanding of causes and consequences of mental illness. Wagner Duveen, Themel, and Verma (1999, 2002) explored social representations of madness in the Indian urban middle class people. The sample comprised of 39 educated middle class residents of Patna, Bihar. The results revealed polymorphic representations of madness. The representation of madness existed in the form of cultural beliefs of ghost or spirit possession. However, at the same time people also held modern representations in the form of awareness regarding psychiatrists, psychiatric medicines, and electroshock therapy for treating madness. The polymorphic representations refer to the set of social thoughts that can have co-existence in knowledge systems. This knowledge system possesses information that can be affirming, contradictory or negating. The society at large is becoming polysemus and an individual can have multiple explanations for various phenomena. Moscovici, 1967, p. 402 refers it to "the dynamic co-existence of modalities of individual knowledge, corresponding to concrete relations between man and his environment".

Representations of Mental Illness

The results of the present study demonstrated polymorphic representations of mental illness. These polymorphic representations resulted in multiple meanings about a particular issue related to mental illness. Sometimes opposing meanings also existed about the same phenomenon. The multiplicity of meanings is discussed below.

(a) According to the participants, mental illness was a common phenomenon and yet they considered it as uncommon or unfamiliar. The participants expressed that everyone in the society had some or the other kind of mental illness. Along with this, they also held the belief that there was a general tendency to avoid discussion on mental illness.

(b) The participants considered mental illness as an illness, but at the same time they did not accept it as an illness that needed to be attended like physical illness.

(c) The participants believed that a mentally ill person should be treated with care and sympathy. However, they commented that due to lack of physical symptoms people expressed less sympathy towards a mentally ill person.

(d) The participants expressed that the nuclear family system has taken over the joint family system in society. They believed that this has led to a rise in various types of mental problems. However, at the same time the participants expressed the benefits of the nuclear family system.

(e) The present study found that dislocation from family for career advancement was a causal factor in creating stress in life that could lead to mental health problems. The participants expressed that though, people were aware of the stresses related to migration and dislocation of family yet, they wished to go abroad for better future prospects that at times resulted in stressful situations. In this context Bhugra and Jones (2001) comment that migration leads to social change whereby an individual moves from one cultural setting to another and this process is inevitably stressful and can lead to mental illness.

(f) The participants described mental illness as a deviance. There were further distinctions in types of deviation. Not abiding by the social norms was one form of deviation. Other type of deviation included homosexuality. According to the participants artists and scientists were also considered as deviants. They did not conform to the norms of society, but were also not mentally ill. The lay participants expressed that such people belonged to some different world. Thus, the concept of mental illness held multiple notions of deviance.

(g) The representations indicated a clear awareness about mental illness. However, there was reluctance to seek professional help. The reluctance to seek help was due to *fear of ostracism from the society*, and *inaccessibility of mental health services*. According to the participants, mild mental problems could be dealt with the support and counselling provided by the family members and friends. In case of severe mental illness participants expressed need for professional intervention.

The conflict in representations of mental illness in the "educated urban middle class society in India" can be explained through the processes of social change. According to Kakar (1997), India has undergone rapid modernization and industrialization. This development has brought positive as well as negative effects. There has been a phenomenal rise of the educated urban middle class and with these changes there has been an increase in social stress and mental problems. He further describes that the rise of the urban middle class with modernization has brought about many changes in the nature of problems which are primarily products of the contemporary social contexts. Kakkar and Kakkar (2007) in their writings on Indian people discuss that though modernization has developed as a way of life in the urban middle class, there still remains a latent desire for the traditional element.

The social representations indicated awareness of mental health services. However, there was reluctance to seek help due to fear of social exclusion from the society. This could be explained in terms of maintenance of individual and social identities of normality. Foster (2001) has provided an explanation for the tendency to differentiate mentally ill people from normal. According to her, people adopt a strategy to maintain self-identity. For maintenance of self identity as normal people categorize mentally ill people as out groups. According to Marwaha (2003), the identity of an Indian individual is enmeshed in the identity of his social group. People conform to the social norms in order to identify oneself a part of a large social group or society. The tendency to label a mentally ill person as crazy or mad reflects the tendency to perceive mentally ill as out groups. The representations revealed that there was a general tendency to differentiate mentally ill person from normal people as this served to maintain self-identity of 'being normal'.

Representations of Mental Health

The results of the present study elucidate the representations of mental health held by the Indian urban middle class. The overall themes of the focussed group interviews revealed a general lack of awareness about mental health. The lay understanding of mental health focussed on psycho-social themes such as *mental health as positive health, self-organization as mental health, abiding by social norms as mental health, spiritual well-being as a state of mental health, and involvement in religious practices to attain mental health*. According to Trainor, Pomeroy, and Pape (1997), efforts need to be made to enhance the literature on mental health promotion for people with mental illness. It is important to promote community research on mental health for positive outcomes in mental illness. A study by Mehrotra, *et al.* (2012), has recently explored the lay meaning of mental health among urban Indian college youths. This study though limited to youth suggests the need to extend the research from the lay perspective. The theoretical models are important in understanding mental illness however, the lay perspective can help in designing intervention programmes targeting specific population. The study mentions the need for further exploration of the concept of mental health in varied contexts so as to design context appropriate intervention programmes.

Representations of Health Seeking Behaviour

The participants expressed that the health seeking behaviour is probable only when there is awareness about mental health. According to the participants, mild mental problems could be dealt with the support and counselling provided by the family members and friends. The participants expressed that, besides taking professional help supportive environment was also essential. With proper support of family, friends and society recovery could be faster. With recovery, rehabilitation in the society by accepting the cured people as normal was considered to be important. WHO (2003) report suggests that providing a supportive environment lessens the severity of mental illness. The participants suggested that the awareness about mental health and illness could be spread through *involvement of the local bodies, involvement of media and creating social support.* The participants expressed the need for formal education for maintaining mental health.

Conclusion

The qualitative exploration revealed the core themes of mental health and mental illness with a prominence of psychosocial explanations. The findings suggest that the urban middle class focussed more on mental illness in comparison to mental health. The findings of the present study revealed that the lay meanings of mental illness were largely polymorphic in nature and derived from the psychosocial context of the educated urban middle class. In the present study, the cognitive polyphasia reflects the polymorphic nature of social thought about mental illness in the educated urban middle class Indians. The explanation for these polymorphic representations lies in the psychosocial and cultural context of the educated urban middle class. According to Kalampalikis and Moscovici (as cited in Kalampalikis & Haas, 2008), the explanation for cognitive ployphasia lies in the belongingness of people to multiple and different groups, playing various roles in daily life where different identities of people come into interplay and sharing common representations to a certain extent.

These polymorphic representations of the concept of mental health, mental illness and health seeking in mental illness can be understood as the versatile social thought in action. People understand and interpret the world depending on the social context. In the present study the knowledge of the mental health issues and health seeking practices indicates the knowledge pertaining to the issues however, the reluctance to use the services and acceptance of mental illness as a concern to be attended professionally is avoided. In order to maintain the identity with the larger social group people abstain from talking about it openly or seeking help. The fear of seclusion and the negative stereotypes are so dominant that the familiar also becomes less familiar. This multifaceted representation gives rise to polymorphic representations. Therefore, the representations are more context (social) specific and not individual specific. The social context determines which representations will be more dominant and operant. According to Kalampalikis & Haas (2008) polyphasia represents the dynamic social thought in changing social contexts. The social representation carries the polysemus views or the social thought which is explicit in polymorphic representations. Wagner (2007) proposed the concept of "discursive polyphasia" that referred to the use of different social representations in different social contexts. According to Provencher (2011) cognitive polyphasia explains how these dynamic representations cohabit in individuals of the same social group.

In present study, the polymorphic representations of mental illness, mental health and the health seeking behaviour explain the complex nature of the social representations shared by a group of people. In order to meet the mental health needs there is a need to engage towards a multifaceted approach that combines the social and cultural needs along with the biomedical. The present study suggests that along with the existing models used to study mental illness, there is a need to understand the lay perspective as well. Only focussing on mental illness is a narrow approach; an understanding of mental health needs of people and their health seeking behaviour is also required. Such lay explorations can provide important insights in designing community specific interventions and thus enriching the health care delivery system that works better with an eclectic approach.

REFERENCES

Bhugra, D. and Jones, P. (2001). "Migration and Mental Illness", *Advances in Psychiatric Treatment*, 7, 216-23.

De Rosa, A. (1987). "The Social Representation of Mental Illness in Children and Adults", in W. Doise and S. Moscovici (eds.), *Current Issues in European Social Psychology*, Cambridge University Press: Cambridge.

Dixit, S. (2005). "Meaning and Explanations of Mental Illness: A Social Representations Approach", *Psychology and Developing Societies*, 17, 1-18.

Flick, U. (1998a). "Everyday Knowledge in Social Psychology", in U. Flick (ed.), *The Psychology of the Social* (pp. 41-59), Cambridge: Cambridge University Press.

Flick, U. (1998b). "The Social Construction of Individual and Public Health: Contributions of Social Representations Theory to a Social Science of Health", *Social Science Information*, 37, 639-62.

Flick, U. (1992). "Combining Methods — Lack of Methodology: Discussion of Sotirakopoulou and Breakwell", *Papers on Social Representations*, 1, 43-48. Retrieved July 7, 2005, from http://www.psr.jku.at/PSR1992/1_1992Flick.pdf

Flick. U. (2000). "Qualitative Enquiry into Social Representations of Health", *Journal of Health Psychology*, 5, 309-18.

Foster, J. (2001). "Unification and Differentiation: A Study of Social Representations of Mental Illness", *Papers on Social Representations*, 10, 3.1-3.18. Retrieved June 23, 2005, http://www.psr.jku.at/PSR2001/10_3Foste.Pdf.

Herzlich, C. (1973). *Health and Illness: A Social Psychological Analysis*, London: Academic Press.

Jodelet, D. (1991). *Madness and Social Representations*, Harvester Wheatsheaf: Hemel Hempstead.

Joffe, H. (1998). "Social Representations and the AIDS Field", *Psychology and Society*, 24, 21-39.

Joffe, H. and Bettega, N. (2003). "Social Representations and the AIDS among Zambian Adolescents", *Journal of Health Psychology*, 8, 616-31.

Kakkar, S. (1997). *Culture and Psyche Selected Essays*, Oxford University Press, Delhi.

Kakkar, S. and K. Kakkar. (2007). *The Indians: Portrait of a People*, Penguin Books: Delhi.

Kalampalikis, N. and Haas, V. (2008). "More than a Theory: A New Map of Social Thought", *Journal for the Theory of Social Behaviour*, 38, 0021-8308.

Kleinman, A. (1980). *Patients and Healers in the Context of Culture: An Exploration of the Borderland between Anthropology, Medicine, and Psychiatry*, London: University of California Press.

Marwaha, S.B. (2003). "Culture and Counselling: The Indian Paradox — Implications for Professional Psychology", in U. Vindhya (ed.), *Psychology in India: Intersecting Crossroads* (pp. 95-107), Concept Publishing Company, New Delhi.

Maurya, A.S. and Dixit, S. (2008). "Lay Understanding of Mental Health and Illness: A Social Representations Approach", *Psychological Studies*, 53, 34-40.

Mehrotra, S., Tripathi, R. and Elias, J. (2012). "Lay Meanings of Mental Health in Urban Indian College Youth: Insights for Mental Health Promotions", *Journal of Community and Applied Psychology*, DOI:10. 1002/casp.

Morant, N. (1998). "Constructions of 'Mental Ill Health' amongst Mental Health Practitioners in Britain and France", *Social Science Information*, 37, 663-85.

Moscovici, S. (1984). "The Phenomena of Social Representations", in R.M. Farr and S. Moscovici (eds.), *Social Representations* (pp. 3-69), Cambridge: Cambridge University Press.

Moscovici, S. (1988). "Notes Towards a Description of Social Representations", *European Journal of Social Psychology*, 18, 211-50.

Mostyn, B. (1985). "The Content Analysis of Qualitative Research Data: A Dynamic Approach", in Brenner, M., Brown, J. and Canter, D. (eds.), *The Research Interview Uses and Approaches* (pp. 115-45), London: Academic Press.

National Council for Applied Economic Research (2006). *Middle Income Group to Grow by 13 per cent NCAER Study*. Retrieved September 30, 2006, from http://www.financialexpress.com/new/middle-income-group-to-grow-by-13-ncaer-study/17

Petrillo, G. (1996). "Changes in Social Representations of Mental Illness: The Last Twenty-five Years on the Italian Press", *Papers on Social Representations*, 5, 99-112. Retrieved July 4, 2006 from http://www.psr.jku.at/PSR1996/5_1996Petri.pdf

Provencher, C. (2011). "Towards a Better Understanding of Cognitive Polyphasia", *Journal for the Theory of Social Behaviour*, 41, 377-95.

Spector, R.E. (1996). "Culture, Health and Illness", *Cultural Diversity in Health and Illness* (p. 65), Appleton and Lange Stamford, CT.

Trainor, J., Pomeroy, E. and Pape, B. (1993). *A New Framework for Support for Persons with Serious Mental Health Problems*, Toronto: Canadian Mental Health Association, National Office.

Wagner, W., Duveen, G., Themel, M., Verma, J. (1999). "The Modernization of Tradition: Thinking about Madness in Patna, India", *Culture & Psychology*, 5, 413-45.

Wagner, W., Duveen, G., Themel, M., Verma, J. (2002). "I have Some Faith and at the Same Time I Don't Believe" — Cognitive Polyphasia and Cultural Change", *Journal of Community and Applied Social Psychology*, 10, 102-314.

Wagner, W. (2007). "Vernacular Science Knowledge: Its Role in Everyday Life Communication", *Public Understanding of Science*, 16, 7-22.

World Health Organization (2003). *Investing in Mental Health, WHO, Geneva*. Retrieved August 9, 2007, from http://www.who.int/mental_health/media/investing_mnh.pdf

Zani, B. (1993). "Social Representations of Mental Illness: Lay and Professional Perspectives", in G.M. Breakwell and D.V. Canter (eds.), *Empirical Approaches to Social Representations* (pp. 315-30), Oxford: Clarendon Press.

Zani, B. (1995). "The Mentally Ill Person and the Others: Social Representations and Interactive Strategies", in I. Markova and R.M. Farr (eds.), *Representations of Health and Illness and Handicap* (pp. 145-62), Chur: Switzerland: Harwood.

APPENDIX A

Semi-Structured Interview Schedule

1. How do you define the concept of mental illness?
2. How and to what extent psychosocial contexts affect mental illness?
3. What are the possible explanations for the stereotypes and negative representations of mental illness in the lay urban middle class?
4. How do you define the concept of mental health?
5. What are the health seeking options present in the society for people suffering from mental illness?
6. What can be the possible measures that can be applied in the current scenario to create awareness towards mental health and mental illness?

SECTION IV

Health Challenges

12

Health and Illness Concerns of Children in India

Issues and Challenges

Sibnath Deb, Anjali Gireesan and *Aneesh Kumar*

When William Shakespeare wrote his famous poem "Seven Ages of Man", he described childhood in just one line, the meaning of which is that this particular stage of life signifies a worry-free world which can be enjoyed with eagerness and enthusiasm. Shakespeare belonged to what we now call an 'archaic era' where technological and scientific revolution was at a bare minimum. The advent of these ideas was meant to simplify life. But life has never been more complicated as today. The simple childhood that was described, has long been lost. Instead, it has become the most vulnerable and worrisome 'age' for the man. Today's child lives in an unstable society. Consequently, the well-being of the child is no longer a simple, but has become a complicated issue, embedded in the mesh of its equally complicated contributing factors. The manifestation of this scenario can be directly observed in the current health and well-being of children.

Worldwide, several measures have been taken to protect children from various hazards so that the innocence of childhood can be maintained and cherished. There is no doubt that child protection has emerged as a priority in many national as well as international conventions. The United Nations convention on child rights is considered to be a milestone in this respect. It was followed by many other policies and programmes for the welfare of children. The sensitivity of the issue has increased in the background of an intricate and entangled web of circumstances. The prevalence of various types of diseases, both communicable and non-communicable, has gradually increased across the world. Children having a developing and vulnerable immune system, tend to be the first victims of infections. These new infections cannot be dealt with instantly. Hence, their perseverance in the population, later on, takes harmful forms. Crimes and offences against children have also increased. This includes all forms of exploitation like abuse (physical, psychological and sexual), child labour and corporal punishment. Children are easy victims because they are considered to be weak and it is perceived that their exploitation can be hidden and they can be dominated. A child interacts with various systems of the society for a holistic development. This includes the self, family, friends, school and community. A misunderstood or negative interaction with any of these systems affects the whole cycle of interaction and thus influences the physical as well as psychological development of children. This might be because of dysfunctional families, lower social support and approval, incompatible school environment or peer pressure.

India has one of the largest child populations in the world. Approximately, 13.1 per cent of India's population is constituted by children. The children require adequate care and support to achieve their full potential. There are many child protection programmes in our country, but there is still more to do in order to address the health needs of children. Problems of malnutrition and anemia are highly prevalent in the country, number of children with HIV infections has shown an increase and child mortality rates are alarmingly high (Ministry of Statistics and Programme Implementation, Government of India, 2012). There are other health concerns for which no reliable statistics is available. In this chapter, various health concerns of different groups of children have been discussed. These groups generally come under the purview of vulnerable children. There is a section on health initiatives for children in India as well.

Victims of Child Abuse and Neglect

Child abuse is a serious social problem as well as a matter of primary importance for public health. It is a very grave and unfortunate global phenomenon. No country has been left untouched by this pandemic which shakes the very core of human civilization, i.e. trust and social interactions. In India, it has affected the population of children with no discrimination between age, gender, region or class. Approximately 20 per cent women and 5-10 per cent men report that they have been sexually abused as children; 25-50 per cent of all children report being physically abused (WHO, 2010). According to the Ministry of Women and Child Development Report on child abuse, children in the age group of 5-12 years have reported higher levels of abuse. Boys are at an equal risk of being abused as girls and the perpetrators principally include persons in trust and authority (MWCD, 2007). When the protectors themselves turn into the perpetrators, saying that a home is the safest place for a child becomes a myth. When these children see that their caregivers are turning negative, it leads to adoption of unhealthy attachment styles (ACF/OPRE, 2012a). Although there are many facets to the consequences of this problem, one of the major issues that emerge out of this pool is the health of these children. It is said that a child is the father of a human being. If this is regarded to be true, then a dysfunctional childhood will definitely pave the way for a dysfunctional life, the starting and significant point of which can be the health of this individual.

Abuse and neglect has detrimental effects on development of brain. Both of these processes are considered toxic stress that deters the brain development for worse and exhibiting negative impact on the child's physical, cognitive, emotional and social growth (Kendall-Tackett, 2002). The fear regions remain overly stimulated (Perry, 2012) and neuro-chemical balance is disturbed (Healy, 2004) which results in negative perception of their own well-being by these children.

Children usually have neuronal pathways in expectation of care, encouragement and reinforcements which die in case children are deprived of them. This refrain them from achieving the usual developmental milestones (Scunnapieco, 2008). Abuse and neglect often result in diminished growth in the left hemisphere which might lead to depression, irritability in the limbic system which may result in panic disorders and a dysfunctional connection between the two hemispheres which may result in Attention Deficit Hyperactive Disorder (Teicher, 2000). The process of brain maturation, if hindered, has a prolonged effect on the cognitive (ACF/OPRE, 2012b), language and academic abilities and also has an implication for the incidence of mental health disorders (Tarullo, 2012).

According to a survey of National Survey on Child and Adolescent Well-being (NSCAW), 28 per cent of children had a chronic health condition after they were subjected to maltreatment (ACF/OPRE, 2007). They are more often sick and are at an increased risk of having one or more pain syndromes (Kendall-Tackett, 2002). Victims of multiple types of abuse are at an increased risk of ischemic heart disease, cancer, stroke, chronic bronchitis, emphysema, diabetes, skeletal fractures and hepatitis (Felitti, *et al.*, 2001; Felitti & Anda, 2009). Child neglect implicates an increased risk of diabetes and poor lung functioning while physical abuse invites a threat of diabetes and malnutrition (Widom, Czaja, Bentley & Johnson, 2012). Children meted out with this type of treatment usually engage in different types of substance abuse like alcohol, psychoactive and intravenous drugs and smoking (Barthlow, *et al.*, 1994; Kendall-Tackett, *et al.*, 2000; Felitti, *et al.*, 2001; Felitti & Anda, 2009). They are more vulnerable to suicidal ideation and suicidal attempts (Brier & Zeidi, 1989; Felitti, *et al.*, 2001). High risk sexual behaviour is one of the most researched upon harmful behaviour as a consequence of child abuse. Its prevalence is evident in both community samples (Fergusan, Horwood & Lynskey, 1997; Fleming, Mullen, Sibthorpe & Bamner, 1999; Girmstad & Schei, 1999) as well specialized samples (Thompson, Potter, Sanderson & Maiback, 1997; Mason, Zimmerman & Evans, 1998). This endangers them towards various diseases like AIDS and other sexually transmitted diseases. The pandemic also affects their sleeping and eating patterns. They have nightmares (Teegan, 1999) and insomnia (Brier & Runtz, 1987) resulting in disrupted sleep which in turn makes them vulnerable to infections and illnesses (National Sleep Foundation, 2000). In the case of food intake, they are prone to eating disorders like bulimia (Miller, McClusky-Fawett & Irving, 1993; Felitti, *et al.*, 2001) as well as obesity (Shin & Miller, 2012). Delinquency, truancy and pregnancy are highly probable in this group of children (ACF/OPRE, 2012b). They are nine times more likely to be involved in criminal activities (Gold, Sullivan & Lewis, 2011).

In addition to all the above mentioned physical manifestations of health concerns of child abuse, there are many psychological implications which may be of direct or indirect concern in the context of their health. Physical or sexual abuse often predisposes a child to an increased risk of Borderline Personality Disorder, depression, Post-Traumatic Stress disorder and other psychiatric disorder (Child Welfare Information Gateway, 2013). Depression is highly prevalent in abuse survivors, (Briere & Elliot, 1994; Gladstone, Parker, Wilhelm & Mitchell, 1999; Zuravin & Fontanella, 1999) which is an immunosuppressor (Weisse, 1992) and affects the level of white blood cells as well (Avissar, Nuhamkin, Roitman & Schreiber, 1997). Cognitively, they are under stress hence, there is an increased stimulation to release cortisol. Constantly elevated cortisol levels can suppress the immune system, slow wound healing, damage the brain and increase the likelihood of the disease (Child Welfare Information Gateway, 2009). Their self-health perception, which is a predictor of both illness and mortality (Moosey &

Shapiro, 1982; Kaplan & Comacho, 1983), is observed to be low. They often suffer from lifelong psychological consequences like low self-esteem and relationship difficulties, which is detrimental to health as a stable and strong social support is a predictor of a better health profile.

Children with Disability

Disability puts people in threat of various health hazards like secondary conditions (pressure ulcers, osteoporosis, pain, etc.), co-morbid conditions, and age related conditions and have higher rate of premature deaths (WHO Factsheet No. 352, 2014). Children with disability constitute a group which is constantly dependent on the people around them. They are in a precarious situation when it comes to their health and well-being. There are several contributing factors which have led to this current scenario.

1. ***Inadequate Statistics and Representation:*** Though we have census every ten years that gives one the statistics of all types of population and associated entities, statistics on population with disability suffer from several problems. In developing countries people with disability are often 'hidden' from census enumerators and identification process is limited by how disability is defined in various constitutional provisions and legislations.
2. ***Lack of Appropriate Legislation and Policies:*** The legislation and policies are formulated, so that, they meet the needs of the target population. The needs have to be understood and then the solutions for it have to be formulated. Children with disability have many needs apart from the financial concerns. Their care and support services involve people from different sections of the society like their parents, service providers, pediatricians, the community that they live in and teachers who are involved in inclusive education.

   A person with disability can avail the benefits provided by the Government on the basis of disability certificate issued by an appropriate authority. The disability categories being issued this certificate include physical, hearing and speech disabilities, visual impairment and mental retardation. All these categories of disability are physically observable. An appropriate authority has not been designated to certify all the other types of disabilities and thus these children are not able to avail even the existing benefits in the system.

3. ***Accessibility to Medical Care:*** Generally, children with disability have greater requirement of medical care than children without disabilities. Children with cerebral palsies have medical conditions like convulsions and seizures. Children with autism have frequent self-inflicted injuries and epileptic attacks. Children with learning disabilities often complain of headaches and lack of concentration. Children with locomotor disabilities experience pain and other related medical conditions. They face unequal access to health promotion programmes, universal health services and appropriate palliative care services. Lack of appropriate services in the area was reported to be the second most significant barrier in accessing health facilities in States of Uttar Pradesh and Tamil Nadu (WHO Factsheet No. 352, 2014).
4. ***Vulnerability to Maltreatment:*** Children with disability are at an increased risk of all types of abuse like physical, psychological, emotional and sexual than children without disabilities (Hershkowitz, Lamb & Horowitz, 2007). The injuries inflicted may often go unnoticed because the child may himself not understand that he has been abused. They also experience neglect, because of lack of awareness about disability and cultural myths associated with this condition.

The challenges and difficulties in the life of children with disability can be reduced if at least their basic health requirements are taken care of. Professionals should be able to recognize their needs and families should be supported. Centre for Disease Control and Prevention reports that individuals with disabilities report poorer overall health, have lower level of physical activity and have increased risk of indulging in smoking. Children with disabilities are 38 per cent more likely to be obese than their counterparts (http://www.cdc.gov/ncbddd/disabilityandhealth/articles.html). According to WHO, health promotion and prevention activities exclude people with disabilities from their purview (WHO Factsheet No. 352, 2014). Hence, an increased vigilance is required to ensure maximum health benefits to children.

Girl Child

The health and living condition of girl child in India is not very encouraging. It stems from age old beliefs of a male child being superior to a female child. The child sex ratio has shown a decline in the census

2011 (Ministry of Statistics and Programme Implementation, Government of India, 2012). This perception is reflected in various health indulging behaviours by the caregivers of a child. Each stage of the life-cycle of a female is substantiated with gender discrimination which further perpetuates other problems like unbalanced sex ratio (Fikree & Pasha, 2004).

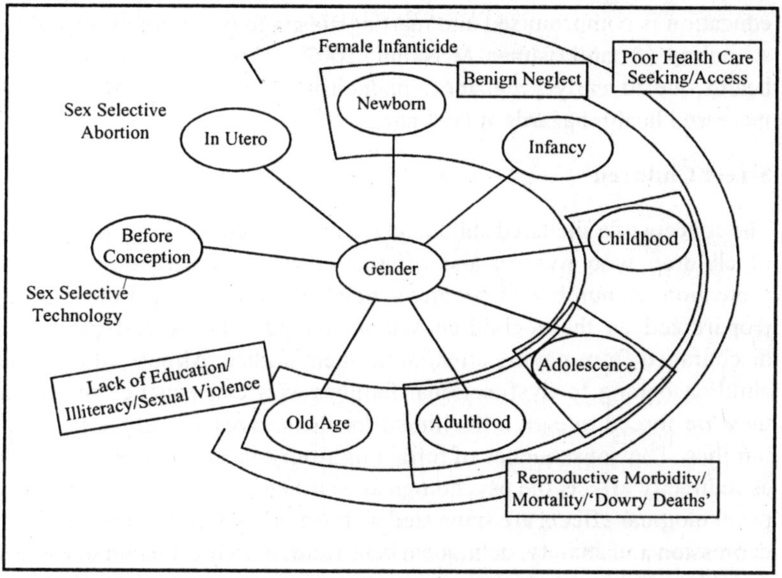

Figure 12.1: Life Cycle of a Girl Child Depicting Concerns at Different Stages

Source: Fikree and Pasha, 2004.

An unwanted girl child is often subjected to selective abortion, female infanticide, and is sometimes severely neglected. This translates into a higher girl child mortality rate (George, 1997). India has the world's largest gender survival gap (Save the Children, 2008). The chances of her dying between first and fifth birthday is 40 per cent more than that of boys (Victora, *et al.*, 2003). Gender gap in mortality is a good indicator of discrimination against the girl child (Agnihotri, 2001). There is also a clear discrimination in provision of medical care to the girl child. For example, during diseases like diarrhoea and acute respiratory infections, if the caregivers have to travel a long distance for qualified professionals they would rather serve the medical needs of a male child than a female child (Gantra & Hirve, 1994; Abbasi, Mirani, Parsram & Sarwar, 1998; Hassan & Khanum, 2000; Premi, 2001; Pande,

2003). Preferential hospitalization and immunization have been observed for male children (Srivastava & Nayak, 1995). Regional patterns exist for immunization. Most pronounced gender differences are found in north and north-central region, and to some extent in eastern regions of the country. For vaccinations like BCG and DPT also there are clear regional patterns which indicate the neglect of the girl child (Arokiasamy, 2004). The regions where her health is not given due importance, her education is compromised and marriage is given more importance than schooling (Anantkrishnan & Nalini, 2002). This in turn affects their health due to early pregnancy, malnourishment among children and increased health hazards at later ages.

Street Children

The concept of a sheltered childhood is a myth. There is a large population of children who live on and off the streets with bare minimum of protection. A number of problems befall these children. Education is jeopardized as these children seldom attend schools and are often discouraged from paying attention to their studies. Almost all of these children belong to dysfunctional families as a consequence of which they are forced to earn a livelihood for themselves as well as for their families. The consequence of refraining from education directly as well as indirectly affects the psychological well-being of these children. The psychological effects are translated as lower self-esteem, prevalence of depression and anxiety, delinquent behaviour, insecure attachment styles and other problems which have long-term effects on their life (Kerfoot, Koshyl, Mikhailichenko, Gorbova & Pottage, 2007). The physical well-being of such children is compromised as well. Street children, in order to attain livelihood, engage in jobs like scavenging, rag picking, in factories, etc. which exposes them to a lot of occupational hazards (D'Lima & Gosalia, 1992; Hunt, 1996). The hazardous nature of waste like presence of fecal, material, hospital waste, industrial waste and waste that includes sharp objects increases their susceptibility to infections (Hunt, 1996). They are susceptible to communicable diseases because of the lack of proper hygiene and sanitation in their surroundings.

Street children suffer from malnutrition which may have a directly observable effect on their health (Kombarakaran, 2004). They have been observed to eat leftover food at places where they work and food from garbage bins, which may lead to problems of food poisoning and other related harmful outcomes. As their economic condition does not permit them to have a proper meal, they often beg or frequently go to

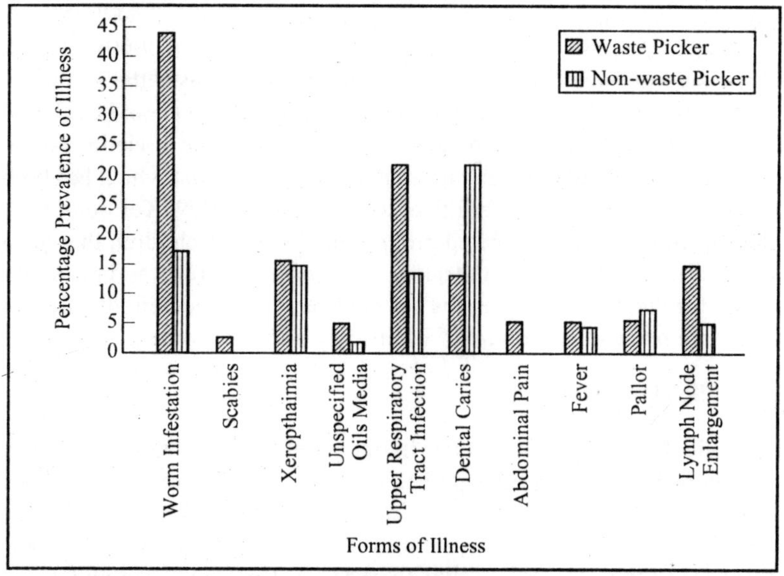

Figure 12.2: Infections that are Contracted by Waste Pickers

Source: Hunt, C. (1996). "Child Waste Pickers in India: The Occupation and Its Health Risks", *Environment and Urbanization*, 8(2), 111-18.

places where the meal is free. The quality of food that is gained from such means is uncertain which again implies that they lack adequate nutrition (Kombarakaran, 2004). Their bruises and injuries often go untreated as they do not have adequate access to medical care which makes them susceptible to several types of infections (Reddy, 1992; Pandey, 1992). Apart from all these, there is a high incidence of risk behaviour amongst these children. The reasons for indulging in such activities range from personal factors like depression and frustration from living on streets to societal factors like peer pressure and conflicts in life. Out of all the factors, peer group influence was found to be the most potent initiation factor in engaging in such behaviour (Kombarakaran, 2004). Also, it has been observed that these children often engage in unsafe sex practices. Exchange sex and survival sex are highly prevalent in this group. Children who are reluctant to work are known to offer sexual favours in exchange of food and gifts (Kombarakaran, 2004; Towe, Hasan, Zafar, & Sherman, 2009).

Reports from different cities of India like Chennai, Bengaluru, Kolkata and Jaipur show a disturbing statistics of abuse of street children (Arimpoor, 1992). For example, in Jaipur city, 98.4 per cent of street children experience moderate to severe category of abuse while 1.6 per cent fall in the mild category (Mathur, Rathore & Mathur, 2009). Though some studies have shown that living in streets increases the resilience capacity of these children, the harm that comes with it cannot be ignored as well. Street children are forced to be in a vicious cycle of victimization, unhealthy circumstances and unsupportive environment which has both short-term and long-term health outcomes (Lalor, 1999; Kerfoot, *et al.*, 2007). India has an integrated programme for street children that have been formulated to assess the needs of children on streets and make life better for them. The programme has not been evaluated periodically and therefore one cannot be sure of its efficacy and functioning.

Juvenile Delinquents

Juvenile delinquency is on a rise in our country. Over 33,000 juveniles, mostly between the age group of 16 to 18, have been arrested for crimes like rape and murder across the country in 2011, the highest in last decade (*The Indian Express*, January 13, 2013). The evidence is clear from December 16, 2012 Delhi (Nirbhaya) gang rape case and many other similar stories. A National Crime Records Bureau (NCRB) study reveals that the number of juvenile raping girls and women has increased over the last three years in India (*The Times of India*, 18 July, 2013). There are many reasons that children become delinquents of which some have been already mentioned in this article. Psychiatrists and women rights activists claim that easy access to pornography, changing food habits can be attributed as two reasons behind the crime (*The Times of India*, 18 July, 2013) The other factors include poor socio-economic status and the family environment of these children. After the crime has been committed, they are generally sent to correctional homes.

In order to ensure wholesome reform and development, children's physical, psychological and social health needs to be taken care of. Apart from conduct disorder, other diagnosable disorders like personality, affective, attention deficit hyperactivity, and substance abuse disorders, and mental retardation have been observed to occur in these delinquents as well females have been observed to suffer from affective disorders like depression (Weirson, Forehand & Frame, 1992). They often meet the diagnostic criteria for substance abuse disruptive behaviour disorders (Kataoka, *et al.*, 2001; Teplin, Abram, McClelland, Dulcan & Mericle, 2002). Poly-Substance abuse is likely to predispose a delinquent to have one or more psychiatric disorders (Neighbors, Kempton, & Forehand, 1992). They may have somatic complaints and suicidal ideation as well

(Cauffman, 2004). They have been reported to have post-traumatic stress disorder (Cauffman, Feldman, Wetherman & Steiner, 1998). Thus, in order to ensure their healthy reform, the root causes of these mental health problems have to be identified and thus treated.

Health Compromising Behaviours in Children

With the advent of globalization, there has been a rapid change in the lifestyle of adults as well as children. Consequently, indulgence in health compromising behaviours has also increased. The first victim in this scenario is nutrition. Balanced diet is a myth nowadays. Children prefer food products like burger, pizza, bread, noodles and other type of fast food rather than the traditional food that used to be cooked at home. Parents also tend to chose processed food products because it is easy on their time. One reason that children tend to be obese these days is that they do not eat food that is in their genes.

The increased media coverage and television shows have changed the perception of life for many people. Inhibitions to engage in high risk behaviours like smoking, drinking and unchecked sexual behaviour is also on the rise in our country. Violence is on the increase among adolescents as in general population which includes physical fights, thought of killing somebody and carrying of weapons (Sharma, Grover & Chaturvedi, 2008; Chaterjee, Paul, Basu & Mukherjee, 2012). Sexual initiation has become early indicating the need for education regarding reproductive health (Sahay, *et al.*, 2013). Weight control has become a fashion statement rather than a fitness parameter and this motivates an accelerated but unhealthy weight loss. Children and adolescents are facing mental health problems as well. The depleted mental health has implications for other developmental and health concerns like educational achievements, substance abuse, violence and poor reproductive and sexual health (Patel, Fisher, Hetrick & McGarry, 2007). Evidence across the globe consistently shows that 20 per cent of children and adolescents suffer from disabling mental illness (Belfer, 2008). Low self-esteem might be one of the reasons for engaging in health compromising behaviour (McGee and Williams, 2000). Mental health issues such as loneliness, worry and suicidal thoughts are prevalent in both urban and rural adolescents in States like West Bengal (Smantha, Mukherjee, Ghosh & Dasgupta, 2012). The rate of suicides is also alarming among youth which correspond to 60 per cent in females of 15-29 years and 40 per cent in males of 15-29 years (*The Hindu,* June 23, 2012).

All of this mandates routine health and awareness camps in different premises like schools, housing localities and other places that the children and adolescents frequently visit. Support from media can augment this process to ensure the health of future of our country.

Health Initiatives for Children

India has one of the most comprehensive legal frameworks for protection of children. This includes constitutional provisions as well as various health initiatives launched by the Government of India. Some of the constitutional provisions are as follows:

- ***Article 21A:*** provides for free and compulsory education for children aged six to fourteen years.
- ***Article 23:*** prohibits human trafficking and bonded labour.
- ***Article 24:*** prohibits child labour.
- ***Article 45:*** provides for early childhood care and education for children until they complete the age of six years.

Though these provisions are there, they lack in specificity of safeguarding the children. Hence, they become quite ambiguous to interpret and difficult to implement in a real situation. There are also several legislations which is an endeavour to indicate and ensure that rights of a child are given due importance. Some of these legislations include:

- The Child Labour (Prohibition and Regulation) Act, 1986.
- The Juvenile Justice (Care and Protection of Children) Act, 2000.
- The Infant Milk Substitutes, Feeding Bottles and Infant Foods (Regulation of Production, Supply and Distribution) Act, 1992.
- The Pre-Conception and Pre-natal Diagnostic Technique (Prohibition of Sex Selection) Act, 1994.
- The Persons with Disabilities (Equal Opportunities, Protection of Rights and Full Participation) Act, 1995.
- The Immoral Traffic (Prevention) Act, 1956.
- The Guardian and Wards Act, 1890.
- The Young Persons (Harmful Publications) Act, 1956.
- The Commissions for Protection of Child Rights Act, 2005.

All these legislations are protective in nature. The problem lies in their awareness. Out of the exhaustive list of all child rights, people are aware of only a handful of them. Hence, the concept of child rights often goes unnoticed.

There is a wide array of policies which have been brought to force with the goal of ensuring health and well-being of the children in India. They are as follows:

- National Policy for Children, 1974.
- National Policy on Education, 1986.
- National Plan of Action to Combat Trafficking & Commercial Sexual Exploitation of Women & Children.
- National Health Policy, 2002.
- National Charter for Children, 2004.
- National Plan of Action for Children, 2005.
- Policy for Children and HIV/AIDS (Strategic Framework), 2007.
- Integrated National Plan of Action to Prevent & Combat Trafficking of Human Beings, with Special Focus on Women & Children, 2008.
- Juvenile Justice (Care and Protection of Children) Act, 2000.
- Commissions for Protection of Child Rights Act, 2005.
- Right of Children to Free & Compulsory Education Act, 2009.
- Protection of Children from Sexual Offences Act, 2012.

All these policies have their basic aim outlined around an adequate physical, mental, social and emotional development and care of children. Despite having such policies, the statistics of vulnerable children and the problems they face, documented after these policies were implemented, are disturbing and disappointing. Apart from the constitutional provisions, legislations and policies, there are different projects and schemes for promoting the welfare of children in India. As health, nutrition and education are all interrelated and interdependent, the following policies have the right direction to lay the foundation of a holistic childhood (Kaul & Shankar, 2009). These are as follows:

Integrated Child Development Scheme

This scheme was initiated in 1975, as a programme to facilitate wholesome early childhood development comprising of education and a better health for all children. It is one of the better and successful measures employed to ensure nutrition to the underprivileged children of the society (Kapil, 2002).

Integrated Child Protection Scheme

This is a policy initiated to govern all the child protection legislations and policies. The scheme is very comprehensive and ensures that the best interests of child are taken care of.

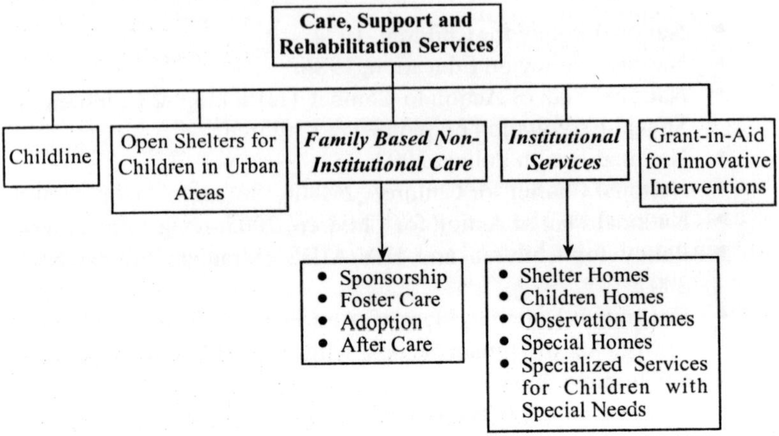

Figure 12.3: One of the Major Aspects of ICPS

Source: https://custom.cvent.com/.../7a6953b120fd486896044b64d6c571ea.ppt

Rajiv Gandhi National Creche Scheme for the Children of Working Mothers

This is a scheme for taking care of children aged 0-6 years who have working mothers. The scheme provides for many centers across the country catering to nutritional, immunization, health, recreation and non-formal pre-school education needs of these children.

Rajiv Gandhi Scheme for Empowerment of Adolescent Girls or SABLA (RGSEAG)

This scheme is at empowering adolescent girls for taking better care of their health. It is aimed at improving their nutrition and health status. Under this scheme, there are provisions for adequate health education including reproductive health issues as well as for periodic health check-ups and referral services. They are also provided life skill education under this scheme.

Mid-Day Meal (MDM)

Mid-Day meal scheme has become a community programme which has a successful implementation in most parts of the country (Pratichi Trust,

2010). Taken as a reinforcement it has helped considerably in improving the enrollment rates and good practices like washing hands before and after eating are imparted in schools (PROBE, ASER, 2010). Not only has this scheme been implemented, it has been evaluated as well. This is a scheme that can become role model for the implementation of other schemes.

Total Sanitation Campaign (TSC)

This is a programme aimed at improving the sanitation facilities and increasing awareness about the health and hygiene among rural as well as urban population though its significance is more in rural set-ups. Rural school sanitation is a major component of this campaign, so that, children get better sanitation facilities and are aware about the importance of such practices through hygiene education provided in schools.

Conclusion

To conclude, it is observed that India has all the machinery in the form of its various health initiatives to take care of the health concerns of her children in an interdisciplinary fashion. The need is to use this 'of the people' machinery, effectively by, 'the people' and for 'the people'.

Health is an important contributing factor in life satisfaction. It is essential to give it its due importance from an early point in life, i.e. childhood. Today, children face increased difficulties in maintaining a good health because of various precarious circumstances. These circumstances predispose the children towards a difficult adulthood as well. It is necessary to identify and regulate these situations in order to facilitate a wholesome development of our children. The scope of the problem is often underestimated because we always think that "this will not happen to me". Instead of thinking about this issue in third person, a first person approach should be used. This will make the problems more relevant and make one sensitive about them. The vulnerable children are often victimized, often, for no fault of theirs. This needs to be curbed because these children, more than anybody else, require support and approval. Health of children is a societal issue, not an individualistic issue. Thus, a society needs to actively contribute towards their health and well-being.

Recommendations

1. Ensuring basic health care facilities, nutrition and safety for all the children through community and institution based approach

and in this regard local health officials should take help from the Panchayat and school authorities.

2. Creating awareness about child rights among people of all sections of the society.
3. Ensuring effective and timely intervention of Government policies and programmes for the needy children and periodic monitoring and evaluation of the same.
4. Involvement of community members for effective implementation of Government policies and programmes like Right to Free and Compulsory Education Act, 2009, Mid-Day Meal Programme, Integrated Child Development Scheme (ICDS), Integrated Child Protection Scheme (ICPS) and so on.
5. Finally, there is an urgent need to bring inclusive policy for welfare and well-being of the vulnerable and disadvantaged children.

REFERENCES

Abbasi, K.A., Mirani, P.H., Parsram, A. and Sarwar, A. (1998). "Causes, Clinical Features and Outcome of 150 Newborns with Birth Asphyxia at Larkana Hospital", *Pakistan Paediatric Journal*, 21, 121-25.

Agnihotri, S.B. (2001). "Declining Infant and Child Mortality in India: How Do Girl Children Fare?" *Economic and Political Weekly*, 36(3), 228-33.

Ananthakrishnan, S. and Nalini, P. (2002). "Social Status of the Rural Girl Child in Tamil Nadu", *The Indian Journal of Pediatrics*, 69(7), 579-83.

Arimpoor, J. (1992). *Street Children of Chennai: A Situational Analysis*, Noida, India: Child Labour Cell, National Labour Institute.

Arokiasamy, P. (2004). "Regional Patterns of Sex Bias and Excess Female Child Mortality in India", *Population* (English edition), 59(6), 831-63.

Avissar, S., Nechamkin, Y., Roitman, G. and Schreiber, G. (1997). "Reduced G Protein Functions and Immunoreactive Levels in Mononuclear Leukocytes of Patients with Depression", *American Journal of Psychiatry*, 154(2), 211-17.

Bartholow, B.N., Doll, L.S., Joy, D., Douglas, J.M., Bolan, G., Harrison, J.S., Moss, P.M. and McKirnan, D. (1994). "Emotional, Behavioural, and HIV Risks Associated with Sexual Abuse among Adult Homosexual and Bisexual Men", *Child Abuse & Neglect*, 18, 747-61.

Belfer, M.L. (2008). "Child and Adolescent Mental Disorders: The Magnitude of the Problem Across the Globe", *Journal of Child Psychology and Psychiatry*, 49(3), 226-36.

Briere, J. and Runtz, M. (1987). "Post Sexual Abuse Trauma: Data and Implications for Clinical Practice", *Journal of Interpersonal Violence*, 2(4), 367-79.

Briere, J. and Zaidi, L.Y. (1989). "Sexual Abuse Histories and Sequelae in Female Psychiatric Emergency Room Patients", *American Journal of Psychiatry*, 146(12), 1602-06.

Briere, J.N. and Elliot, D.M. (1994). "Immediate and Long-term Impacts of Child Sexual Abuse", *The Future of Children*, 4(2), 54-69.

Cauffman, E. (2004). "A Statewide Screening of Mental Health Symptoms among Juvenile Offenders in Detention", *Journal of the American Academy of Child & Adolescent Psychiatry*, 43(4), 430-39.

Cauffman, E., Feldman, S., Watherman, J. and Steiner, H. (1998). "Post-traumatic Stress Disorder among Female Juvenile Offenders", *Journal of the American Academy of Child & Adolescent Psychiatry*, 37(11), 1209-16.

Chatterjee, C., Paul, S., Basu, G. and Mukherjee (2012). "A Study on Inter-personal Violence among School Going Adolescents in a Rural Block of West Bengal", *Journal of Dental and Medical Sciences*, 3(3), 41-44.

Child Welfare Information Gateway (2010). *Understanding the Effects of Maltreatment on Brain Development*, Washington, DC: U.S. Department of Health and Human Services. Retrieved from: https://www.childwelfare.gov/pubPDFs/brain_development.pdf

Child Welfare Information Gateway (2013). *Long-term Consequences of Child Abuse and Neglect*, Washington, DC: U.S. Department of Health and Human Services. Retrieved from: https://www.childwelfare.gov/pubpdfs/long_term_consequences.pdf

D'lima, H. and Gosalia, R. (1992). *Street Children of Mumbai: A Situational Analysis*, Study for the Ministry of Welfare, Government of India and UNICEF, College of Social Work, Mumbai, National Labour Institute (Child Labour Cell), New Delhi.

Felitti, V.J. and Anda, R. (2010). "The Relationship of Adverse Childhood Experiences to Adult Medical Disease, Psychiatric Disorders, and Sexual Behaviour: Implications for Healthcare", in R. Lanius, E. Vermetten and Pain, C. (eds.), *The Impact of Early Life Trauma on Health and Disease: The Hidden Epidemic* (pp. 77-87), Cambridge: Cambridge University Press.

Felitti, V.J., Anda, R.F., Nordenberg, D., Williamson, D.F., Spitz, A.M., Edwards, V., Koss, M.P. and Marks, J.S. (2001). "Relationship of Childhood Abuse and Household Dysfunction to many of the Leading Causes of Death in Adults", in K. Franey, R. Geffner and R. Falconer (eds.), *The Cost of Child Maltreatment: Who Pays? We All Do* (pp. 53-69), San Diego, CA: Family Violence and Sexual Assault Institute.

Fergusson, D.M., Horwood, L.J. and Lynskey, M.T. (1997). "Childhood Sexual Abuse, Adolescent Sexual Behaviours and Sexual Revictimization", *Child Abuse & Neglect*, 21(8), 789-803.

Fikree, F.F. and Pasha, O. (2004). "Role of Gender in Health Disparity: The South Asian Context", *BMJ: British Medical Journal*, 328(7443), 823-26.

Filmer D., King E.M. and Pritchett, L. (2004). *Gender Disparity in South Asia: Comparisons between and within Countries*. Retrieved from: www.worldbank.org/html/dec/Publications/Workpapers/WPS1800series/wps1867/ wps1867.pdf (World Bank Policy Research Working Paper No. 1867.)

Fleming, J., Mullen, P.E., Sibthorpe, B. and Bammer, G. (1999). "The Long-term Impact of Childhood Sexual Abuse in Australian Women", *Child Abuse & Neglect*, 23(2), 145-59.

Ganatra, B. and Hirve, S. (1994). "Male Bias in Health Care Utilization for Under-fives in a Rural Community in Western India", *Bulletin of the World Health Organization*, 72(1), 101-04.

George, S.M. (1997). "Female Infanticide in Tamil Nadu, India: From Recognition Back to Denial?" *Reproductive Health Matters*, 5(10), 124-32.

Gladstone, G., Parker, G., Wilhelm, K. and Mitchell, P. (1999). "Characteristics of Depressed Patients Who Report Childhood Sexual Abuse", *American Journal of Psychiatry*, 156(3), 431-37.

Gold, J., Sullivan, M.W. and Lewis, M. (2011). "The Relation between Abuse and Violent Delinquency: The Conversion of Shame to Blame in Juvenile Offenders", *Child Abuse & Neglect*, 35(7), 459-67.

Grimstad, H. and Schei, B. (1999). "Pregnancy and Delivery for Women with a History of Child Sexual Abuse", *Child Abuse & Neglect*, 23(1), 81-90.

Hasan I.J. and Khanum A. (2000). "Health Care Utilization during Terminal Child Illness in Squatter Settlements of Karachi", *Journal of the Pakistan Medical Association*, 50(12), 405-09.

Healy, J.M. (2004). *Your Child's Growing Mind: Brain Development and Learning from Birth to Adolescence*, New York: Broadway Books.

Hershkowitz, I., Lamb, M.E. and Horowitz, D. (2007). "Victimization of Children with Disabilities", *American Journal of Orthopsychiatry*, 77(4), 629-35.

Hunt, C. (1996). "Child Waste Pickers in India: The Occupation and Its Health Risks", *Environment and Urbanization*, 8(2), 111-18.

Kapil, U. (2002). "Integrated Child Development Services (ICDS) Scheme: A Programme for Holistic Development of Children in India", *The Indian Journal of Pediatrics*, 69(7), 597-601.

Kaplan, G.A. and Camacho, T. (1983). "Perceived Health and Mortality: A Nine-year Follow-up of the Human Population Laboratory Cohort", *American Journal of Epidemiology*, 117(3), 292-304.

Kataoka, S.H., Zima, B.T., Dupre, D.A., Moreno, K.A., Yang, X. and McCracken, J.T. (2001). "Mental Health Problems and Service Use among Female Juvenile Offenders: Their Relationship to Criminal History", *Journal of the American Academy of Child & Adolescent Psychiatry*, 40(5), 549-55.

Kaul, V. and Sankar, D. (2009). "Early Childhood Care and Education in India", *Education for All Mid-Decade Assessment*, New Delhi, India: National University of Educational Planning and Administration (NUEPA).

Kendall-Tackett, K.A. (2000). "Physiological Correlates of Childhood Abuse: Chronic Hyperarousal in PTSD, Depression and Irritable Bowel Syndrome", Invited review. *Child Abuse & Neglect*, 24(6), 799-810.

Kendall-Tackett, K.A., Marshall, R. and Ness, K.E. (2000). "Victimization, Healthcare Use, and Health Maintenance", *Family Violence & Sexual Assault Bulletin*, 16, 18-21.

Kendall-Tackett, K. (2002). "The Health Effects of Childhood Abuse: Four Pathways by which Abuse can Influence Health", *Child Abuse & Neglect*, 26(6), 715-29.

Kerfoot, M., Koshyl, V., Roganov, O., Mikhailichenko, K., Gorbova, I. and Pottage, D. (2007). "The Health and Well-being of Neglected, Abused and Exploited Children: The Kyiv Street Children Project", *Child Abuse & Neglect*, 31(1) 27-37.

Kombarakaran, Francis A. (2004). "Street Children of Mumbai: Their Stresses and Strategies of Coping", *Children and Youth Services Review*, 26(9), 853-71.

Lalor, Kevin J. (1999). "Street Children: A Comparative Perspective", *Child Abuse & Neglect*, 23(8), 759-70.

Mason, W.A., Zimmerman, L. and Evans, W. (1998). "Sexual and Physical Abuse among Incarcerated Youth: Implications for Sexual Behaviour, Contraceptive Use, and Teenage Pregnancy", *Child Abuse & Neglect*, 22(10), 987-95.

Mathur, M., Rathore, P. and Mathur, M. (2009). "Incidence, Type and Intensity of Abuse in Street Children in India", *Child Abuse & Neglect*, 33(12), 907-13.

McGee, R.O.B. and Williams, S. (2000). "Does Low Self-esteem Predict Health Compromising Behaviours among Adolescents?" *Journal of Adolescence*, 23(5), 569-82.

Miller, D.A., McClusky-Fawcett, K. and Irving, L.M. (1993). "The Relationship between Childhood Sexual Abuse and Subsequent Onset of Bulimia Nervosa", *Child Abuse & Neglect*, 17(2), 305-14.

Ministry of Statistics and Programme Implementation (2012). *Children in India, 2012 — A Statistical Appraisal*, Government of India.

Ministry of Women and Child Development (2007). *Child Abuse: India 2007*, Government of India.

Mishra, A.N. (2013, July 18). "Juvenile Delinquency on the Rise", *The Times of India*, Ranchi. Retrieved from: http://articles.timesofindia.indiatimes.com

Mossey, J.M. and Shapiro, E. (1982). "Self-rated Health: A Predictor of Mortality among the Elderly", *American Journal of Public Health*, 72(8), 800-08.

National Sleep Foundation (2000). *The Nature of Sleep*. Retrieved from: www.sleepfoundation.org

National Survey of Child and Adolescent Well-Being (2007). "Special Health Care Needs among Children in Child Welfare", *NSCAW Research Brief No. 7*. Retrieved from http://www.acf.hhs.gov/sites/default/files/opre/special_health.pdf

National Survey of Child and Adolescent Well-Being (2012a). "Instability and Early Life Changes among Children in the Child Welfare System", *NSCAW Research Brief No. 18*. Retrieved from http://www.acf.hhs.gov/sites/default/files/opre/early_life.pdf

National Survey of Child and Adolescent Well-Being (2012b). *Adolescents with a History of Maltreatment have Unique Service Needs that may Affect their Transition to Adulthood*. Retrieved from https://www.acf.hhs.gov/sites/default/files/opre/youth_spotlight_v7.pdf

Neighbors, B., Kempton, T. and Forehand, R. (1992). "Co-occurrences of Substance Abuse with Conduct, Anxiety, and Depression Disorders in Juvenile Delinquents", *Addictive Behaviours*, 17(4), 379-86.

Pande, R.P. (2003). "Selective Gender Differences in Childhood Nutrition and Immunization in Rural India: The Role of Siblings", *Demography*, 40(3), 395-418.

Patel, V., Flisher, A.J., Hetrick, S. and McGorry, P. (2007). "Mental Health of Young People: A Global Public-health Challenge", *The Lancet*, 369(9569), 1302-13.

Perry, B. (2012). "Supporting Maltreated Children: Countering the Effects of Neglect and Abuse", *Adoption Advocate, No. 48*. Retrieved from: https://www.adoptioncouncil.org/images/stories/documents/NCFA_ADOPTION_ADVOCATE_NO48.pdf

Premi, M.K. (2001). "The Missing Girl Child", *Economic and Political Weekly*, May 26, 1875-80.

Probe, T. (1999). *Public Report on Basic Education in India/PROBE Team in Association with Centre for Development Economics*, Oxford University Press.

Sahay, S., Nirmalkar, A., Sane, S., Verma, A., Reddy, S. and Mehendale, S. (2013). "Correlates of Sex Initiation among School Going Adolescents in Pune, India", *The Indian Journal of Pediatrics*, 80(10), 814-20.

Samanta, A., Mukherjee, S., Ghosh, S. and Dasgupta, A. (2012). "Mental Health, Protective Factors and Violence among Male Adolescents: A Comparison between Urban and Rural School Students in West Bengal", *Indian Journal of Public Health*, 56(2), 155-58.

Scannapieco, M. (2008). "Developmental Outcomes of Child Neglect", *The APSAC Advisor*, Winter. Elmhurst, IL: American Professional Society on the Abuse of Children.

Sharma, R., Grover, V. L. and Chaturvedi, S. (2008). "Risk Behaviours Related to Interpersonal Violence among School and College-going Adolescents in South Delhi",

Indian Journal of Community Medicine, Official Publication of Indian Association of Preventive & Social Medicine, 33(2), 85-88.

Srivastava, S.P. and Nayak, N.P. (1995). "The Disadvantaged Girl Child in Bihar: Study of Health Care Practices and Selected Nutritional Indices", *Indian Pediatrics*, 32, 911-13.

Tarullo, A. (2012). "Effects of Child Maltreatment on the Developing Brain", *Child Welfare 360°. Using a Developmental Approach in Child Welfare Practice, 11*. Retrieved from: http://www.bu.edu/cdl/files/2013/08/Tarullo-CW360-2012.pdf

Teicher, M.D. (2000). "Wounds that Time Won't Heal: The Neurobiology of Child Abuse", *Cerebrum: The Dana Forum on Brain Science*, 2(4), 50-67.

Teplin, L.A., Abram, K.M., McClelland, G.M., Dulcan, M.K. and Mericle, A.A. (2002). "Psychiatric Disorders in Youth in Juvenile Detention", *Archives of General Psychiatry*, 59 (12), 1133-43.

Thompson, N.J., Potter, J.S., Sanderson, C.A. and Maibach, E.W. (1997). "The Relationship of Sexual Abuse and HIV Risk Behaviours among Heterosexual Adult Female STD Patients", *Child Abuse & Neglect*, 21(2), 149-56.

Towe, Vivian L., Hasan, S., Zafar, S. Tariq and Sherman, S.G. (2009). "Street Life and Drug Risk Behaviours Associated with Exchanging Sex Among Male Street Children in Lahore, Pakistan", *Journal of Adolescent Health*, 44(3), 222-28.

Victora, C.G., Wagstaff, A., Schellenberg, J.A., Gwatkin, D., Claeson, M. and Habicht, J.P. (2003). "Applying an Equity Lens to Child Health and Mortality: More of the Same is not Enough", *The Lancet*, 362(9379), 233-41.

Weisse, C.S. (1992). "Depression and Immunocompetence: A Review of the Literature", *Psychological Bulletin*, 111(3), 475-89.

WHO (2010). *Child Maltreatment*. Retrieved from: www.who.int/mediacentre/factsheets/fs150

WHO (2014). *Disability and Health*. Retrieved from: http://www.who.int/mediacentre/factsheets/fs352/en/

WHO (2014). *Disability and Health — Fact Sheet No. 352*. Retrieved from http://www.who.int/mediacentre/factsheets/fs352/en/

Widom, C., Czaja, S., Bentley, T. and Johnson, M. (2012). "A Prospective Investigation of Physical Health Outcomes in Abused and Neglected Children: New Findings from a 30 Year Follow-up", *American Journal of Public Health*, 102(6), 1135-44.

Wierson, M., Forehand, R.L. and Frame, C.L. (1992). "Epidemiology and Treatment of Mental Health Problems in Juvenile Delinquents", *Advances in Behaviour Research and Therapy*, 14(2), 93-120.

Xiangming, F. and Corso, P. (2007). "Child Maltreatment, Youth Violence, and Intimate Partner Violence: Developmental Relationships", *American Journal of Preventative Medicine*, 33(4), 281-90.

Zuravin, S.J. and Fontanella, C. (1999). "The Relationship between Child Sexual Abuse and Major Depression among Low-income Women: A Function of Growing up Experiences?" *Child Maltreatment*, 4(1), 3-12.

13

Early Childhood Mortality in India

Recent Trends and Prospects for the Near Future

P.M. Kulkarni

Typically, the risk of mortality is high during infancy and early childhood, it declines during young adulthood and rises again in old age. While this is the general pattern, the level varies considerably across populations and the long-term trends have shown a decline over time though there have been periods during which the level has been stagnant and some when it has actually risen. In the recent years, such rise has been seen in parts of the world affected by the HIV. While mortality at all ages is desired to be low and sought to be reduced, a number of public programmes have focusesd on improving child survival. This covers infancy, including neonatal and post-neonatal periods, and early childhood up to the age of five years. While neo-natal mortality is primarily influenced by endogenous factors, including maternal ones, exogenous factors play a major role in post-neonatal infant mortality and early childhood mortality when infectious diseases dominate the causes of death.

India's Maternal and Child Health Programme, later renamed as Reproductive and Child Health (RCH) programme, focussed on both child health and maternal health, and given the importance of maternal health for child health, was expected to lower childhood mortality substantially. The various strategies included professional assistance at deliveries, immunization for pregnant women, pre-natal and post-natal check-ups, supplementary nutrition to pregnant and lactating women, supplementary child nutrition, health and nutrition education, and curative services. These have evolved over time with new components added and some strengthened. In 2005, a major initiative, the National Rural

Health Mission (NRHM) was introduced with the *Janani Suraksha Yojana* as an important component. The thrust of this was on professional care at delivery with facilities for transport to health institutions, along with improved ante-natal and post-natal care with the aim of lowering maternal mortality and accelerating the decline in infant and child mortality. Over time, infant and early childhood mortality has declined in India. In the early 1970s, the Under-five Mortality Rate (U5MR) was 210 per thousand as seen from the life tables for 1970-75 which fell to 125 by 1990 and further to 55 in 2011 (Registrar General, 1984, 1998, 2013). But there are wide variations across States; the broad pattern among large States is that the U5MR is relatively low in Kerala and fairly low in Maharashtra, Tamil Nadu, West Bengal, and Punjab, and relatively high in Madhya Pradesh, Uttar Pradesh, Odisha, Rajasthan, and Assam. Besides, childhood mortality has been higher for girls than for boys in India. This is against the world pattern of lower female than male mortality during childhood; this anomaly and reasons for it have long been recognized in India.

The inclusion of lowering early childhood mortality in the Millennium Development Goals in the U.N. Millennium Declaration gave impetus to programmes on child and maternal health. The specific goal, numbered fourth, or MDG 4, is to reduce U5MR by two thirds by the year 2015 from the level in the base year 1990. Though India has set specific measurable goals for lowering mortality from time to time, including the goal of lowering the Infant Mortality Rate (IMR) to 30 by 2010, the MDG on the U5MR has received considerable attention in the media and by programme managers. Therefore, this chapter seeks to examine recent trends in the U5MR and see how close India and large States have moved to achieving this goal.

The Under-five Mortality Rate (U5MR) as the Indicator of Early Childhood Mortality

For long, the expectation of life at birth, labelled as the life expectancy, has been used as the summary measure of the level of survival of a population and is commonly used for mortality comparisons across populations and over time. This is a synthetic measure that takes into account mortality in all age groups, infant and child, middle ages, and older ages and has a clear meaning. The popular Human Development Index (HDI) also uses this indicator of survival. However, the computation of life expectancy does require considerable data, in particular, age-specific death rates in all age groups, which are not available for many countries, especially the developing ones. Therefore, often the infant mortality rate (IMR), which may be available from surveys or as an indirect estimate, is used for comparisons. As the name clearly indicates, this refers only to mortality during infancy and is by no means a comprehensive measure; yet the wider availability of estimates of the IMR and the fact that high infant mortality is a matter of public concern justifies its use. However, the relatively high mortality during early childhood beyond the first year of life has also drawn attention of policy-makers and programme managers and a measure that incorporated mortality during these ages was felt to be necessary. The U5MR that measures mortality up to the age of five years, encompassing mortality both during infancy and ages one to five, has now emerged as the most commonly cited measure of early childhood mortality. This is simply the probability of dying before completing five years of age, or proportion dying before completing the fifth year of life, usually multiplied by 1,000 so that the U5MR becomes the number dying before completing five years of age per 1,000 births. Its computation requires the age-specific death rates in the conventional age groups 0 and 1-4 and if a life table has been constructed, the U5MR is obtained from the life table terms simply as U5MR = $[1 - l_5/l_0] \times 1{,}000$. Often, information on mortality during early childhood is collected in surveys allowing the computation of this measure. Besides, the Brass-type indirect estimation that is based on questions on children ever born and children surviving which are asked in many censuses and surveys also permits the estimation of the U5MR [the $q(5)$ value in the Brass method]. In fact, the Brass method is more suited to the estimation of the U5MR than of the IMR. The inclusion of reduction in under-five mortality as one of the Millennium Development Goals (MDGs) set by the Millennium Declaration of the United Nations in 2,000 has made the U5MR the most talked about measure in media and among policy-makers and programme administrators since then. The credit for popularizing the U5MR as a key indicator of childhood mortality, though not for inventing it, should indisputably go to the U.N. Millennium Declaration.

Data and Methods

There are a number of sources of data on early childhood mortality in India. While the civil registration system is to collect information on all deaths along with age and sex, separate tabulations of under-five deaths are not available. Numbers of infant deaths are reported by the system but the coverage is poor in most States; some districts have not reported any infant death in a few years. Therefore, the civil registration system is a poor source of data on early childhood mortality. The Sample Registration System (SRS) has shown good coverage and over the years the data have been widely accepted as of good quality. The SRS has been providing estimates of the crude death rate and IMR at the national level and for States and Union Territories and estimates of age-sex specific death rates for India and large States. The estimates are available since the 1970s for most States though for some no estimates have been provided for a few periods (notably for West Bengal and Bihar in the 1970s, for Jammu & Kashmir in the 1990s, and for some small States in a few years). For quite some time, U5MR as such was not published by the SRS. However, the life tables provided by the SRS (Registrar General, various years) allow computation of the U5MR as $[1 - l_5/l_0] \times 1{,}000$. The SRS life tables are available for five-year periods (based on average age-sex-specific death rates for the five years) in the 1970s, and the first quinquennium of the 1980s, and as five-year moving averages since 1986 (for the periods 1986-90, 1987-91, 1988-92, ...). An error had crept in the SRS life tables constructed for the periods 1995-1999 onwards (Kulkarni, 2008; Saikia, Singh & Ram, 2010) but this has since been rectified and the corrected tables are released by the SRS. Thus, a time series of estimates can be obtained from the SRS data, by treating the five-year average as referring to the middle year. From 2008, the annual reports of the SRS give estimates of the U5MR (Registrar General, 2009a; 2011; 2012a, 2013).

Besides, a number of demographic and health surveys give estimates of the U5MR. Most cited are those by the three rounds of the National Family Health Survey, nationwide sample surveys conducted in 1992-93, 1998-99, and 2005-06 (IIPS, 1995; IIPS and ORC Macro, 2000; IIPS and Macro International, 2007). These estimates are obtained from the detailed fertility histories collected in the surveys and refer to periods up to 15 years prior to the survey date, calculated for five-year segments, 0-4 years, 5-9 years and 10-14 years before the respective survey dates. The recent Annual Health Surveys also give estimates of the U5MR but these are only for nine States and for districts in these. Some other surveys also give estimates; however, ad-hoc surveys carried out at different time points do not allow an assessment of trends since the methodologies differ. Further, survey estimates are subject to sampling errors which could be large if sample sizes are small. In addition, beginning 1981, India's decennial censuses have asked questions on number of children ever born and number surviving to ever married women and this information has been used to estimate childhood mortality rates including the U5MR indirectly *via* the Brass method or its variants. The Office of the Registrar General publishes these estimates for India, States and districts (Registrar General, 2009b). The estimates of U5MR [called $q(5)$] refer to dates prior to the respective census; the Feeney method allows estimation of the reference date and in case of U5MR this is generally about 5 years before the census date.

The MDG Target 4A is stated as: "Reduce by two-thirds, between 1990 and 2015, the under-five mortality rate" (U.N., 2013). This is a relative goal, and the achievement is to lower the rate by 2015 to one-third of the base level of 1990. For a country, thus, the goal set is one-third the value of the 1990 level.

Now that estimates up to 2011 are available (the latest figures from the SRS are for the year 2011), one needs to essentially extrapolate the series to 2015 to see whether the goal would be reached. For this purpose, recent trends should be used. There are various ways of extrapolation. The simplest approach is to use the linear function; this yields the function $\text{U5MR}(t) = a - b^* (t - T_0)$, where T_0 is the baseline time point and b is the slope which gives annual decline. Such a linear function implies a constant numerical annual change (actually decline) in the U5MR. For achieving a decline by two-thirds in the 25 year period, from 1990 to 2015, b should equal [U5MR(1990)*(2/3)]/25 or U5MR(1990)/37.5. However, intuitively, as the level falls, the annual decrement should also fall. At high levels of mortality, the decline could be large but once a low level is reached further progress is bound to be slower. In such case, a negative exponential function seems appropriate; this is given by:

$\text{U5MR}(t) = a \, . \, e^{-r^*(t - T0)}$, where r is the rate of annual decline. For achieving a decline of two-thirds over 25 years (from 1990 to 2015), that is, for the U5MR in 2015 to be one-third of the rate in 1990, the value of r should equal $[-\ln(1/3)/25]$ or 0.044. The pattern of recent trends could guide the choice of function.

Results

India

Since, a number of sources give estimates of the U5MR, directly or indirectly, an examination of these is in order. Three major sources are: SRS, NFHS (three rounds) and census (indirect estimates). The SRS life tables are for five-year periods. Each of the three rounds of the NFHS gives estimates for three-five-year periods prior to the surveys. The indirect estimates from the censuses refer to three to five years before the census date (the exact reference point estimated using the Feeney's method varies but is around this period). A set of estimates of the U5MR for India has been provided in Table 13.1.

Table 13.1: Estimates of Under-Five Mortality Rates from Various Sources, India, 1970-2011

Period	*Source*				
	SRS	*NFHS-1*	*NFHS-2*	*NFHS-3*	*Census Indirect*
1970-75	210				
1976-80	193				152*
1977-82		144			
1981-85	161				
1982-87 or 1983-88		128	122		
1986-90	137				94*
1987-91 or 1987-92	132	109			
1988-92 or 1988-93			107		
1989-93	118				
1990-94	114				
1991-95 or 1991-96	113			107	
1992-96	111				
1993-97 or 1993-98	107		95		
1994-98	105				
1995-99	102				
1996-2000 or 1996-2001	98			95	96*
1997-2001	95				
1998-2002	91				
1999-2003	88				
2000-2004	86				
2001-05 or 2001-06	84			74	
2002-06	81				
2003-07	78				
2004-08	74				
2005-09	71				
2006-10	67				
2008	69				
2009	64				
2010	59				
2011	55				

Note: The time periods are not necessarily equidistant or of equal width.

* : The census based indirect estimates refer to time points 3-5 years before the respective census dates, 1981, 1991, 2001.

Sources: SRS: Registrar General (1984, 1985, 1989, 1994, 1998, 2009a, 2011, 2012a, 2012c, 2013); NFHS: IIPS (1995), IIPS and ORC Macro (2000), IIPS and Macro International (2007); Census indirect: Registrar General (2009b).

The SRS estimates for the 1970s are quite high, 210 and 193. The census based estimate for the mid-late 1970s is relatively lower, 152, which is close to the estimate of 144 for 1977-82 from the NFHS-1. The SRS estimate for 1981-85 is 161, much higher than the NFHS-1 estimate of 128 for 1982-87 and the NFHS-2 based estimate of 122 for 1983-88. The census based estimate is even lower, 94. Essentially, no consistency is seen across the various sources. However, estimates for periods after 1990 show a high degree of consistency though the SRS estimates are slightly higher than other estimates. Therefore, it is preferable to use the trends since 1990 for extrapolation. As the MDG has set 1990 as the baseline, using the series from 1990 is convenient. Since, the SRS series is available for the entire period up to 2011, it is preferred for this purpose.

For the study of trend, first, the initial value (for 1990) is to be identified. For India, the SRS life table for 1988-92, the mid-point of which period is 1990, yields 125 per thousand as the U5MR (the 15 value for both sexes together is 87494 giving (1 – 87494/100000)*1000 as 125 per thousand. Perhaps this value, rounded to 126 has been accepted in the U.N. documents (UNICEF, 2013). Taking 125 as the base level (for 1990), the goal for 2015 works out to 41.67 or 42. Some researchers have used 115 as the baseline value; this is probably because the 1990-94 life table yields an U5MR of 115; but the mid-year for the 1990-94 life table is 1992 rather than 1990.

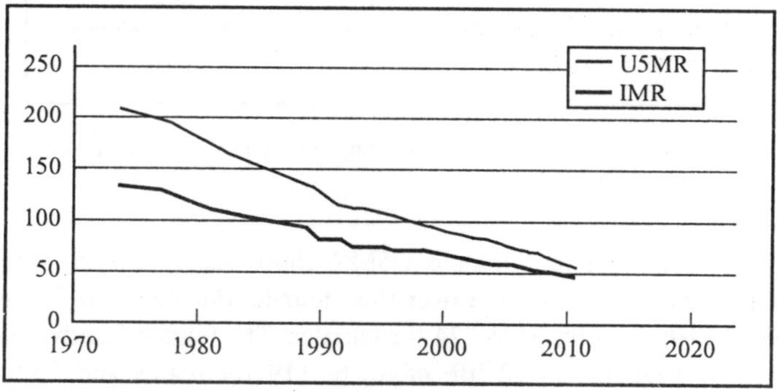

Figure 13.1: Trends in U5MR and IMR, India, 1973-2011

Source: See Table 13.1.

The SRS series shows a smooth declining trend in U5MR. This is partly due to the use of moving averages but even the annual estimates show a smooth trend (see Fig. 13.1). Both the linear and exponential trends were applied to the series from 1990 to 2011. In the linear trend, the (negative) slope coefficient is 3.09; for the decline from 125 to 42 to be achieved in 25 years, the coefficient should be 3.32 and thus the actual decline is less steep. Similarly, the rate of exponential decay is 0.036 whereas for the two-thirds decline it should be 0.044. The linear fit was found to be excellent (see Fig. 13.2) and better than the exponential form though the latter is intuitively more appealing. Applying the linear function for extrapolation beyond 2011 (the latest value available) yields a value of 43 for 2015 which is fairly close to the goal of 42, only slightly higher. Application of the exponential curve yields the extrapolated value of 48 for 2015.

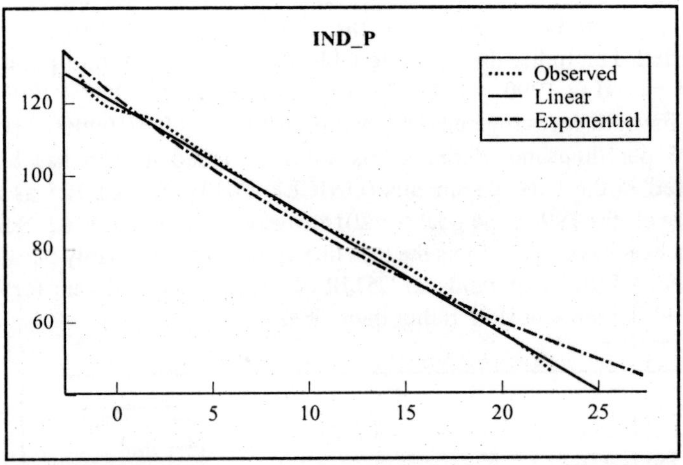

Figure 13.2: Trends in U5MR for India and Fitting of Linear and Exponential Functions, 1990-2011

Trends for male and female U5MR show nearly similar results except that male mortality is lower than female; during 1970-75 male U5MR was 196 in contrast to 224 for females. The female disadvantage persisted in 1990 (1988-92 life table) to 119 for males and 132 for females. The MDG targets also differ, 40 and 44 respectively for males and females. In both the cases, the linear fit is excellent (Figures 13.3 and 13.4). The extrapolated (using the linear function) value for males is 39, just below the target and for females 46, just above the target. Thus, for both males and females the target would be nearly achieved though the disparity is expected to prevail.

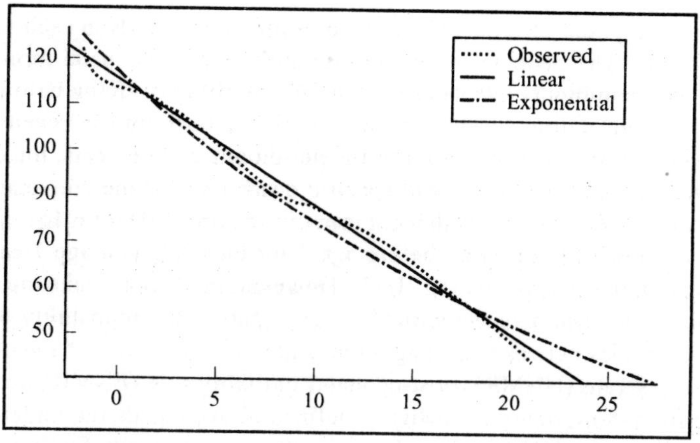

Figure 13.3: Trends in U5MR for India, Males, and Fitting of Linear and Exponential Functions, 1990-2011

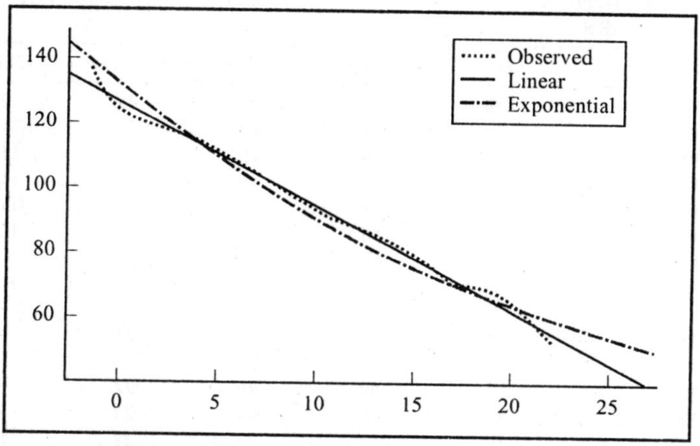

Figure 13.4: Trends in U5MR for India, Females, and Fitting of Linear and Exponential Functions, 1990-2011

Components of Early Childhood Mortality

Three distinct components of under-five mortality are recognized: neonatal period (up to four weeks or about one month), post-neonatal infancy period (one month but less than one year), and one year to below five years. As noted earlier, the influences of various factors on the risk of mortality in these segments differ considerably. Therefore, conceivably, the trends in mortality rates in these segments could vary.

Fortunately, the SRS data allow us to examine the trends in each of the segments. The neonatal mortality rate and the post-neonatal mortality rates are commonly used and measure probabilities of dying before the completion of four weeks (or one month) of birth and between four weeks and one year of birth. For the period one to five years, the child mortality rate, that is, the age-specific death rate for the conventional age group 1-4 years is available. From this the life table term 4q1 which is the probability of dying before age 5 for those alive at age 1 can be obtained; this is given by $(l_1 - l_5)/l_1$. However, in order to make the rates additive, we use here the term $(l_1 - l_5)/l_0$; this is the probability that a newborn dies between exact ages one and five. The sum of the neonatal mortality rate (NNMR), post-neonatal mortality rate (PNMR) and the rate for 1-5 mortality (1-5MR) as defined above equals the under-five mortality rate (U5MR). Trends in the three components for India are shown in Table 13.2 and Figure 13.5.

Table 13.2: Trends in Components of Early Childhood Mortality, India, 1990-2011, SRS

Year	*IMR*	*NNMR*	*PNMR*	*1-5MR*	*U5MR*
1990	80	53	27	45	125
1991	80	51	29	38	118
1992	79	50	29	35	114
1993	74	47	26	39	113
1994	74	48	26	37	111
1995	74	48	26	33	107
1996	72	47	25	33	105
1997	71	46	25	31	102
1998	72	45	27	26	98
1999	70	45	24	25	95
2000	68	44	23	23	91
2001	66	40	26	22	88
2002	63	40	24	23	86
2003	60	37	23	24	84
2004	58	37	21	23	81
2005	58	37	22	20	78
2006	57	37	20	17	74
2007	55	36	19	16	71
2008	53	35	18	16	69
2009	50	34	16	14	64
2010	47	33	14	12	59
2011	44	31	13	11	55
Extrapolated to 2015 (linear)	37.4	27.1	10.4	5.2	42.6
Extrapolated to 2015 (exponential)	39.7	28.3	11.6	8.7	47.6

(Contd.)

Table 13.2 (*Contd.*)

Note: IMR: Infant Mortality Rate, NNMR: Neonatal Mortality Rate, PNMR: Post-Neonatal Mortality Rate, 1-5MR: Mortality rate between ages 1 and 5, U5MR: Under-five Mortality Rate

Source: Registrar General (Annual Statistical Reports of the Sample Registration System, various years).

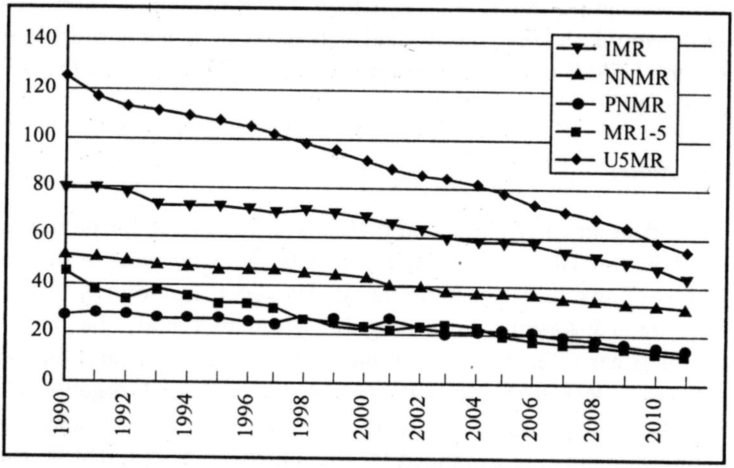

Figure 13.5: Trends in Neonatal, Post-neonatal, Infant, 1-5 and Under-five Mortality Rates, India, 1990-2011

Source: See Table 13.2.

It is seen that while decline has occurred in all the components, it is steeper in the mortality in the age range 1-5 than in neonatal and post-neonatal periods. Overall, in the U5MR, the fall has been large. Commonly, the initial decline in the mortality in age group 1-5 is relatively higher than in the neonatal period and this has been the case here. Further, the fall in the individual components is not as smooth as in the case of the U5MR. There are some years of stagnation and some of sharp fall.

Given that the trends in the three components are different over the period 1990-2011, it makes sense to extrapolate the rates separately. Again, both linear and exponential fits were attempted. Neither the linear nor the exponential curve gives a good fit in the case of the under-five mortality (U5MR) as such; note that the departures from the straight line in the components get smoothed in the sum of these, the U5MR, which shows a very smooth linear trend. The extrapolated values for 2015 of the components are shown in the bottom rows of Table 13.2.

Linear extrapolation shows lower values than the exponential. In particular, for 1-5MR, adopting the linear extrapolation gives a value of 5.2 whereas the exponential curve gives 8.7, a relatively large difference. The 1-5MR has reached a very low level and further declines are expected to be at a slower pace which is well captured by the exponential curve. Accepting this line of argument, the extrapolated value of the U5MR would also be slightly higher than 43 as noted earlier. In any case, the U5MR is likely to be only marginally higher than the MDG target of 42.

Large States

Similar data on early childhood mortality are available for large States (population of 10 million or more) from the SRS for most of the years and this allows us to examine trends. However, for some years, data from Jammu & Kashmir are missing. Besides, until recently, the published data for Bihar referred to Bihar and Jharkhand together and those for Madhya Pradesh to Madhya Pradesh and Chhattisgarh together. This prevents an assessment of trends for these four States separately. Therefore, trends are examined for the undivided States, that is, Bihar and Jharkhand together and Madhya Pradesh and Chhattisgarh together.

In the early 1970s, the U5MR (based on the life table for 1970-75 for which comparable data are available for most large States) varies substantially across States. The highest level, over 300, was found in Uttar Pradesh, followed by Madhya Pradesh, Rajasthan, Gujarat, Odisha, Assam all with U5MR exceeding 200. Kerala had the lowest level, just below 100 at the time. There has been notable decline in all the States (Table 13.3). However, the degree of fall varies. Looking at States with relatively high mortality in the 1970s, that is, U5MR over 200, one can see that by 2011 the U5MR had fallen below 100 in all the States and was around 70 in most (see Figure 13.6); besides, in Gujarat and in India as a whole, it had fallen close to 50 and is likely to fall below 50 by 2015. In States with moderate level (U5MR below 200) in the 1970s, the U5MR was well below 50 in 2011 in all the States except Haryana (Figure 13.7). Tamil Nadu and Maharashtra have shown remarkable progress with U5MR falling below 30; Kerala had low mortality even earlier.

Table 13.3: Trends in U5MR, Extrapolated Values, and MDG Targets for 2015, India and Large States

India/ State	*1970-75* [1973]	*1988-92* [1990]	*1998-2002* [2000]	*2011*	*Extrapolated Value for 2015*	*MDG Target for 2015 = 1/3* [1990 value]*	*Ratio: Extrapolated 2015 value/ 1990 value*
India — Both sexes	210	125	91	55	43	42	0.34
India — Male	196	119	87	51	39	40	0.33
India — Female	224	132	96	59	46	44	0.35
Andhra Pradesh	195	97	73	45	37	32	0.39
Assam	212	141	108	78	66	47	0.47
Bihar + Jharkhand	na	128	91	58	45	43	0.35
Gujarat	234	116	81	52	42	39	0.36
Haryana	158	104	91	51	41	35	0.40
Himachal Pradesh	173	91	63	46	38	30	0.42
Jammu & Kashmir	121	Na	60	45	—	—	—
Karnataka	153	107	74	40	29	36	0.27
Kerala	97	27	16	13	11	9	0.41
Madhya Pradesh + Chhattisgarh	250	185	131	72	53	62	0.28
Maharashtra	170	81	57	28	18	27	0.23
Odisha	223	156	114	72	57	52	0.36
Punjab	162	84	70	38	31	28	0.36
Rajasthan	243	157	110	64	50	52	0.32
Tamil Nadu	195	80	54	25	16	27	0.20
Uttar Pradesh + Utterakhand	306	161	120	73	58	54	0.36
West Bengal	na	97	66	38	26	32	0.26

Note: Estimates for Bihar and Jharkhand are combined as are those for Madhya Pradesh and Chhattisgarh.
na: Not available.
Estimates for Jammu & Kashmir are not available for 1990.
Source: Registrar General (1984, 1998, 2012c, 2013).

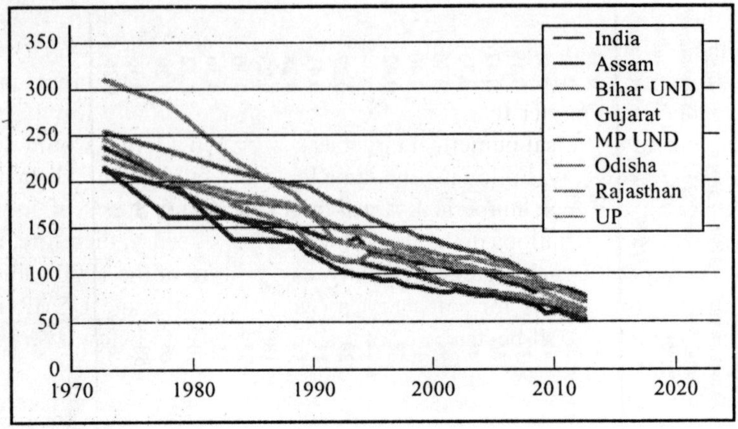

Figure 13.6: Trends in U5MR, States with Relatively High Initial Level, 1973-2011

Source: See Table 13.3.

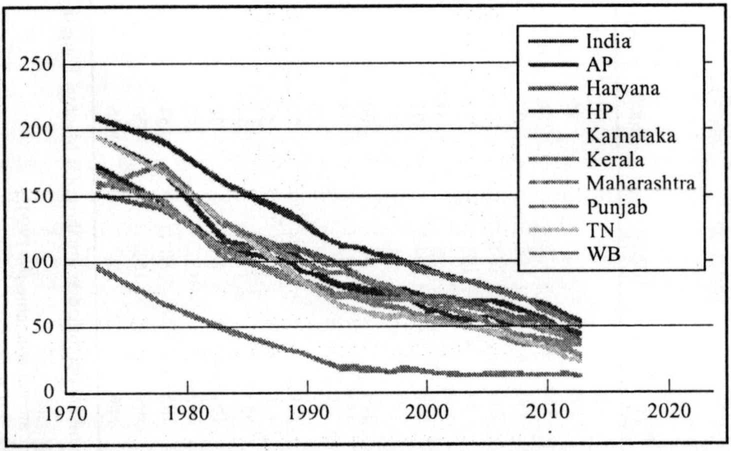

Figure 13.7: Trends in U5MR, States with Relatively Low Initial Level, 1973-2011

Source: See Table 3.3.

What about the progress towards achieving the MDG target for U5MR? To answer this question, we must first see what the target is. In most of discussions, it is implicitly assumed that the numerical target for India (42 or 38.5 as stated in literature) applies to States (and districts) as well (see, for example, Ram, *et al.*, 2013). But it must be noted that the MDG target is stated in relative terms, as "Reduce by two-thirds, between 1990 and 2015, the under-five mortality rate". Thus, the target depends on the level in the base year, 1990, and equals (1/3)*(U5MR in 1990). In the U.N. reports, targets for various countries are specified exactly in this manner. Clearly, the numerical targets for countries with initial high levels are also higher than those for countries with initially low level. There is no universal numerical target as such. Such a target would not be realistic anyway. Following the same logic, it would be unrealistic to presume a common numerical target for regions and States of India given the vast variations in the initial level. It makes sense, therefore, to set the target for each State individually, as one-third of the 1990 value. Note that this means for some States (with above average U5MR in 1990) the target will be above 42 and some other (with below average U5MR in 1990) it will actually be *lower* than the national target.

The extrapolation exercise has been carried out for large States based on the series 1990-2011. The trends for many States are not as smooth as the national series as there are some short periods of stagnation or slowdown. Overall, the linear fit is fairly good (though not as close as for the national trend). Utilizing this, the extrapolated values are computed and shown in Table 13.3. For many States with initially moderate levels, the extrapolated value is below or marginally above the target and thus the target seems achievable or nearly so. These are: Tamil Nadu, Maharashtra, West Bengal and Karnataka. In these States, the U5MR is expected to be fall below one-third of the 1990 level, and also be well below 42 given their initial levels. Kerala has long had low mortality and even in 1990 U5MR in the State was 27, much below the national target of 42. It has often been said that Kerala has already achieved the target. But given its initial level, the target for Kerala must also be low, 9; the State will move close to it though achieving it is a difficult task as further progress from a low level is difficult. Punjab, Himachal Pradesh, Andhra Pradesh and Haryana are likely to cross the level of 42, the national numerical target, but fall short of their respective State targets.

Among States with initially high levels, Rajasthan and Madhya Pradesh are expected to achieve their respective targets though not cross the national target. Bihar and Gujarat are likely to be close to achieving the target. However, Assam, Uttar Pradesh and Odisha are not expected to achieve the target. In particular, in the last two decades, the progress of Assam in raising the level of child survival has been very poor.

Discussion

There is no doubt that India has achieved substantial progress in improving child survival. Yet India has a long way to reach the level of the developed world. Moreover, India lags behind most developing countries of Asia and Latin America as well. Lack of recognition of the problem is not an issue as programmes aimed at raising child survival have been in place for long, augmented and recast from time to time. Given the close link between child health and maternal health, most of the programmes addressing child health are integrated with those on maternal health as the titles 'Maternal and Child Health', 'Child Survival and Safe Motherhood', 'Reproductive and Child Health', and '*Janani Shishu Suraksha Karyakramma*' show. Undoubtedly, the efforts have not been adequate. The recognition of early childhood mortality as a goal in the Millennium Declaration of 2000 and setting a specific target to be achieved by 2015 gave an impetus to global efforts to improve child survival. One must acknowledge that though the targets as such are not sacrosanct, they do serve a purpose since policy-makers begin to view the matter in more concrete terms and pressures are put on programme managers for implementation of programmes and for monitoring progress. It is true that goals and quantitative targets have been set in the past; the Indian policy and plan documents generally specify targets which are revised from time-to-time. The National Population Policy 2000 had set a clear target for the IMR that was included in the National Health Policy documents as well. But the U.N. targets put greater pressures as these are widely accepted by the international community and development organizations and national governments feel the need to be responsive to the global sentiment. A consequence is that the national achievement begins to be assessed in terms of progress towards the target. The MDG target expressed in terms of the under-five mortality rate, namely reducing the U5MR by two-thirds between 1990 and 2015, needs to be viewed in this context.

The trends in the U5MR in India show that the country is close to achieving the target though it may fall a bit short. Early childhood mortality has fallen substantially as the recent data clearly show and by 2011 it had reduced by 55 per cent since 1990 level, treated as the baseline by the U.N. The trends suggest that by 2015, the level is likely to fall by about 65 per cent, close to the desired quantum of decline. Improvement has been seen both among males and females, but it is disturbing to note that in spite of the overall decline, the male-female gap persists. As is widely known, childhood mortality is generally lower for the female child than the male child world-wide and India is among the exceptions. This state is likely to continue as girls in India continue to suffer from relative disadvantage as compared to boys. It should be recognized that gender disparities are the result of discrimination against girls at home elimination of which calls for major social change.

There has been better progress in lowering mortality during ages between one and five than during infancy. But further progress must come primarily from improvements in infant survival. Various Government programmes including the *Janani Shishu Suraksha Yojana* of the National Rural Health Mission (NRHM) address this issue. The NRHM introduced certain schemes to enhance pre-natal and post-natal care and to support institutional and professional assistance at delivery with provision for transport to institutions. The introduction of the Accredited Social Health Activist (ASHA) was to promote local support to facilitate maternal and child health care. The NRHM was introduced in 2005 and it took some time for the ASHA and other services to be in place. There is evidence from the Annual Health Survey 2010-11 that institutional deliveries have increased in all States (Registrar General, 2012b). How well this translates into improvements in child survival (and also reduction in maternal mortality) needs to be seen. Perhaps, one needs to wait for some more time to assess the impact.

Besides, interstate disparities persist. Setting a common numerical target for States with huge variations in initial levels implies that a convergence is expected. Some of the discussions in India treat the national target as the target for all States. This is clearly unrealistic. While convergence in the long-term is desirable, achieving convergence in a short period is clearly not feasible; since the Millennium Declaration was made in the year 2000 and the MDG4 target set for 2015, the time available was only 15 years. But the wording of the statement on the target clearly shows that the target is meant to be relative and a look at the numerical targets set for various countries in U.N. documents confirms this.

Therefore, one should see whether regions or States are on track to achieve their targets rather than the single national target. The trends for different States reveal that a number of States, e.g. Tamil Nadu, Maharashtra, West Bengal, Karnataka, Rajasthan and Madhya Pradesh, are likely to achieve their respective targets by the year 2015. While the first four of these have already crossed the national target and are expected to reach the respective targets, Rajasthan and Madhya Pradesh may fall short of the national target, but are expected to achieve the respective State targets; note that the initial levels in these States were much above the national average. A few States will come close to the targets. Some States that had lower than national U5MR may achieve the national target (Kerala has done so long ago and Punjab has also now achieved the level), but not the State target which is lower than the specific numerical national target. Thus, they seem to be losing the advantage that they enjoyed. The case of Kerala is altogether different as the U5MR has reached a fairly low level; as the probability of survival improves considerably, further improvement in it becomes more and more difficult. On the other hand, progress in some States with high levels of U5MR in 1990, Assam, Odisha, and Uttar Pradesh has been tardy. These States are certainly far from the national target but also far from their State targets which are higher than the national one.

It is pertinent to note here that the wide variations in child survival have long been acknowledged and have been factored in Government programmes in India. The NRHM identified certain States as high focus group States and brought in special schemes for these along with financial inputs. Earlier, States pooled under the Empowered Action Group (EAG) were recognized for intensive inputs. The intention to minimize inter-State disparities was clearly evident. Yet the differences persist. Has the special attention not made much impact? It is perhaps too early to pass a judgement. Obviously, the disparities are too sharp to be eliminated. While some States have made relatively greater progress than others, some have been slow. Clearly, implementation of programmes is a matter of concern.

We thus see a mixed picture. At the national level, India seems to have done fairly well in lowering early childhood mortality and is on track or very close to it in achieving the MDG target for U5MR. But some States are far from it in spite of the special efforts under the NRHM. In particular, Assam, Uttar Pradesh, and Odisha are in need of efforts beyond the normal programme and the NRHM, and further intensification of effort or a 'very high focus' is necessary.

What about the future? A rather unexpected observation on the recent trends is that the decline in the past few decades has continued to be linear. It has normally been seen that as the level of mortality declines so does the gradient since further improvements are difficult. This means that the trend would be close to exponential. But the continuation of the linear trend implies that India is still in the phase of moderate level of child mortality. At the same time, as the slopes for States with moderately low mortality, not to mention Kerala, are lower than the national one, the pace of decline at the national level is expected to be slower in the future. Therefore, while India is quite likely to achieve the MDG goal, if not in 2015 itself, certainly soon after the date, a very high level of child survival is quite distant.

REFERENCES

IIPS (1995). *National Family Health Survey 1992-93: India*, Health and Family Planning, Mumbai: IIPS.

IIPS and ORC Macro (2000). *National Family Health Survey 1998-99 (NFHS-2): India*, Mumbai: IIPS.

IIPS and Macro International (2007). *National Family Health Survey 2005-06 (NFHS-3)*, Mumbai: India.

Kulkarni, P.M. (2008). "Infant and Child Mortality in India: Recent Trends and Prospects", Paper presented at a *National Seminar on Methodological Issues in Measuring Millennium Development Goals (MDG) in Districts of India*, 12-13 December, Mumbai: IIPS.

Ram, U., Jha, P., Ram, F., Kumar, K., Awasthi, S., Shet, A., Pader, J., Nansukusa, S and Kumar, R. (2013). "Neonatal, 1-59 Month, and Under-5 Mortality in 597 Indian Districts, 2001-12: Estimates from National Demographic and Mortality Surveys", *The Lancet*. Retrieved from: www.thelancet.com/lancetgh

Registrar General, India (1984). *SRS Based Abridged Life Tables 1970-75. Census of India 1981, Occasional Paper No. 1 of 1984*, New Delhi: Office of the Registrar General.

Registrar General, India (1985). *SRS Based Abridged Life Tables 1976-80. Census of India 1981, Occasional Paper No. 1 of 1985*, New Delhi: Office of the Registrar General.

Registrar General, India (1989). *SRS Based Abridged Life Tables 1981-85. Census of India 1981, Occasional Paper No. 1 of 1989*, New Delhi: Office of the Registrar General.

Registrar General, India (1994). *SRS Based Abridged Life Tables 1986-90. SRS Analytical Studies Report Series, Occasional Paper No. 1 of 1994*, New Delhi: Office of the Registrar General.

Registrar General, India. (1998). *SRS Based Abridged Life Tables 1990-95. SRS Analytical Studies Report No. 1 of 1998*, New Delhi: Office of the Registrar General.

Registrar General, India (2009a). *Sample Registration System Statistical Report 2008*, New Delhi: Office of the Registrar General.

Registrar General, India (2009b). *District Level Estimates of Child Mortality in India based on the 2001 Census Data*, New Delhi: Office of the Registrar General, India.

Registrar General, India (2011). *Sample Registration System Statistical Report 2009*, New Delhi: Office of the Registrar General, India.

Registrar General, India (2012a). *Sample Registration System Statistical Report 2010*, New Delhi: Office of the Registrar General, India.

Registrar General, India (2012b). *Annual Health Survey 2010-11*, New Delhi: Office of the Registrar General, India.

Registrar General, India (2012c). *Sample Registration System, Abridged Life tables, 1995-99 to 2006-10*, Retrieved from: www.censusindia.gov.in

Registrar General, India (2013). *Sample Registration System Statistical Report 2011*, New Delhi: Office of the Registrar General, India.

Saikia, N., Singh, A. and Ram, F. (2010). "Has Child Mortality in India Really Increased in the Last Two Decades?" *Economic and Political Weekly*, 45(51), 62-70.

United Nations (2013). *The Millennium Development Goals Report 2013*, New York: United Nations.

United Nations Children's Fund (2013). *Committing to Child Survival: A Promise Renewed, Progress Report 2013*, New York: UNICEF.

14

Psychological Aspects of Reproductive and Sexual Health

Nutan Prabha Jain, S.D. Gupta and *Snigdha Pareek*

The reproductive health research has predominantly included "eligible couple" focussing on married women of childbearing age. Men's reproductive health and the interrelationships between women's and men's reproductive health are seriously underinvestigated. Research studies focussing on single women or men, adolescents, and women who have passed the age of childbearing, are meagre.

The recently introduced reproductive, maternal, new born, child and adolescent health (RMNCH+A) strategy by Government of India provides an understanding of 'continuum of care' to ensure equal focus on various life stages in a gender-sensitive manner. If this strategy is implemented with complete understanding of adolescence from psychological perspective, it is most likely that our country will achieve the health outcome goals established in the Twelfth Five Year Plan.

> Reproductive health is a state of complete physical, mental and social well-being and not merely the absence of disease or infirmity, in all matters relating to the reproductive system, and to its functions and processes. Reproductive health therefore implies that people are able to have a satisfying and safe sex life and that they have the capability to reproduce and the freedom to decide if, when and how often to do so. (http://www.who.int/topics/reproductive_health/en/)

For the first time, the International Conference on Population and Development (ICPD) held in Cairo in 1994 marked the acceptance of a clear focus on the needs of individuals (every individual is unique). It raises the importance of a life-cycle perspective beyond the childbearing years. It also refers to the complex links between direct and indirect determinants of health and between the individual and the environment. It suggests that the awareness of, and entitlement to health — as well as the provision of appropriate services — need to be informed to the general public. To have access to safe, effective, affordable and acceptable methods of family planning of their choice, as well as other methods of their choice for regulations of fertility which are not against the law, are also part of reproductive health. This will enable women to go safely through pregnancy and childbirth and provide couples with the best chance of having a healthy infant.

This chapter aims at understanding psychological aspects of reproductive and sexual health using life-cycle and gender-sensitive approach.

Social Determinants of Reproductive and Sexual Health

Psychology is the study of the mind and behaviour and "the understanding of behaviour" is the enterprise of psychologists. Health in general and reproductive and sexual health in particular, is part of quality of life. The World Health Organization (WHO, 1997) has included bodily image and appearance, negative feelings, positive feelings, self-esteem, thinking, learning, memory and concentration as "psychological" issues under quality of life. The WHO's framework of social determinants of health framework includes psychological factors as shown in the Figure 14.1. The framework draws attention of policy-makers towards three broad approaches: (i) targeted programmes for disadvantaged populations; (ii) closing health gaps between worse-off and better-off groups; and (iii) addressing the social health gradient across the whole population to reduce health inequities.

Sexual health is a central element in reproductive health formulations. Statements about sexual health can be drawn from a WHO Technical Report (1975), which included the concept of sexual health as something "enriching" and that "enhance(s) personality, communication and love". It went further by stating that "fundamental to this concept are the right to sexual information and the right to pleasure".

Reproductive health conditions make a major contribution to the global burden of disability, particularly for women. Psychological capacities that are acquired across the life course greatly influence the way in which people age through various stages of life.

Reproductive health is a lifetime concern for both women and men, from infancy to old age. A life-course perspective calls on policy-

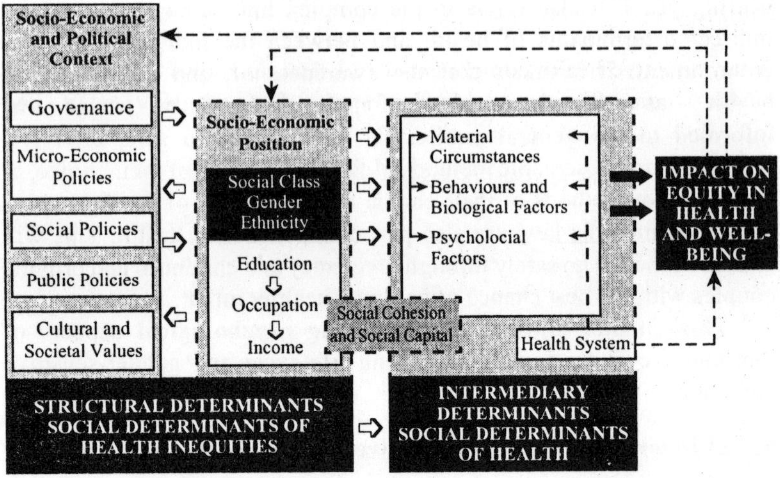

Figure 14.1: Psychological Factors as One of the Components of Social Determinants

Source: A *Conceptual Framework for Action on the Social Determinants of Health*, WHO, 2010, p. 6.

makers and civil society to invest in the various phases of life, especially at key transition points when risks to well-being and windows of opportunity are greatest. These include critical periods for biological, psychological and social development, including *in utero*, the first six years of life, adolescence, transition from school to the workforce, motherhood, menopause, the onset of chronic illnesses and widowhood.

Methods

A desktop review of the published and gray literature was used for this chapter. The literature review employed a web-based search of over 268 documents. Relevant evidence from related topics such as psychological aspects of health and the broader reproductive health literature was reviewed when relevant to the topic. Publications like journal, reports, documents, books, as well as relevant policies, legislation, and national demographic and health surveys published by governments, organizations, and individuals were reviewed. Main search terms included the following: psychological aspects/mental health, social determinants, reproductive health, sexual health, RMNCH+A, life-cycle approach, early marriage, Knowledge, Attitude and Practices (KAP) studies or survey, continuum of care, gender-sensitive, and quality of life (Table 14.1). More than half of the studies were international.

Findings

A reproductive health component-wise break-up shows that a majority of the studies were available for family planning, HIV/AIDS, and followed by "sexual health".

Table 14.1: Per cent Distribution of List of Keywords

Key Words	*Per cent*
KAP survey/study	76 (28%)
Reproductive and sexual health	59 (22%)
Psychological aspects/mental health	47 (18%)
RMNCH+A	23 (8%)
Gender-sensitive	21 (7%)
Social determinants	20 (7%)
Early marriage	17 (6%)
Continuum of care	5 (2%)
Total	**268**

The existing evidence base derives from the fact that research on reproductive health has predominantly been carried out on married women of childbearing age. Evidence on the reproductive health of adolescent girls, single women, and women who have crossed the age of childbearing is meagre. Moreover, men's reproductive health and the interrelationships between women's and men's reproductive health are seriously underinvestigated. There are significant differences in the prevalence of disability between men and women (men have higher prevalence rate than their counterparts), especially during the reproductive period. As women enter into the age-group of 50+ years, more women report the disability irrespective of type of the disabilities (Census of India, 2011). The review has been summarized and discussed in the following sections:

Life-cycle Approach to Reproductive and Sexual Health

There are multiple points using life-cycle approach and of intersection between psychological health and reproductive and sexual health: for example, psychological issues related to pregnancy, childbirth and the postpartum period, and the mental health effects of violence, including sexual violence, adverse maternal outcomes, such as stillbirths and miscarriage, surgery and removal of reproductive organs, sterilization, premarital pregnancies in adolescents, Human Immunodeficiency Virus (HIV) infection and Acquired Immunodeficiency Syndrome (AIDS), menopause and infertility (Patel & Oomman, 1999).

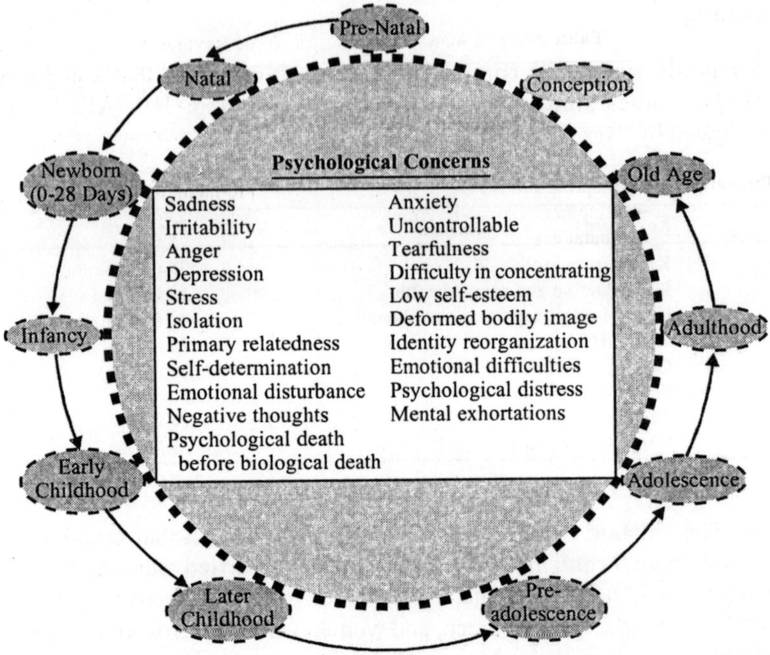

Figure 14.2: Life-cycle Approach of Reproductive and Sexual Health and Psychological Concerns

The authors argue that life-cycle approach may even consider "status before conception" which is basically "planning" phase where couple's knowledge, attitude, beliefs, and practices matter. The decision to terminate a pregnancy, most often, is a heart-wrenching decision, which sometimes results in a mental repercussion for the woman involved. It is not a proposition to be made casually by men and feminist proponents who do not have to feel the full force of a decision to terminate the life of one's own unborn child. However, Figure 14.2 is about the life-cycle of a person's starting since conception till death. It is important to recognize that components of the reproductive and sexual health cannot be addressed in isolation as these are closely linked to the psychosocial status of the population in various stages of life-cycle.

This is also important that in the case of a person (either man or woman) with psychotic disorder(s), health service providers inquire about sexual and reproductive functioning and not show reluctance in this regard. There are 11 stages in all and a person may have various psychological experiences at different stages using life-cycle approach by reproductive, sexual health and psychological aspects or concerns. Some of the common psychological concerns across the stages are mentioned in the center (Table 14.2).

Table 14.2: A Summary of Results of the Review

Life Stages	*Reproductive Health Concerns*	*Sexual Health Concerns*	*Psychological Concerns*
(1)	*(2)*	*(3)*	*(4)*
Pre-natal	Appropriate growth and development, complete antenatal care	Sex-determination	Pre-natal learning, pregnant women's morning sickness — nausea and vomiting protects both mother and foetus from infection and dangerous chemicals, maternal nutrition and maternal emotions, Seriously stressed women often have babies who are restless, irritable, and having feeding problems
Natal	Physical condition of baby, 37-gestational period, weight of the baby, normal *Vs.* C-section, skill-birth attendance, ectopic pregnancy, obstructed labour, sepsis/ infections, hypertensive disorders, maternal morbidity and complications	Sex of the baby	Presence of father of the baby can be a source of physical and psychological support for the mother
Newborn (up to 28 days)	Neonatal toxicity/ neonatal withdrawal, growth and development, exclusive breast feeding, immunization, hypothermia, jaundice, umbilical cord, morbidity and mortality, gender-discrimination		Expectations of parents for their babies determine how they treat them and these expectations have important physical, cognitive and psychosocial consequences, Detachment *Vs.* attachment, anxiety, depression, post-traumatic stress disorder, breast-feeding
Infancy (up to 1 year)	Growth and development, Breast feeding, weaning, immunization, morbidity and mortality,	Bodily sensations provide pleasure, explorations of own body	Basically helpless, yet the child's instinctive responses (e.g. sucking) set off physiological changes in mother and subsequent social

(*Contd.*)

Table 14.2 (*Contd.*)

(1)	*(2)*	*(3)*	*(4)*
	infanticide, gender-based discrimination		bonding. Begins to react differently to family caretakers and strangers, Trust *Vs.* Mistrust conflict, "Can I trust the people around me?" hope
Early Childhood (up to 5 years)	Growth and development, Immunization, gender-based discrimination	Sexual abuse	Dependency on parents, becomes upset when separated, conscious of adult approval, sense of possessiveness, developing a greater sense of personal control: mastering fear, controlling eating, restricting drinking, refusing drugs. Psychosocial conflict between Autonomy *Vs.* Shame and Doubt, "Can I do things myself or am I reliant on the help of others?" Basic virtue: Will. Important event: Toilet Training. Begins to incorporate social attitudes and prejudices, begins to comprehend his/her expected role in the adult world and to play out roles worth imitating
Later Childhood (6-9 years)	Immunization, deworming, awareness, gender-based discrimination	Sexual abuse	Pre-moral and moral development, A concern for how things work and how to make things
Pre-Adolescence (10-12 years)	Physical changes around puberty, growth spurts, increase in weight, height, heart size, lung capacity, muscular strength. Bone growth is faster than muscle development — can result in lack of coordination and awkwardness, early marriage, gender-based discrimination	Sexual abuse	Conventional moral development, integrating various aspects of one's self in to a sense of who has been and who one may become

(*Contd.*)

Table 14.2 (*Contd.*)

(1)	*(2)*	*(3)*	*(4)*
Adolescence (13-19 years)	Change in Hormonal balance, Menstruation, capable of conception, Hair growth begins on the upper lip, change in voice, enlargement of genitals/breast development, age at marriage, teenage pregnancy, menstrual hygiene, contraceptives, gender-based discrimination	Sexual maturation, breast elevation, rounding of the hip begins, beginning of downy auxiliary hair, nipple pigmentation begins, Nocturnal emissions (ejaculation of semen during sleep), Sperm production becomes sufficient for fertility, sexual abuse	Pre-menstruation syndrome shows strong feelings and intense emotions at different times, unpredictable moods, emotional ups and downs can lead to increased conflict. This is partly because child's brain is still learning how to control and express emotions in a grown-up way, more self-conscious, especially about his physical appearance and changes, decision-making skills are still developing, searching for self-identity, Comprehends abstract ideas/ ideation and reasoning about the future, curiosity, experimentation, physical and mental pain
Adulthood (20-49 years)	"Continuum of Care" for reproductive, maternal, newborn and child health (RMNCH), nutrition, breast-feeding, family planning, infertility, prolonged and difficult vaginal deliveries, hysterectomy, cervical cancer, breast cancer, HIV/AIDS, partner treatment for STI and RTI, fertility regulation, abortion, use of assisted reproductive technologies, utero-vaginal prolapsed, lack of attention for widows and singlehood, gender-based violence, pregnancy loss, fear of pregnancy outcome, gender-based discrimination	Sexual activity and interest remain high, Extra-marital relationship, sexual abuse decreased interest in sex, sexual dysfunction	Accepted as "adult" socially, role change — spouse, and then parent, develop a style and their standard of living, emotional stress, lack of decision-making, expectation of the "good" mother, suicide, mother-child interaction disorder, somatic complaints, pre-operative psychological distress, anticipatory anxiety, fear related to physical appearance and disfigurement, fear and shock, physical and emotional pain, intense self-disgust, powerlessness, worthlessness, depression and chronic anxiety, feelings of vulnerability, impaired sense of self, nightmares, chronic mental disorders, endangering their lives

(*Contd.*)

Table 14.2 (*Contd.*)

(1)	*(2)*	*(3)*	*(4)*
Old age (49+ years)	Hormonal changes, Menopause, poor knowledge on menopause among the elderly women, Gender-based violence, gender-based discrimination, lack of attention for widows and singlehood, utero vaginal prolapsed	Vaginal dryness	Anxiety, depression, sadness, difficulty in concentrating, overreacting to minor upsets, angen and irritability, forgetfulness and mood swings, dependability, behavioural complication, sleeplessness, no longer being useful, distorted body image, fear of death, insomnia, feeling 'unemployable', low self-worth, hot flushes, loss of friends and family

In order to further accelerate progress towards Millennium Development Goals (MDGs) and redefine the national agenda, a new strategy, namely, Reproductive, Maternal, Neo-natal, Child Health plus Adolescents (RMNCH+A) has been implemented to come up with a coordinated approach. Mutually linked interventions are required at various stages of life-cycle. According to the strategy, there are two dimensions to healthcare: (a) stages of the life-cycle, and (b) places where the care is provided. These together constitute the 'Continuum of Care'.

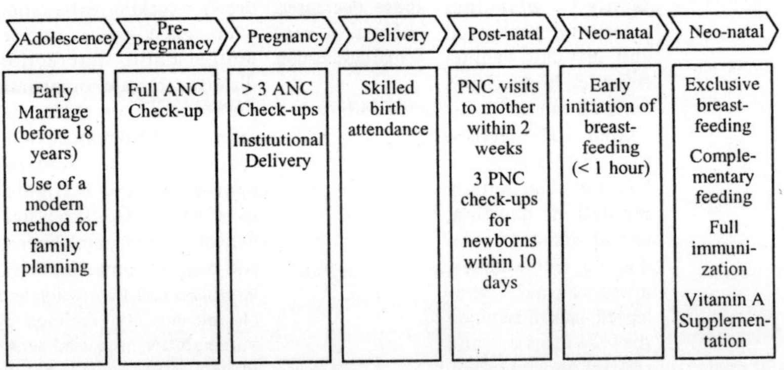

Figure 14.3: Life-cycle Approach under RMNCH+A

The RMNCH+A strategy focusses on adolescence which is one of the important stages of the life-cycle in terms of health interventions because there are a number of important issues that emerge during the adolescent period that comprises of pre-adolescence (10-12 year) and adolescence (13-19 years) phases. Psychology literature review discusses three distinct stages (early, mid, and adolescence) in the psychological development of an adolescent. Even though there is a great deal of overlap in the stages, and they may not occur during the age span indicated. During early adolescence (ages 11-13 years), development usually involves developing a new self-image due to the physiological changes. Adolescents need to make use of their newly acquired skills of logical thinking and ability to make judgements rationally. When they reach the ages of 14 and 15 (the period known as mid-adolescence), adolescents strive to loosen their ties to their parents. At this stage, their emotions and intellectual capacities increase. The adolescents become adventurous, and experiment with different ideas. This plays an important role in finding one's relations to oneself, groups, and opposite sex. During this time, the adolescents battle over their own set of values *versus* the set established by parents and other adult figures. They also begin to take on more control of educational and vocational pursuits and advantages. It is during this time that adolescents' self-dependence and a sense of responsibility become apparent, along with their quest to contribute to society and find their place in it.

It is important to understand the 'plus' in the strategic approach. It denotes: (1) the inclusion of adolescence as a distinct 'life stage' in the overall strategy; (2) linking of maternal and child health to reproductive health and other components (like family planning, adolescent health, HIV, gender and Preconception and Prenatal Diagnostic Techniques (PC&PNDT); and (3) linking of community and facility-based care as well as referrals between various levels of health care system to create a continuous care pathway, and to bring an additive/synergistic effect in terms of overall outcomes and impact.

It may be argued that in the Indian culture, there is no such period as adolescence. Adolescence or '*youvana*' is discussed in terms of poetry and *shringar rasa*. Culturally, children remain children before their marriage and once they are married they are considered adults. Unfortunately, many children are producing children because of legal age of marriage (18 years for girls and 21 years for boys). A girl or a boy who due to early marriage loses her/his childhood, and all the pleasurable emotions attached to it, will have a difficult time developing a self-concept with personality traits of concern and care which allows for creating an environment that leads to the enhancement of others including her/his own children. All the physical and mental pain that early marriage inflicts on girls gets multiplied several fold when its impact overflows to the next generation and perpetuates itself to destroy a girl's fair chances to life. The impact of early marriage on girls' psyche is wide-ranging, like denial of childhood and adolescence, curtailment of personal freedom, and lack of opportunity to develop a sense of selfhood as well as the denial of psychosocial and emotional well-being, reproductive health and educational opportunity. It often signifies an end to their individual will and aspirations. Early marriage plunges them into a cycle of early pregnancy, frequent childbearing, poor health, and somewhere in between, the possibility of an untimely death. For both girls and boys, early marriage has profound physical, intellectual, psychological and emotional impact due to reduced chances of educational opportunity and personal growth.

Knowledge, Attitude and Practices *Vs.* Behaviour Change Communication

It has been observed that, generally, psychological aspects are considered under mental health except Knowledge, Attitude and Practices (KAP) studies. "Information, education and communication (IEC)" is a major activity to create knowledge, and influence attitudes and practices. Many KAP studies are available on different health problems like, adolescence, family planning, and HIV/AIDS. Information alone cannot provide protection, but it is certainly a first step towards empowerment. Measurement of attitudes (including construction of attitude scales) towards various health issues is a technical issue and needs extensive training. Nonetheless, adolescents and young people continue to have limited knowledge of reproductive health issues and the risks they face. Further, this is the era of Behaviour Change Communication (BCC). A well implemented behaviour change communication strategy has the potential to improve knowledge and practices and consequently accelerate the health outcomes. The challenge with behaviour change efforts is that it has largely been implemented in silos and in segmented approaches.

Gender-sensitive Approach to Reproductive and Sexual Health

The psychology of people regarding women is limited to their reproductive role only. For example, in most of the studies, all pregnant women are called "mothers". It is important to remember that all pregnancies may not result in live births. There are many other outcomes like miscarriage, abortion, and stillbirth. The societal attitude of looking at women as means and not ends is even more pervasive. Compared with men, women more frequently experience certain kinds of negative life events, such as physical and sexual abuse, poverty, and gender discrimination (Figure 14.3). It reflects that reproductive health is a matter of concern to women only which is not true as reproductive health is a couple's affair.

Gender discrimination can be observed across the life-cycle. It starts with the sex ratio at birth. Per thousand boys, there are 952 girls, born naturally. However, due to the cultural preference for sons, misuse of the modern diagnostic tools for pregnancy have made it possible to determine a child's sex in the early phase of pregnancy which can facilitate female foeticide. Even after the girl babies' birth, family and society's discriminatory behaviour reflects in terms of child sex ratio for the age group of 0-6 years of children. It is argued that PCPNDT Act is able to restrict misuse of ultrasound services to determine sex of the foetus, but what could be done for those who murder the girl baby through their regressive thinking and attitude towards the girls. We assume that they are psychologically sick people; otherwise, a person with normal capabilities would easily understand that without girls/ women the world will not survive as only women can give birth to a baby.

Those girls who survive face abuse, exploitation and violence, and lack vital knowledge about sexual and reproductive health, including HIV/AIDS, experience significant challenge in terms of adolescence development. Adolescents exploited in the commercial sex industry, are subjected to neglect, sexual violence and physical and psychological abuse (UNICEF, 2006).

Life-skill based education is being promoted by Central Board of Secondary Education and UNICEF (CBSE, 2013). In 2005, life skills focussed on adolescence education was introduced as a separate subject in the senior secondary curriculum across approximately 4500 government schools in the state of Rajasthan and the subject is now institutionalized within the government schools (IIHMR, 2013).

Parents believe that marriage will protect girls from sexual assault and pregnancy outside marriage, extend girls' childbearing years or ensure obedience to their husband's household. Premature pregnancy and motherhood are an inevitable consequence of child marriage. Girls under 15 are five times more likely to die during pregnancy and childbirth than women in their twenties (World Health Organization, UNICEF, UNFPA and The World Bank, 2012). If a mother is under 18, her baby's chance of dying in the first year of life is 60 per cent greater than that of

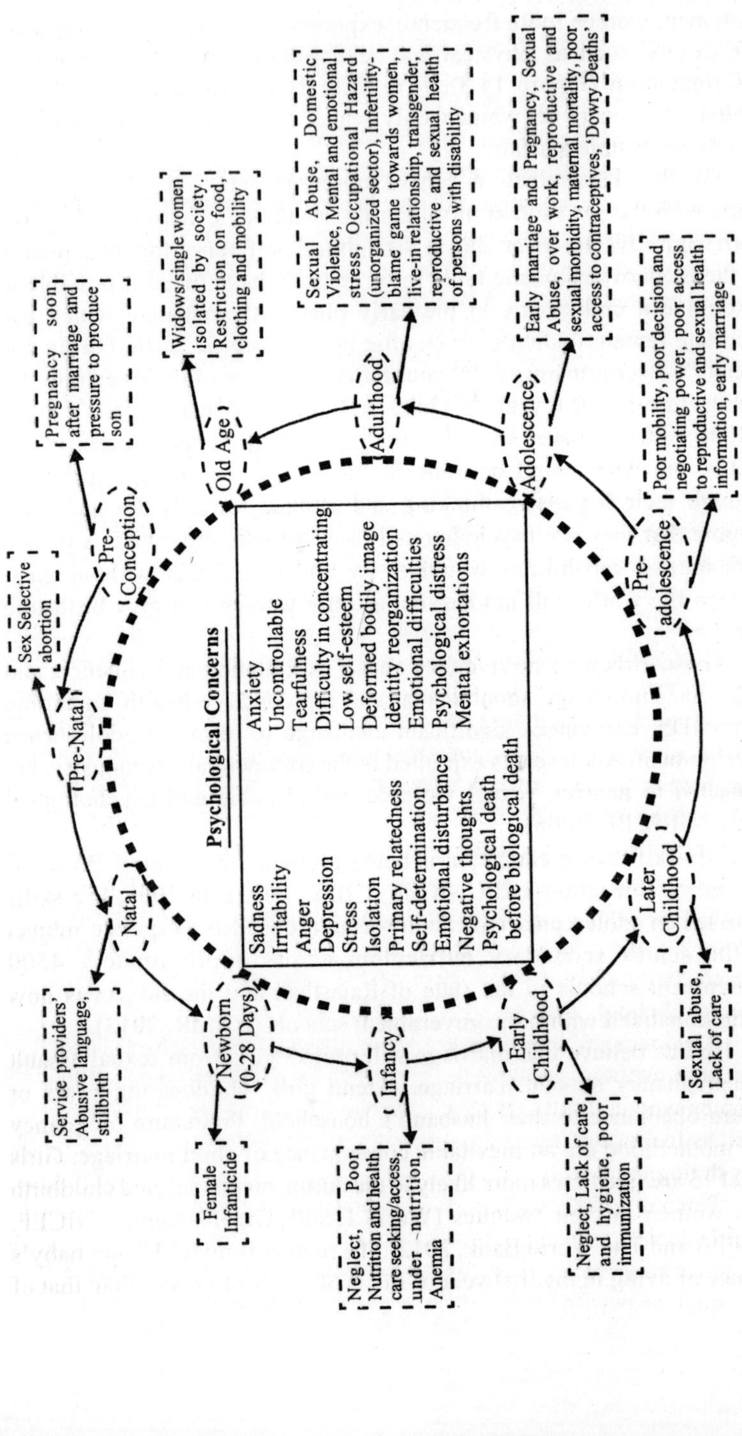

Figure 14.4: Life-cycle Approach, Psychological Concerns and Gender Perspectives

a baby born to a mother who is above 19 years of age. Even if the child survives, he or she is more likely to suffer from low birth weight, under-nutrition and late physical and cognitive development.

Women who have had experiences of physical or sexual violence, or both, by a partner are significantly more likely to have contemplated suicide than women who did not have such experiences in the past. Further, among all women who have ever contemplated suicide, women who have experienced violence are also significantly more likely to have attempted suicide (WHO, 2005).

It is hypothesized that changes in hormone levels in women are a contributing factor for the differences in depression prevalence across a woman's lifetime. A dramatic shift in depression prevalence is apparent during adolescence in girls sometimes between the ages of 10 and 15 years (Keita, 2007). During early adulthood, depression becomes most prevalent, with a typical onset between the second and third decades. Women of childbearing age are at heightened risk of experiencing a depressive episode.

There are many psychologically vulnerable groups among the women are available whose reproductive and sexual health issues like infertility, differently-abled women, and single women are not dealt with adequate care. Infertile couples were found different from non-infertile subjects with respect to psychological distress, stress, depression, self-esteem, marital satisfaction and sexual satisfaction (Kormi, 2000). For infertility, a woman is blamed, even though it may be because of the male partner. For seeking treatment, both are required but generally, male partner shows resistance due to notions attached to the 'masculine image' in the society. When the problem is diagnosed with the wife, husband does not feel as distressed as the wife does. But when men learn that they are the ones who are infertile, they experience the same levels of low self-esteem, stigma, and depression as the infertile women do (Harvard Medical School, 2009).

A woman may enter into surrogacy arrangements because of financial hardship without being fully aware of its potential risks. For those women who do relinquish the child, the risk of post-natal depression, as well as feelings of anger or guilt, may add further strain to the woman's psychological health.

Persons with disabilities, those who have long-term physical, mental, intellectual, or sensory impairments which, in interaction with various barriers, may hinder their full and effective participation in society on an equal basis with others, make-up a significant part of the population.

To quote in terms of percentage, only 2.21 per cent of the total population is differently-abled, but in terms of number, it becomes 2,68,10,557 persons.

Table 14.3: Percentage of Disabled to Total Population in India, 2011

	Persons	*Men*	*Women*
Rural	2.24	2.43	2.03
Urban	2.17	2.34	1.98
Total	**2.21**	**2.41**	**2.01**

This part of population has been extremely neglected and this leaves persons with disabilities among the most marginalized groups when it comes to reproductive and sexual health services. Persons with disabilities have sex too. Like everyone else, persons with disabilities have their needs throughout their lives, and these needs change over a lifetime.

Adolescents with disabilities need to know about the changes in their bodies and emotions and about the choices they make concerning sexual and reproductive health. They also may need special preparation concerning sexual abuse and violence and the right to protection from it. For persons with disabilities, social barriers may increase the chances of mental health difficulties in these circumstances. It is crucial to pay close attention to the mental health or psychological well-being of persons with disabilities, their families, and other care providers.

Women tend to live longer than men, may lack control of family resources and can face discrimination from inheritance and property laws. Elderly women may face double discrimination on the basis of both gender and age. They may face psychosocial death before biological death. Rumination of negative experiences related to reproductive and sexual health is one of the significant reasons of psychological ill-health among women. Understanding that mental health and mental illness are the results of complex interactions among biological, psychological, and socio-cultural factors is important for ageing women.

Although mental health is widely recognized as closely linked to reproductive health, in many countries it remains, at best, a marginal concern. RMNCH+A strategy is not an exception and deals with the general indicators, except one: per cent of adolescents accessing Adolescent Friendly Health Clinic (AFHCs) for SRH, nutrition, mental health, substance misuse, injuries, violence, and non-communicable disease related problems. It is also argued that increased migration from rural to urban, urban to metro for various reasons like employment, and higher education has exposed the public made them more vulnerable to psychological ill-health. The existing reproductive and sexual health services are not gender-sensitive and not favourable to widow/widower, separated, unmarried persons within the purview of health system. Live-in relationship is another upcoming issue to be dealt with carefully by policy-makers to achieve the WHO health definition. In recent times, "live-in-relationship" — a living arrangement in which an un-married couple lives together in a long-term relationship that resembles a marriage — has become popular due to the most obvious contributing factor of the transformed urban life which itself is growing from factors associated with urbanization and increased income, long hours of work, often late in the night and virtually no time for family. Those in live-in relationship think that marriage is too big a commitment. If people are shying away from marriages — one reason could be that people are scared of commitments that come along with marriage and are worried if it does not work out?

Besides woman and man, there are transgender issues/gender-identity disorders and psychological aspects need to be understood. A key problem transgender people face is ignorance of gender identity issues among medical staff. Very few studies have been done in the field of HIV/ AIDS Prevention on Transgender population as a component of the disciplines such as Psychiatry and Social Work (Lakshmanan & Victor, 2011).

Conclusion

It is very much clear that psychological/mental health and reproductive and sexual health are closely linked, influencing each other in powerful and complex ways. Reproductive problems may be linked to antenatal care, delivery, postpartum care, family planning; infertility, unsafe abortion, sexually transmitted infections, including HIV, reproductive tract infections, cervical cancer and other gynecological problems. These can have major psychological, social, emotional and physical consequences. Reproductive and sexual health and psychological and emotional aspects of the differently-abled population, need a comprehensive research.

In our country, research evidence related to psychological issues related to sexuality, childbirth, sexual violence, adverse maternal outcomes (such as stillbirths and abortions), sexually transmitted infections, including HIV/AIDS, family planning, reproductive tract surgery, sterilization, premarital pregnancy, menopause and infertility, need to be created for both men and women (including vulnerable population) at various stages of life.

REFERENCES

Central Board of Secondary Education. (2013). *Teachers Manual: Life Skills for Class VI*, Shiksha Kendra, 2, Community Centre, Preet Vihar, Delhi.

Fazli Khalaf, Z., Shafiabadi, A. and Tarahomi, M. (2008). "Psychological Aspects of Surrogate Motherhood", *Journal of Reproduction and Infertility*, 9(1), 43-49.

Garcia-Moreno, C., Jansen, Henrica A.F.M., Ellsberg, M., Heise, L. and Watts, C. (2005). *WHO Multi-country Study on Women's Health and Domestic Violence against Women: Initial Results on Prevalence, Health Outcomes and Women's Responses*, Geneva: World Health Organization. Retrieved from: http://www.who.int/gender/violence/who_multicountry_study/Introduction-Chapter1-Chapter2.pdf

Harvard Medical School (2009). "The Psychological Impact of Infertility and Its Treatment", *HEALTHbeat*, Harvard Health Publications. Retrieved from http://www.health.harvard.edu/newsletters/Harvard_Mental_Health_Letter/2009/May/The-psychological-impact-of-infertility-and-its-treatment

Keita, G.P. (2007). "Psychosocial and Cultural Contributions to Depression in Women: Considerations for Women Midlife and Beyond", *Journal of Managed Care Pharmacy*, 13(9 Suppl. S-a), S12-S15.

Kormi Nouri R. (2000). "Psycho-Social Aspects of Infertility", *Journal of Reproduction and Infertility*, 1(2), 57-68.

Lakshmanan R.M., Karthik and Victor, J. (2010). *A Study on General Well-being of Male to Female Transgenders Living in Chennai*, Dept. of Counselling Psychology, Madras School of Social Work, University of Madras, Chennai. Retrieved from http://www.medindia.net/news/healthwatch/mental-health-concerns-of-transgender-population-living-in-chennai-south-india-a-study-78981-1.htm#ixzz3GUZDs935

Office of the Registrar General, India (2011). *Census of India 2011*, Government of India Census of India, Ministry of Home Affairs, Government of India.

Patel, V. and Oomman, N. (1999). "Mental Health Matters Too: Gynaecological Symptoms and Depression in South Asia", *Reproductive Health Matters*, 7, 30-38.

Reproductive Health. *Western Pacific Region: World Health Organization*. Retrieved from: http://www.wpro.who.int/topics/reproductive_health/en/

UNICEF (2006). "The State of the World's Children 2007: Women and Children", *The Double Dividend of Gender Equality*, New York, NY: UNICEF. Retrieved from: http://www.unicef.org/sowc07/docs/sowc07.pdf

World Health Organization (2006). *Defining Sexual Health: Report of a Technical Consultation on Sexual Health*, 28-31 January, 2002, Geneva. Retrieved from: http://www.who.int/reproductivehealth/publications/sexual_health/defining_sexual_health.pdf

World Health Organization (1975). *Education and Treatment in Human Sexuality: The Training of Health Professionals*, World Health Organization (WHO Technical Report Series No. 572), Geneva: Switzerland. Retrieved from: http://apps.who.int/iris/bitstream/10665/38247/1/WHO_TRS_572_eng.pdf

World Health Organization (1997). *WHOQOL — Measuring quality of life*, Division of Mental Health and Prevention of Substance Abuse, WHO. Retrieved from: http://www.who.int/mental_health/media/68.pdf

World Health Organization and UNFPA (2009). *Mental Health Aspects of Women's Reproductive Health: A Global Review of the Literature*, Geneva, Switzerland: World Health Organization. Retrieved from: http://whqlibdoc.who.int/publications/2009/9789241563567_eng.pdf

World Health Organization, UNICEF, UNFPA and The World Bank (2012). "Giving Birth should not be a Matter of Life and Death", *Trends in Maternal Mortality: 1990-2010*. Retrieved from: http://www.unfpa.org/sites/default/files/resource-pdf/EN-SRH%20fact%20sheet-LifeandDeath.pdf

15

Causes and Prevention of Suicides in the Military
An Overview

Updesh Kumar

Suicide is one of the major human problems. It is estimated that worldwide between 5,00,000 and 1.2 million people died by suicide each year (United Nations, 1996). WHO figures show that a suicide takes place somewhere in the world every 40 seconds (Befrienders Worldwide, 2009). According to WHO estimates, in the year 2000, approximately one million people died by suicide, and 10 to 20 times more people attempted suicide worldwide. This represents one death every 40 seconds and one attempt every 3 seconds, on an average. The World Health Organization (WHO) estimated in 2002 that in the year 2020 there will be approximately 1.53 million people who will die by suicide, according to current trends. Worldwide, suicide attempts will be about 10-20 times more than deaths by suicide. This is an average of one suicide every 20 seconds and an attempt every 1-2 seconds. In all countries, suicide is now one of the three leading causes of death among people aged 15-34 years. There are variations in suicide rates across nations, highest being in Europe's Baltic region (40/lakh), followed by Sub-Saharan Africa (32/lakh). The lowest rates are reported for Latin America and a few countries in Asia. Suicide rates in India have shown an ascending trend from 8.9/lakh in 1989 to 10.8/lakh in the year 2007. Suicide is one of the ten main causes of death in India. One of the every three cases of suicide reported every 15 minutes is committed by a youth in the age group of 15 to 29. The total numbers of 1,54,000 suicide cases were recorded throughout India in the year 2002. Some 50,000 people in the four states of Kerala, Karnataka, Tamil Nadu, and Puducherry kill themselves every year. In 2002, there were 11,300 suicides in Kerala, 10,982 suicides in Tamil Nadu, 10,934 in Karnataka, and 9,433 in Andhra Pradesh. Some 32 people commit suicide in Kerala everyday. As per these evidences, Kerala, the country's first fully literate state has the highest number of suicides.

A lower rate of suicide is usually reported for the military personnel in comparison to the civilian population of the same region. Scoville, Gubata, Potter, White, and Pearse (2007) in a study of U.S. Armed Forces from 1980 through 2004, reported lower suicide rates for military personnel as compared to a matched civilian population. This holds true for the Indian Army as well. As per the data reported in the media (*The Hindustan Times*, 23 July, 2014) the annual number of suicides in the Indian Army has hovered around 100, while for the year 2013 it was reported as 86. With the strength of thirteen lakh soldiers this roughly translates to a rate of 6 or 7 suicides per lakh. Mehlum and Nrugham (2009) associate the trend with the phenomenon of 'healthy worker effect' and selection effect that rules out many psychiatric conditions, and the continuous health monitoring facilities provided by the armed forces.

Present chapter briefly traces the dynamics of suicide and provides an overview of studies conducted in the area. Drawing upon the extensive research conducted by the author in the field a conceptual model is proposed explicating the dynamic interplay of life conditions, stressors, support systems and coping resources in a soldier's life. Further, deriving from the extant literature and based upon empirical research, the chapter proposes certain strategies for preventing suicidal behaviours in the military organization. On a larger level, it is proposed that the military needs to be evolved as a positive organization that places the onus of soldiers' well-being not only on the individual, but on the organization as a whole.

It may be anticipated that almost everyone at intolerable and difficult moments in his or her life entertains the idea that it might be best to put an end to it all. Yet, it is only a handful of individuals that actually take the plunge, and attempt to end their own lives. In layperson terms, suicide stands for ending one's own life or killing oneself. It is a self-inflicted, life-threatening act which results in death. In suicidology, and even its study within the field of psychology, there has been conceptual disagreement on how exactly to define suicide and what the field of suicidology does and does not encompass (Maris, Berman & Silverman, 2000; Silverman, 2006). These definitional discrepancies can lead to differences in methodologies and difficulty in communicating, generalizing, and synthesizing research findings across the diverse field, hindering progress in the field (Silverman, 2006; Silverman, Berman, Sanddal, O'Carroll, & Joiner, 2007).

Suicide may be defined differently depending on the purpose of the definition — medical, legal, administrative, etc. In most countries reporting to the WHO, suicide is defined (by a medical examiner or coroner) as one of four possible modes of death — Natural, Accidental, Suicidal and Homicidal. Suicide can be more elaborately defined as an act with a fatal outcome, that is deliberately initiated and performed by the deceased him- or herself, in the knowledge or expectation of its fatal outcome, the outcome being considered by the actor as instrumental in bringing about desired changes in consciousness and/or social conditions (Retterstol, 1993).

Heerringen (2001), in his edited volume on understanding suicidal behaviour, provides a comprehensive overview of the definitional issues in suicide research. According to him, suicidality comprises of "cognitive and behavioural characteristics, which may manifest as suicidal ideation and suicidal behaviour" (p. 4). The wide spectrum of suicidal behaviours begins with suicidal ideation. Suicidal ideation refers to thoughts and ideas about ending one's life. Such ideas may be vague or be accompanied by concrete plans. Such ideations may sometimes be communicated by way of verbal or non-verbal threats through signs, behaviours or actions. Suicidal threats include spontaneously reported suicidal thoughts.

The term 'attempted suicide' is an umbrella term that covers a number of different behaviours. Common to these behaviours is that people inflict acute harm upon themselves, poison or injure themselves, or try to do so, with non-fatal outcome. Also common is that such behaviours occur in conditions of emotional turmoil. For laypersons, attempted suicide is an activity which involves acts of intentional self-injury and with the objective of causing death, but where the result is not death (Hammerlin & Enerstvedt, 1988). In other words, it is a consciously self-inflicted, self-destructive and life-threatening act which does not result in death. Suicide attempts many times result in death of the person and that is termed as committed suicide.

Suicidal Process

The suicidal process describes suicidal behaviour as a development from suicidal ideation or suicidal thoughts and attempted suicide through to accomplished suicide. The concept of suicidal process places the progression of suicidality from ideation to attempted and completed suicide within the individual. Certain phases of the suicidal process remain beyond observation, and others are visible as they exist above the threshold of observation (Heeringen, 2001). The threshold may vary for different individuals and is considered to be determined by personality related and social factors. There are three phases that precede a suicide:

1. ***Narrowing and Isolation:*** Scope of actions is narrowed, the view of world becomes more and more one-sided. The narrowing of human contacts means that there is a tendency to avoid others and seek more and more isolation.
2. ***Aggression:*** There is aggression of various kinds, primarily directed against oneself and ultimately there is unsatisfactory discharge of aggression outwards.
3. ***Flight from Reality:*** The individual is far from reality with fantasies and daydreams about suicide. The individual also dreams about committing suicide. The process is completed with the suicidal act itself.

According to Poldinger (1968), the pre-suicidal progression has three stages:

1. ***The Deliberation Stage:*** The individual starts considering that suicide is the possible answer to his problems.
2. ***The Ambivalence Stage:*** A struggle takes place between self-building and self-destructive forces. Suicidal thoughts emerge in this stage.
3. ***The Decisive Stage:*** At this stage the person takes the decision to either carry on living or end one's life.

Factors Leading to Suicidal Behaviour

The existing literature suggests that the particular stressful events that precede suicidal behaviour are those that signal defeat; no escape; and a feeling of 'no rescue' increases hopelessness through biased judgements of future. Various interpersonal and psychological causes of suicidal behaviour are like (a) loss of meaning and hope, (b) depression and anger, (c) interpersonal crises, (d) failure and devaluation, and (e) insoluble inner conflict. Many kinds of personality variables and cognitive factors may also be associated with the arousal of suicidal thoughts.

Personality Variables Associated with Suicidal Behaviour

1. ***Impulsivity:*** Impulsivity is one of the personality attributes

that gives most cause for concern in preventing self-destructive behaviour. Studies conclude that impulsivity is associated with suicide risk and that the manner in which people manifest their anger and hostility is generally intropunitive and covert, with high levels of guilt and depression.

2. ***Dichotomous Thinking:*** It is the tendency to think in all-or-nothing terms. Suicide attempters display cognitive styles of 'extremeness' according to some studies. It is generally found that suicidal individuals are more rigid and extreme in their thinking than non-suicidal persons. Most people have the capacity to moderate or ignore dichotomies, but suicidal people lack this flexibility, and so if they are dissatisfied with something in their lives, they find it difficult or impossible to modulate their expectancies or to imagine compromise. Thus, when faced with a problematic situation, suicidal individuals will experience their environment as offering few opportunities for relief or change.
3. ***Cognitive Rigidity:*** Dichotomous thinking is closely related to another cognitive variable of cognitive rigidity. The suicidal subjects are more rigid and inflexible in their thinking, and they are less able to change their problem solving strategies. Young suicide attempters are generally more field-dependent (that is, their decisions are more influenced by their environment).
4. ***Problem Solving:*** Suicide attempters see themselves as less confident in their problem solving skills, less systematic and active in their problem solving attempts, and feel less in control in problematic situations. Cognitive deficits make it difficult for a depressed individual to generate new or alternative solutions to the problems that face them. Increase in negative life events in combination with reduced problem solving ability may place an individual at risk for suicidal behaviour.

Risk Factors for Suicidal Behaviour

Research in the United States has shown that approximately 15 per cent of their population seriously considers suicide at some point in the course of their life (Nock, *et al.*, 2008), though only 1.4 per cent of the population actually dies by suicide (Nock, *et al.*, 2008). Importantly, the suicide attempt to completion ratio is estimated to be 25 to 1, further indicating that a substantial number of people try to die by suicide, but only a few do, many of whom do so only after multiple previous attempts (McIntosh, 2009). Thus, there appears to be something preventing many suicidal people from dying by suicide, despite their desire. Leenaars (2004) gave the following factors in understanding suicidal behaviour.

Biological Roots: Brain Dysfunction, Learning Disabilities, Physical Disability and Illness

Rourke, Young, and Leenaars (1989) have shown that one possible adolescent and adult outcome of childhood central processing difficulties is suicidal behaviour as well as other socio-emotional problems. Current research suggests that some physical illnesses are associated with suicidal behaviour, including anorexia, bulimia, diabetes, epilepsy, traumatic brain injury and muscular dystrophy (Barraclough, 1986). Some individuals with physical disability who are at risk are those with limb amputations or spinal injuries resulting in quadriplegia. Individuals with terminal illnesses such as AIDS appear also to be at high risk (Fryer, 1986).

Depression

Lester (1992) has noted that depression distinguishes many suicidal people from non-suicidal groups. Depression can be noted in mood and behaviour, verbal expression, and fantasy. Most suicides occur due to the experience of unbearable pain, but not necessarily depression (Shneidman, 1985). The unbearable emotion might be hostility, anxiety, despair, shame, guilt, dependency, hopelessness or helplessness. A critical factor in this regard is the unbearable nature of emotion — pain.

Specific Environmental Precipitating Events

Shneidman (1985) has noted that the common consistency in suicide is not the precipitating event, but lifelong coping patterns. People who kill themselves experience a steady toll of threats, stress, failure, challenge, and loss that gradually undermines their adjustment process. This view does not mean to suggest that environmental stimulus is not critical; it may in fact be, to use the common metaphor, the last straw that breaks the camel's back.

Family Background

After a review of literature Leenaars (2004) suggests that the family system and its functioning is a central factor associated with suicide and suicidal behaviour in children, adolescents and even older people, although by no means do all families show these characteristics — some none at all.

1. There is at times lack of generational boundaries in suicidal families.
2. The family system is often inflexible. Any change is seen as a threat to survival of the family.
3. Long-term disorganization (malfunctioning) has been noted in these families; for example, mother's or father's absence, divorce, alcoholism or mental illness.

Gender

The basic sex difference in suicide is that males kill themselves more than females. In contrast, females attempt suicide more often than males, and this sex difference has been found in almost all nations (Lester, 1988, 1992)

Risk Factors in Military Setting

Soldiers deployed in low intensity conflict operations are exposed to innumerable stresses which affect their endurance and mental health to a great extent. The situation in Low Intensity Conflict (LIC) operations is diametrically opposite to the conventional operations of war where the battle lines are clearly drawn, the enemy is clearly identifiable, aggression is well channelized, the goals of war are very much clear, the unit operates from a firm base, and the soldier regards himself as a symbol of patriotic pride. The prolonged exposure of soldiers to LIC environment modifies their perception and judgement of the conditions. The protracted service in counter insurgency operations, coupled with the rigours of inhospitable conditions, and other personal, domestic and organizational pressures, leads to increased stress and psychological imbalance in soldiers. The prolonged prevalence of such conditions before the soldier results in deviant behaviour.

In contrast to the field areas, peace areas are remarkably different for the troops. There is no constant threat of sudden traumatic event. Nature of job changes from 'offensive' to 'defensive'. But it has been found that troops are not at ease at peace situations. In peace areas soldiers face a tight routine of tasks to be performed by them. This leaves little time to be spent in leisure activities. The other factor is that the event of getting posted to a peace session after serving a tenure in field area, brings with it an expectation of a posting with relatively less pressures and more time to relax. The demands placed by peace stations and the requirements of duty, though different from field areas are no lesser in putting the soldier under stress. The soldiers get hardly any time to spend with their families and shortage of manpower results in additional duties to the soldiers. The steep hierarchy of command and control and dearth of social support increase the pressure on a soldier.

Rapid Changes in Social Integration

Although a high level of social integration is a protective factor of suicidal behaviour, rapid decreases in levels of social integration may result in higher suicide rates (Durkheim, 1897). The military lifestyle with frequent moves and relocations implies constant change in the social environment which may be perceived as enriching but which may also make it difficult for usual social relationships to be developed or maintained and for family structures to survive.

Loss of Individualism and Conformity Pressure

In a military setting, the uniformity expected and required may disturb the balance between interdependence and autonomy. This threat of eradication of individualism may by itself, if large and intense enough, or in combination with several other factors such as loss of social support and loss of meaning, lead to the consideration of suicide as a valid option (Mehlum, 1992).

Traumatic Stress Exposure

The exposure of military personnel to high rates of traumatic events during combat and peacekeeping options is logically expected and scientifically documented (Mehlum & Weisaeth, 2002). Exactly how much such exposure contributes to later mental health issues has been extensively investigated, with much evidence for a positive association (Mehlum & Weisaeth, 2002).

Psychopathology

The variable 'mental disorders' had the strongest association with suicide in a review of psychological autopsy studies (Cavanagh, Carson, Sharpe, & Lawrie, 2003). Five constructs have been consistently associated with completed suicide: impulsivity/aggression, depression, anxiety, hopelessness and self-consciousness/social disengagement (Connor, Duberstein, Conwell, Seidlitz, & Caine, 2001). A greater risk of suicidal acts was found in the combination of major depression, PTSD and a cluster B personality disorder than major depression alone among outpatients (Oquendo, *et al.*, 2005).

Uncertainty and Fear of Death and Injury

The anxiety and fear of not knowing if and when an attack might occur comprises a major stressor for the soldiers. Awareness about the dangers involved in military operations and the chances of death and injury is a significant stressor among personnel deployed in Counter Insurgency (CI) environments (Britt & Adler, 1999; Robinson, 2004).

Constrained Resources and Inhospitable Terrain and Climate

Basic facilities like food, accommodation, weather appropriate clothing, and transport are often found lacking in quantity as well as quality in forward areas. Weather conditions faced by military personnel are extreme with regards to heat, cold, as well as rains. Further the location of these deployments is often inaccessible by any modes of transport, thus depriving soldiers of adequate resources to cope with harsh weather.

Long Hours of Work and Resultant Fatigue

Military operations have almost always been associated with long hours of work and resultant fatigue (Pflanz & Ogle, 2006). The extensive work load due to inadequate staffing and shortage of manpower coupled with lack of sleep and rest significantly affects the stress levels and performance of soldiers in field deployment. To make matters worse, these deployments are often scheduled for long periods of time, as a result of which soldiers go months without a break.

Stress and Suicide in the Military

The experience of stress is subjective and varies from person to person and so are the coping strategies. Studies show that individuals exhaust all their resources in the process of coping, though the stress is not abetted in the process. As the resources available to an individual deplete and get exhausted, hopelessness increases in the individual. The individual starts feeling that there is no way to deal with the threatening event and that the only way to deal is to escape. It often results in suicide. The threat of eradication of individualism may by itself, if large and intense enough, or in combination with several other factors such as loss of social support and loss of meaning lead to the consideration of suicide as viable option (Mehlum, 1992).

Loss of meaning is the term used to describe the concept of existential vacuum espoused by Frankl (1967), which he believed could arise when an individual experiences a sense of loss of meaning in life, a sense of complete emptiness and an absence of purpose for continuing to live, wherein suicide may appear as a plausible alternative to the distress generated by such experiences of loss.

Military environment is composed of jobs having high stress, low autonomy, little personal control over workplace, stretched working hours, and prolonged deployment in combat or insurgency areas which results in chronic exposure to potentially traumatizing events. Armed forces personnel serve in stressful situations irrespective of being posted in combat, training or peace stations. Their duties go beyond normal duty hours and they work in environment of 7 × 24 × 365 day's work culture. Military as an organization is authoritative in nature. The foundation of this organization lies on adherence of 'discipline' and the most sought behaviour is of 'compliance' to the commands of the higher rank and working diligently till the peril of the life. The nature of military job itself creates a baseline level of stress in military personnel that is higher than the civil population. This holds true especially for the Other Ranks (ORs), who are minimally prepared to face the hardships of military life, and have the minimum of resources to cope up with the stressors. This baseline level of stress is their work or occupational stress.

Military stress has mainly three environments in which they operate, i.e. garrison, training exercises, and deployment. Those personnel deployed in routine/peace time duties face unique military stressors and other life stressors that are similar to those found in non-military (civilian) settings such as troubled family relations, financial or legal issues, serious changes in physical health or injury and organizational issues like old mindset of officers, their discourteous conduct toward subordinates, and deteriorating military grievance redressal mechanism. Certain aspects of routine military environment are also potential stressors or source daily hassles, such as work overload, lack of control over duty assignment, periodic transfers, role stress, perceived unfairness or injustice in superior *vs.* subordinate conflict resolution, subjective performance evaluation, poor command and control. In military, stress can be attributed to deployment or combat related factors as well as routine aspect of military life. It could be that occupational stress in military has less to do with the fact that military personnel deal with the difficult business of war and may stem more from subtle and intrinsic aspects of military culture that foster them (Pflanz & Sonnek, 2002). There is a paucity of research regarding the stress of routine military personnel. The assessment of perceived severity and the frequency of occurrence of stressful events in military domain can help to identify possible and desired changes in work environment and other interventions that will reduce psychological distress and increase job performance (Spielberger, Vagg, & Wasala, 2003). Recently, Paflanz and Ogle (2006) estimated that about one quarter of the US military personnel suffered significant job stress and related consequences. An enhanced individual vulnerability to military situations is most likely to be determined by one's genetic disposition, developmental history, substance abuse, female gender, job rank, duty type, service branch as well as by pre-existing mental conditions manifested as anxiety, neuroticism, anger/hostility, depression and the like (Pflanz, 2001). On the contrary, the existence of qualities such as resilience and military hardiness in individual can provide courage and strategies to turn stressful circumstances from disaster into growth opportunities (Maddi, 2007). Social or organizational support (e.g. support system) also matters in the stress-strain relationship.

Emotionally distressed military personnel are likely to exhibit decreased productivity, increased armed force turnover, higher rates of absenteeism, more accidents, lower morale, and greater interpersonal conflict with colleagues and supervisors. Recent research has established that combat, exposure to heavy casualties, deployment of units in a war zone, and unexpected mobilizations of reserve units are all correlated with higher levels of psychological distress. More recently, as the role of military personnel in disaster relief missions has increased, so has the focus on the stressful nature of these missions. According to a study conducted by the Department of Defense, 32.3 per cent of military members stated that their military duties were more stressful than their personal or family lives (Bray, *et al.*, 2002). A study conducted by Manning, *et al.* (1981), in Europe among the troops posted in peace stations found that military personnel suffering from mental health problems identified work-related problems as the primary contributor to their emotional problems. These workers complained of problems with job satisfaction and relations with supervisors and co-workers. McCarroll, Orman and Lundy (1993) reported that 23 per cent of military mental health patients in a stateside military mental health clinic were given the sole diagnosis of occupational problem.

Soldier Stressor Model

On the basis of the findings of a series of empirical studies conducted by the author and his colleagues in the area of stressors being faced by soldiers and the coping resources available to them, a model of soldiers' stressors is being proposed, which schematically explains the dynamics involved. Keeping in view the inherent stressors in the life of a soldier, the proposed model lays down the various pathways that lead to adaptive or maladaptive consequences. Figure 15.1 depicts the same.

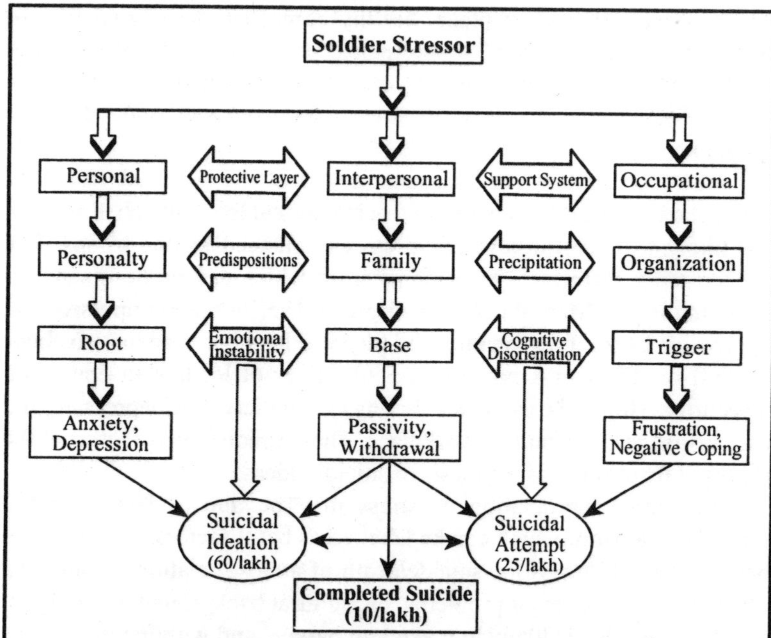

Figure 15.1: Soldier Stressor Model

In military settings, a soldier encounters stress which may arise due to personal, familial, interpersonal, occupational and environmental issues. The personal attributes of a troop, his relationship at the interpersonal front and the sort of occupational conditions that he is exposed to, serve as a protective layer on the extent of stress experienced by the troop. The factors which create a protective layer at the personal front are: Personal resilience and problem-solving skills, good physical and mental health, a sense of personal control and self-efficacy, a strong faith in spirituality, a strong sense of meaning and purpose in life, an optimistic outlook, easy temperament, a high level of self-esteem and social/emotional competence.

At the interpersonal front, the support system is provided by the soldiers' family and the society he comes from. If there are strong family bonds, a health style of coping is being followed. Presence of children and a supportive spouse, existence of healthy communication patterns at home and a strong sense of spiritual connectedness in the family moderate the level of stress experienced by a soldier to a great extent.

At the occupational front, if there is cohesiveness in the unit, the buddy system is well in place, healthy communication patterns exist between the superiors and subordinates, stress management strategies are being followed and there is an easy access to assistance services in times of need, then the level of stress experienced is moderated to a great extent.

However, certain predisposing factors at the personal front and precipitants at the interpersonal and occupational front, which if interact, are likely to raise the level of stress experienced by the troops. The predisposing factors at the personal front which can be designated as root factors are: Marital isolation, decreased self-esteem, impulsive and aggressive bend of personality, bad physical health, a tendency to abuse alcohol or drugs or a previous suicidal attempt leading to emotional insecurity. He may experience feelings of anxiety and depression and may refuse to contribute at workplace. These predisposing factors at the personal front serve as a genesis to suicidal ideas.

The same aggravation of stress may be due to factors at the interpersonal front which can be labelled as basal factors, primary ones being: financial stressors, suicide/death of a close relation, breakdown of a close relation, legal problems, his cultural background and religion and the like. This is likely to make him passive and withdrawn.

The workplace can also provide triggers like, loss of self-respect and efficacy, a bad evaluation, disciplinary problem, discharge from service, inability to get leave when needed. These triggers make the soldier vulnerable to cognitive disorientation. He may start misperceiving orders. In a state of frustration, he is likely to adopt emotion focussed ways of coping. He may become impulsive, critical, and unaware of his strengths and weaknesses may become sensitive and take things personally; thus leading to suicide attempts. These suicidal ideas and attempts, if not handled at an early stage are likely to result in successful cases of completed suicides.

The key lies not in acknowledging events that may precipitate a suicide, but in understanding the relationship between current stress and the underlying vulnerabilities and resourcefulness that a person brings to a crisis. It is important to be able to recognize when someone may be on a path to suicidal behaviour and to intervene in ways that give the person the resources to address their pain and difficulties in other ways.

Preventing Suicides in Military

Suicide affects the unit's readiness, devastates the morale of troops and affects the family, friends and leader of the suicide victim. A reasonable number of suicides can be prevented by identifying at-risk individuals, recognizing warning signs and taking direct action. The task of suicide prevention is a major challenge for military leaders as he is expected to foresee suicide attempts and protect the soldiers from death by suicide. This is possible by addressing the complex issue of suicide at three levels: Primary, Secondary and Tertiary.

Primary Intervention

Primary prevention refers to anticipation of potential times of crisis and structuring pre-emptive military support systems. This is the ideal method of protection against suicide. It involves reduction in number of new suicide cases. It includes targeting causal as well as modifiable risk factors. Support is a primary prevention strategy for the military. It serves to reduce the incidence of suicidal thoughts and behaviours by moderating the individual's responses to stress. It involves the promotion of protective factors that consist of internal and external resources that can help an individual cope with challenges, changes and feelings of stress, e.g. promotion of a healthy lifestyle and problem-solving coping skills. This support needs to be present prior to, during and after a crisis. Support can be provided by the leader in terms of a caring and protective climate with improved job conditions in terms of grant of leave, provision of basic amenities and recreational facilities.

Gatekeeper Training: Gatekeepers are people in contact with high-risk people. In case of military personnel, they are the immediate leaders, religious teacher, buddies and other members of the unit. If they are trained in recognition of risk for suicide, mental illness, or signs that depict high level of distress, the incidence of suicides can be checked at an early stage. As a gatekeeper, the person is also responsible for improving links between the personnel in distress and available mental health services.

Crisis Hotlines: Crisis hotlines that provide an immediate access to support services to the distressed soldier help a great deal in initial catharsis of the problem, thus preventing a serious event.

Periodic Surveillance of Well-being of Soldiers or General Stress Audit: Well-being and stress evaluation of the unit will help in diagnosing a soldier manifesting symptoms of suicidal risk. Early signs and behavioural markers of anxiety, anger and depression in soldiers can be detected either by their immediate supervisors or medical officers during their routine medical check-up. Interventions can be tailored to specifically address areas of elevated risk. The services of military psychologists and psychiatrists can be employed for developing and administering *Military Suicide Risk Assessment Protocols* to screen soldiers for symptoms associated with depression, substance abuse and the like.

Initial Screening at Time of Selection: With a selection system calibrated to screen out candidates showing personality dispositions indicative of suicidal risk, incidences of negative behaviour can be reduced to a great extent.

Training in Mental Resilience: The troops need to be trained not only in physical resilience but also in mental resilience at the training stage.

Secondary Intervention

The goal of secondary prevention is to decrease the likelihood of a suicide attempt in the high-risk group. It involves recognition of obvious signs and symptoms of distress and potential emotional disorder while providing caring support and needed interventions. The continuum of suicidal behaviour ranges from ideas, to gestures, to risky lifestyles, suicide plans, attempts and finally suicide completion.

Spotting of At-risk Soldier: Suicide attempts can be identified early through indirect self-destructive behaviours, like chronic alcohol and substance abuse in case of military personnel. The management of suicidal personnel includes assessment of suicide risk and diagnosis and treatment of existing psychiatric illness, e.g. depression and mood disorders.

Promoting Social Support: Since, the command climate acts as a protective factor, it is the leader's responsibility to have a supportive climate in the unit where the soldier feels involved and secure in times of need. He should know the problems being faced by his men whom he can refer to a specialist. The leader should pay close attention to the personal needs of personnel and be on the lookout for signs of stress. Not only the leaders, the other personnel down the chain also need to recognize the signs of stress and depression so that they are likely to spot their buddies who are in need of help.

De-stigmatizing and Rewarding Help-seeking Behaviour: Military personnel are highly reluctant to ask for help because they do not want to be seen as weak. The leader should dispel the stigma from the minds of his men by communicating that recognizing the problems of life is acceptable and a sign of strength. Help seeking behaviour needs to be encouraged by the leader and he should handle it in a confidential manner. He should encourage soldiers to seek help from mental health professionals if the problem is serious enough.

Promoting a Norm of Mutual Buddy Care: The military personnel have to be taught to spot the buddy who is distressed and escort him through the chain of command or take him to a religious teacher or a counsellor.

Tertiary Intervention

It involves recognizing and treating psychiatric disorders that result in acute suicidal behaviour.

Assistance to Family Members of Suicide Victim: Post-event intervention activities involve the therapeutic work with survivor victims of a suicide. Open discussion with mental health worker allows the survivors to express their underlying grief and feelings of guilt, if any. The complete resources of the military community must be mobilized to assist the family. Focus can be directed on family life education to improve family functioning in areas of parenting, communication skills, assertiveness training, stress management training and financial management assistance.

Critical Incidence Stress Debriefing: Critical Incidents have the power to overwhelm the normal coping abilities of even the most experienced professional. Typically, these rare, but overwhelming events, especially those which may end with a tragic outcome, often have the power to completely immobilize the professional or potentially an entire group of people. One such critical incident is suicide in military setting which creates an adverse impact on the morale and readiness of a military unit. Critical Incidence Stress Debriefing needs to be provided to troops of the unit where a suicide has taken place. Debriefing teams can provide assistance to events such as combat deployments, serious accidents, suicides, trauma and the like.

Psychological Autopsy: The purpose of psychological autopsy is to enable the unit commander to know the exact reason of death, the motivation of perpetrator, his intent and the lethality of suicide. It helps to develop future prevention programmes and lessons learnt, so that, family members are better served. It facilitates bereavement counselling too.

A re-look at the intervention strategies reveals that approximately 80 per cent of the problems can be tackled by the military leaders at the primary prevention stage. The role of a psychiatrist, psychologist and psychiatric social worker comes later on in the tertiary prevention phase. Since, suicidal act is a complex phenomenon, which is initiated by a host of stressors and precipitants, a coordinated programme of suicide prevention is needed, wherein the coordinated efforts of Commanding Officer, the psychiatrist, the psychiatric social worker, the religious teacher, the military psychologist, the counsellor and mental health officer are needed.

Military is a unique organization, different from other organizations in the manner in which it makes claim on thc timc and life of the soldier. Being a soldier, it is said, is not a job, but is a lifestyle. It is logical to assume, then, that the military organization accept the responsibility for alleviating the distress a soldier faces, but also for providing an environment that not nurtures capabilities, enhances well-being, optimizes work output and helps the soldier flourish in life. It is proposed that efforts need to be made that go beyond providing intervention for suicide and other self-harming behaviours, and develop the military as a positively oriented organization.

Building Military as a Positive Organization

The World Health Organization emphasizes that optimum functioning of an individual can only be ensured through "a state of well-being in which the individual realizes his or her own abilities, cope with the normal stresses of life, work productively and fruitfully and is able to make a contribution to his or her community" (WHO, 2001). It is imperative that along with providing appropriate interventions in times of crisis and breakdown, a programme may be developed and implemented that focusses on recognizing, maintaining and enhancing the existing psychological strengths of the soldier. Optimum effectiveness of the soldier can be ensured only by ensuring a strong foundation of well-being and resilience.

Well-being is a dynamic process centered in the person that gives people a sense of how their lives are going. This perspective is achieved through an ongoing appraisal of interaction between the life circumstances and activities on one hand and available psychological resources on the other. An individual who is well aware of his strengths/weaknesses will be more able to respond to difficult circumstances in a more effective manner and will innovate and constructively engage with other people and the world around him. Generating awareness thus becomes an essential first step to ensure a healthy working environment which is conducive to the individual.

Psychological resilience refers to an individual's capacity to withstand stressors and not manifest psychological dysfunction, such as mental illness or persistent negative mood. The positive approach refers to this as an individual's capacity to thrive and fulfil potential despite or perhaps even because of such stressors. Resilience is considered to be a dynamic characteristic, which makes resilient individuals demonstrate dynamic self-renewal, whereas less resilient individuals find themselves worn down and negatively impacted by life stressors. Resilient individuals are more inclined to see problems as opportunities for growth and cope well with unusual strains and stressors. Whilst some individuals may seem to prove themselves to be more resilient than others, it needs to be emphasized that resilience is a dynamic quality, not a permanent capacity. Resilience research is expanding beyond the traditional psychopathology perspective, and emergent research examines the construct of resilience as a dynamic developmental process (Werner & Smith, 1992).

A study by Meredith, *et al.* (2011), elaborates about the factors contributing to soldier resilience based on extensive literature review and empirical evidence. They suggest that the baseline assumptions for designing a resilience building programme for the military must involve a shift from the deficiency approach to efficiency approach towards soldier mental health. The new model must focus on psychological health rather than illness and psychological dysfunction. A programme based on the efficiency approach focusses on optimal functioning by enhancing peak performances, inculcating high stress tolerance levels, and imbibing optimism at the organizational as well as the individual levels. Along with providing support for recuperation and recovery in cases of breakdown or dysfunction such strength building approaches shall also provide pathways for the soldier to regain levels of optimal functioning or be resilient in facing the imminent distressing situations. Inculcation of mental hardiness in the face of difficult life circumstances and constraining professional obligations coupled with an early diagnosis at the stage before the stress levels lead to dysfunction would help the soldier to live his life as an optimum experience.

Snyder, Lopez and Pedrotti (2011) emphasize the need to develop prevention programmes for ensuring mental health that would not only prevent the bad but would also enhance the good. They divide the possible intercessions into two broad categories — 'Stopping the bad before it happens' and 'Making life good'. Primary prevention refers to the actions that are taken to lessen or remove the likelihood of subsequent psychological difficulties (Heller, Wyman, & Allen, 2000). Primary prevention can be universal (aimed at entire community) or selective (aimed at selective vulnerable sections). Effective primary prevention programmes typically provide knowledge to the target populations about the risky behaviours, have motivational potential, teach problem solving skills and garner social support in order to prevent regressing into previous counter-productive behaviours. Secondary prevention is synonymous with psychotherapy, and is the current model being followed by the Armed Forces wherein action is aimed at eliminating, reducing or containing the problem once it has appeared. A discussion of the current model is not warranted here. Pursuit of enhancement involves seeking optimal performance and satisfaction *via* a quest for attaining desired goals and maximizing the pleasurable. Primary and secondary enhancements operate on a temporal continuum and secondary enhancements involve augmenting the already positive levels to reach the ultimate in performance and satisfaction. Building up resilience entails effective implementation of primary prevention as well as enhancement strategies.

The World Health Organization defines mental health as "A state of complete physical, mental and social well-being, and not merely the absence of disease". It emphasizes the efficiency of the individual, including sense of well-being and feelings of optimum functioning. It is related to the promotion of well-being, the prevention of mental disorders, and the treatment and rehabilitation of people affected by mental disorders. While defining well-being WHO goes beyond 'absence of illness', rather it defines well-being in its broadest sense as health. Subjective well-being refers to the degree to which individual judges the overall quality of his/her life as positive and favourable. Since, it is subjective, it is within the individual, and depends on people's judgements on what it means to be 'well' (Diener & Suh, 2000).

The prevalent deficiency approach that follows the medical model of conceptualizing mental health merely as breakdown of 'normal' day-to-day functioning proves grossly inadequate for the purpose of ensuring well-being of the individual. This holds especially true in the organizational context, where the ultimate goal is to improve organizational output through ensuring optimum functioning of its personnel.

Recently, the domain of organizational behaviour has seen expansions in consonance with the positive psychology movement initiated by Seligman and Csikszentmihalyi (2000), wherein they proclaimed "psychology of positive human functioning will arise that achieves a scientific understanding and effective interventions to build thriving in individuals, families, and communities" (p. 5), with a focus on recognizing and building upon the inherent potentialities of the individuals in order to help them attain happiness, fulfilment and well-being. Luthans (2002) emphasized that psychology in organizations needed to go beyond managing negativity, and concern it with fostering positive behaviours like hope, optimism, resilience, and confidence in order to develop positive and thriving organizations (Positive Organizational Behaviour Paradigm). Another approach by Cameron and colleagues (Cameron, Dutton & Quinn, 2003) emphasizes the need to include extra organizational as well as intra-organizational factors in its analysis of positive outcomes (Positive Organizational Studies Paradigm). The positive framework in the organizational set-up has been divided into four broad areas, namely — Positive traits, positive state — like psychological resource capacities, positive organization, and positive behaviours.

Military is a huge organization, and any modern military realizes the importance of maintaining and enhancing the capabilities of its human resources. Due to the very nature of their duties the soldiers are exposed to innumerable stresses which affect their endurance and mental health to a great extent. Prolonged exposure to war or low intensity conflict environments modifies their perception and judgement of the conditions. The protracted service in counter insurgency operations, coupled with the rigours of inhospitable conditions, and other personal, domestic and organizational pressures, leads to increased stress and psychological imbalance in soldiers. There is no constant threat of sudden traumatic events in the peace stations, yet soldiers face a tight routine of tasks to be performed leaving little time to be spent in leisure activities. The soldiers get hardly any time to spend with their families and shortage of manpower results in additional duties to the soldiers. The steep hierarchy of command and control and dearth of social support increase the pressure on a soldier.

Despite being inducted into the military through a screening and selection procedure, and despite being trained for facing the tough military life, the stressors prove strong enough to break the poise and balance of many soldiers. The impact usually leads to breakdown only for a very small percentage, while a few remain vulnerable hovering near the periphery. A positively geared approach of developing the latent strengths of the majority of the soldiers pays to enhance the organizational effectiveness as well as ensures the well-being of the soldiers.

Concluding Comments

Suicide is not only a mental health issue, but a larger human problem as well. Suicides and suicidal behaviours in the military make a larger impact as these affect not only the soldier and the family, but leave a negative mark on the entire surrounding environment through the close knit organizational ties. Despite being constituted of a selected work force screened for behavioural anomalies at the time of selection, the work pressures and stressors add to the vulnerabilities of a soldier. In the times of increasing global conflict and multiplicity of tasks a soldier is required to accomplish, it is absolutely essential that the organization provides support to the soldier and his family in times of distress; yet, it is more crucial that the organization helps the individual prepare for facing tough times by inculcating positive behaviours and strengths. Also, there is an absolute need to augment the organizational environment with positive practices, which would increase organizational efficiency and nurture the soldier. Well formulated preventive strategies, timely professional interventions and a positively geared environment would go a long way in dealing with the issues of suicidal behaviours in military settings.

REFERENCES

Barraclough, B. (1986). "Illness and Suicide", in J. Morgan (ed.), *Suicide: Helping those at Risk* (pp. 61-65), London: King's College.

Befrienders Worldwide (2009). *Suicide Statistics*. Retrieved on December 22, 2009 from http://www.befrienders.org/suicide-statistics

Bray, R., Hourani, L., Rae, K., Dever, J.A., Brown, J. M.,Vincus, A.A. Pemberton, M.R., Marsden, M.E., Faulkner, D.L. and Vandermaas-Peeler, R. (2003). *The 2002 Department of Defense (DoD) Survey of Health Related Behaviours Among Military Personnel*. Retrieved on December 22, 2009, from DoD Military Health System: http://www.tricare.osd. mil/ main/ news/2002WWFinalReport.pdf

Britt, T. and Adler, A.B. (1999). "Stress and Health during Medical Humanitarian Assistance Missions", *Military Medicine*, 164(4), 275-79.

Cameron, K., Dutton, J. and Quinn, R. (eds.) (2003). *Positive Organizational Scholarship: Foundations of a New Discipline*, San Francisco: Berrett-Koehler Publishers, Inc.

Cavanagh, J.T., Carson, A.J., Sharpe, M. and Lawrie, S.M. (2003). "Psychological Autopsy Studies of Suicide: A Systematic Review", *Psychological Medicine*, 33(3), 395-405.

Connor, K.R., Duberstein, P.R., Conwell, Y., Seidlitz, L. and Caine, E.D. (2001). "Psychological Vulnerability to Completed Suicide: A Review of Empirical Studies", *Suicide and Life Threatening Behaviour*, 31(4), 367-85.

Diener, E. and Suh, E.M. (2000). *Culture and Well-being*, Cambridge: The MIT Press.

Durkheim, E. (1897). *Le Suicide*, Paris: Alcan.

Frankl, V.E. (1967). *Psychotherapy and Existentialism: Selected Papers on Logotherapy*, New York: Simon and Schuster.

Fryer, H. (1986). "AIDS and Suicide", in J. Morgan (ed.), *Suicide: Helping those at Risk* (pp. 193-200), London: King's College.

Hammerlin, Y. and Enerstvedt, R.T. (1988). *Selvmord [Sucide]*, Oslo: Falken Forlag.

Heeringen, K.V. (ed.) (2001). *Understanding Suicidal Behaviour: The Suicidal Process Approach to Research, Treatment and Prevention*, West Sussex; England: Wiley.

Heller, K., Wyman, M.F. and Allen, S.M. (2000). "Future Directions for Prevention Science: From Research to Adoption", in C.R. Snyder and R.E. Ingram (eds.), *Handbook of Psychological Change: Psychotherapy Processes and Practices for the 21st Century* (pp. 660-80), New York: Wiley.

Leenaars, A.A. (2004). *Psychotherapy with Suicidal People*, Chichester: John Wiley & Sons.

Lester, D. (ed.) (1988). *Why Women Kill Themselves*, Springfield IL: C.C. Thomas.

Lester, D. (1992). *Why People Kill Themselves* (3rd ed.), Springfield IL: C.C. Thomas.

Luthans, F. (2002). "The Need for and Meaning of Positive Organizational Behaviour", *Journal of Organizational Behaviour*, 23(6), 695-706.

Maddi, S.R. (2007). "Relevance of Hardiness Assessment and Training to Military Context", *Military Psychology*, 19(1), 61-70.

Manning, F.J., Kukura, F.C., DeRouin, E.M., McCarroll, J.E., Zych, K.A. and Edwards, F. (1981). "Occupational Mental Health Facilities in the U.S. Army. Europe: Patient Characteristics, Complaints and Dispositions at three Sites", *Military Medicine*, 38, 7-13.

Maris, R.W., Berman, A.L. and Silverman, M.M. (2000). *Comprehensive Textbook of Suicidology*, New York: Guilford Press.

McCarrol, J.E., Orman, D.T. and Lundy, A.C. (1993). "Clients, Problems and Diagnosis in a Military Community Mental Health Clinic: A 20-Month Study", *Military Medicine*, 158(11), 701-05.

McIntosh, J.L. (for the American Association of Suicidology) (2009). *U.S.A. Suicide 2006: Official Final Data*, Washington, DC: American Association of Suicidology, dated April 19, 2009, downloaded from http://www.suicidology.org.

Mehlum, L. and Nrugham, L. (2009). "The Suicidal Soldier", in U. Kumar and M.K. Mandal (eds.), *Suicidal Behaviour: Assessment of People-At-Risk*, New Delhi: Sage Publication.

Mehlum, L. (1992). "Prodromal Signs and Precipitating Factors in Attempted Suicide", *Military Medicine*, 157(11), 574-77.

Mehlum, L. and Weisaeth, L. (2002). "Predictors of Post-traumatic Stress Reactions in Norwegian U.N. Peacekeepers 7 Years after Service", *Journal of Traumatic Stress*, 15(1), 17-26.

Meredith, L.S., Sherbourne, C.D., Gaillot, S., Hansell, L., Ritschard, H.V., Parker, A.M. and Wrenn, G. (2011). "Promoting Psychological Resilience in the U.S Military", *Santa Monica*, CA: RAND Corporation.

National Crime Records Bureau (2007). *Suicides in India*. Retrieved from: http://ncrb.nic.in/ADSI2007/Suicides 07.pdf

Nock, M.K., Borges, G., Bromet, E.J., Cha, C.B., Kessler, R.C. and Lee, S. (2008). "Suicide and Suicidal Behaviour", *Epidemiologic Reviews*, 30(1), 133-54.

Nock, M.K., Borges, G., Bromet, E.J., Alonso, J., Angermeyer, M., Beautrais, A., Bruffaerts, R., Chiu, W.T., de Girolamo, G., Gluzman, S., de Graaf, R., Gureje, O., Haro, J.M., Huang, Y., Karam, E., Kessler, R.C., Lepinc, J.P., Levinson, D., Medina-Mora, M.E., Ono, Y., Posada-Villa, J. and Williams, D. (2008). "Cross-national Prevalence and Risk Factors for Suicidal Ideation, Plans, and Attempts", *The British Journal of Psychiatry*, 192(2), 98-105.

Oquendo, M., Brent, D.A., Birmaher, B., Greenhill, L., Kolko, D., Stanley, B., Zelazny J., Burke A.K., Firinciogullari S., Ellis S. P. and Mann, J.J. (2005). "Post-traumatic Stress Disorder Comorbid with Major Depression: Factors Mediating the Association with Suicidal Behaviour", *American Journal of Psychiatry*, 162(3), 560-66.

Pflanz, S. (2001). "Occupational Stress and Psychiatric Illness in Military: Investigation of the Relationship between Occupational Stress Mental Illness Among Mental Health Patients", *Military Medicine*, 166(6), 457-62.

Pflanz, S. and Sonnek, S. (2002). "Work Stress in Military: Prevalence, Causes, and Relationship to Emotional Health", *Military Medicine*, 167(11), 877-82.

Pflanz, S.E. and Ogle, D.D. (2006). "Job Stress, Depression, Work Performance, and Perceptions of Supervisors in Medical Personnel", *Military Medicine*, 171(9), 861-65.

Poldinger, W. (1968). *Die Abschatzung der Suizidalitat*, Huber, Bern.

Record-breaking Suicides in US Army (2009). Retrieved from: http://www.zeenews.com/news580360.html

Retterstol, N. (1993). *Suicide: A European Perspective*, Cambridge University Press.

Robinson, S.L. (2004). *Hidden Toll of War in Iraq: Mental Health and the Military*, Washington, DC.: Centre for American Progress. Retrieved from: www.americanprogress.org/kf/hiddentoll91404.pdf

Rourke, R., Young, G. and Leenaars, A. (1989). "A Childhood Learning Disability that Predisposes those Affected to Adolescent and Adult Depression and Suicide Risk", *Journal of Learning Disability*, 22(3), 169-75

Scoville, S.L., Gubata, M.E., Potter, R.N., White, M.J. and Pearse, L.A. (2007). "Deaths Attributed to Suicide among Enlisted U.S. Armed Forces Recruits, 1980-2004", *Military Medicine*, 172(10), 1024-31.

Seligman, M.E.P. and Csikszentmihalyi, M. (2000). "Positive Psychology: An Introduction", *American Psychologist*, 55(1), 5-14.

Shneidman, E. (1985). *Definition of Suicide*, New York: John Wiley & Sons.

Silverman, M.M. (2006). "The Language of Suicidology", *Suicide and Life-Threatening Behaviour*, 36(5), 519-32.

Silverman, M.M., Berman, A.L., Sanddal, N.D., O'Carroll, P.W. and Joiner, T.E. (2007). "Rebuilding the Tower of Babel: A Revised Nomenclature for the Study of Suicide and Suicidal Behaviours Part 1: Background, Rationale, and Methodology", *Suicide and Life-Threatening Behaviour*, 37(3), 248-63.

Singh, R. (2014). "Enemy Within: Army Grapples with Suicide Cases", *The Hindustan Times*, New Delhi, July 23rd, 2014.

Snyder, C.R., Lopez, S.J. and Pedrotti, J.T. (2011). *Positive Psychology: The Scientific and Practical Exploration of Human Strengths*, Thousand Oaks, CA: Sage.

Spielberger, C.D., Vagg, P.R. and Wasala, C.F. (2003). "Occupational Stress: Job Pressure and Lack of Support", in J.E. Quick and L. Tetrick (eds.), *Handbook of Occupational Health Psychology* (pp. 185-200), Washington DC: American Psychological Association.

United Nations (1996). *Prevention of Suicide: Guidelines for the Formulation and Implementation of National Strategies*, New York: United Nations.

Werner, E. and Smith, R. (1992). *Overcoming the Odds: High-Risk Children from Birth to Adulthood*, New York: Cornell University Press.

WHO (2001). *Mental Health: New Understanding, New Hope*, The World Health Report, Geneva: World Health Organization.

WHO (2002). *Figures and Facts about Suicide*. Retrieved from: www.lifee.org.nz/suicide/suicide4

INDEX